GOVERNING MIGRATION IN THE LATE OTTOMAN EMPIRE

Edinburgh Studies on the Ottoman Empire
Series Editor: Kent F. Schull

Published and forthcoming titles

The Ottoman Canon and the Construction of Arabic and Turkish Literatures
C. Ceyhun Arslan

Migrating Texts: Circulating Translations around the Ottoman Mediterranean
Edited by Marilyn Booth

Ottoman Translations: Circulating Texts from Bombay to Paris
Edited by Marilyn Booth and Claire Savina

Death and Life in the Ottoman Palace: Revelations of the Sultan Abdülhamid I Tomb
Douglas Scott Brookes

Ottoman Sunnism: New Perspectives
Edited by Vefa Erginbaş

Jews and Palestinians in the Late Ottoman Era, 1908–1914: Claiming the Homeland
Louis A. Fishman

Governing Migration in the Late Ottoman Empire
Ella Fratantuono

Spiritual Vernacular of the Early Ottoman Frontier: The Yazıcıoğlu Family
Carlos Grenier

The Politics of Armenian Migration to North America, 1885–1915: Sojourners, Smugglers and Dubious Citizens
David Gutman

The Kizilbash-Alevis in Ottoman Anatolia: Sufism, Politics and Community
Ayfer Karakaya-Stump

Çemberlitaş Hamami in Istanbul: The Biographical Memoir of a Turkish Bath
Nina Macaraig

Hagia Sophia in the Long Nineteenth Century
Edited by Emily Neumeier and Benjamin Anderson

The Kurdish Nobility in the Ottoman Empire: Loyalty, Autonomy and Privilege
Nilay Özok-Gündoğan

Nineteenth-Century Local Governance in Ottoman Bulgaria: Politics in Provincial Councils
Safa Saraçoğlu

Prisons in the Late Ottoman Empire: Microcosms of Modernity
Kent F. Schull

Ruler Visibility and Popular Belonging in the Ottoman Empire
Darin Stephanov

The North Caucasus Borderland: Between Muscovy and the Ottoman Empire, 1555–1605
Murat Yasar

Children and Childhood in the Ottoman Empire: From the 14th to the 20th Centuries
Edited by Gülay Yilmaz and Fruma Zachs

euppublishing.com/series/esoe

GOVERNING MIGRATION IN THE LATE OTTOMAN EMPIRE

Ella Fratantuono

EDINBURGH
University Press

Edinburgh University Press is one of the leading university presses in the UK.
We publish academic books and journals in our selected subject areas across the
humanities and social sciences, combining cutting-edge scholarship with high editorial
and production values to produce academic works of lasting importance. For more
information visit our website: edinburghuniversitypress.com

© Ella Fratantuono, 2024

Edinburgh University Press Ltd
The Tun – Holyrood Road
12 (2f) Jackson's Entry
Edinburgh EH8 8PJ

Typeset in Jaghbuni by
Cheshire Typesetting Ltd, Cuddington, Cheshire,
and printed and bound by CPI Group (UK) Ltd, Croydon, CR0 4YY

A CIP record for this book is available from the British Library

ISBN 978 1 3995 2184 0 (hardback)
ISBN 978 1 3995 2186 4 (webready PDF)
ISBN 978 1 3995 2187 1 (epub)

The right of Ella Fratantuono to be identified as author of this work has been asserted
in accordance with the Copyright, Designs and Patents Act 1988 and the Copyright and
Related Rights Regulations 2003 (SI No. 2498).

Contents

List of Illustrations	vi
Acknowledgements	vii
Introduction: Labelling Mobility in a Regime in Motion	1
1. *Muhacir* as Colonist	25
2. *Muhacir* as Problem	62
3. *Muhacir* as Victim	98
4. *Muhacir* as Failure	134
5. *Muhacir* as Muslim	176
6. *Muhacir* as Possibility	203
Conclusion: Categories of Movement and Categories of Belonging	238
Bibliography	250
Index	268

Illustrations

Figures

0.1	Ottoman provinces, c. 1900	x
2.1	The Balkans in 1860	64
2.2	Midhat Pasha's sample register	88
4.1	Map, Garipler Mezarlığı, 1888	136
4.2	Ferik Muzaffer Pasha's irrigation project, 1891	140
4.3	Ankara-Eskişehir branch of the Anatolian Railway and Imperial Stud Farms	143
4.4	Muzaffer Pasha's map of *miri* farms along projected railroad, 1891	145
4.5	Map of immigrant housing, Ankara, 1901	165
4.6	Blueprints for migrant housing, Ankara, 1901	166
4.7	Blueprint for migrant village, Tripoli, c. 1902	167
5.1	Territorial changes following the Treaty of Berlin	179

Table

4.1	Register: available *miri* land along projected railroad, 1891	146

Acknowledgements

It is a joy to be able to thank the many mentors, colleagues, scholars, organisations, friends and family who played a role in making this book happen.

My editors at Edinburgh University Press have been a pleasure to work with, and I am extremely pleased this book will appear as part of the Edinburgh Studies on the Ottoman Empire series. I am grateful to series editor Kent Schull for believing in the project several years before it came to fruition. The professionalism and expertise of acquisitions editor Rachel Bridgewater, assistant editor Isobel Birks and managing desk editor Eddie Clark have made the publishing process transparent, navigable and smooth. I appreciate the ways all four have guided me through each stage of the process. I thank the anonymous reviewers, whose insights have strengthened the book and whose commentary on an earlier version was thoughtful, clear and constructive.

The research in this book would not have been possible without the assistance and expertise of librarians and archival staff. I am indebted to Ali Osman Çınar, Umut Soysal, İsmail Hakseven, and many others at the Başbakanlık Osmanlı Arşivi, Atatürk Kitaplığı, TDV İslam Araştırmaları Mekerzi and SALT Research in Istanbul; the Milli Kütüphane/National Library of Türkiye and Kızılay/Red Crescent Archives in Ankara; and the National Archives of the United Kingdom at Kew and the British Library in London. My thanks to the Inter-Library Loan staff at Michigan State University (MSU) and the University of North Carolina (UNC) at Charlotte and to Amanda Binder for help obtaining research materials.

Language acquisition, travel, research and writing of this book were made possible by MSU's University Distinguished Fellowship, the University of Richmond's Woodfin-Lough grant for Graduate Study, the Fulbright Institute of International Education, the Mellon Foundation through the

Governing Migration in the Late Ottoman Empire

Council of European Studies, the American Philosophical Society and UNC Charlotte's Faculty Research Grant and Junior Faculty Development Award. I thank the *Journal of Genocide Research* and the *Middle East Journal of Refugee Studies* for permission to republish material in this book.

Many teachers and mentors contributed to my trajectory and that of this work. I got my start as a historian at the University of Richmond, where Yücel Yanıkdağ introduced me to the Ottoman Empire. Yücel, Carol Summers and Nicole Sackley showed me the joy that emerges from distilling archival research into interpretation. The project that eventually became this book began at MSU. I am grateful to my entire dissertation committee – Emine Evered, Leslie Moch, Lewis Siegelbaum and Kyle Evered – each of whom shaped this project. Emine was a model advisor and extraordinarily generous with her time. Her approach to understanding late Ottoman history has deeply influenced my own. In seminars and independent readings and through close critical reading of my papers, proposals and chapters, Leslie, Lewis and Kyle encouraged me to situate my research within global patterns and processes of migration, empires and state-building. Alongside Leslie and Lewis, Steven Gold, Stephanie Nawyn and Mara Leichtman contributed to my engagement with migration studies. I am thankful to Karrin Hanshew for organising the European History Colloquium as an informal venue for graduate students to discuss works in progress and to Michael Stamm's support as Graduate Director during my final years in the program. During my time at MSU, I was lucky to work among a cohort of supportive graduate students focused on migration studies, including Svetla Dimitrova, Rachel Elbin, Emily Elliot, Linda Gordon, April Greenwood, Helen Kaibara, Kitty Lam, Adrienne Tyrey and Brian Van Wyck. The cohesiveness of this group was facilitated above all by the efforts of my dear and inspiring friend Alison Kolodzy. David Baylis and Douglas Priest also commented on this work in its early stages.

At UNC Charlotte, I am grateful to be surrounded by supportive colleagues who have proven over and again their willingness to read and comment on material and who lighten each semester with kind words and a fair amount of humor. I appreciate the guidance I received as an assistant professor from two History Department chairs, Jurgen Buchenau and Amanda Pipkin, and I thank Dan Du, Dan Dupre, Maren Ehlers, Peter Ferdinando, Christine Haynes, Carol Higham, Jill Massino, Gregory Mixon, Steve Sabol, Tina Shull, Peter Thorsheim and Mark Wilson for their commentary on parts of the manuscript. Thank you to John Cox, Karen Cox, Carol Higham, David Johnson, Oscar Lansen, Caitlin Schroering and Carmen Soliz for pranks, sweets, drinks, furry friends and

Acknowledgements

other forms of moral support. John David Smith has been a most generous colleague and friend, whose close readings and advice were crucial as I moved through the publication process. I am indebted to Ritika Prasad for her honest feedback on large portions of the manuscript. Any faults that remain are my own.

Many individuals have been particularly helpful to me in my intellectual journey as mentors, scholars whose work has inspired my own, friends and fellow travelers among archives, at conferences, in reading and writing groups, and over email. I apologise for any omissions I may commit in thanking them here. My gratitude to Patrick Adamiak, Oscar Aguirre-Mandujano, Elçin Arabacı, Emily Arauz, Alexander Balistreri, Nora Elizabeth Barakat, Lily Balloffet, Isacar Bolaños, Lale Can, Lucia Carminati, Frank Castiglione, Dawn Chatty, Yaşar Tolga Cora, Dzovinar Derderian, Sotirios Dimitriadis, Samuel Dolbee, Madeleine Elfenbein, Michael Ferguson, Matthew Ghazarian, Chris Gratien, Carlos Grenier, Zoe Griffith, David Gutman, Vladimir Hamed-Troyansky, Barbara Henning, Hadi Hosainy, Polina Ivanova, Martin Lemberg-Pederson, Chris Low, Helen Makhdoumian, Jared Manasek, A. Dirk Moses, Emily Neumeier, Ramazan Hakkı Öztan, Graham Autumn Pitts, Michael Polcynzki, Laura Robson, James Ryan, Alex Schweig, Nir Shafir, Nicole Beckmann Tessel, Ben White, Seçil Yılmaz and Fatih Yucel. I am grateful to Selim Kuru and Yorgos Dedes for their endeavors to teach me Ottoman Turkish. I also thank the scholars whom I have not been able to meet in person, yet whose work on the Ottoman Empire and migration has been so crucial to my own.

In the many years it has taken to research and write this book, I would have escaped neither the dark forests of partially written chapters nor the existential crises that accompany them if not for the love, patience, generosity and support of friends and family in Charlotte, Detroit, Durham, Istanbul, Lansing and elsewhere. I am grateful to have met my caring and brilliant friends Emek Ergun and Ritika Prasad so soon after arriving in Charlotte. Allison Swaim's general enthusiasm for the project, many laughs and steadiness were essential as I approached the finish line. I am grateful for family members Beria, Hikmet, Karen, Remzi and Eren Sipahi, Suraj Bhatt and Sergio Torres. My life is enriched by Shravani and Karnika Bhatt, who have delighted me for eight (!) and six (!) years respectively. I thank my grandmother, Anna, my parents, Michael and Rebecca, and my sisters, Moira and Julia, whose teasing is both humbling and the finest form of affection, especially when coupled with unconditional support. And finally, I thank Levent, who has been a part of this project since before it existed, and whose inspiring curiosity, delight in debating ideas, kindness and love have helped me see it through to its end.

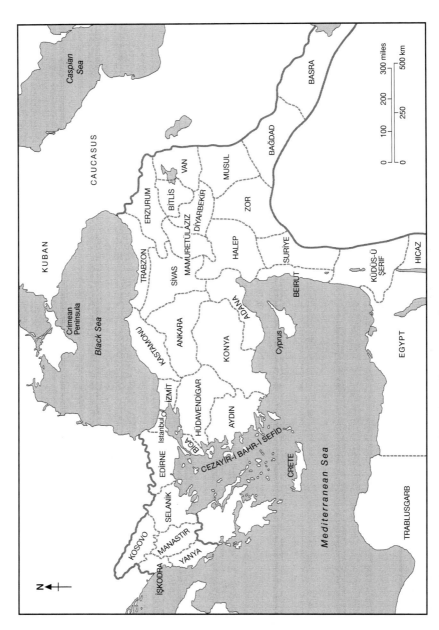

Figure 0.1 Ottoman provinces, c. 1900. Hejaz and Yemen not shown.

Introduction
Labelling Mobility in a Regime in Motion

In January 1918, the upper house of the Ottoman Parliament weighed a proposal to increase the budget of the General Directorate of Tribes and Migrants (AMMU). According to its director, Hamdi Bey, the AMMU oversaw a population of over a million 'immigrants and refugees' (*muhacirin* and *mülteciler*), roughly one third of whom needed direct support from the government. After several minutes of debate on the proposal itself, one senator asked for clarification on a fundamental point: Whom did these terms describe? Were *muhacir* those fleeing from invaded countries? Did *mülteci* refer to a different group? Hamdi Bey offered clarification. *Muhacir* were those who arrived in the empire officially and in accordance with the empire's treaties with other states. *Mülteci* referred to anyone, regardless of type or sect, who fled due to the conditions of war. At the heart of the matter was the question of whom should receive assistance from the state. Pressed for further explanation, the director assuaged concerns about whom the budget increase supported. According to Hamdi Bey, the *mülteci* came from border provinces within the Ottoman state rather than from 'enemy countries'.[1]

As director of the AMMU, Hamdi Bey fielded the question about terminology with some confidence. Nevertheless, his terms did not align with a law enacted just five years earlier. The 1913 Migrant Settlement Regulations (*İskan-ı Muhacirin Nizamnamesi*) distinguished between two types of *muhacir*, both of which referred to an individual who had crossed into Ottoman territory. The first type (*muhacir*) signified an individual who had received documentation and permission from his or her original government and the Ottoman state in advance. The second arrived as 'a refugee' (*mülteci*) without such documentation or permission, sought to become an Ottoman subject, and received official *muhacir* status only after a state investigation confirmed his or her identity.[2] The Ottoman historian, as much

1

Governing Migration in the Late Ottoman Empire

as the Ottoman parliamentarian, might be justifiably confused about the categories used to describe those under the purview of the AMMU.

Although situated in the upheaval of World War I, the question of 'who is an immigrant' was informed by more than a half century of mass migration into the Ottoman Empire. From the Crimean War (1853–6) to 1913, some five million individuals arrived in the empire.[3] When they arrived, their status as *muhacir* meant they were entitled to free land, settlement assistance and a period of tax exemptions, a set of benefits intended to turn migrants into productive, loyal Ottoman subjects. Thus, the question of who exactly was a *muhacir* remained of considerable importance.[4]

As this book demonstrates, within Ottoman sources, the term *muhacir* (pl. *muhacirin*) encompassed a range of movements, including Muslims, Jews and Christians fleeing varying degrees of coercion throughout the nineteenth and twentieth centuries and European colonisers invited to settle in the empire beginning in 1857. While the term was capacious, most of the five million individuals who arrived in the empire during the period were Muslim. Many fled an encroaching Russian Empire in the Caucasus and Crimean Peninsula or conflict in the Balkans. As migrants entered the empire en masse, they became for Ottoman officials a problem to solve and a resource to carry out reform projects. As a result, Ottoman statesmen developed the 'policies, practices, and infrastructures designed to both foster and limit human movement' of a sophisticated migration regime.[5] The *muhacir* became an essential element of Ottoman governance.

This book approaches the question of 'who was a *muhacir*' as crucial to understanding the development of the nineteenth- and early twentieth-century Ottoman state. Rather than a challenge to understanding Ottoman governance and the broader story of the relationship between state-building and mobility, the meaning of such categories and labels reveals how officials and statesmen understood Ottoman society and the migrants' role within it. Despite the number of individuals who arrived in the empire in the nineteenth and early twentieth centuries, the Ottoman migration regime is largely overlooked in histories of state-building and migration. This oversight has emerged in part because those who arrived in Ottoman territory did not neatly fit the categories many migration scholars use to label and study human mobility.

Labelling Migrants and Refugees

From the vantage point of the twenty-first century, Ottoman officials' questions about the terms used to describe those on the move seem both strange and familiar. Seventy-odd years after the mass population

Introduction

displacement of World War II, the ensuing creation of the United Nations High Commissioner for Refugees (UNHCR), and that same body's 1951 convention's defining of 'refugee' and refugee rights, the term refugee conjures a set of attributes in today's legal, scholarly and popular circles. A refugee is 'someone who is unable or unwilling to return to their country of origin owing to a well-founded fear of being persecuted for reasons of race, religion, nationality, membership of a particular social group, or political opinion'.[6] According to this definition, a refugee is an individual defined by their reason for movement, their ongoing displacement and a rupture in the relationship between citizen and state.

Though the meaning of 'refugee' appears straightforward, closer examination reveals that the distinction between coerced and voluntary movement is not so clear-cut. The term refugee is a policy-oriented status rather than an empirical condition. Asylum seekers, refugees, stateless persons and irregular migrants travel in much the same manner over the same routes, and many of the world's most desperate are never designated refugees. Labels such as refugee, asylum seeker and irregular migrant determine the distribution of resources and rights long after displacement.[7] When aid workers, state officials and UNHCR representatives apply asylum laws, 'reasonable fear' and 'social group' are subjective interpretations, incentivising certain performances of refugee-ness among asylum seekers and breeding suspicion among those who evaluate claims.[8] Individuals on the move recognise the material significance of those categories and contribute to the discursive, legal and popular meaning of refugee and migrant.[9] In liberal democracies, the question of who is a refugee and what responsibilities that label might entail creates fractures within political landscapes often framed in terms of a polity's self-definition.

The categorical distinction between migrant and refugee is of relatively recent vintage. People have long been on the move, yet historians have traced tremendous changes in patterns of human mobility from the nineteenth century forward, capturing a sense of ever more movement and ever more significant social transformation. New technologies contributed to the era of mass migration (c. 1840–1940), and a 'general increase in mobility ... is now widely recognized as the defining feature of the twenty-first century'.[10] Sandwiched between the nineteenth and twenty-first centuries, the twentieth century earns the unfortunate designation of 'the century of the refugee'.[11] In an era of upheaval, the consolidation of modern states and the elevation of citizenship as the primary means of political belonging gave rise to the phenomenon of the refugee as a 'new social category of concern' and to international attempts and apparatuses to resolve the problem of displacement across state lines.[12]

The phenomenon of the refugee is closely tied to the history of the modern international state system. Modern states are defined in part by their capacity to organise the circulation of people, goods and resources in and through their territories.[13] The formation of new states was a 'refugee-generating process', and refugees contributed to the forging of new states after World War I, World War II and periods of decolonisation.[14] States emerge through expulsions, forced sedentarisation, racialisation and migrant illegality, though official histories often require forgetting the population movements that defined territorial and social boundaries. The erasure of forced migrations helps to create the seemingly 'natural' borders of contemporary nation states. Movement and displacement are reduced to anomalous and unnatural conditions rather than recognised as an inherent feature of human history.[15]

Refugees help constitute the meaning of modern state sovereignty. The casting of refugees as a social problem in the nineteenth and twentieth centuries opened a venue for state intervention in society and reified particular forms of sovereignty and control. In the interwar Middle East, for example, the presence of refugees contributed to state authority among mandate powers, serving as a justification for intervention.[16] The interwar era saw the emergence of international entities intended to deal with the problem of the refugee. With the creation of the formal and informal arrangements, laws and institutions of an international refugee regime, *events of human displacement* ... were rearticulated (reinscribed) as a specific *refugee problem* characterized in terms of images, identities, and subjectivities that support the sovereign state'.[17] Refugees help naturalise the borders of contemporary nation states; the notion of the refugee as exceptional in their 'right' to cross state lines reinforces the sense that states can and should restrict the majority of movement across borders. Refugees become aberrations that uphold the norm, exceptions that prove the rule of the state and that render categories of state, citizen and migrant seemingly natural and without history.

'The refugee' seems to conjure a clearly demarcated social concept because it is defined in opposition to another category: 'the migrant'. The 'migrant/refugee binary' distinguishes between 'voluntary (often economically motivated) migrants' and 'forced (often politically motivated) refugees'. Rebecca Hamlin argues that this conceptual dichotomy influences state policy – who can be 'excluded' and 'who should be let in' – and popular conceptions of those on the move.[18] The migrant/refugee binary contributes to a sense that the categories of migrant and refugee are naturally and fundamentally distinct from one another, and it gives rise to a set of assumptions about trauma, need, motivation, obligation and the

Introduction

capacity to objectively and correctly designate who is a refugee and who is not. The meaning of the category is reified by policies, humanitarian workers, individuals crossing international borders and scholars, all of whom treat the distinction between refugee and migrant as meaningful.[19]

The migrant/refugee binary endures despite its limitations in describing migration experiences. While scholars recognise the inadequacy of these categories and their inability to describe fundamental attributes of mobile individuals, their scholarship continues to distinguish between voluntary and coerced migration. The binary plays out in disciplinary distinctions between the field of refugee studies, on the one hand, and migration studies, on the other. The distinction between free and coerced migration has implications for how scholars establish their research questions and conceptually separate different regions, migrations and groups. For example, the history of the nineteenth-century era of mass migration posits free labour migration as the norm for white Europeans across the liberal societies of the North Atlantic and coerced migration as the norm in other corridors. In this telling, the twentieth century was an aberration in European history that gave rise to the international refugee regime. The problem solved, Europe 'naturally' returned to patterns of free migration. Coerced migration in the rest of the world is then also a 'natural' state, rather than an outcome of an interconnected system in which the ease of border crossing for some is created by the conditions that give rise to forced displacement for others.[20]

The nineteenth- and early twentieth-century Ottoman Empire is an essential and overlooked site to consider histories of migrations and states outside of the migrant/refugee binary. By and large, Ottoman officials used the term *muhacir*, an Arabic-origin word with connotations of forced flight within early Islamic history, to refer to the groups and individuals who arrived in the empire. While historians writing in English have translated *muhacir* as im/migrant, colonist, refugee, exile and asylum seeker, a vocabulary that draws upon the causes and motivations for movement, Ottoman officials remained interested in the outcomes of *muhacir* arrival. Their responses to mass migration centred on the question of how migrants, by virtue of their acceptance and permanent settlement in Ottoman territory, could contribute to the consolidation and perpetuation of Ottoman sovereignty.

In his work on Ottoman migrants, Isa Blumi offers an expansive definition of the refugee, which collapses spiritual, economic and physical removal to include all those in exile. In this, Blumi to some extent anticipates Thomas Nail's depiction of the 'figure of the migrant', a political figure emerging through the forces of territorial, political, juridical and economic expulsion.[21] For Nail, this expansive terminology does not reduce all those on the move to an indistinguishable mass. Nor is it intended to undermine existing systems of protection for vulnerable populations. Instead, taking an expansive view of the 'figure of the migrant' allows for consideration of how regimes contribute to movement and shape belonging in specific historical settings.

The numbers and varied experiences of migrants to the empire, the emergence of institutions and policies to respond to mass movement, and the terminology used by Ottoman officials all shed light on the intertwining of displacement and governance in an era prior to the consolidation of the meaning of 'refugee'. Rather than applying contemporary distinctions based on the causes of movement, this book prioritises other aspects of migration administration, allowing the causes of mobility to serve as a component but not the defining characteristic of the *muhacir*. Instead, the book traces the changing use of the term within Ottoman governance over time. It shows that changing realities faced by Ottoman officials – the extension of the purview of the central state, on the one hand, and the emergence of separatist movements and the financial, diplomatic and military realities of European imperialism on the other – shifted how officials defined the characteristics and utility they ascribed to the *muhacir*. This book focuses on the history of a migration regime and the history of a social category within Ottoman governance. To better situate that discussion, it is essential to examine the contours of Ottoman reform and state-building in the nineteenth and early twentieth centuries.

The Making of a Modern Ottoman State

The nineteenth-century *muhacir* entered the Ottoman Empire in the midst of an extended era of administrative, economic, legal and military reform. Ottoman sultans and statesmen, spurred by internal decentralisation and by a relative loss of military and economic power vis-à-vis the empire's European rivals, designed wide-ranging projects intended to centralise and standardise government, efficiently extract taxes, augment the productivity of the population, and encourage the loyalty of the empire's religiously and linguistically diverse communities. The reform era was influenced by international as well as domestic dynamics. The Eastern Question, or the diplomatic wrangling of the European powers over the potential demise of the Ottoman Empire, influenced European intervention in Ottoman politics and society at large. Wars, European imperialism and the many social transformations associated with the centralising reforms influenced the

Introduction

course of ongoing and emergent fiscal problems, uprisings and nationalist movements through to the end of the empire in 1922.

The reform era began with Sultans Selim III (r. 1789–1807) and Mahmud II (r. 1808–1839), but centralisation efforts shifted to the bureaucracy in the early nineteenth century. In 1839, Sultan Abdülmecid I (r. 1839–61) promulgated the Gülhane Rescript, an edict typically designated as the starting point for the period of administrative reorganisation and wide-ranging legislative changes known as the *Tanzimat* (1839–76). The Tanzimat era saw the adoption of legal equality and political representation among the empire's religious-administrative groups, culminating in the 1876 constitution. Two years later, in the midst of the 1877–8 Russo-Ottoman War, Sultan Abdülhamid II (r. 1876–1909) suspended the constitution and the parliament. Nevertheless, Abdülhamid II continued the trajectory of centralising reforms throughout his thirty-year reign, until he was ousted by the Young Turks, a cohort of reformers opposed to the sultan's authoritarianism. A coup in 1908 reinstated the constitution and recalled the parliament, and the revolutionary-era government deposed Abdülhamid II in 1909.

Throughout the reform era, organising cross-border migration was but one facet of how Ottoman statesmen approached movement. Population mobility served as a source of strength and a target of reform throughout Ottoman history. As Reşat Kasaba has shown, nomadic pastoralists contributed to the empire's expansion, supplied animals and facilitated the movement of goods from the empire's origins in fourteenth-century Anatolia. Beginning in the final decades of the eighteenth century, Ottoman administrators made greater efforts to forcibly settle nomadic pastoralists in order to better identify the population and increase the amount of cultivated land. Nevertheless, these settlement efforts were not widely effective until the late nineteenth century, and successful sedentarisation of some tribes often required granting expanded rights to others. During the Tanzimat and Hamidian eras, administrators dispatched *muhacirin* to internal frontiers, embracing immigration as a means to settle tribes and further develop the Ottoman agricultural economy. To that end, administrators placed entire villages of immigrants in highlands and lowlands traditionally traversed by pastoralists. While migrations and population mobility were fluid, spontaneous and relatively organic processes in the empire's earlier centuries, migrants and mobile subjects in the last century of Ottoman rule encountered an increasingly inflexible state interpreting and valuing identity in fundamentally new and different ways.[22]

The Ottoman state's approach to migration management aligned with global historical trends. Documents, such as internal passes and passports, contributed to modernising states' monopolisation of 'the legitimate "means of movement"', and policies determining who could cross international borders became an essential component of state-building and social engineering in the nineteenth and twentieth centuries.[23] The principle that sovereignty included state control over mobile subjects emerged through contingent and ad hoc responses to demands for labour and concerns about nationality, belonging and citizenship in an era of state-building and mass migration.[24] While historians generally have overlooked Ottoman migration policies in this history, in his recent examination of Armenian migration to and from the Ottoman Empire and United States, David Gutman has shown that the Ottoman Empire was one more participant in a global shift towards a system of borders, documentation and restricted migration.[25]

Migration and mobility are useful in considering the questions of loyalty, identity, subjecthood and nationality in empires and nation states at the turn of the twentieth century. During the nineteenth and early twentieth centuries, Ottoman statesmen sought to cultivate new sources of legitimacy and loyalty among the empire's subjects. During the Tanzimat era, major legislation in 1839 and 1856 encouraged a supra-ethnic identification with the Ottoman state (Ottomanism/*Osmanlılık*) by asserting the legal equality of all subjects regardless of religion. While the ideology of Ottomanism persisted into the Hamidian and Young Turk eras (1909–18), statesmen also appealed to other ideologies, rhetoric and symbols as they sought to encourage social unity. Broadly, Hamidian-era Islamic Ottomanism adopted symbols and rhetoric drawn from Islam to appeal to Muslims within and outside the empire. During the Young Turk era, some statesmen advocated for Turkification policies ranging from requiring the use of the Turkish language in state institutions to forcibly relocating or deporting non-Turkish or non-Muslim individuals and communities. Mobile subjects offer insight into the implications and limitations of those unifying ideologies over time.

In the age of European imperialism, the Ottoman state struggled to gain equal footing in an inter-imperial competition over legal jurisdiction. At a historical moment when individual subjects began to experience nationality as a legal standing activated via international encounters, nationality emerged as a 'contingent and strategic' practice.[26] Under whose authority were individuals who traversed imperial borders? The question had practical implications for pragmatic migrants navigating the legal possibilities of nationality. Despite Ottoman policies establishing unilateral authority over naturalised migrants, 'transimperial Muslims' could simultaneously become Ottoman subjects and retain Russian subjecthood, allowing those

Introduction

who emigrated to the Ottoman Empire to maintain the option of return.[27] Mobile subjects challenged assertions of Ottoman nationality, territoriality and sovereignty. Work on the Hamidian-era hajj reveals limits and contradictions in Ottoman strategies to manage mobility. Lale Can's work on Central Asian hajj pilgrims has shown how two countervailing impulses, an interest in crafting a narrower definition of Ottoman subjecthood on the one hand and appeals to a Muslim community beyond the empire's borders one the other, paralleled each other.[28] As Michael Christopher Low explains, even in the Hijaz, the geographic centre of Ottoman claims to caliphal authority, mobile Muslim subjects revealed the limits of Hamidian Islamic Ottomanism as a strategy of imperial rule.[29]

By and large, Ottoman statesmen prioritised the outcomes of migration rather than its causes. The imperial competition for legal authority over individuals within Ottoman territory shaped statesmen's view of the *muhacir*. Subjecthood was a defining criterion, and concern over sovereignty and subjecthood were perennial components in statesmen's understanding of the ideal *muhacir*. For officials, the *muhacir* signified someone who intended to become unambiguously Ottoman.

Migration Regimes: Governmentality, Social Engineering and Failure

This book places migration and settlement politics at the centre of Ottoman state-building and governance in the nineteenth and early twentieth centuries. The Ottoman reform era witnessed attempts to build a modern state, one with an extended capacity to intervene widely in the everyday life of the empire's subjects through new and reformed institutions, policies, programmes and tools, in venues ranging from the army and prisons to vocational orphanages and schools.[30] One such change was the development of institutions and policies intended to centrally coordinate immigration and immigrant settlement. In 1860, faced with large-scale migration from the Crimean Peninsula and Caucasus, statesmen established the Migrant Commission (Muhacirin Komisyonu). Across the next six decades, Ottoman officials continued to develop institutions and policies to administer immigrant reception and settlement. In order to understand how officials conceptually and geographically placed migrants within the Ottoman state and to trace the ways that that changed over time, I rely on three conceptual frames: governmentality, social engineering and failure.

GOVERNMENTALITY

The effort to organise migration and settlement reflected one component of how, for Ottoman officials in the nineteenth century, the purview of governance encompassed the health, loyalty and productivity of the population. Michel Foucault identifies 'governmentality', a rationale of governance that elevates the population as a site of rule, as central to the development of modern states. This rationality places population as the 'ultimate end of government', and finds the purpose of government in 'the welfare of the population, the improvement of its condition, the increase of its health, longevity, wealth, etc.'[31] Within such states, including the Ottoman Empire, population became 'a kind of living entity with a history and a development, and with possibilities of pathology'; it became newly knowable, with characteristics that could be evaluated through categorisation and the collection of statistics.[32]

SOCIAL ENGINEERING

Whereas 'governmentality' provides insight into Ottoman officials' identification of the population, its welfare and its development as the purview and purpose of government, the concept of social engineering draws attention to the criteria officials identified as they attempted to manipulate the population in order to strengthen the state. As officials began to engage in new ways of understanding Ottoman population and territory, they endeavoured to not only manage society but to mould it 'into an ideal image'.[33] Their efforts to do so required creating new categories and identifying and attributing characteristics to specific groups within the population.

Frequently, historians have used the concept of social engineering to characterise the goals, mechanisms and pathologies of states responsible for genocide and ethnic cleansing in the twentieth century. Scholars exploring those ideologies, tactics and technologies used to transform populations employ Zygmunt Bauman's metaphor of the state as 'gardener'.[34] As Bauman noted, the gardener 'impose[s] a design on formlessness, order and structure on chaos and randomness ... The gardener *designs* order and *enforces* it on reality ... The gardener focuses ... on dividing extant creatures into proper and improper, useful and harmful, desirable and unwelcome, deserving protection or earmarked for annihilation.'[35] Gardening states transform society through a range of prescriptive and proscriptive policies intended to eradicate certain cultures and ways of living. Their tactics include (but are not limited to) generating and affix-

Introduction

ing population labels, economic development, arrest and murder of individuals and ethnic cleansing.[36] Because regimes of government 'elicit, promote, facilitate, foster, and attribute various capacities, qualities, and statuses to particular agents', labelling and categorising groups is essential to identifying and targeting for change behaviours, cultures and identities among the population.[37]

Although historians have linked 'gardening' to the homogenising ethos of the nation state, ethnic, religious and national categories are not the only criteria states have use to enact social engineering. When defined more broadly, social engineering captures the processes by which certain groups or individuals are identified variously as beneficial, in need of reform or unimprovable and subject to expulsion. Ottoman officials linked immigration to the economic development and security of the Ottoman state. Thus, the question of 'who is a *muhacir*' was also always a question of 'who is the ideal Ottoman.' The history of migration administration reveals how, when and why certain individuals and groups within Ottoman society became targets of social engineering techniques. Thus, while I identify governmentality as a rationality and approach to governance tied to officials' interest in intervening in the population overall, I rely on the concept of social engineering to trace the emergence and implications of Ottoman officials' identification, elevation and/or problematisation of groups within the population. In their engagement with migration, officials adopted the rationality of governmentality and the underlying logic of social engineering. Exploring how officials imagined, identified, described and problematised migrants lends insight into how Ottoman social engineering changed over time.

FAILURE AND THE 'WILL TO IMPROVE'

Mass migrations and the vast project of settlement radically changed Ottoman society. Sometimes, it did so along the lines envisioned by administrators. Nevertheless, failure features prominently in the history of migration administration. The archive is rife with examples of migrant sickness, death, unauthorised movement, contributions to social unrest and eventual departure from the Ottoman Empire. Administrative, infrastructural and economic limitations reduced the empire's capacity to govern migration, and migrants themselves shaped Ottoman history. During the Hamidian period, bans on Armenian emigration yielded unintended outcomes, including smuggling networks that stretched from Anatolia to the Americas, while 'Ottoman refugees' 'compelled various strata of regional, local, and imperial government to adapt'.[38] Mass migrations overwhelmed the state's administrative capacity; nevertheless, in its failures to actualise plans, policies and proposals, the Ottoman state was hardly alone. For example, though state-generated border controls are fundamental to modern states' migration regimes and to migrants' experiences, government attempts to regulate movement fully are frequently aspirational. Legal restrictions barring immigration influence paths rather than ending cross-border mobility. The limited capacity of Ottoman governance echoed in the states that succeeded it after World War I. In Mandate Palestine, migrants and refugees used and subverted an emerging documentary regime, while in the early Turkish Republic, international contexts influenced the enactment of settlement laws.[39]

In their analysis of governmentality, Peter Miller and Nikolas Rose describe governance as 'a congenitally failing operation'.[40] In gardening, as well as in governing, 'a 'fully controlled' garden is never attained, and the struggle for full control never ends'.[41] Governmentality and social engineering rely fundamentally on administrators' 'discovery' of problems and the creation of techniques to bring about solutions to those problems; the diagnosis of problems and the development of solutions are interdependent. This 'will to improve' operates in the gaps between ideal and outcome, gaps that create the space for the development of new or 'enhanced' projects, policies and techniques of management. In the nineteenth and early twentieth centuries, border controls, documentary regimes (e.g. passports) and states' management of mobility emerged through administrators' contingent and contested concerns about labour, nationality and citizenship in an era of state-building and mass migration.[42]

The propulsive dynamic of failure is essential in the consolidation of regimes and states. State-building does not arise strictly as an outcome of human intention and rationality but is rather a process that emerges through complex interactions and outcomes.[43] Limits on the Ottoman state's capacity to intervene successfully in its subjects' lives do not negate the importance of officials' attempts to do so. In the Ottoman Empire and elsewhere, 'the articulation of government [was] bound to the constant identification of the difficulties and failures of government'.[44] Officials' responses to critiques of Ottoman administrative or infrastructural failure contributed to their renewed efforts to know and manipulate the characteristics of the Ottoman population. That is, faced with 'failures' in migration and settlement projects, officials devised programmes to improve governance itself. For statesmen and officials, improved plans, scientifically informed administrative practices and more precise instruments of calculation could resolve existing problems. In this way, the identification of failure was fundamental to the entrenchment of governmentality and extension of social

Introduction

engineering projects. In the face of obstacles and failures in migration and settlement, officials reasserted the state's prerogative to manipulate the population and furthered their development of tools and mechanisms to categorise, tabulate and 'improve' Ottoman subjects.

Governmentality, social engineering and failure provide a framework to consider how Ottoman administrators understood governance and how their understanding of and approaches to the Ottoman population changed over time. In the past decade, historians of the Armenian Genocide and the early Turkish Republic have explored broader trends in Ottoman population politics to better situate the genocide within the totality of Ottoman social engineering.[45] This book builds on those insights, exploring institutions and policies of migration administration to better understand Ottoman population management prior to the Balkan Wars and World War I. The history of Ottoman migration administration reveals how over time Ottoman officials developed the ideological and infrastructural capacity to engage in mass expulsion and genocide. The unique specificities of the empire – its precarious sovereignty, administrative difficulties and internal and external dynamics across the nineteenth and twentieth centuries – are crucial in considering how certain groups became insiders and outsiders in projects of Ottoman social engineering.

Throughout the sixty years that this book covers, migrants offered a useful tool in officials' attempts to engineer the population, though the vision of what the future of the Ottoman state might look like, and the ways migrants could be useful, changed in response to internal and external politics. The question of how to mould the population turned on the question of who might comprise the ideal subject. As this book argues, the meaning of the *muhacir* changed in turn.

Ottoman Mass Migrations

One of the great challenges of Ottoman migration administration was that it emerged alongside moments of upheaval and mass migration events, revealing the limits of Ottoman infrastructure, administrative capacity and funding. Motion characterised life in the Black Sea region for centuries, but these movements grew vastly in scale in the eighteenth and nineteenth centuries. The 1774 Treaty of Küçük Kaynarca and the Russian annexation of Crimea in 1783 increased pressure on Muslims in the peninsula, and several hundred thousand Crimean and Nogay Tatars immigrated to the Ottoman Empire in the several decades following the 1774 treaty.[46] In the early decades of the nineteenth century, the Russian and Ottoman Empires redistributed Christians and Muslims within border regions in an informal process of colonisation and border securitisation.[47] The Crimean War (1853–6) marked a shift in the scale of population redistribution. In 1859, 50,000 Nogay Tatars left the Kuban. During the war, 10,000–20,000 Crimean Tatars sought asylum in the Ottoman Empire, and between 1856 and 1862, nearly two thirds of the Crimean Tatar population left the peninsula. The end of the Crimean War coincided with a redoubling of Russian efforts to control the North Caucasus.[48] Historians have struggled to establish definitive figures, but perhaps 223,000 Tatars left Crimea for the Ottoman Empire during this period, and between 1861 and 1866 more than one million Circassians departed from the North Caucasus.[49]

Although a general climate of fear, discrimination and upheaval prompted movements from both the Crimean Peninsula and the Caucasus, the Russian Empire's policies and actions fluctuated according to time and place. The mass migration of Crimean Tatars following the Crimean War was a complex and multi-causal phenomenon. In the decades prior to the war, Crimean Tatars faced land confiscations, while during the war, they endured forcible relocation and attacks from Cossack squadrons.[50] The devastation of the Crimean War, deteriorating trust in the Russian-Tatar relationship, and social upheaval in the peninsula contributed to mass exodus in 1860. Nevertheless, as the Muslim peasantry fled the peninsula, the same landowning class that had originally encouraged Tatar emigration realised that the mass departure was economically devastating. The central government stopped issuing passports to Crimean Tatars, thus forcibly maintaining the remaining population.[51]

Like Tatars, Muslims in the Caucasus faced disruption from the war and Russian colonisation. Far more so than they did with the Tatars, however, Russian officials viewed removal of the Muslim Caucasus population as essential to Russian state security. Nomadic pastoralist mountaineers engaged in full-scale armed opposition to Russian forces and assisted the Ottomans during the Crimean War. Following the war, the Russian Empire launched a strong offensive in the Caucasus. To a far greater extent than the migrations of the Tatars, the 1861 to 1866 migrations of the Circassians and other Caucasus groups were expulsions planned and enacted by the Russian Empire. Entire villages were destroyed. Conquered tribes, faced with a 'choice' of resettlement in the Kuban valley in the north, military service in the Tsar's army or conversion to Christianity, decided instead to depart for the Ottoman Empire.[52]

Large-scale migrations likewise followed the 1877–8 Russo-Ottoman War. The Ottoman military was unable to match Russian forces on its western and eastern borders. In the west, the Russian Army halted less than ten miles from Istanbul; its approach was ultimately checked by

Introduction

British warships. In the east, the cities of Kars and Erzurum fell to Russian forces soon after the start of the war. The war and its aftermath led to movement from both theatres of an estimated two million people in total.[53]

Aside from the concentrated movements of the 1860s and 1870s, throughout the following decades Muslims continued to arrive from Russia and former Ottoman territories, with potentially 500,000 arriving from the Caucasus between 1880 and the start of World War I. The unification of Bulgaria and Eastern Rumelia in 1885 and the creation of autonomous Crete in 1898 continued the empire's trend of territorial loss and contributed to large-scale cross-border movement. Following the Balkan Wars of 1912–13, another half million Muslims took refuge in Istanbul and Anatolia. In total, from 1783 to 1913, some five to seven million Muslims immigrated into Ottoman lands. An estimated 3.8 million of these migrants were former Russian subjects.[54] Mass migrations and loss of land radically changed the composition of the Ottoman population. Though the population of the empire in 1914, twenty-six million, was approximately the same as it had been in 1800, population density effectively doubled during the period.[55]

The periodisation suggested by these mass migration reveals the importance of conflict and coercion within Ottoman immigration. It reflects as well how individuals experienced the changing nature of imperial governance, as states increased their capacity 'to count, to extract, and to exterminate' populations.[56] Conflict influenced the timing and extent of migrations as well as the likelihood that newcomers arrived with capital, moveable property or relatives. The question of resources figured largely in the policies statesmen designed as they sought to turn migrants into productive and loyal subjects of the Ottoman state. Although officials retained their overarching vision of the utility of the *muhacir*, they also distinguished among migrants based on factors of class, social systems and places of origin.

The Ottoman migration regime unfolded across repeated 'crisis' moments. In response to the difficulties of mass migration and settlement, officials sought to refine their efforts by extracting more information about the population. As the empire contracted, new ideas about governing the population coincided with new ideas of what the most governable population might be. The elevation of those characteristics that administrators believed comprised the ideal *muhacir* and their approaches to fostering that ideal revealed and contributed to lines of inclusion and exclusion in the empire's last decades.

Governing Migration in the Late Ottoman Empire

Outline of the Study

This book progresses through six semi-chronological and thematic chapters, each of which highlights immigration as a component of Ottoman social engineering and considers a different aspect of the meaning of the *muhacir*. It traces the generative aspects of 'failure' and 'crisis' on migration policies and settlement strategies by highlighting how *muhacirin* and other Ottoman subjects critiqued immigration policies and settlement outcomes, exhuming the idiosyncrasies of individual Ottoman officials, and underlining the ways in which Ottoman administrators applied the 'will to improve' to governance itself.

Chapter 1 focuses on the enactment and outcomes of the Ottoman Migrant Regulations of 1857. The Tanzimat Council passed the law in order to attract European and North American settlers to colonise the empire. The chapter situates the underpinning logic of the Migrant Regulations – that the state should facilitate migration, that migration could enhance agricultural development and that settlement could render the population more legible – within the broader context of the Tanzimat reform era. Officials viewed colonisation as a way to develop agriculture, and Ottoman statesmen, consuls and potential migrants situated the regulations within their understanding of European trans-Atlantic migration. In this context, *muhacir* was synonymous with colonist. When officials faced mass immigration from Russia beginning in the late 1850s, they transposed the essence of the law – immigration as a path to shaping a productive, legible and loyal population – onto the newcomers. Ultimately, those migrants became the colonists Tanzimat officials had hoped to attract.

The logic of the Migrant Regulations featured in how officials responded to unanticipated movement in the following decades. Chapter 2 traces that response in terms of *muhacir* settlement during the migrations of Crimean Tatars in 1860–1 and Circassians in 1863–5. In 1860, the establishment of the first administratively independent institution for migration management, the Migrant Commission (Muhacirin Komisyonu), cast mass migration as a realm of governance for the central state. The chapter follows the career of Nusret Bey/Pasha, the Director of Migrant Settlement in Rumelia from 1860–4, who played a role within migration administration across the next several decades. During Nusret's tenure as Settlement Director, some 120,000 immigrants arrived in Rumelia, the empire's territories in south-eastern Europe. The chapter shows how settlement protocols encompassed emergency aid and long-term investment in migrants' economic productivity. Officials were challenged by the numerous difficulties of actualising large-scale settlement. As the *muhacir* became a problem

Introduction

in need of a state-driven solution, Nusret and other officials sought to improve administration by mapping territory and collecting data. Their efforts to turn refugees into colonists attached certain rights and resources to the *muhacir* category overall and to subcategories based on factors such as class, occupation, gender and age. While migrants remained a resource in colonising Ottoman territory, the *muhacir* also became a problem for officials to solve.

Chapter 3 analyses how international dynamics influenced Ottoman migration governance from the perspectives of public health and migrant welfare. In the nineteenth century, public health became a field for the Ottoman state to manage its population and to fashion its international image as a 'civilised' state. At the same time, international protocols and institutions such as the Constantinople Superior Health Council provided pathways for Great Power influence over the empire and its territory. These factors affected the empire's management of mobility. In the 1860s, the Health Council and the Ottoman government cast the *muhacir* as a public health threat, and administrators developed techniques to confine and administer migrants. When the empire again faced mass migration in the late 1870s, officials maintained and expanded those techniques. During and after the 1877–8 Russo-Ottoman War, at a moment when the dynamics of the Eastern Question threatened the empire's sovereignty in the Balkans and in Anatolia, the arrival in Edirne and Istanbul of hundreds of thousands of displaced individuals rendered the *muhacirin* and their welfare essential to the Hamidian-era government's framing of its administrative efficacy and overall legitimacy. In that context, the *muhacir* became a preoccupation of philanthropic enterprises, including the İane-i Muhacirin Encumeni (Migrant Aid Committee) and the Turkish Compassionate Fund, which addressed migrant suffering as a humanitarian concern and as a form of political power. Thus, during the migration crises of the early 1860s and late 1870s, the *muhacir* and the *muhacir*'s welfare were crucial in Tanzimat and Hamidian-era arguments for the Ottoman right to rule.

Moving from spaces of representation to spaces of settlement, Chapter 4 focuses on the last two decades of the nineteenth century to consider how *muhacir* settlement unfolded via claims to territory. Settlement was crucial to social engineering; officials sought to organise space in order to shape the population and its behaviours. Policies, procedures and reports reveal officials' belief that they could rely on science and careful planning to execute large-scale settlement projects. The chapter weaves together reports written by multiple officials, such as General Muzaffer Pasha, an individual who discovered 'empty land' for settlement across Anatolia in

Governing Migration in the Late Ottoman Empire

the 1890s. The chapter describes the tools, documents, institutions and projects officials deployed to render visible the distribution of the population. It also explores how obstacles, failures and contestations reinforced and challenged documentary regimes and ideologies of land use in the 1880s and 1890s. Officials, migrants, peasants, notables and others levied critiques as plans unfolded. Their diagnoses of failure generated grounds for further intervention, solidifying officials' sense that success was ever just slightly out of reach. The rhetoric of failure contributed to the positioning of the state – and officials as its representatives – as outside of and acting upon society, elevated by regularity, standardisation and the binding qualities of legal codes and documentary evidence.

Though Muzaffer Pasha's efforts aligned with the Ottoman government's established interest in facilitating immigration, Hamidian-era anxieties over state security and legitimacy encouraged the development of restrictions at the Ottoman border and led administrators to elevate criteria of religion and motivation in their approach to the *muhacir*. Chapter 5 assesses exclusion in border control and migrant settlement. During the Hamidian era, the sultan and Ottoman statesmen responded to the terms of the 1878 Treaty of Berlin, the emergence of national separatist organisations and the continued threat of Great Power intervention by identifying Muslims as uniquely beneficial to Ottoman security and sovereignty. Consequently, the Hamidian state's migration policies and institutions sought to change population distribution on the basis of religion and prioritised the economic development of Muslim subjects. Administrators developed institutions and policies intended to encourage Muslim immigration, including the Commission for Muslim Migrants (Muhacirin-i İslamiye Komisyonu), and updated Migrant Regulations. Nevertheless, administrators' attempts to prevent Armenian return migration from North America undermined the facilitation of Muslim migration. Passport and visa requirements encouraged officials' control and surveillance over Muslims as well as non-Muslims at the border. At this moment of migration restriction, officials relied on the *hijra* – religiously obligatory migration – to advocate for the immigration of certain Muslims. Though this too reflected the effort to facilitate Muslim migration, the selective application of the *hijra* to certain populations reveals that the empire did not seek to facilitate Muslim immigration at any cost. Instead, sovereignty, nationality and legal jurisdiction remained primary concerns in the Ottoman border regime.

In the years immediately following the Young Turk Revolution of 1908, Ottomans once more posed and responded to the question of 'what does *muhacir* mean?' Chapter 6 explores how this question provided

Introduction

perspectives from which to detect flaws in Ottoman society and to consider possibilities for an Ottoman future. Self-identified *muhacirin* writing in the newspaper of the Society for Rumelian Muslim Migrants (RMIC) used the question to consider the role of the individual and the citizen within Ottoman society. Personal experiences of displacement were fundamental to the writers' identification as *muhacir*; nevertheless, they deployed the concept to diagnose problems and propose solutions in the Ottoman state, thus retaining a forward-looking, instrumentalised understanding of the migrant's role in Ottoman society. Members of the Ottoman General Assembly likewise considered the meaning of *muhacir* as they debated whether the government was discriminatory in its migration and settlement policies. Though 'what does *muhacir* mean' was a matter of debate, politicians' approaches to that question were constrained by hegemonic understandings of migration and the state: that immigration was closely tied to the empire's economic development, and that careful planning and information-driven administration could unlock the innate potential of the *muhacir*. Though the revolution initiated rapid change and political upheaval, these durable assumptions, drawn from sixty years of mass migration, influenced how Ottoman politicians, administrators and subjects considered issues of migration management in the years prior to the Balkan Wars.

The book concludes by revisiting the narrative's essential insights, discussing Ottoman social engineering and migration administration in the empire's last decade, and commenting on the ongoing significance of categories of movement in the Turkish Republic in the twentieth and twenty-first centuries. Taken together, the chapters narrate the development of rationalities of governance and posit why and how the identification and exclusion of population groups was attached to the figure of the *muhacir*. The narrative reveals continuities and changes across a sixty-year period of mass migration and administration, offering insight into a system that was originally designed to facilitate orderly immigration and settlement in the Ottoman Empire yet became a tool for exclusion, deportation and genocide.

* * *

The nineteenth- and early twentieth-century Ottoman state provides an opportunity to 'deliberately explore instances in which the categories, concepts, and motivations of migration are confused'.[57] In the anecdote that began this Introduction, an Ottoman parliamentarian's question about the meaning of *muhacir* and *mülteci* arose because the official and legal definitions of those terms were in flux. In contrast, the contemporary

Governing Migration in the Late Ottoman Empire

Ottoman historian finds ambiguity in the term *muhacir* because of the durability of the migrant/refugee binary and a nearly unshakable tendency to differentiate and describe migrants based on the causes of their movement. The changing meaning of *muhacir* offers insight into Ottoman processes of state-building and statecraft. By tracing a series of meanings attached to the term *muhacir* – colonist, problem, possibility, health threat, victim, forced migrant, Ottoman and Muslim – the book describes Ottoman officials' interest in social engineering practices, their growing capacity to intervene in society and their shifting criteria of who could be transformed for the sake of the empire.

Notes

1. *Meclis-i Ayan Zabıt Ceridesi*, 3.4.1.16, 3 January 1918, 206–7. Quoted in Fuat Dündar, *İttihat ve Terakki'nin Müslümanları İskan Politikası (1913–1918)* (İstanbul: İletişim Yayınları, 2001), 227–8.
2. İskan-ı Muhacirin Nizamnamesi, *Düstur*, 2, vol. 5 (Istanbul: Matbaa-i Amir, 1332/1913), 377. Russian and Austro-Hungarian officials likewise employed now unfamiliar distinctions between refugees and other migrants during the era, in part because 'forced migration' and resettlement were essential to war-time governance. For Tsarist officials, refugees were 'spontaneous' and unplanned. In the Austro-Hungarian context, 'evacuees' were forced from their home, while 'refugees' left of their own accord. Peter Gatrell, *The Making of the Modern Refugee* (Oxford: Oxford University Press, 2013), 30.
3. Kemal Karpat, *Ottoman Population, 1830–1914: Demographic and Social Characteristics* (Madison, WI: University of Wisconsin Press, 1985), 60–77.
4. The parliamentarian's question also highlights pitfalls in translating terms that now wield much different meanings. In modern Turkish, the term *mülteci* refers largely to international refugees, whereas a newer word, *göçmen*, refers to im/migrant, leaving *muhacir* a term largely used to describe the historical migrations covered in this book.
5. Lewis Siegebaum and Leslie Page Moch, *Broad Is My Native Land: Repertoires and Regimes of Migration in Russia's Twentieth Century* (Ithaca, NY: Cornell University Press, 2014), 3.
6. 'What Is a Refugee?', UNHCR, accessed 9 September 2021, unhcr.org/en-us/what-is-a-refugee.html.
7. Roger Zetter, 'Refugees and Refugee Studies: A Label and an Agenda, Editorial Introduction to the *Journal of Refugee Studies*', *Journal of Refugee Studies* 1, no. 1 (1988): 1–6; Zetter, 'Labelling Refugees: Forming and Transforming a Bureaucratic Identity', *Journal of Refugee Studies* 4, no. 1 (1991): 39–62; Oliver Bakewell, 'Conceptualising Displacement and Migration: Processes, Conditions, and Categories', in *The Migration-*

Introduction

Displacement Nexus: Patterns, Processes, and Policies, ed. Khalid Koser and Susan Martin (Oxford: Berghahn Books, 2011), 14–28; Giulia Scalettaris, 'Refugee Studies and the International Refugee Regime: A Reflection on a Desirable Separation', *Refugee Survey Quarterly* 26, no. 3 (2007), 36–50.

8. Shahram Khosravi, *'Illegal' Traveller: An Auto-Ethnography of Borders* (Basingstoke: Palgrave Macmillan, 2010), 31–5.

9. Ilana Feldman, 'Difficult Distinctions: Refugee Law, Humanitarian Practice, and Political Identification in Gaza', *Cultural Anthropology* 22, no. 1 (2007): 129–69; Victoria Abrahamyan, 'Citizen Strangers: Identity Labelling and Discourse in the French Mandatory Syria, 1920–1932', *Journal of Migration History* 6, no 1 (2020); 40–61.

10. Thomas Nail, *The Figure of the Migrant* (Stanford, CA: Stanford University Press, 2015), 2.

11. Panikos Panayi, 'Imperial Collapse and the Creation of Refugees in Twentieth-Century Europe', in *Refugees and the End of Empire: Imperial Collapse and Forced Migration in the Twentieth Century*, ed. Panikos Panayi and Pippa Virdee (Basingstoke: Palgrave Macmillan, 2011), 3.

12. Gatrell, *Making of the Modern Refugee*, 2.

13. John Torpey, *The Invention of the Passport: Surveillance, Citizenship, and the State* (Cambridge: Cambridge University Press, 2000).

14. Aristide Zolberg, 'The Formation of New States as a Refugee-Generating Process', *The Annals of the American Academy of Political and Social Science* 467 (1983): 24–38; Gatrell, *Making of the Modern Refugee*.

15. Liisa Malkki, 'National Geographic: The Rooting of Peoples and the Territorialization of National Identity among Scholars and Refugees', *Cultural Anthropology* 7.1 (1992): 24–44.

16. Laura Robson, *States of Separation: Transfer, Partition, and the Making of the Modern Middle East* (Oakland: University of California Press, 2017); Benjamin White, *The Emergence of Minorities in the Middle East: The Politics of Community in French Mandate Syria* (Edinburgh: Edinburgh University Press, 2011); Keith Watenpaugh, *Bread from Stones: The Middle East and the Making of Modern Humanitarianism* (Oakland: University of California Press, 2015).

17. Nevzat Soğuk, *States and Strangers: Refugees and the Displacements of Statecraft* (Minneapolis: Minneapolis University Press, 1999), 119. Emphasis in the original.

18. Rebecca Hamlin, *Crossing: How We Label and React to People on the Move* (Stanford, CA: Stanford University Press, 2021), 1.

19. Ibid., 4.

20. For discussions of forced migration and the segmentation of scholarship see Ulbe Bosma, 'Beyond the Atlantic: Connecting Migration and World History in the Age of Imperialism, 1840–1940', *International Review of Social History* 52, no. 1 (2007): 116–23; and Adam McKeown, 'Global Migration, 1846–1940', *Journal of World History* 15, no. 2 (2004): 155–89.

21. Isa Blumi, *Ottoman Refugees, 1878–1939: Migration in a Post-Imperial World* (London: Bloomsbury Academic, 2013); Thomas Nail, *Figure of the Migrant*.

22. Reşat Kasaba, *A Moveable Empire: Ottoman Nomads, Migrants, and Refugees* (Seattle: University of Washington Press, 2009); Chris Gratien, *The Unsettled Plain: An Environmental History of the Late Ottoman Frontier* (Stanford, CA: Stanford University Press, 2022). Janet Klein also describes how attempts to co-opt Kurdish leaders ended up reinforcing their power. Janet Klein, *The Margins of Empire: Kurdish Militias in the Ottoman Tribal Zone* (Stanford, CA: Stanford University Press, 2011).

23. Torpey, *The Invention of the Passport*, 4. See also Cristoph Herzog, 'Migration and the State: On Ottoman Regulations Concerning Migration since the Age of Mahmud II', in *The City in the Ottoman Empire: Migration and the Making of Urban Modernity*, ed. Ulrike Freitag, Malte Fuhrmann, Nora Lafi and Florian Riedler (London: Routledge, 2011), 117–34. For a discussion of eighteenth-century Ottoman regulatory policies, see Andrew Robarts, *Migration and Disease in the Black Sea Region: Ottoman-Russian Relations in the Late Eighteenth and Early Nineteenth Centuries* (London: Bloomsbury Academic, 2017).

24. Radhika Mongia, *Indian Migration and Empire: A Colonial Genealogy of the Modern State* (Durham, NC: Duke University Press, 2018). See also Adam McKeown, *Melancholy Order: Asian Migration and the Globalization of Borders* (New York: Columbia University Press, 2008); Aristide Zolberg, *A Nation by Design: Immigration Policy in the Fashioning of America* (Cambridge, MA: Harvard University Press, 2006).

25. David Gutman, *The Politics of Armenian Migration to North America, 1885–1915: Sojourners, Smugglers, and Dubious Citizens* (Edinburgh: Edinburgh University Press, 2019).

26. Will Hanley, *Identifying with Nationality: Europeans, Ottomans, and Egyptians in Alexandria* (New York: Columbia University Press, 2017).

27. James Meyer, *Turks across Empires: Marketing Muslim Identity in the Russian-Ottoman Borderlands, 1856–1914* (Oxford: Oxford University Press, 2014).

28. Lale Can, *Spiritual Subjects: Central Asian Pilgrims and the Ottoman Hajj at the End of Empire* (Stanford, CA: Stanford University Press, 2020).

29. Michael Christopher Low, *Imperial Mecca: Ottoman Arabia and the Indian Ocean Hajj* (New York: Columbia University Press, 2020).

30. Nazan Maksudyan, 'Orphans, Cities, and the State: Vocational Orphanages (*Islahhanes*) and Reform in the Late Ottoman Urban Space', *IJMES* 43, no. 3 (2011): 493–511; İpek K. Yosmaoğlu, 'Counting Bodies, Shaping Souls: The 1903 Census and National Identity in Ottoman Macedonia', *IJMES* 38, no. 1 (2006): 55–77; Eugene L. Rogan, 'Aşiret Mektebi: Abdülhamid II's School for Tribes (1892–1907)', *IJMES* 28, no.1 (1996): 83–107; Emine Ö. Evered, *Empire and Education under the Ottomans: Politics, Reform, and Resistance from the Tanzimat to the Young Turks* (London: I. B. Tauris,

Introduction

2012); Kent Schull, *Prisons in the Late Ottoman Empire* (Edinburgh: Edinburgh University Press, 2014).

31. Michel Foucault, 'Governmentality', in *The Foucault Effect: Studies in Governmentality*, ed. Graham Burchell, Colin Gordon and Peter Miller (Chicago: The University of Chicago Press, 1991), 100.

32. Dean Mitchell, *Governmentality: Power and Rule in Modern Society* (London: Sage, 1999), 10; Foucault, 'Governmentality', 102.

33. Amir Weiner, 'Nature, Nurture, and Memory in a Socialist Utopia: Delineating the Soviet Socio-Ethnic Body in the Age of Socialism', *The American Historical Review* 104, no. 4 (1999): 1116.

34. Amir Weiner, ed., *Landscaping the Human Garden: Twentieth-Century Population Management in a Comparative Framework* (Stanford, CA: Stanford University Press, 2003); see also, Uğur Ümit Üngör, *The Making of Modern Turkey: Nation and State in Eastern Anatolia, 1913–1950* (Oxford: Oxford University Press, 2011), x–xi.

35. Zygmunt Bauman, 'In the Court Where Multi-Ethnic Polities Are On Trial the Jury Is Still Out', interview by Sergei Glebov, *Ab Imperio* 2008, no. 1 (2008): 20.

36. Nicholas Breyfogle, 'Enduring Imperium: Russia/Soviet Union/Eurasia as Multiethnic, Multiconfessional Space', *Ab Imperio* 2008, no. 1 (2008): 109–12.

37. Mitchell, *Governmentality*, 32.

38. Gutman, *Politics of Armenian Migration*; Blumi, *Ottoman Refugees*, 48.

39. Lauren Banko, 'Refugees, Displaced Migrants, and Territorialization in Interwar Palestine', *Mashriq & Mahjar* 5, no. 2 (2018): 19–49; Ramazan Hakkı Öztan, 'Settlement Law of 1934: Turkish Nationalism in the Age of Revisionism', *Journal of Migration History* 6, no. 1 (2020): 82–103.

40. Peter Miller and Nikolas Rose, *Governing the Present: Administering Economic, Social, and Personal Life* (Oxford: Polity Press, 2008), 17.

41. Bauman, 'In the Court', 21.

42. McKeown, *Melancholy Order*; Mongia, *Indian Migration and Empire*.

43. James Scott, *Seeing Like a State: How Certain Schemes to Improve the Human Condition Have Failed* (New Haven, CT: Yale University Press, 1998); Timothy Mitchell, *Rule of Experts: Egypt, Techno-Politics, Modernity* (Berkeley: University of California Press, 2002); Tania Murray Li, *The Will to Improve: Governmentality, Development, and the Practice of Politics* (Durham, NC: Duke University Press, 2007); Miller and Rose, *Governing the Present*.

44. Miller and Rose, *Governing the Present*, 61. For similar discussions, see Li, *The Will to Improve*, and Scott, *Seeing Like a State*.

45. Dündar, *İttihat ve Terakki'nin*; Nesim Şeker, 'Demographic Engineering in the Late Ottoman Empire and the Armenians', *Middle Eastern Studies* 43, no. 3 (2007): 461–74; Üngör, *The Making of Modern Turkey*; Taner Akçam, *The Young Turks' Crime against Humanity: The Armenian Genocide and*

Ethnic Cleansing in the Ottoman Empire (Princeton, NJ: Princeton University Press, 2012).

46. The largest estimate for this migration is 500,000. There is surprisingly little secondary literature mentioning this movement, and Fisher notes there is almost no evidence in the Ottoman archive responding to such a large number of arrivals. Alan Fisher, 'Emigration of Muslims from the Russian Empire in the Years after the Crimean War', *Jahrbücher für Geschichte Osteuropas* 35.3 (1987): 357.

47. Mark Pinson, 'Demographic Warfare – An Aspect of Ottoman and Russian Policy, 1854–1866' (PhD diss., Harvard University, 1970).

48. James Meyer, 'Immigration, Return, and the Politics of Citizenship: Russian Muslims in the Ottoman Empire, 1860–1914', *IJMES* 39 (2007): 16.

49. The term Circassian is a blanket term, encompassing Circassians, Abazins and Abkhaz. Other groups from the Caucasus who journeyed to the Ottoman Empire in the 1860s and after include Ossetians, Chechens and Daghestanis. For migrant population estimates, see Karpat, *Ottoman Population, 1830–1914*, 67–9.

50. Hakan Kırımlı, 'Emigrations from the Crimea to the Ottoman Empire during the Crimean War', *Middle Eastern Studies* 44.5 (2008): 755.

51. Brian Glyn Williams, 'Hijra and Forced Migration from Nineteenth-Century Russia to the Ottoman Empire: A Critical Analysis of the Great Crimean Tatar Emigration of 1860–1861', *Cahiers du Monde Russe* 41.1 (2000): 79–108; Fisher, 'Emigration of Muslims'; Kırımlı, 'Emigrations from the Crimea'.

52. Karpat, *Ottoman Population*, 69.

53. Nedim İpek, *Rumeli'den Anadolu'ya Türk Göçleri, 1877–1890* (Ankara: Türk Tarih Kurumu, 1994), 41; Karpat, *Ottoman Population*, 70.

54. Donald Quataert, 'The Age of Reforms: 1812–1914', in *An Economic and Social History of the Ottoman Empire*, vol. 2, ed. Halil İnalcık and Donald Quataert (Cambridge: Cambridge University Press, 1994), 793.

55. Ibid., 777.

56. Peter Holquist, 'To Count, to Extract, and to Exterminate: Population Statistics and Population Politics in Late Imperial and Soviet Russia', in *A State of Nations: Empire and Nation-Making in the Age of Lenin and Stalin*, ed. Ronald Suny and Terry Martin (New York: Oxford University Press, 2001), 111–44.

57. Hamlin, *Crossing*, 69.

1

Muhacir as Colonist

On June 2, 1856, several hundred Prussian families sought permission from the Ottoman state to immigrate to and settle permanently in the empire. A factory owner from their town submitted a petition on their behalf to Davud Pasha, the Ottoman consul in Vienna, who forwarded the request to Istanbul. The Foreign Minister took up the matter in the Tanzimat Council, the empire's central legislative body. The Prussian families seem to have been inspired by the Imperial Reform Edict (*Islahat Fermanı*) of 1856. The edict, one of the legislative hallmarks of the Tanzimat period, promised equality to all Ottoman subjects regardless of creed. According to the factory owner's petition, the families aspired, like so many others, to move in search of a better life. They struggled to get by, and so sought to leave for a land where 'compassion and rights extended to all subjects' and where they would be 'able to make a better living'.[1]

From the mid-nineteenth century to the mid-twentieth, mass long-distance migrations shaped world history. What some scholars refer to as the 'age of mass migrations' (c. 1840–1940) witnessed some fifty million Europeans emigrating to the Americas, but mass migration was not just a trans-Atlantic phenomenon. Numerically comparable migrations around the Pacific and Indian Oceans, internal migration in land-based empires and intra-continental movements occurred in Europe, Southeast Asia, Manchuria and Siberia.[2] Ottoman officials in the Foreign Ministry and the Tanzimat Council were keen observers of these global population trends. As the Prussians' request moved through the Ottoman bureaucracy, officials compared them to the many Europeans who had emigrated to America. The families had witnessed others embark on transatlantic journeys, which inspired them to likewise try their luck 'outside of Europe'.[3] Despite the families' willingness to leave home, the sheer distance of the Americas rendered the decision daunting. Why should European migrants

Governing Migration in the Late Ottoman Empire

travel across the sea, when plentiful land, new opportunities and a government promising equal rights for all awaited in a far closer location?

For the members of the Tanzimat Council, the lack of regulations governing immigration was a clear factor deterring families from making the empire their new home. What awaited potential migrants upon arrival within Ottoman territory? Would they receive permission to settle permanently? Would they obtain land? Would that land match their needs? The scale of the journey required some clarity. In short, the council believed setting out the conditions of subjecthood and settlement would assuage the fears and hesitations of potential immigrants. The council and the grand vizier decided to issue a law to clarify the questions raised by the petition.[4]

Aside from easing the fears of a few thousand Prussians, statesmen welcomed the chance to more widely regulate, standardise and advertise immigration in order to encourage a larger flow of settlers from Europe. That Ottoman officials placed the Prussians' petition within the context of trans-Atlantic immigration from Europe to America signalled their interest in benefiting from the age of mass migration. As the Tanzimat Council considered the Prussians' request, they shifted from a discussion of the families to one regarding a much larger, undifferentiated group of 'Europeans' who would be drawn to participate in the Ottoman economy after hearing about the opportunity from Ottoman representatives and newspapers throughout the continent.[5] Within a few months, the Tanzimat Council issued the Migrant Regulations (*Muhacirin Nizamnamesi*), which promoted colonisation by inviting Europeans and others to settle on available, arable land in the empire.

The Prussians' petition, dispatched four months after the issuing of the *Islahat Fermanı* and three months after the Treaty of Paris concluded the Crimean War, offers evidence of an Ottoman role during the first decades of the mid-nineteenth-century global migration boom. Though the gravitational pull of the Ottoman Empire was fainter than that of North or South America, Eastern Europe was within its orbit. Nor were Tanzimat officials' hopes of European colonisation so far-fetched. During the era of mass trans-Atlantic migration, England, France and Imperial Germany attracted workers from Ireland, Italy, Sweden and Poland. Nearly half the Italians who left Italy from 1876 to 1920 went to nearby European countries.[6] The Prussians' petition highlights European interest in migrating to the Ottoman Empire. The Tanzimat Council's response reveals Ottoman statesmen's view of immigration as something to be regulated and manipulated for the benefit of the economy and in conjunction with the distribution of Ottoman land.

Muhacir *as Colonist*

This chapter explores the background, parameters and significance of the 1857 *Muhacirin Nizamnamesi* within Ottoman governmentality and social engineering. The law serves to place the Ottoman state within a global era of mass migration and reveals self-conscious interest on the part of Ottoman officials in internal colonisation. The regulations, although they targeted economic migrants, provided an ideological, bureaucratic and policy framework when the Ottoman state began to respond to mass immigration in the same era. In the years immediately following the Crimean War, the *muhacir* was, first and foremost, a colonist.

Developing a Population

The *Muhacirin Nizamnamesi* aligned with the economic and population concerns held by Ottoman statesmen during the Tanzimat Reform Era (1839–76). The very entities that considered the Prussians' request and the issue of immigration indicated the empire's nineteenth-century bureaucratic expansion in fields ranging from foreign relations to education. The Ministry of Foreign Affairs was established in 1836, and the Tanzimat Council, established in 1854, was one iteration of a series of new central legislative bodies intended to increase expertise in the investigation and drafting of laws.[7] The Tanzimat Council's purpose – 'to consider the reform of the affairs of the subjects and to increase the prosperity of the Empire' – signalled the alignment between the Migrant Regulations and the era's general ethos.[8] The 1850s witnessed several key pieces of legislation – key not so much for their immediate influence on Ottoman society, which, much like the Migrant Regulations, initially was limited, as for revealing the Tanzimat's ideological trends. Ottoman officials saw in the offer of colonisation a solution to some of the empire's most urgent economic issues.

Ottoman reforms of the eighteenth and early nineteenth centuries were intended to address the empire's relative military deficits, and in so doing contributed to a changing understanding of the relationship between state and subject. The reforms, while significant, had the associated effect of plunging the empire into debt. The 1850s were a watershed moment in the long-term integration of the empire into a capitalist world economic system, and the Crimean War contributed to the empire's extended economic crisis.[9] To pay for the war, the Ottoman Empire entered into foreign debt for the first time in its history, initiating a series of loans that culminated in the empire's bankruptcy in 1875. During the Crimean War, military expenditures accounted for 67 per cent of the budget, and the state paid for half of those expenditures via foreign loans.[10]

Governing Migration in the Late Ottoman Empire

Faced with debt and reliant largely on the revenues of the agricultural tithe (*öşür*), Tanzimat statesmen attempted to improve revenue collection by appointing salaried tax collectors, shifting land from tax exempt status, reforming excise taxes and assessing taxes on traditionally exempt urban populations.[11] Agricultural experts engaged by the Ottoman state also advised the government to populate uncultivated land in order to increase economic production.[12] In conceiving of how to augment tax revenue, Ottoman officials considered two main solutions: first, increasing the sheer number of people cultivating the land, and second, creating more direct relationships among people, land and state.

The Migrant Regulations were half law and half aspiration. The Tanzimat Council issued the *Muhacirin Nizamnamesi* to address quantitative and qualitative aspects of the population. The council proposed that colonists could serve as new producers whose land claims and tax payments would be offered directly to state institutions. In presenting the case for the drafted regulations, the council framed the law's potential benefits in terms of financial gain. Given that 'Germans' were 'peerless in their honour and industriousness among the people of Europe', the Council predicted the Prussian migrants would rapidly improve the land they received.[13] In this light, the regulations reflected the Tanzimat Council's interest in cultivating the productive capacity of the population and reaping the economic benefits of population management. Immigration served as a straightforward route to agricultural development and improved revenues. The new law was a pro-immigration social engineering tool, a means to facilitate colonisation and to establish criteria to filter immigration requests through the Ottoman bureaucracy.

AN ATTAINABLE PROMISED LAND

In order for the *Muhacirin Nizamnamesi* to succeed in its intent, officials had to attract colonists to Ottoman territory. To this end, the Tanzimat Council called upon the empire's ambassadors, envoys, ministers, charges d'affaires and consuls general in London, Paris, Vienna, St Petersburg, Madrid, The Hague, Berlin, Athens, Brussels, Turin, Naples, Malta, Livorno and Corfu to publish translations of the regulations in leading journals and newspapers in March of 1857. The regulations, perhaps because they were intended to serve as promotional material as well as law, contained just fourteen articles. The first three articles established the immigrants' relationship to the central state – requiring from them an oath of loyalty and submission to the empire's laws and in return protecting the exercise of their professed religion. Subsequent articles established the immigrants' relationship to land and locality. The law guaranteed fertile land distributed according to the means of each settler, given free of charge and without imposed taxes for a set period. Migrants were offered exemptions from military conscription for the same period. The regulations included an injunction against selling the land for twenty years: settlers had to cede parcels, including buildings they had constructed on land, back to the government if they left the country during this probationary period. Newcomers also had to submit to local governance and could expect to be treated as Ottoman subjects. Though migrants were allowed to resettle elsewhere within the empire, their tax and military exemptions dated from when they received their first land allocation. The law's final articles addressed eligibility and logistics. Migrants were to be honest agriculturalists or artisans. Each family had to possess sixty gold *mecidiye* (1,350 *francs*), and each had to be registered according to 'their names, qualities, means and occupations'. Settlers were entitled to free passports and assistance in the transportation of goods and baggage, for which the government required at least two months between initial application and arrival to determine each colonist's settlement location.[14]

Observers responded to the new law by echoing the same language of economic development and population improvement espoused by the Tanzimat Council. In the spring of 1857, weeks after the council issued the regulations, Andreas David Mordtmann, a German Orientalist, charge d'affaires for the Hanseatic League and later a judge in the Ottoman commercial court, wrote to the Foreign Ministry to praise the regulations and to comment on the qualities of his own compatriots as potential colonists.[15] Mordtmann outlined the benefits the regulations could have for the empire, referring to them as 'proof of the good intentions' of the empire to 'move forward on the path of progress'. The regulations promised not only to increase the population, but, more importantly, to improve its quality by attracting settlers whose work habits and new, experience-driven methods would 'increase the Empire's resources' and 'improve [its] cultural state'. Luckily for the Ottoman Empire, Mordtmann noted, the industrious, sober colonists it most needed were departing en masse from Bavaria, Wurttemberg, Saxony, Prussia and elsewhere.[16]

Like the Tanzimat Council, Mordtmann situated the regulations and their potential outcomes within the context of trans-Atlantic migration. In his commentary, Mordtmann identified classic 'push factors' for these thousands of German peasants. According to Mordtmann's observations, though a few Germans emigrated for religious or political reasons, most of those who left for the Americas or Australia were farmers or petty craftsmen. These 'quiet people' did not bother themselves with politics or religious fanaticism. Instead, they merely sought a country and land that 'allowed them to work, to feed themselves and their families, to fulfil their duty to their superiors, and to exercise their religion without hindrance'. They came from areas that simply could no longer house the entire population, due to laws of inheritance that divided the land beyond the point of sustainability.

Lack of land and the difficulties of life in the German countryside drove people to leave; thus, desperation, rather than the particular draw of the Americas, determined peasants' destinations. Unfortunately, Mordtmann asserted, travel to the New World held no guarantee of material improvement. He focused on the conditions of those who made it to the United States. Little did these 'simple' folk know, but US laws and institutions did not protect them from corrupt and cunning speculators, and their ignorance of English left them unable to plead for the scant protections offered by the US government. With that in mind, Mordtmann argued that the Ottoman Empire could offer a far safer home for aspiring migrants.

Though the language issue was not be resolved by journeying to the Ottoman Empire, Mordtmann believed that Ottoman institutions offered far greater protections to German colonists than the American system. This was especially true if the Sublime Porte took the step of creating a secular, German *millet* (an administrative grouping traditionally based on confessional community), appointed a *vekil* (representative) and charged that *vekil* with coordinating the arrival, registration and settlement of German immigrants. It just so happened that the ideal *vekil* shared many of Mordtmann's qualities. In order to avoid 'misunderstanding' between the colonists and the Ottoman state, it was 'absolutely essential' that the *vekil* have 'perfect mastery of the German language, and that he understand the needs, feelings, ideas and views of the German colonists, that, in a word, he be a native German'.[17] Mordtmann, a model for anyone considering how to pitch a position for themselves to fill, articulated observations, concerns and goals shared by his audience at the Foreign Ministry. In their response to the Prussians' request, members of the Tanzimat Council had likewise referenced the economic and geographic factors contributing to European emigration. Agreement with Mordtmann regarding the causes of migration extended to accord about its potential benefits, not only for newcomers who had struggled to eke out an existence in Europe but for the Ottoman state as well.

Like Mordtmann, Ottoman consuls and potential migrants inserted the Ottoman regulations into their understanding of global patterns of migration and colonisation. In 1864, a Swiss lawyer by the name of Dormann Gasparini wrote to Rüstem Pasha, the Ottoman consul in Turin, to propose

Muhacir *as Colonist*

the establishment of a Swiss colony in the Ottoman Empire. Gasparini, a major in the Swiss Army and a member of the Grand Council and Criminal Tribunal of the Canton of St. Gallen, hoped to bring some 2,000 individuals to the empire over the subsequent year. Gasparini touted his experience in coordinating the emigration of Swiss peasants to the Americas, and he speculated that the Ottoman Empire could choose from a number of colonisation strategies, including founding settlements, chartering colonies via individuals and corporations, or establishing military colonies of the type seen in Algeria and Russia.[18]

Gasparini emphasised the appeal of the Ottoman Empire for potential immigrants: Switzerland was too crowded, and the Ottoman Empire was rich in available land. Moreover, like the Prussian families whose request had initiated the Migrant Regulations, he believed that the Swiss found the prospect of a transoceanic voyage daunting. A large number of Swiss left their homeland each year headed for the New World, but 'the long and treacherous voyage' caused the emigrants all manner of evils. The Ottoman Empire, on the other hand, promised 'the convenience of a short trip by land, fertility of soil, and a benevolent government', which would 'encourage all the emigrants from Switzerland to choose to ... settle there definitively'. Commenting on Gasparini's plans, Rüstem echoed the idea that the empire could divert the stream of Swiss migrants headed to the New World simply by offering a more attainable and familiar option to a largely 'continental' people.[19]

Gasparini and Rüstem employed the language of civilisation and development in making the case for the Swiss project. In his pitch, Gasparini emphasised that a Swiss colony would be 'more advantageous' than any other, since the Swiss were a hardworking, politically neutral, loyal and religiously tolerant people, which would allow them to live among the empire's Muslim subjects. Rüstem generously echoed Gasparini's assessment of the Swiss, painting them as 'more likely than other colonists to take Ottoman nationality'. Though they were in possession of 'a conciliatory character' that would allow them to live in 'perfect harmony' with the Ottoman population, they would also be eager to complete their Ottoman military service because of their 'naturally martial spirit' and 'familiarity with weapons since childhood'.[20] Despite Gasparini's best efforts and Rüstem's enthusiastic support, the Swiss colony was not to be. Citing the sheer number of Circassian refugees arriving in the empire by 1864, Ali Pasha, then Foreign Minister, rejected Gasparini's proposal.

Gasparini's direct comparison between the Ottoman Empire and the Americas was more than just a failed rhetorical ploy undone by poor timing. Reference to the transoceanic movements of the era framed how potential migrants, entrepreneurs, observers and Ottoman officials understood the benefits and significance of the *Muhacirin Nizamnamesi*. In an era of mass migration, officials believed the Ottoman Empire could attract otherwise transatlantic emigrants by promoting the Ottoman Empire as an attainable promised land. This possibility appealed to migrants themselves. While Gasparini, Mordtmann, the Prussians and others writing to the Sublime Porte were prudent to weigh the Ottoman Empire favourably in their comparisons with the New World, the fact remains that those petitioning for permission to immigrate believed in the opportunities they would find in the empire. They trusted the Ottoman state to provide security and ensure religious freedom, and they bore no great qualms about pledging loyalty to the Sultan.

TAXES, TERRITORY AND PEOPLING THE LAND

The Migrant Regulations featured in Ottoman social engineering. Ottoman officials coupled their understanding of the era of global mass migration with a sense that the *Muhacirin Nizamnamesi* could augment the quantity and quality of the Ottoman population. They believed that immigration would improve the empire's productive capacity and enhance the military through population increase. While the promise of development through colonisation was clear, the regulations were tied to another overarching trend of the reform period: the establishment of a more direct relationship between subjects and the central state. In order for officials to manipulate characteristics of the population, they first had to administratively locate Ottoman subjects. It was not enough that the newcomers be loyal and hardworking. They should also be legible: capable of being 'identified, observed, recorded, counted, aggregated, and monitored'.[21] The colonisation plan and the terms of the Migrant Regulations coincided with the Land Code of 1858 and other legislative attempts to extend the extractive capacity of the Ottoman state through the identification and registration of people and land.

Land was fundamental to the *Muhacirin Nizamnamesi*. It was the boon offered to lure potential settlers, and it was the primary driver in inviting migrants in the first place. Over and again, potential colonists and officials framed the colonisation plan as a pairing between surplus populations in Europe and the vast, fertile, available lands of the Ottoman state. Land reform and tax reform were closely tied. The Land Code of 1858 required that individual users register title deeds, which increased the state's ability to tax the population through establishing one-to-one relationships between subjects and the central state.[22] Likewise, inviting migrants peopled the

Muhacir *as Colonist*

land by making known the population dwelling within Ottoman territory. The *Muhacirin Nizamnamesi*'s registration requirements and expectations of long-term settlement worked in tandem with the broader Ottoman attempt to make land ownership legible, to influence land usage, and to collect taxes through new cadastral surveys and the centralisation of title deeds within the Imperial Cadastral Office.[23] The regulations contributed to the generation of knowledge about the land and the people who lived within it by encouraging long-term settlement, attending to patterns of population distribution and providing impetus for land surveys.

The *Muhacirin Nizamnamesi* also corresponded to Tanzimat-era shifts in the legal framework of subjecthood. Two signature pieces of Tanzimat-era legislation, the 1839 Gülhane Rescript and the 1856 *Islahat Fermanı*, extended equal rights to subjects. Both decrees were intended to reduce foreign intervention on behalf of Ottoman non-Muslim subjects and to foster a shared imperial identity among the empire's religiously diverse population. While asserting the civil equality of all subjects, the Ottoman state formalised the arrangements of the *millet* system. Prior to the nineteenth century, Ottoman officials used the term *millet* (religious community) to describe Ottoman Muslims and *dhimmi* to refer to non-Muslim monotheist 'People of the Book'. Religious minorities were allowed some autonomy over their educational and judicial practices. During the Tanzimat, the state shifted from ad hoc, localised relationships with non-Muslim minorities to an institutionalised, centralised structure for each community (*millet*).[24] The Ottoman *millet* reforms corresponded to a trans-imperial trend of formalising state oversight over communal administration.[25] Though Tanzimat-era legislation elevated 'Ottoman' – a term that did not distinguish between Muslims and non-Muslim subjects – and *ecnebi* (foreigner) as new legal categories, the reformed *millet* system continued to allow for state recognition of distinctions among the empire's subjects.[26]

These new legal and social categories emerged in the context of imperial competition for sovereignty over Ottoman subjects. In particular, Tanzimat reformers used the promise of equal rights to address the problem of the Capitulations: treaties that allowed European states legal authority over their subjects residing in Ottoman domains and allowed those subjects certain privileges. By the eighteenth century, the capitulatory agreements granted European powers authority over not only their own subjects but also over Ottoman subjects who served as their representatives/protégés. A large number of foreigners and non-Muslim Ottoman subjects received tax privileges and avoided the jurisdiction of Ottoman courts. In response, Tanzimat statesmen issued a series of laws to address the problem of

European intervention on behalf of Ottoman subjects. The 1863 Protégé Law was intended to dismantle further the privileges of the protégé system, and the 1869 Nationality Law was meant to clarify who was an Ottoman, and thus who was subject to Ottoman law.[27] The Ottoman fight for sovereignty over Ottoman subjects continued in the next several decades. Officials waged the battle internally, at the empire's borders and overseas, as they confronted jurisdictional disputes over emigres in the Americas and non-Ottoman Muslim pilgrims in Ottoman territory.[28]

The *Muhacirin Nizamnamesi* contributed to the emergence of the 'secular, state-centred membership regime' envisioned in the Protégé and Nationality Laws.[29] By requiring settlers to change their subjecthood, the Tanzimat Council attempted to prevent the emergence of a new population with ambiguous legal status. In its deliberations, the council emphasised that settlers' change in subjecthood was a necessary precondition for the Ottoman state to obtain the benefits offered by immigration.[30] The expectation of changed subjecthood became essential to the legal meaning of *muhacir* within the Ottoman bureaucracy.

The Migrant Regulations addressed the need for long-term settlement, and its tenets were intended to facilitate migrants' success. Colonists received temporary exemptions from taxation and military conscription. While both exemptions were tactics to entice newcomers, waiving military service also served to keep settlers working on their land. The importance of encouraging long-term settlement of new Ottoman subjects emerged in further addenda to the regulations, which elaborated the issue of inheritance for migrants who died prior to farming the land for the twenty-year period required in the regulations. If an individual died before completing the twenty-year term, their heirs had several options. They could fulfil the rest of the time individually or in common with other inheritors, or they could sell the land to another migrant. In either case, upon fulfilment of the original twenty-year loan, the individual received the usufruct rights to that plot. Inheritors who lived outside the Ottoman Empire did not hold any claim to the property of the deceased.[31] The addenda prioritised long-term development and long-term productivity for property usage within the empire.

In drafting the *Muhacirin Nizamnamesi*, the Tanzimat Council targeted Anatolia for migrant settlement, seeking to reverse the outcome of centuries-long demographic trends. Beginning in the late sixteenth century, widespread upheaval, rebellion, environmental change and rural-to-urban migration led to the depopulation of the Ottoman countryside. Population registers from north-central Anatolia record household numbers falling some 70 to 80 per cent, and 30 to 40 per cent of villages populated in the 1570s were left abandoned or ruined by the 1640s. In Anatolia, the crises of the seventeenth century contributed to the resurgence of nomadic pastoralism in Central and Eastern Anatolia, Syria and Iraq.[32] A series of conflicts in the eighteenth and nineteenth centuries slowed demographic recovery. As the Tanzimat Council weighed the terms of the regulations, its members considered how to encourage immigrants to settle in Anatolia, where they believed the improvements Europeans could bring to the land would be especially beneficial. The council's solution was to differentiate the tax and conscription exemptions for each area, sweetening the appeal of Anatolia with a twelve-year exemption period as opposed to a six-year period for settlement in Rumelia.[33]

The regulations reveal the council's attempt to shape the population through entry criteria and careful management. The *nizamname* encouraged immigration, but it also established standards to determine the circumstances under which individuals could immigrate and regularise their status. The criteria through which the regulations filtered immigrants were neither religious nor ethnic; instead, the law specified economic and moral characteristics, such as the capital requirement, agricultural or small-scale industrial professional credentials and intentions, and stipulations of 'honesty' and industriousness.[34] Three signals suggest that the council and officials recognised standardisation, selection and organisation as integral to the colonisation project. First, the Tanzimat Council attempted to regulate the flow of border crossers. The council stipulated that colonists had to relay their request at least three months in advance of a potential move date. Consuls registered the colonists two months prior to their arrival in the empire to facilitate travel within the country and to prevent newcomers from suffering a 'loss of time' or other hardship.[35] Second, consuls and prospective immigrants took selection criteria seriously, framing requests to the Foreign Office in terms of applicants' industriousness, prosperity, respectability, moral conduct and potential to be model contributors to the advancement of Ottoman agriculture.[36] Third, officials sought to ensure successful, productive colonisation by evaluating land and organising settlement.

In the years immediately following the Crimean War, the Ottoman state faced an ongoing revenue crisis. Ottoman officials embraced colonisation as a route to economic development and agricultural productivity and as a means to overcome debt, decentralisation and foreign incursion. In a global era of mass migration, colonisation and the facilitation of immigration became tools to address some of the most urgent issues facing the Ottoman state. The regulations revealed officials' growing effort to engage in social engineering through placing productive, legible

Governing Migration in the Late Ottoman Empire

populations on the empire's available land. Colonists themselves were interested in the attainable promised land of the Ottoman Empire – a land rendered attractive by proximity and availability, by the promise of equal treatment under law, and by belief in the administrative capacity of the Ottoman state.

Obstacles

While the goals of the *Muhacirin Nizamnamesi* were clear to Ottoman officials and potential migrants alike, it is a truth universally acknowledged that policies create unanticipated effects. That is, Ottoman officials, in possession of a good plan, must be in want of the means to enact it. As happened repeatedly during the development of the Ottoman migration regime, rather than offering a straightforward pairing of people and land, enacting colonisation presented unanticipated challenges for officials, migrants and the populations among whom they settled. These obstacles reflected the complications of translating the ideology of the Migrant Regulations into action, and emerged in four main capacities: limited ability to prepare and organise large-scale settlement, reliance on individual European recruiters, ongoing mediation by European consuls, and the emergence of mass migration from around the Black Sea.

QUESTIONS FOR CONSULS

The first issue Ottoman officials encountered was born of an appealing problem: interest in the plan quickly eclipsed the Ottoman state's preparation. Soon after the Tanzimat Council called upon its envoys to publicise the *Muhacirin Nizamnamesi* in the spring of 1857, Ottoman representatives abroad submitted calls for clarification to the Foreign Ministry, commenting on the appeal of the regulations for capitalists and potential colonists. While the members of the Tanzimat Council intended the regulations to encourage immigration by establishing standardisation and clear processes, potential colonists' desire for clarification outstripped the plan's enactment. Though the availability of land was not in question, exactly where it might be found was. Ottoman land-surveying efforts lagged behind migrants' desire to relocate.

Weeks after the publication of the regulations, Florentine readers of the *Turin Journal* peppered Pierre Tausch, the Ottoman consul general in Livorno, with questions too specific for him to answer. He duly passed them on to Istanbul. First, the Florentines wondered where they might settle. They ranked several appealing regions, inquiring about the availability of land northeast of Bergama/Pergamon, and, if not there, land close to other cities near the Dardanelles. Aside from the question of location, they sought clarity regarding the amount of land each family was to receive, whether those apportionments were to be mixed use or exclusively farmland, and whether large groups or even entire villages could anticipate settling together. Finally, they asked for clarification on the relationship between the state and newcomers. Citing rumours that farmers in the Ottoman Empire were frequently subjected to exploitation, they wondered what laws protected colonists from the extortion faced by other Ottoman subjects.[37]

The Migrant Regulations sought to ensure careful settlement and avoid long delays for interested colonists, but the issuing of the regulations preceded the administrative capacity to realise this goal. The logistics of settlement, especially the selection of land for potential colonists, revealed how little surveying officials had completed in advance. The Foreign Ministry's response to the Florentines' questions about where they might settle centred on the inevitability of delay, as Ottoman surveyors encountered 'various difficulties' in their attempts to demarcate and map available land.[38] One imagines some frustration on the part of consular agents tasked first with promoting the law, then with gathering information about applicants' wealth and moral character, and finally with delaying any actual movement for months-long periods. The specificity Florentines articulated in their questions to the beleaguered Tausch emerged in similar requests for information from across the continent; the response, generated by the Foreign Ministry and echoed by Ottoman envoys, was 'wait and see'.

Though the need to populate Anatolia with a productive, hard-working group of colonists was clear, the availability of specific land was unknown. In an era when the Ottoman state sought to uncover who held claim to particular spaces, the colonisation effort corresponded to the need to record who lived where. The *Muhacirin Nizamnamesi* relied upon populating unfilled or unproductive space within the empire, and doing so required first determining where those spaces were. By the end of March, 1857, the Tanzimat Council dispatched seven officers to uncover and map available land in the provinces. The officers were sent to Adana, Izmir, Salonica, Tırhala and Yanya, Silistre, Edirne, and Bursa. With the exception of Adana, the provinces were concentrated in Rumelia and West Anatolia. Though the Tanzimat Council had incentivised settlement in Anatolia, they recognised colonists from Central and Eastern Europe likely preferred territories closer to home.[39]

While dispatching the officers was the first step in determining available land, provincial administrators soon pointed out that the job was more complicated than just 'distinguishing and separating' (*temyiz ve tefrik*) empty from claimed land. Surveyors had to account for issues such as the local use of pastureland, and for this they relied on local knowledge. In Edirne, the provincial council designated a Haci Shakir Efendi as a local escort for Captain (*Yüzbaşı*) Tahsin Efendi and proposed an appropriate monthly salary for his work to be paid by the imperial treasury. Additionally, the provincial council noted, Captain Tahsin required another escort when he moved on to evaluating villages elsewhere in the province. Given the importance of rapidly completing the surveys and ensuring justice for Ottoman subjects who already laid claim to land, the Tanzimat Council endorsed hiring Haci Shakir Efendi and other local escorts.[40]

AGRICULTURAL COLONIES

A second obstacle to quick enactment of the regulations emerged from officials' reliance on individual entrepreneurs. Whether the original request on the part of the Prussians, the Florentine's inquiries or Dormann Gasparini's idea for a Swiss colony, Europeans petitioned the Ottoman Foreign Ministry for permission to establish agricultural colonies within Rumelia, Anatolia and the Levant. These individuals, while offering to recruit large numbers of migrants, directly promote agricultural development and defray some risk on the part of the state, could divert resources towards proposed plans that never came to fruition.

A successful agricultural colony required a good-faith actor to furnish information about settlers, ensure timely settlement and guarantee the capital requirement for all potential colonists. Such an individual was not always easy to find. In October of 1858, Sir Alexander Baggio of Turin sought permission to establish an agricultural colony in Albania. Over the course of a year, the Turin consul Rüstem Pasha struggled to collect the necessary information about the colonists, to confirm Baggio's means of capital and to finalise the deal. In the end, Rüstem lost patience and contacted the Foreign Ministry to recommend the state look elsewhere for settlers; Baggio, it seemed, would never have sufficient means.[41]

While Ottoman officials endorsed concessions as a means to rapid agricultural development, potential entrepreneurs saw in the Migrant Regulations a route to free land and tax and military exemptions. In October of 1862, Thomas Lane, former British vice consul at Larnaca, sought a concession for 130,000 donums (roughly 32,000 acres) of uncultivated land to grow cotton on Cyprus, and he promised to bring 300 Irish families with him to work as farmers. Lane's knowledge of the region and fluency in Ottoman Turkish may have convinced officials of the likelihood of his success; rapidly rising global cotton prices caused by the American Civil War and the projected revenue of the concession likewise made the project alluring. Lane estimated that each donum of land would generate fifty okka of clean cotton, yielding a total of 6,500,000 okka (832,000 kg) for the entire concession.[42] Thus when the land became eligible for taxation, the tithe would provide 650,000 okka of cotton to the treasury, valued at 4,550,000 *kuruş*/piasters (roughly 35,600 British pounds sterling).[43] The Council of Public Works noted the excellent opportunity Lane's proposal offered. If successful, the colony could become a model for capital and labour-heavy projects throughout the empire. With that benefit in mind and the always-welcome advantage of importing 'a colony of industrious and intelligent farmers', the Council of Public Works endorsed enacting the concession immediately.

The Council of Public Works evaluated Lane's request with reference to the legal framework of the Migrant Regulations, arguing that nothing within the regulations prohibited a settler/colonist from being a capitalist, so long as the concession increased agricultural or industrial productivity. The size of the concession and the 'large agglomeration' of families necessitated making the colonists subject to Ottoman law. The terms of Lane's concession asserted this status, requiring Lane and the Irish families to become Ottoman subjects and prohibiting Lane from selling the land for twenty years. The council reasoned that the terms of the concession and Lane's position reduced risk for the Ottoman state, as it was in Lane's interest to use as much land for cotton as possible. Additionally, Lane's personal motivation to ensure the capital requirement for potential settlers protected the government against an 'invasion of miserable families' who might become a burden to the state.

But for two unforeseen events, Cyprus could have become home to several hundred Irish families. As the Council of Public Works was finalising the concession in December of 1862, the Ottoman Empire entered its second consecutive year of mass immigration from the Crimean Peninsula and the Caucasus. Given the arrival of hundreds of thousands of migrants, the Tanzimat Council wondered whether it was best to divert those newcomers to Cyprus rather than waiting for the Irish farmers. To this end, the Council requested that Kostaki Musurus Pasha, Ottoman Ambassador in London, vet Thomas Lane one more time before moving forward with the concession plan. To his surprise, Musurus learned that Thomas Lane had passed away during the winter of 1862. Though Thomas was survived by his brother, who expressed interest in the project, Musurus advised against transferring the concession to the other Lane and put a stop to the colony before it began.[44]

Governing Migration in the Late Ottoman Empire

SUBJECTHOOD

The *Muhacirin Nizamnamesi* was a colonisation endeavour intended to promote agricultural development. Still, one of the most important provisions of the regulations was the very first: settlers had to pledge loyalty to the Sultan and become naturalised Ottoman subjects upon arrival in the empire. Over and again, Ottoman sources describe potential settlers as those who wished to leave their homes, establish themselves in the empire and adopt Ottoman subjecthood. After all, it was the large-scale agricultural concession's relationship to migration and subjecthood that made Thomas Lane's proposal subject to the terms of the *Muhacirin Nizamnamesi.* Agricultural concessions offered a potential shortcut to recruiting large numbers of immigrants, but they laid bare a tension between facilitating rapid development and rendering settlers exclusively subject to Ottoman law. Large-scale migration complicated the likelihood of individual migrants adopting the imperial identity articulated in the *Islahat Fermanı* of 1856 and the unambiguous subjecthood aimed for in the Protégé Regulation of 1863 and the Nationality Law of 1869. While the concessions promised the rapid creation of thousands of Ottoman subjects, Ottoman reliance on intermediaries undermined the likelihood that newcomers severed legal ties and representational claims with their former states.

An empire that had created equality under law still had to rule over a diverse population, and the question of how individuals and groups might be represented in such a state remained unresolved into the early twentieth century. Responses to the Migrant Regulations signalled complexities in the search for an imperial identity and the promotion of an unmediated relationship between newcomers and the central state. For example, when A. D. Mordtmann identified the *millet* system as a means to insert German colonists into the workings of the empire, he coupled integration and long-term settlement with administrative differentiation based on secular, ethno-linguistic groups rather than religious difference. Mordtmann believed language was crucial to the successful administration of immigrant populations. On these grounds, he dismissed the possibility of German representation within the Catholic *millet*s, such as those that existed for Armenians or Melkites. Instead, Mordtmann envisioned a secular *millet* tied together by shared language and culture; religious distinction was not an issue, as Catholic and Protestant Germans 'considered themselves brothers'.[45] For Mordtmann and others, good governance and justice emerged through representation and even mediation with the central state.

Muhacir *as Colonist*

In practice, despite their status as newly minted Ottoman subjects, colonists turned to the representatives of their former homes in times of need. In 1874, the Austro-Hungarian Ambassador contacted the Foreign Ministry on behalf of a number of Austro-Hungarian subjects in Tulça/ Tulcea. According to the Ambassador, despite the Austro-Hungarians' long-term residence in the district, the governor of the subprovince (*sancak*) of Tulça claimed that as foreign subjects they were not eligible to own land or other immovable property in rural districts. In response to the ambassador's letter, the Foreign Ministry pointed out that the issue was not one of foreign subjects owning property in the Ottoman Empire, but rather of colonists fulfilling the terms of the *Muhacirin Nizamnamesi*. As colonists, the individuals in question received their property on loan from the government, and they had surrendered Austro-Hungarian subjecthood as a condition of that loan. The Austro-Hungarian Ambassador and the Governor of Tulça eventually agreed to this perspective, and communicated it to the petitioners. Those who wished to maintain their status as Austro-Hungarian subjects were welcome to settle in the town of Tulça, but at least four individuals renounced their Austro-Hungarian subjecthood and retained their land concessions in the villages.[46]

In another case from 1875, a handful of German colonists sought intercession with the German Consul. Upon arrival in the empire the previous year, they were promised 13,575 donums of land for their thirty-seven families, but a Bulgarian claimed the land the settlers had been promised. Despite having officially taken Ottoman subjecthood, the group of colonists, frustrated with the lack of support of the Ottoman government, planned to send two individuals to Istanbul to petition the German Ambassador to intervene on their behalf.[47] Thus, despite the stipulation of subjecthood, colonists continued to seek intercession through their former representatives, a challenge to the Ottoman state's role as sole recourse in issues of property, rights and justice.

Mass Migration

In 1862 and 1864, respectively, Lane and Gasparini's agricultural concessions faced the same obstacle – the arrival of a large, unanticipated population from the Crimean Peninsula and the Caucasus. Given the urgency of resolving the migration crisis, Ottoman statesmen questioned whether the empire could devote resources and land to European colonisation. The Crimean War was particularly devastating to populations on the peninsula.[48] In 1855–6, some 20,000–40,000 left Crimea for the Ottoman Empire. In 1859, 50,000 Nogay Tatars left the Kuban and travelled through the Crimean Peninsula on their way to the Ottoman territory. The Nogay Tatars' experiences, the social upheaval brought by devastation of the war, deteriorating trust in the Russian-Tatar relationship and stories of the Russian treatment of Muslims in the Caucasus contributed to the belief among Crimean Tatars that they faced imminent removal. Their mass exodus to the Ottoman Empire began in 1860. Between 1860 and 1861 some 200,000 Tatars emigrated to the Ottoman Empire.[49]

Following the Crimean War, the Russian state redoubled its efforts to control the Caucasus, leading to the mass departure of Circassians from the region. Like Tatars, Muslims in the Caucasus faced disruption from the war and Russian colonisation. Russian officials viewed removal of the Muslim, pastoralist population in the Caucasus as essential to Russian state security after decades of anti-colonial armed resistance to Russian forces. To a far greater extent than the forced migration of the Tatars, the 1861–6 migrations of the Circassians and other Caucasus groups were an expulsion planned and enacted by the Russian Empire. Entire villages were destroyed. Conquered tribes, faced with a 'choice' of resettlement in the Kuban valley in the north, military service in the Tsar's army or conversion to Christianity, instead emigrated to the Ottoman Empire. Forced mass migrations began in 1862 and peaked in 1863–4. Between 1861 and 1866, more than one million Circassians and other groups departed from the Caucasus.[50]

Thus, as requests to immigrate via the Migrant Regulations languished within consular offices in Vienna, Turin, Livorno and Paris, groups outside of the formal system established by the colonisation plan pled with the Ottoman state for entry. The migrants diverted the state's attention from the large-scale colonisation envisioned by the *Muhacirin Nizamnamesi* and rendered the impetus to invite settlers obsolete.

An Unorthodox Settler State?

Is the *Muhacirin Nizamnamesi* a footnote in the history of the migrations that made the modern Middle East? The regulations generated interest on the part of potential immigrants, who saw in them an opportunity to create a new life while avoiding the trans-Atlantic voyage. Though the Tanzimat Council's overarching aims for the regulation were hindered by lack of preparation, incomplete bureaucratic infrastructure and mass displacement around the Black Sea, the law was not a complete failure. Some Europeans were encouraged by the regulations to make a cross-continental trip. They remained embedded in the legal framework of the regulations decades after their passing.

Muhacir *as Colonist*

Rather than the 'failure' of the law to attract large numbers of Europeans, it is the conceptual distinction between 'free' and 'forced' migrations that conceals the Ottoman Empire's participation in the mass migrations of the nineteenth century. If the regulations are read only in terms of inviting colonists – and if colonists are defined only as financially independent, state regulated, economic or European migrants – then the influence of the *Muhacirin Nizamnamesi* was indeed limited. If, however, historians approach the *muhacir* population as Ottoman officials did in 1856, without separating migrants according to religion or assumed levels of coercion, the narrative changes. Similarly, by recognising that modern migration regimes emerged as much from facilitation of movement as from restricting the movement of certain groups, scholars may approach the regulations to understand how Ottoman officials took part in tactics of state-building adopted around the globe. The *Muhacirin Nizamnamesi* was a harbinger of change within the Ottoman state; the Ottoman plan for colonisation and officials' response to mass migration situate Ottoman state-building within a global history of the making of modern mobility regimes.

LABELLING MOVEMENT

To what extent did Ottoman officials distinguish between colonists and refugees? In contemporary, popular parlance, the juxtaposition of the label of refugee and colonist is an uneasy one. While the term refugee positions an individual as a *victim* of state violence, the term colonist positions an individual as an *agent* of state violence. The international legal framework established by the UNHCR recognises the right to seek asylum as a human right; the fate of refugees and asylum seekers is a morally trenchant issue from which to critique state policy. Even in the first two decades of the twenty-first century, within a global political climate of increased hostility towards migrants of all kinds, refugees have maintained some of their elevated moral position, meriting protection and compassion above other types of migrants. Nevertheless, focusing on the role coercion played in motivating mass immigration into the empire obscures the ways Ottoman policies purposefully aligned with nineteenth-century state-building practices.

In the twentieth and twenty-first centuries, ethnic cleansing and genocides rendered displacement a relatively well-known tool of statecraft; however, refugee recognition, aid and settlement have long served as essential components in state-building. In the late eighteenth century, for example, the United States government passed a 'refugee' act for individuals from the British territories of Canada and Nova Scotia who had supported the American Revolution. The 1798 act encouraged Anglo-American settlement of the Northwest Territory by offering the refugees land grants in the region. The policy aligned with the US government's goals of westward expansion and dispossession of Native Americans.[51] There are multiple twentieth-century examples of refugee settlement projects used in demographic engineering, for economic development, and as political tools to undermine the legitimacy of competing states and ideologies, including the Greek-Turkish Population Exchange, massive repatriations in Europe after World War I and World War II, and the migration of Holocaust survivors to Israel.[52] Close in time and space to the Ottoman case, Laura Robson has argued compellingly that refugees, as the *raison d'être* of the League of Nations, offered European mandate authorities the space and population to enact 'visions of ethnicity and nationhood' as they recolonised the Middle East after World War I.[53] Seventy years earlier, Ottoman statesmen similarly used displaced populations to change the state's relationship to the population and to enact the underlying ideology of the *Muhacirin Nizamnamesi*.

The religious significance of the term *muhacir* has contributed to the ambiguities of its application in the Ottoman context. The term recalls the migration (*hijra*) of Muhammad and his followers from Mecca to Medina in the year 622. The Islamic calendar (*Hijri*) begins in 622, marking the significance of the *hijra* for the establishment of the Muslim community (*umma*). Those who accompanied the prophet became known as the *muhajirun*, a title reflecting the permanence of their move, their abandonment of property and connections in order to follow Islam, and the new community they formed with the inhabitants of Medina. Though *muhacir* and other terms derived from *hijra/hicret* maintained religious relevance and significance internal to the practice of Islam, those terms became part of the vocabulary of movement, religiously inflected or otherwise. Thus, in the nineteenth century, the Ottoman state applied the term *muhacir* to individuals from a range of ethno/religious categories, regardless of whether they were motivated by religion or whether they were coerced into leaving their homes. Neither religion nor coercion *defined* the category, to the extent that the phrase 'Muslim migrants' (*muhacirin-i İslamiye*) was a relevant distinction within a wider *muhacir* population.

Both refugee and colonist are terms whose valence has shifted over time, and as such neither can function as free-standing, static analytical categories. Following the mid-twentieth-century consolidation of the modern international refugee regime, scholars have debated how the term 'refugee' shapes categories of practice and categories of analysis within

Muhacir *as Colonist*

studies of forced migration. The current migrant/refugee binary elevates *motivation* and *causation* for movement as the primary means of classifying migrants, yet motivation and causation were neither the only nor the most salient characteristics Ottoman officials employed in responding to migrant populations.

For Ottoman officials, *muhacir* was a label that emphasised the *outcomes* of human mobility. Indeed, the term gained coherence in its relationship to settlement. That is, *muhacir* was a status attached to permanence and Ottoman subjecthood. Ottoman officials described those to whom the *Muhacirin Nizamnamesi* applied as 'families coming from abroad who will accept subjecthood and settle in the Ottoman Empire'. For example, when the Foreign Ministry responded to the Austro-Hungarian Ambassador's question about foreigners' rights to own land in 1874, the Ministry described the individuals in question as those migrants (*muhacirin*) who 'entered under the protection of the Ottoman Government and were given free land by the government'.[54] Officials expressly connected the *Muhacirin Nizamnamesi* and colonisation. Consuls and other members of the Ottoman Foreign Ministry used the term colonist and colonisation to describe Americans, Western Europeans and Germans from the Russian Empire seeking permission to immigrate.[55] In discussing Thomas Lane's agricultural concession, the Supreme Council (Meclis-i Vala-yı Ahkam-ı Adliye, successor to the Tanzimat Council) referred to the Migrant Regulations as the 'Colony Regulations' (*Koloni Nizamnamesi*).[56] Regardless of religion or place of origin, Ottoman officials labelled as *muhacir* individuals who intended to live permanently in the empire.

As much as officials employed '*muhacir*' to evoke permanence and stability, the meaning of terms describing individuals on the move was in flux in the Ottoman state and elsewhere. Scholars concerned with the history of 'the refugee' as a distinct social category take care to distinguish between the emergence of the word 'refugee' and its attachment to specific, often legally delineated meanings. The practice of seeking refuge, protection and asylum 'is ancient', but 'the idea that an individual is a "refugee" is not'.[57] Nevzat Soguk notes that prior to the twentieth century, 'refugees ... went by many different names. They were called refugees, exiles, fugitives, and/ or emigres, in a practice of naming that, in effect, neither represented, nor engendered or afforded any clear-cut, formal, institutionalized distinctions among these categories of displacement.'[58] European states welcomed as 'exiles' the well-to-do political émigrés of the mid-nineteenth-century age of revolutions. Similarly, Ottoman officials used terms such as *mülteci* (refugee) and *firari* (deserter) to describe the Hungarian, Polish and Italian political refugees who arrived in the empire after the Revolutions of 1848.[59]

Governing Migration in the Late Ottoman Empire

The best-known English–Ottoman dictionaries from the era reveal the indeterminate nature of the terminology at play. In his 1856 English–Turkish dictionary, Sir James Redhouse defined *muhacir* in English as 'one compelled to abandon his country', the plural *muhacirin* as 'those inhabitants of Mecca who fled to Medina and joined Muhammad' and *mülteci* as 'a refugee'.[60] Precisely what 'refugee' meant to Redhouse is not clear. Despite describing *muhacir* as one compelled to leave, the definition he provided for 'refugee' in Ottoman was *mülteci*. Redhouse did not provide an Ottoman definition for 'immigrant' or 'emigrant'. Whereas in 1856 Redhouse defined *muhacir* in terms of coerced movement, his 1861 English-Turkish lexicon described the opposite. He provided definitions in Ottoman Turkish for 'emigrant': 'someone who leaves their country *by choice* [emphasis added] and settles in another land, *muhacir*' and for 'immigrant': 'someone who comes from elsewhere and settles, one who comes to settle, *muhacir*'. He retained the definition of 'refugee' as '*mülteci*'.[61]

When Ottoman officials made terminological distinctions between potential settlers and refugees, their categories neither remained stable nor conformed easily to the terminology of free-versus-coerced migration. Documents moved quickly through a range of terms. In a translation of the Prussian Ambassador's response to the *Muhacirin Nizamnmasi* in 1857, the French '*colons Allemands*' was initially translated as 'German immigrants' (*Almanyalı Muhacirin*). Subsequently, the scribe crossed out all instances of *muhacir/muhacirin* and replaced them with *mülteci/mülteciyat*.[62] Likewise, in the course of rejecting Gasparini's plan for a Swiss colony in 1864, the Supreme Council distinguished between the European colonists and the Circassian refugees, referring to the former as *mülteciler* and the latter as *muhacirin*.[63] While the Supreme Council referenced the Colony Regulations in commenting on Thomas Lane's concession, it referred to the settlers circuitously as 'families from Europe', again in distinction to the *muhacir* population, while the concession's French translation referred to the Europeans again as *colons*.

Though the resonance of *muhacir* within Islamic history may have underpinned officials' use of the term *muhacir* to distinguish between Muslims fleeing from the Russian Empire and non-Muslim settlers, the population arriving from the Crimean Peninsula in the 1850s and 1860s included Muslims and non-Muslims such as Jews, Germans and Romanians. Jared Manesek notes that after the Eastern Crisis (1875–8), Ottoman officials referred to Ottoman Balkan Christians who fled to the Austro-Hungarian Empire as *mülteci* rather than *muhacir*, a distinction he attributes to the 'communal inclusion' evoked by *muhacir*.[64] Indeed,

Muhacir *as Colonist*

as subsequent chapters of this book will show, following the Eastern Crisis, Ottoman officials narrowed their vision of the ideal *muhacir* along religious lines. Nevertheless, Şemsettin Sami's 1900–1 Ottoman Turkish dictionary defined *muhacir* as 'an individual who came to settle with their family from another land', for example 'Crimean and Bosnian migrants', and 'European migrants in America'.[65] Sami's examples imply that even some fifty years into *muhacir* settlement, the term was neither tied exclusively to Muslims nor dependent on coercion.

For Ottoman officials, the consolidation of migration terminology was still underway, such that the term '*mülteci*', with its implication of flight and refuge, could apply to potential colonists seeking to migrate under the auspices of the *Muhacirin Nizamnamesi*. A distinction among migrants based on motivations for movement, familiar to contemporary readers, was not the trait most significant in categorising mobility for Ottoman officials. This is not to say that the labels Ottoman officials applied held no meaning. Rather, the conceptual divisions among migrant populations, to the extent that they were salient from the perspective of governance, were emergent within historical contingencies of nineteenth-century relationships between state and subject. From the perspective of Ottoman officials, immigrants, regardless of their motivations, were a tool to engage in state-building. Officials' emphasis on permanence reflected the goals the Ottoman state held for migration management: population increase, with its associated economic and security benefits, and population loyalty, via the legal establishment of subjecthood.

COLONISATION AMIDST CRISIS

The nineteenth-century Ottoman migration regime developed from the ideals articulated in the Migrant Regulations and in response to unforeseen mass migration. In the decades after the passing of the *Muhacirin Nizamnamesi*, officials capitalised on the large-scale movement of migrants. As potentially productive subjects, the displaced could stand in for the colonists anticipated by the *Muhacirin Nizamnamesi*. The arrival of migrants from around the Black Sea diverted resources away from an ideal of carefully organised colonisation, yet despite the challenges mass migration presented, Ottoman officials and others soon recognised that the newcomers could furnish the population the Ottoman state had sought for colonisation.[66] Indeed, aspects of the Migrant Regulations reflected practices Ottoman statesmen simultaneously applied to unanticipated movement. The establishment of the city of Mecidiye in Dobruca (a historical region spanning Eastern Romania and North Eastern Bulgaria) in 1856

Governing Migration in the Late Ottoman Empire

was an early example of officials' coupling of immigrant settlement with economic development.

The making of Mecidiye reflected the Ottoman embrace of opportunity amidst crisis. In early May of 1856, as Tatars arrived from the Crimean Peninsula, the Tanzimat Council sent instructions to the governor of Silistre that set forth key principles in accommodating their entry and streamlining their placement. The governor's responsibility began when migrants arrived in Balchik, a port on the southwestern coast of the Black Sea. The port served as a key anchorage for the British and Ottoman navies during the Crimean War, and it became a major centre for migrant arrival. Official reports estimated that 4,140 people had traversed through Balchik by mid-May and predicted an increase in numbers of arrivals.[67] From the port, the governor of Silistre temporarily housed migrants and organised their rapid transfer to nearby towns and villages.

The urgency of transferring the arrivals away from Balchik did not dissolve the Tanzimat Council's sense of the long-term promise of successful settlement. From the very beginning, officials sought to facilitate the well-being of the migrants and the central state by treating migrants as potential colonisers, echoing the principles they articulated in the Migrant Regulations. Like other potential colonists, the Crimean immigrants were entitled to military and tax exemptions, though the instructions to the governor of Silistre accommodated the more precarious position of the refugees by establishing tax and military exemptions more generous than those of the *Muhacirin Nizamnamesi*. Impoverished migrants were entitled to financial assistance and benefits in kind, including short-term food assistance, money and supplies for housing, and farming implements and seed.[68] Whether Crimean refugee or European colonist, state officials viewed immigration as an investment, though different groups required varying levels of initial outlay.

The imperial decree founding Mecidiye described its purpose as a site of migrant settlement, and Muslim, German and Jewish immigrants soon populated the town and its surrounding villages. Ottoman officials identified Dobruca as ripe for economic development. Intermittent warfare between Russia and the Ottoman Empire had emptied out the villages and cities of the region, leaving a historically low population of roughly 100,000 people in the 1830s. In 1855, the Crimean War contributed to further population loss once Russian troops arrived in Silistre Province.[69] Despite its low population, Dobruca remained economically important. The Ottoman state had commissioned a comprehensive survey of its districts of Tulça and Silistre in 1850 from Ion Ionescu de la Brad, famed Moldavian revolutionary and Romanian agronomist, who argued the

Muhacir *as Colonist*

economic potential of the region could be unlocked through colonisation and careful administration.[70] Officials selected the location for Mecidiye based on its proximity to a newly constructed railroad line. They promoted the area as a commercial centre in Silistre Province by organising merchant fairs and encouraging warehouse construction through free land grants.[71] To complete Mecidiye's transformation into a new, viable commercial centre, officials directed migrants to the city centre and to its rural environs. The state offered land and seed allotments, assistance in procuring draft animals and agricultural implements, and temporary tax exemptions to those arriving from the Crimean Peninsula. Led by Colonel Nusret Bey, who became Director of Migrant Settlement in Rumelia several years later (see Chapter 2), officials placed more than 290 Crimean Tatar families in Mecidiye and its surrounding villages by the spring of 1857, and they continued to assess where to place migrants arriving in Varna and Balchik.[72]

Other observers similarly envisioned using refugees as resources. In 1860, tens of thousands of Circassians remained in encampments in Trabzon, Samsun and other Black Sea towns, and officials anticipated hundreds of thousands more making the journey. Paul de Anino, adjutant in the Ottoman navy, proposed deploying Circassians in a military colony along the Euphrates to facilitate trade and taxation and to serve as a barrier between the city of Baghdad and various nomadic tribes.[73] Similarly, in the spring of 1864, Henry Bulwer, British Ambassador to the Ottoman Empire, suggested that the refugees could 'furnish a new resource to the Turkish armies', thereby reducing the strain on the Ottoman peasantry. More importantly, the Circassians could provide labour for road construction between the Black Sea port of Trabzon and the inner Anatolian city of Erzurum. By settling the refugees in the vicinity of the two cities, the Ottoman state could rely on a source of cheap labour, and in so doing facilitate trade and address an issue of 'interest to the world'. Bulwer envisioned an aid movement in Europe to assist with the cost of the project, which he estimated would cost one-and-a-half million pounds sterling. According to Bulwer, the French Ambassador had considered the same scheme, and Grand Vizier and Foreign Minister Fuat and Ali Pashas 'showed a hearty willingness' to enter into it.[74]

In an era when statesmen from Japan to Brazil embraced colonisation as a component of statecraft, Ottoman officials likewise saw mass migration as a colonising opportunity. Tanzimat officials drafted the *Muhacirin Nizamnamesi* as similar laws and institutions emerged in Mexico, the United States, Australia, Canada and Russia.[75] While the United States is an outlier, in terms of numbers, the Ottoman experience is comparable to other well-known 'immigrant-receiving' states and regions.

Such comparisons must be drawn with caution, given differences in terms of geographic size, population density and modality of colonisation; nevertheless, on the surface, the numbers are striking. From the mid-1850s to 1913, Muslim migrations across Ottoman borders totalled an estimated five million people. Between 1820 and 1932, some 6.5 million Europeans arrived in Argentina, 4.3 million went to Brazil and some 5 million headed to Canada. An estimated six million peasants resettled in Siberia between 1801 and 1913. About 1.5 to 2 million Europeans went to Cuba, Australia and South Africa.[76]

In her work on Indian migration in the British Empire, Ridhika Mongia argues that studying migration by analysing state's 'technologies of regulation ... allows one to consider patterns of migration often held to be distinct (for instance, indentured and "free migration") within the rubric of one project'.[77] The *Muhacirin Nizamnamesi* is one such technology of regulation, revealing that Ottoman state ideologies and technologies encompassed 'forced' and 'free' migration. In the mid-nineteenth century, a *muhacir* was one who (in theory) moved permanently into Ottoman territory and took up Ottoman subjecthood and, on this basis, was entitled to land and certain tax and military exemptions from the central state.

Mobility regimes and the labels that emerge from them are the outcome of contingencies. As will become clear in subsequent chapters of this book, the institutionalisation of the state's response to large-scale movement had implications for migrants' experiences within the empire, and the endeavour to turn refugees into colonists contributed to the consolidation of a meaning of *muhacir* attached to certain rights, resources and behaviours. In his history of the Ottoman and Austro-Hungarian responses to migration during and after the Eastern Crisis of 1875–8, Manasek argues the very meaning of refugee emerged not only through international policy but via 'the domestic practice of refugee aid and population management' established in the two empires.[78] Coercion had implications for the resources migrants received, but only as Ottoman officials sought to mitigate the newcomers' material conditions, to stabilise their contribution to the empire and to render them successful settlers.

MIGRATION REGIMES: LIBERALITY AND RESTRICTION

The conceptual dichotomy between coerced and free movement has many repercussions for how historians narrate the global history of migration and state-building in the nineteenth and twentieth centuries. In a classic telling of the period, the North Atlantic established a unique pattern; European migration to the New World was largely a story of 'free' agents

seeking new economic markets. This is a story written into the justifications of racially exclusive immigration legislation in North America, in
which the regulation of Chinese and Asian immigration was defended as
a response to systems of unfree labour. Eventually, this stereotype spilled
over from racist legislation into some migration scholarship, which
treated the North Atlantic system as a unique example of industrialisation
and understood migration in other parts of the world as an outcome of
European expansion. Despite assumptions to the contrary, 'free white
(labour) was historically far from universal', and white indentureship
and government-assisted migration were tools in shoring up whiteness
in America, Canada, Australia, Brazil and Argentina.[79] Just as regulations that contributed to the historical segmentation of global migration
patterns can contribute to the further segmentation of their study, the
language of liberality and liberalism – attached to the nineteenth-century
values of free commerce, free mobility and the free movement of labour –
can likewise influence how scholars approach and categorise historical
migration regimes.

In August 1858, the Ottoman Consul in New York, J. Hosford Smith,
wrote to the Ottoman Foreign Ministry on behalf of a group of 'industrious' men who wished to grow cotton in Syria. The climate and soil made
the plan attractive to the settlers – Smith himself claimed to have grown
eight-foot-high cotton in the region – but Smith credited the 'liberality' and pro-immigration stance of the Ottoman government as the true
catalyst for the settlers' request.[80] In December, Smith wrote once more
on behalf of potential colonists. He again commented on the 'liberal'
conditions under which emigrants could settle within the empire before
inquiring 'whether persons of colour [*sic*], who are natives of this country,
or others, are included in those conditions, and may avail of the benefits to
be derived from them'. The Tanzimat Council and Fuat Pasha, the Foreign
Minister, succinctly affirmed that people of colour were likewise eligible
under the regulations.[81]

Smith did not elaborate on the characteristics of the individual who
inquired about the policy, but it is easy to speculate on the 'push factors'
experienced by 'persons of colour' seeking to leave the United States in
the two decades following Cherokee Removal and the years immediately
prior to the American Civil War and Emancipation Proclamation. After a
long morning in the archives, faced with Smith's inquiry and Fuat Pasha's
perfunctory response, the historian's mind drifts briefly to counterfactual
fantasy, imagining the Ottoman Empire, a supposedly uncivilised, repres-
sive, authoritarian and 'Oriental' regime, welcoming America's oppressed
racial minorities as 'huddled masses yearning to be free'.[82]

Whether or not Smith's inquiry has drawn other historians to similar flights of fancy, Smith's repeated characterisations of the 'liberality' of the *nizamname* signify why the regulations hold a certain appeal for scholars of Ottoman migration. In considering the historical importance of the 1857 law, scholars have tended to focus on the 'migration' aspect far more so than the 'regulations' aspect. Echoing Smith, they emphasise the law's ideology of free movement and lack of religious requirements as outcomes of the Tanzimat period's Ottomanist ideological orientation. 'Liberal', however, is necessarily a relative term. Within historians' characterisation of liberality is often an explicit comparison with the Ottoman state's migration restrictions and shift towards Islamism during the reign of Sultan Abdülhamid II and an implicit comparison with restrictive, race-based migration policies of late nineteenth- and early twentieth-century settler-colonial societies.[83] Emphasising the liberality of the *Muhacirin Nizamnamesi* offers a route for historians to comment on the deferred dream of the Tanzimat – perhaps overemphasising the inclusivity of the reformers' vision – and even to position the Ottoman and eventual Turkish state as anticipatory of contemporary human rights protections.[84] However, given historians' emphasis on restriction as fundamental to migration management, underscoring the liberality of the regulations obscures the law's role within Ottoman social engineering and risks missing the *nizamname*'s relationship to global trends in states' management of migration.

Migration regimes encompass mechanisms to promote as well as to restrict movement. However, because migration studies as a field has 'assumed that state control over migration is a defining and definitive element of state sovereignty', historians have tended to focus on the emergence of racial and ethnic restrictions in pinpointing the origins of modern immigration regimes.[85] Chief among these are immigration laws in the United States, which began to restrict entry based on nationality and ethnicity in the 1880s.[86] Mongia has recently offered an important corrective to this trend, tracing the emergence of modern immigration regimes to colonial settings and describing how they operate within a 'logic of facilitation' and a 'logic of constraint'. Restrictionist regimes based on categories of race, religion or ethnicity did not emerge suddenly and fully formed in the 1880s. They were layered upon tools of population management, including a much longer history of facilitating and managing enslaved/indentured migration in the eighteenth and nineteenth centuries.[87]

The Migrant Regulations emerged from a logic of facilitation, yet they relied on standardisation and filtration, albeit filtration that was not initially

Muhacir *as Colonist*

racial or religious. In reducing the significance of immigration restriction to the history of racial exclusion in settler-states, historians risk overlooking how 'immigration restriction laws have always been about other, and more, criteria of restriction and exclusion'.[88] J. Hosford Smith's reference to industrious workers is a reminder that the Tanzimat Council issued the *Muhacirin Nizamnamesi* not only to invite but also to control movement, to standardise the qualities of border crossers, and to exert authority over border-crossing procedures themselves. The regulations served as a route to condition, coordinate and, if necessary, constrain immigration and settlement. Enactment of the regulations barred Alexander Baggio and Thomas Lane's brother based on their lack of capital and entrepreneurial expertise. In transmitting immigration requests, consuls verified the industriousness and moral character of potential settlers. Recording information and vetting potential colonists offered modes to deny immigration to those who did not conform to the idealised population invited in the regulations. For example, in late September of 1866, the *mutasarrif* of Jerusalem detained and questioned a group of forty Americans who planned to establish a colony near Ramallah. He warned the Foreign Ministry that the group had no interest in becoming Ottoman subjects, that they would not register, that they wished to buy land and that these aspects of their potential settlement would undermine the welfare of the indigenous people of the area.[89]

Historians contrast the liberality of the 1857 *nizamname* with later Ottoman migration policy. In later decades, the empire introduced restrictions on mass immigration and denied requests to settle in certain locations. A well-known example is the restriction of non-Ottoman Jewish immigration to Palestine. In 1876, Ottoman officials rejected a proposal for a Jewish colony in Palestine on the grounds that the proposal would create a semi-autonomous colony.[90] By 1899, the Ottoman state attempted to prevent all non-Ottoman Jewish immigration into Palestine.[91] Officials framed these limitations as an extension of the general prohibition against group immigration dating to regulations issued in 1884, 1887 and 1888.[92] Given the emergence of Zionist claims to territory within Palestine, the influence of the Great Powers in assisting nationalist separatist movements and the increasing role of demographics in asserting territorial rights, an Ottoman rejection of mass immigration is not surprising. Despite these Ottoman-specific conditions, the Ottoman shift in 'liberality' fits a global pattern in immigration regulation.

Globally, the 1860s–1880s were an era of 'limited border controls' and a moment of institutional consolidation that located identity verification with central authorities.[93] Following the 1880s, border regulation became a tool in generating standardised, categorisable and retrievable bureaucratic identities.[94] In the Ottoman case, both the initial Migrant Regulations and subsequent changes in policy were similar efforts to establish the state's control over mobility. Requiring individuals or individual families to petition for entry elevated the central state as the mediator of movement, while the Ottoman injunction against mass immigration contributed to extracting the individual from collectives (foreign, nationalist and non-Ottoman) that threatened Ottoman sovereignty. Thus, new regulations in the 1880s were not just a by-product of Hamidian repression. Ironically, as David Gutman has noted, it was when the revolutionary Ottoman government of 1908 readopted the liberal principle of freedom of mobility that Ottoman migration policies fell out of step with the prevailing trend among many immigrant-receiving societies.[95]

The conceptual isolation of free and forced migration has shaped the field of migration history. It has contributed to the historical markers many scholars use in defining the era of mass migration (1846–1924), the narrative of the primacy of European trans-Atlantic migration in the nineteenth and early twentieth centuries, and the positing of ethnic and race-based migration restrictions as natural outcomes in the development of modern nation states. That the Ottoman Empire responded to unanticipated and coerced movements of Muslims should not exclude it from global inquiries into the roles refugees and migrants played in the consolidation of modern state apparatuses. The emergence of mass migration from around the Black Sea precluded the empire's need to attract large numbers of colonists from Europe or the Americas. Nonetheless, the underpinning logic of the Migrant Regulations – that the state should facilitate migration, that migration could lead to agricultural development and that settlement could render the population more legible – remained. Regimes are outcomes of contingent events and responses; the Ottoman migration regime developed from the ideals articulated in the regulations and in response to extraordinary situations created by mass migration. In this way, the *Muhacirin Nizamnamesi* served as foundational to an unfolding Ottoman mobility regime.

Conclusion

In Beatrice, Nebraska, the US Homestead National Monument pays homage to the passing of the 1862 Homestead Act, which offered up to 160 acres of federal territory to any qualified person willing to cultivate the land for a period of five years. The monument, which includes a museum, three miles of trails, several historical structures, and an extensive online

Muhacir *as Colonist*

presence to facilitate digital education, stands near the site of the first successful Homestead Act claim, filed by Daniel Freeman just after midnight on 1 January 1863. The Homestead Act successfully transferred an estimated 270,000,000 acres of public land to private hands, or roughly 10 per cent of the territory of the United States.[96]

The terms of the Homestead Act resemble the *Muhacirin Nizamnamesi*'s expectations of the long-term settlement of a legible, productive population. The law offered land to anyone aged twenty-one or older who was a United States citizen or who intended to become one, so long as they paid a ten-dollar fee and stayed on the land for five years. The act accommodated naturalisation and drew large numbers of immigrants to the American West.[97] The Homestead Act, like colonisation plans in Mexico, Canada, New Zealand and Brazil, shared with the Ottoman regulations a path to transfer 'empty'/waste/collectively owned lands to individuals. As a tool of empire and state-building, the Homestead Act contributed to the removal of indigenous populations and the taming of the frontier. Together with the Dawes Act (1887), it was essential to Native American removal, dispersal and restriction. Despite the violence embedded in its passage, the Homestead Act was long remembered as a part of the grand project of settling the American frontier and a component in the making of Americans by 'free' European migrants.

The comparatively muted legacy of the *Muhacirin Nizamnamesi*, I argue, emerges less from the peripheral status of the Ottoman Empire in the nineteenth-century era of mass migration and more from scholars' conceptual divisions among colonist, settler, immigrant and refugee. The Ottoman Empire was remade not by settlers from Western Europe but rather by individuals and families from around the Black Sea. This chapter elaborated the ideology and practical difficulties accompanying the Tanzimat Council's embrace of population management and social engineering within the *Muhacirin Nizamnamesi*. The chapter encourages historians to consider – as statesmen and migrants did – the Ottoman Empire as a potential destination for those seeking to improve their lives during the global era of mass migration.

The Migrant Regulations highlight premises that shaped Ottoman migration management into the twentieth century. Tanzimat statesmen embraced migration to foster economic development, change land-use patterns and identify Ottoman subjects. Though the enactment of the colonisation plan met the reality of administrative limitations, ambiguous subjecthood and intervention on the part of foreign consuls, and mass migration, officials' interest in managing mobility remained. The regulations and the Ottoman Empire's eventual response to large-scale migrations created criteria to select populations, organise mobility and elevate the conceptual-legal status of the individual over collectivities. Ottoman institutions were repeatedly overwhelmed by mass population movements, yet the ideal of a self-sufficient, economically productive and unambiguously Ottoman settler established in the *Muhacirin Nizamnamesi* shaped officials' approach to and understanding of migrants across the next five decades.

During those decades, the word *muhacir* took on additional meanings, as officials attempted to manage unanticipated movement and to overcome administrative, environmental and diplomatic obstacles to settlement plans. The next chapter examines more closely how officials sought to turn refugees into the settlers envisioned by the Tanzimat Council. The development of an aid and settlement regime and the difficulties of actualising its premises contributed to the ongoing making of the Ottoman *muhacir*.

Notes

1. I.MMS 9.362, p. 3, 24 Cemaziyülahır 1273/19 February 1857.
2. McKeown, 'Global Migration, 1846–1940', 156.
3. I.MMS 9.362, p. 2.
4. Ibid., 1.
5. Ibid., 2.
6. Dirk Hoerder, *Cultures in Contact: World Migrations in the Second Millennium* (Durham, NC: Duke University Press, 2002), 333–6; Stephen Castles, Hein de Haas and Mark J. Miller, *The Age of Migration: International Movements in the Modern World*, 5th ed. (New York: Guilford Press, 2014), 93.
7. There were four major legislative bodies organised during the Tanzimat: the Supreme Council of Judicial Ordinances, or Supreme Council (Meclis-i Vala-yı Ahkam-ı Adliye), active 1838–54; the Tanzimat Council (Meclis-i Tanzimat), active 1854–61; another iteration of the Supreme Council (Meclis-i Vala-yı Ahkam-ı Adliye), active 1861–7; and the Council of State (Şurayı Devlet), active 1867–76. Stanford Shaw, 'The Central Legislative Councils in the Nineteenth Century Ottoman Reform Movement before 1876', *IJMES* 1, no. 1 (1970): 51–84.
8. Quoted in Shaw, 'Central Legislative Councils', 64.
9. Edhem Eldem, 'Ottoman Financial Integration with Europe: Foreign Loans, the Ottoman Bank, and the Ottoman Public Debt', *European Review* 13, no. 3 (2005): 431–45.
10. Candan Badem, *The Ottoman Crimean War (1853–1856)* (Leiden: Brill, 2010), 295–8.
11. Stanford Shaw, 'The Nineteenth Century Ottoman Tax Reforms and Revenue System', *IJMES* 6, no. 4 (1975): 421–59.

Muhacir *as Colonist*

12. Kemal Karpat, 'Ottoman Immigration Policies and Settlement in Palestine', in Karpat, *Studies on Ottoman Social and Political History: Selected Articles and Essays* (Leiden: Brill, 2002), 785.
13. I.MMS 9.362.
14. HR.ID 24.13, 11 February 1864. See also, Karpat, 'Ottoman Immigration', 786; Başak Kale, 'Transforming an Empire: The Ottoman Empire's Immigration and Settlement Policies in the Nineteenth and Early Twentieth Centuries', *Middle Eastern Studies* 50, no. 2 (2014): 258. A gold *mecidiye* was worth 100 *kuruş*. The daily wage for a day labourer in Istanbul in the 1840s was 6 *kuruş*; it rose to 10–12 *kuruş* by the beginning of World War I. Şevket Pamuk, *A Monetary History of the Ottoman Empire* (New York: Cambridge University Press, 2000), 208.
15. Christoph Herzog, 'Notes on the Development of Turkish and Oriental Studies in the German Speaking Lands', *Türkiye Araştırmaları Literatür Dergisi* 8, no. 15 (2010): 14.
16. HR.TO 313.52, 24 March 1857.
17. Ibid.
18. HR.ID 24.13.
19. Ibid.
20. Ibid.
21. Scott, *Seeing Like a State*, 183.
22. F. Ongley and Horace Miller, *The Ottoman Land Code* (London: William Clowes and Sons, 1892), 8.
23. Anton Minkov, 'Ottoman *Tapu* Title Deeds in the Eighteenth and Nineteenth Centuries: Origin, Typology and Diplomatics', *Islamic Law and Society* 7, no. 1 (2000): 65–101.
24. Benjamin Braude, 'Foundation Myths of the *Millet* System', in *Christians and Jews in the Ottoman Empire*, abridged ed., ed. Benjamin Braude (Boulder, CO: Lynne Rienner, 2014), 65–86.
25. See Aylin Koçunyan, 'The *Millet* System and the Challenge of Other Confessional Models, 1856–1865', *Ab Imperio* 2017, no. 1 (2017): 59–85.
26. Ibid., 66.
27. Will Hanley, 'What Ottoman Nationality Was and Was Not', *JOTSA* 3, no. 2 (2016): 277–98.
28. For a provocative and wide-ranging discussion of Ottoman sovereignty and international law, see Lale Can, Michael Christopher Low, Kent F. Schull and Robert Zens, eds, *The Subjects of Ottoman International Law* (Bloomington: Indiana University Press, 2020).
29. Hanley, 'Ottoman Nationality', 278.
30. I.MMS 9.362.
31. A.DVN.MKL 74.17, 18 Ramazan 1274/2 May 1858.
32. See Sam White, *The Climate of Rebellion in the Early Modern Ottoman Empire* (New York: Cambridge University Press, 2011); Oktay Özel,

'Population Changes in Ottoman Anatolia During the 16th and 17th Centuries: The "Demographic Crisis" Reconsidered', *IJMES* 36, no. 2 (2004): 183–205.

33. I.MMS 9.362, 5.
34. HR.ID 24.13, 11 February 1864.
35. Ibid.
36. HR.ID 24.5, 17 August 1858; HR.ID 24.13; HR.ID 24.16, 2 March 1872.
37. HR.ID 24.3, 14 April 1857.
38. Ibid.; HR.ID 24.23, 9 December 1857.
39. I.MVL 373.16365, 16 Şevval 1273/9 June 1857.
40. I.MVL 376.16515, 4 Zilhicce 1273/26 July 1857.
41. HR.ID 24.6, 14 October 1858; HR.ID 24.8, 20 January 1859; HR.ID 24.9, 17 November 1859. See also Karpat, 'Ottoman Immigration.'
42. An okka is a unit of weight equal to 1.28 kg. A *dönüm* is just under one square km.
43. In 1862, the exchange rate of a British pound to an Ottoman *kuruş* was 1:124.88. Markus Denzel, *Handbook of World Exchange Rates, 1590–1914* (Farnham: Ashgate, 2010), 394.
44. HR.ID 24.12, 12 February 1863.
45. HR.TO 313.52, 24 March 1857.
46. HR.ID 24.18, 23 May 1874.
47. HR.ID 24.19, 19 June 1875.
48. See Kırımlı, 'Emigrations from the Crimea', 751–73; Mara Kozelsky, 'Casualties of Conflict: Crimean Tatars during the Crimean War', *Slavic Review* 67, no. 4 (2008): 866–91.
49. Kırımlı, 'Emigrations from the Crimea', 767; Williams, 'Hijra and Forced Migration', 88; Kemal Karpat, 'The Crimean Emigration of 1856–1862 and the Settlement and Urban Development of Dobruca', in *Passé Turco-Tatar, Présent Soviétique: Études Offertes à Alexandre Bennigsen*, ed. Ch. Lemercier-Quelquejay, G. Veinstein and S. E. Wimbush (Paris: Éditions Peeters, 1986), 287.
50. Karpat, *Ottoman Population*, 67–9.
51. Evan Taparata, '"Refugees as You Call Them": The Politics of Refugee Recognition in the Nineteenth-Century United States', *Journal of American Ethnic History* 38, no. 2 (2019): 9–35.
52. For a global range of examples, see Peter Gatrell's *The Making of the Modern Refugee*.
53. Robson, *States of Separation*, 34.
54. HR.ID 24.18.
55. HR.ID 1.1, 7 March, 1860; HR.ID 1.5, 31 December 1860.
56. HR.ID 24.12. The Meclis-i Vala replaced the Tanzimat Council in 1861.
57. Hamlin, *Crossing*, 27.
58. Soğuk, *States and Strangers*, 65. See also Michael Marrus, *The Unwanted: European Refugees from the First World War through the Cold War*, 2nd ed. (Philadelphia: Temple University Press: 2002), 15–22.

Muhacir *as Colonist*

59. Abdullah Saydam, 'Osmanlıların Siyasi İlticalara Bakışı ya da 1849 Macar-Leh Mültecileri Meselesi', *Belleten* 61, no. 231 (August, 1997): 339–85.
60. James Redhouse, *An English and Turkish Dictionary* ... (London: Bernard Quaritch, 1856). The 1880 expanded edition of his dictionary offered the same definitions for *muhacir* and *mülteci*, and defined the English term emigrant in Ottoman as 'muhacir'. The 1880 dictionary also defined migration as *göç*. James Redhouse, *Redhouse's Turkish Dictionary* ... , 2nd ed., ed. Charles Wells (London: Bernard Quaritch, 1880).
61. Redhouse additionally defined 'deserter' as 'firari or kaçkın'; 'exile' as 'one absent from his country'; and 'colonist' as 'one who settles outside of their land of subjecthood (*memalik-i tabiya*). James Redhouse, *A Lexicon, English and Turkish* ... (London: Bernard Quaritch, 1861). The second edition of the lexicon, published in 1877 in Istanbul by American missionaries, retained the same definitions in Ottoman Turkish for emigrant, immigrant and refugee. Redhouse, *A Lexicon, English and Turkish* ... , 2nd ed. (Constantinople: A. H. Boyajian, 1877).
62. HR.TO 313.55, 4 April 1857.
63. HR.ID 24.13.
64. Jared Manasek, 'Protection, Repatriation, and Categorization: Refugees and Empire at the End of the Nineteenth Century', *Journal of Refugee Studies* 30, no. 2 (2017): 303–4.
65. Sami also defined *mülteci*, 'one who flees from a place or person and seeks refuge', and *firari*, 'a fugitive, runaway, deserter'. Şemsettin Sami, *Kamus-ı Türki* ... (Istanbul: İkdam Matbaası, 1318/1900–1). Sami's Turkish–French dictionary, published in 1883, defined *muhacir* as '*émigré, fugitif*', and referenced the companions of the Prophet. It defined *mülteci* as '*qui se réfugie, réfugié*'. Sami, *Kamus-ı Fransavi: Türkçeden Fransızcaya Lügat, Dictionnaire Turc-Français* (Istanbul: Mahran Matbaası, 1883).
66. The *Muhacirin Nizamnamesi* required an immediate change in subjecthood. The 1909 revision of the Nationality Law made naturalisation contingent on a ten-year residency, but those arriving as *muhacir* could naturalise after a five-year period. Hanley, 'What Ottoman Nationality Was and Was Not', 293.
67. Abdullah Saydam, *Kırım ve Kafkas Göçleri, 1856–1876* (Ankara: Türk Tarih Kurumu, 1997), 121.
68. Ibid., 119–20. See also I.DH 343.22622, 27 Şaban 1272/3 May 1856.
69. Karpat, 'Crimean Emigration', 281.
70. Catalina Hunt, 'Changing Identities at the Fringes of the Late Ottoman Empire: The Muslims of Dobruca, 1839–1914' (PhD Diss. The Ohio State University, 2015), 37–9, 94–7.
71. Kemal Karpat, 'Ottoman Urbanism: The Crimean Emigration to Dobruca and the Founding of Mecidiye, 1856–1878', in *Studies on Ottoman Social and Political History*, 214–18.
72. I.MVL 382.16743, 3 Rebiyülahir 1274/21 November 1857.
73. HR.ID 1.5, 31 December 1860.

Governing Migration in the Late Ottoman Empire

74. Sir H. Bulwer to Earl Russell, 3 May 1864, in Great Britain, *Papers Respecting the Settlement of Circassian Emigrants in Turkey* (London: Harrison and Son, 1864), 4–5.
75. See Willard Sunderland, *Taming the Wild Field: Colonization and Empire on the Russian Steppe* (Ithaca, NY: Cornell University Press, 2004); Siegelbaum and Moch, *Broad Is My Native Land*; Jose Angel Hernandez, *Mexican American Colonization during the Nineteenth Century: A History of the U.S.-Mexico Borderlands* (New York: Cambridge University Press, 2012); Jose Moya, *Cousins and Strangers: Spanish Immigrants in Buenos Aires, 1850–1930* (Berkeley: University of California Press, 1998); Stuart Banner, *Possessing the Pacific: Land, Settlers, and Indigenous People from Australia to Alaska* (Cambridge, MA: Harvard University Press, 2007).
76. Moya, *Cousins and Strangers*, 46; Bosma, 'Beyond the Atlantic', 119.
77. Mongia, *Indian Migration and Empire*, 3.
78. Jared Manasek, 'Empire Displaced: Ottoman-Hapsburg Forced Migration and the Near Eastern Crisis, 1875–1878' (PhD diss., Columbia University, 2013), 19.
79. Bosma, 'Beyond the Atlantic', 117. See also McKeown, 'Global Migration, 1846–1940'; McKeown, *Melancholy Order*; Mongia, *Indian Migration*; Kornel Chang, 'Enforcing Transnational White Solidarity: Asian Migration and the Formation of the U.S.-Canadian Boundary', *American Quarterly* 60, no. 3 (2008): 671–96.
80. HR.ID 24.5, 17 August 1858.
81. HR.ID 24.7, 7 December 1858.
82. Phrase from Emma Lazarus, 'The New Colossus', written in 1883 and mounted in a plaque on the platform of the Statue of Liberty in 1903.
83. Karpat 'Ottoman Immigration', 798; Kale, 'Transforming an Empire', 261.
84. Writing in 1966, Ahmet Cevat Eren wrote that the *Muhacirin Nizamnamesi* and history of immigration to the Ottoman Empire revealed that, 'No matter the period, the Turkish nation has always extended a helping hand to those left without a country, regardless of race, sect, or religion.' Eren, *Türkiye'de Göç ve Göçmen Meseleleri: Tanzimat Devri, İlk Kurulan Göçmen Komisyonu, Çıkarılan Tüzükler* (Istanbul: Nurgök Matbaası, 1966), 92.
85. Radhika Mongia, 'Historicizing State Sovereignty: Inequality and the Form of Equivalence', *Comparative Studies in Society and History* 49, no. 2 (2007): 387.
86. Anna Boucher and Justin Gest, *Crossroads: Comparative Immigration Regimes in a World of Demographic Change* (Cambridge: Cambridge University Press, 2018), 42.
87. Mongia, *Indian Migration*, 9.
88. Alison Bashford, 'Immigration Restriction: Rethinking Period and Place from Settler Colonies to Postcolonial Nations', *Journal of Global History* 9, no. 1 (2014): 29.
89. HR.ID 24.14, 28 November 1866.
90. Karpat, 'Ottoman Migration', 794; Kale, 'Transforming an Empire', 259.

Muhacir *as Colonist*

91. Kale, 'Transforming an Empire', 260–1.
92. Karpat, 'Ottoman Immigration', 794.
93. McKeown, *Melancholy Order*, 42.
94. Ibid., 12.
95. Gutman, *Politics of Armenian Migration*, 168.
96. Blake Bell, 'Homestead National Monument of America and the 150th Anniversary of the Homestead Act', *Western Historical Quarterly* 43, no. 1 (2012): 72–8.
97. Blake Bell, 'America's Invitation to the World', accessed 5 July 2020, https://www.nps.gov/home/upload/Immigration-White-Paper.pdf.

2

Muhacir as Problem

In 1896, Nusret Pasha, the former Inspector of the 6th Army, passed away in Baghdad. It is unlikely he was mourned by the governor of the province or the local notables, with whom he had been feuding nearly since his arrival there in 1888. Described by a contemporary as 'pernicious and insane', Nusret Pasha seems to have spent his final years in Iraq acquiring land through 'legal and illegal means', seeking the removal of the province's governor, and generally making enemies.[1] Born in 1824 as one of the last *mamluks* of Sultan Mahmud II (r. 1808–39), 'Deli' (Mad) Nusret Pasha was Circassian by birth. He was educated in the Palace School and the Officer's College (Mekteb-i Harbiye). He completed his education with a five-year stint in Paris and returned to the Ottoman Empire by the beginning of the Crimean War, during which he rose in rank, becoming a colonel (*miralay*) and an inspector in Niş, a town within the autonomous Principality of Serbia. Later in his career, he served as governor in Salonica, Ankara, Trabzon and Adana and as aide-de-camp to Sultan Abdülhamid II.[2]

'Educated, loyal, direct, and shrewd', Nusret Pasha was a polymath who seemed to excel equally in cartography, translation and burning bridges. Though he charmed British Ambassador Henry Layard and remained a confidant of Abdülhamid II, Nusret quarrelled with Midhat Pasha, the well-known Tanzimat reformer and 'founding father' of the 1876 Constitution.[3] He was part of a cadre that accused Gazi Osman Pasha, a war hero, of corruption, and he curried disfavour among his colleagues with frequent denunciations (*jurnals*) of other high-ranking officials. In a thirteen-page memorandum he addressed to Abdülhamid II soon after the 1877–8 Russo-Ottoman War, he lamented the lack of quality men in the Hamidian administration and catalogued the limitations of his contemporaries, describing the deficiencies of those at the very

Muhacir *as Problem*

upper echelons of the Ottoman state.[4] Nusret used his stint in Baghdad to pen another long report, this one outlining a major reform programme for the province. He recommended the creation of a special commission to take on the work of reinforcing the army and gendarmerie, registering the population, distributing land to settle tribes, developing the economy, and educating and winning over the people of the province.[5]

Earlier in his career, before he had the chance to accrue his litany of enemies or envision wide-scale reform in Iraq, Nusret served the Ottoman state in Rumelia, the empire's territory in south-eastern Europe. In the summer of 1856, the governor of Vidin described that province as roiled by highway robbery so pervasive it might slip into sedition. Accompanied by scribes, officers and two divisions of sharpshooters, Colonel Nusret set out to restore peace.[6] Nusret soon found that bringing security to the area encompassed more than merely imprisoning brigands. As Rumelia became the site of arrival for thousands of Tatar migrants after the Crimean War, the colonel worked on *muhacir* settlement, helping to establish the city of Mecidiye and 'a large number of villages and hamlets' in the region.[7]

On January 5 of 1860, the Tanzimat Council announced the establishment of the Migrant Commission (Muhacirin Komisyonu), and Colonel Nusret took up a new and newly created role: Director of Migrant Settlement in Rumelia. With the creation of the independent, centralised Migrant Commission came a more far-reaching view of how immigrant settlement could transform Rumelia and Anatolia. The Tanzimat Council's vision for the project emerged in its lengthy description of Nusret's responsibilities. The council began by noting that merely distributing aid would not resolve the intricacies of the *muhacir* question. Instead, Nusret and his associated retinue had to demarcate and define space, organise populations and collect data in order to settle newcomers and maintain order within Rumelia's towns and villages. The Tanzimat Council instructed Nusret to disperse the migrants arriving in the towns of Varna, Köstence (Constanta) and Mecidiye to permanent settlement locations in Edirne, Silistre and Vidin Provinces (see Figure 2.1). Given that the Tanzimat Council envisioned placing anywhere from 25,000 to 50,000 newcomers within a few months, the scope of his position matched the scope of radical change officials envisioned in Ottoman territory.[8]

Nusret's previous experience in security and settlement made him the ideal candidate to take on the challenge. The role of settlement director required a discerning mind, a delicate hand and a decisive attitude – qualities folded into the Tanzimat Council's description of the colonel as a man of 'comprehension and intelligence'.[9] A discerning mind allowed Nusret to interpret land assessments – including those conducted

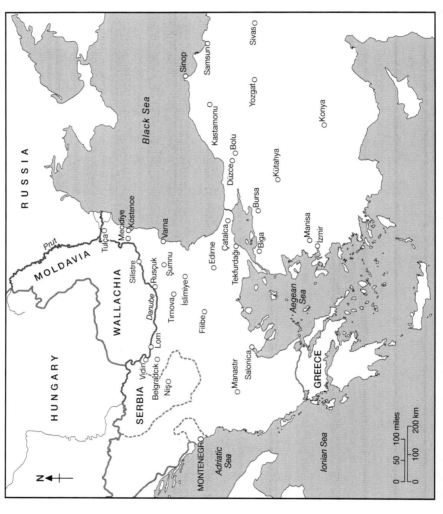

Figure 2.1 The Balkans in 1860.

Muhacir *as Problem*

by provincial and local power holders – to determine the availability and viability of potential settlement areas. A delicate hand allowed him to avoid sowing inter-communal conflict. According to land registers, the people of Dobruca had pasturelands beyond their immediate needs, but Nusret needed to strike a balance between respecting local land use and appropriating land for migrant settlers.[10] Similarly, Nusret had to weigh the benefit of placing migrants in existing villages with the risk of overburdening villagers. As he had in Mecidiye, he was to design newly established migrant villages in the so-called 'new style' (*usul-i cedid*), regularly arranging houses and creating the wide streets popular in Tanzimat-era city planning.[11] Finally, despite the need for delicacy and deliberation, a decisive attitude allowed him to resolve quickly the crisis of migrants left without food, money or housing.

This chapter's narrative is drawn from sources created across multiple offices within the Ottoman government, but it is grounded in the words and actions of Nusret Bey/Pasha during his time in Rumelia. The area was an important and early site for colonisation-based economic development and urban planning. The economic importance of the region, its location on the empire's borders in the Balkans, the high proportion of non-Muslims, and Ottoman anxieties about separatism and outside interference rendered migrant settlement a high-stakes endeavour. During Nusret's tenure, some 120,000 migrants arrived in Rumelia during three main episodes: Crimean and Nogay Tatars immediately after the Crimean War, Crimean Tatars from 1860–1 and Circassians from the Caucasus from 1863–5. Once Nusret left, the region hosted a signature Tanzimat project: the creation of the Danube Province as a pilot programme of administrative, legal, infrastructural and economic reform overseen by Midhat Pasha.[12]

Nusret's star rose alongside his work in the Migrant Commission. Though Ottoman migration institutions changed over time, Nusret kept a watchful eye on the course of settlement into the 1880s. As such, his archival mark is clear enough to consider how he situated the *muhacir* within his vision of a well-run state. For Nusret, the ideal scenario was one in which migrant settlement helped to craft a governable and productive population. Nevertheless, Nusret, like other Tanzimat officials, was an Ottoman, not an automaton. 'Pernicious and insane' on the one hand, discerning and intelligent on the other, Nusret was a complicated figure, a villain or a hero depending on which sources the historian examines.

Narrating the story of the vast enterprise of migrant settlement from the perspective of an individual bureaucrat demystifies and personalises the Ottoman state. Those who made up the modernising, centralising and standardising Ottoman government, who collected information, created new institutions, solved problems and developed policy were complex individuals. Their contributions to governance were spurred on by their own interests and animosities as well as their political visions. They could serve the state and call for action to assuage migrant suffering. They could also be self-serving. This is a story visible at every level in the making and unfolding of policy; as men like 'Deli' Nusret in turn remained dependent on local officials and participants to provide information and to carry out their projects. These individuals and their contributions to the institutions of a developing migration regime influenced migrants' arrival, placement and daily experiences in their first years of settlement within the empire.

This chapter describes the institutions and ideologies of the Ottoman migrant settlement regime in the 1850s and 1860s to consider two overlapping tracks in officials' conception of the *muhacir*. The first of these tracks is the continued view of the *muhacir* as a resource to enact wide-scale reform. The second is the emergence of the *muhacir* as a '"problem" amenable to a "solution"'.[13] The significance of the *muhacir* shifted as officials devised programmes to turn newcomers into colonists. Administrative practices changed as well, as officials encountered the infrastructural, financial and ecological challenges that accompanied large-scale movements and as migrants sought to exert control over settlement. The interaction of policies, challenges and responses is essential in the making of modern bureaucracies. This interaction creates the process by which officials identify the tools and categories they use to simplify reality and to render it 'legible and hence more susceptible' to careful management, control, and manipulation.[14] Faced with the *muhacir* as opportunity and as problem, officials continued to hone tools to map Ottoman territory and to know the Ottoman population, further developing their capacity to engage in social engineering.

Institutionalising an Aid Regime

As discussed in Chapter 1, Ottoman immigration policy during the Tanzimat relied on a logic of facilitation. The 1857 Migrant Regulations embraced the immigration of colonists, but the unanticipated arrival of migrants from the Crimean Peninsula and Caucasus diverted attention and resources away from the planned movement envisioned by the Tanzimat Council. The newcomers could still bring the benefits of immigration, but the magnitude of mass migration and the difficulties migrants faced as they fled Russian expansion added aid and settlement to the contours of the Ottoman migration regime. While these contingencies guided the Ottoman administrative response, the empire's response to mass

Muhacir *as Problem*

migrations, especially from 1856 to 1860, was influenced by a longer history of managing mobility in the empire.

As early as the seventeenth and eighteenth centuries, both the Ottoman and Russian Empires attempted to sedentarise nomads as a component in establishing and safeguarding their borders.[15] Aside from sedentarisation, population removal and colonisation became increasingly visible tactics of state policy. Throughout the eighteenth century, Ottomans and Russians engaged in acts of 'demographic warfare', described by Mark Pinson as exchanges 'of populations, used to bolster the position of one state in territories either threatened by or recently acquired from the other state'.[16] Through these informal population exchanges, Christians and Muslims swapped positions along the changing Ottoman-Russian border. The longer history of cross-border migrations was a factor influencing the direction of migrants' paths into the empire.

Beginning in the late 1850s, the Ottoman state began to experience periods of intense migrant arrival for which it was unprepared (Chapter 1). In their encounters with migrants, officials called forth a language of shared humanity and the special responsibility of the Ottoman state to stem the suffering of those 'destitute and friendless' people who sought the protection of the Ottoman state.[17] Officials described assisting migrants as an act of humanity and generosity and a source of joy.[18] In 1864, already overwhelmed by 25,000 migrants in Trabzon and expecting 270,000 more, Grand Vizier Fuat Pasha nevertheless asserted that refusing the Muslim population and leaving them to suffer under the 'oppressive hands of their enemies' was incompatible with Islam and humanity.[19] The obligations of humanity filtered down from the highest offices in the empire to villages in Rumelia and Anatolia, where individuals and communities were enjoined to support newcomers with reference to traditions of hospitality within Islam, and officials like Nusret publicised the kindness and public-mindedness of those who aided migrants.[20]

Ottoman statesmen were inspired not only by the obligations of humanity but also by their interests in legitimising and improving the Ottoman state. Accepting Muslim refugees was a politically powerful statement of the Ottoman sultan's role within a worldwide Muslim community. The state's extension of mercy was integral to Ottoman political ideology, in which the idealised state acted as a guardian and protector of its subjects. Turning away migrants undermined the empire's claim to civilised, compassionate governance.[21] For Nusret, migrant settlement offered the opportunity to extend better governance throughout Rumelia. In 1861, he described establishing a village of 350 migrant households on the shores of the Danube River near the mountain pass (*derbent*) and monastery of

Dobri dol, near the border of the Principality of Serbia. The settlement, he suggested, promised to bring benefits in terms of security, politics and the administration of land. He proposed naming the new village after Sultan Abdülaziz's son, Yusuf İzzeddin, whose existence had been revealed publicly two months earlier upon Abdülaziz's ascension to the sultanate. Like the arrival of a viable successor to the throne, migrant settlement held the promise of the perpetuation of the Ottoman state. In choosing the name İzzeddin, Nusret noted that place names that reflected 'the language of rule' assisted in administering Rumelia during a 'new century' of Ottoman governance.[22]

When Nogay and Crimean Tatars and Circassians began to arrive in the empire en masse, officials recognised that migrants, many of them forced to leave behind property and further impoverished by the circumstances of their flight, needed assistance in order to become the self-sufficient colonists envisioned in the 1857 Migrant Regulations. Regardless, the Tanzimat Council's goal remained the same: efficient, planned placement that would contribute to the empire's financial well-being within a generation. By instituting and institutionalising a comprehensive aid regime, Ottoman officials sought to save migrants while turning them to their advantage in the larger project of reform.

MIGRATION INSTITUTIONS IN THE TANZIMAT (1860–75)

Nusret's decades-long career encompassed changing iterations of migration administrative entities in the Ottoman Empire. The Tanzimat Council created the Migrant Commission in the winter of 1859–60. Prior to 1860, immigration was handled primarily at local and provincial levels; the central state issued directives as needed. Even after the founding of the Migrant Commission, local leaders, particularly governors and district heads, performed key duties, and local communities aided newcomers.[23] By the end of the Crimean War in 1856, the Istanbul Municipality (Şehremaneti, founded in 1855), the Police Ministry (Zaptiye Nezareti) and the Trade Ministry (Ticaret Nezareti) organised migrant settlement within and outside the capital city.[24] In 1859, the Şehremaneti requested more personnel, citing the work it had put into settling 15,000 migrants in the provinces between September of 1858 and December of 1859 and estimating that another 10,000 might winter in Istanbul. When the request came before the Tanzimat Council, it resolved to create a new, specialised institution to coordinate migrant management in Istanbul with migrant reception and settlement in other port cities.[25] Subsequent resolutions enumerated the tasks of the Migrant Commission: organising the dispersal

Muhacir *as Problem*

and settlement of migrants who arrived in Istanbul, collecting information about newcomers, distributing aid, advertising the need for donations, and publishing the names and contributions of those who donated assistance in two newspapers, *Takvim-i Vekayi* and *Ceride-i Havadis*. While the commission was initially attached to the Trade Ministry, it became an independent organisation in July of 1861.[26]

The commission's reach extended into the provinces, and it established branches in major centres like Trabzon and Samsun. In the early 1860s, Nusret Bey was one among other ministers dispatched to areas of intense migrant arrival and settlement, including Bursa, Biga, Salonica, Çatalca, Kütahya, Izmir, Adana, Tekfurdağı, Gallipoli, Sinop, Samsun, Silistre and Konya. These ministers facilitated migrants' transport to permanent settlement locations, organised the logistics of aid and determined when to cut migrants' stipends and provisions. The army assisted in mobilising and provisioning the newcomers. Like Nusret, the commission's provincial officials were largely army officers, drawn from the ranks of general, colonel, lieutenant colonel and major.[27]

Nusret remained involved in migrant administration across several decades as the personnel, administrative home and name of the Migrant Commission shifted over time. Four different individuals headed the organisation in its first five years.[28] David Cuthell notes that heads of the Migrant Commission were drawn from and reappointed to those provinces that faced the brunt of migrant arrival and settlement, a strategy to ensure that 'those best acquainted with the problems were kept within those posts most affected'.[29] While never head of the commission, Nusret's career followed this trend. After several years as a Settlement Director in Rumelia, he transferred to Eastern Anatolia in the spring of 1865 to oversee settlement of Chechen migrants coming through Kars to Erzurum. He held the post for ten months.[30] Following recognition for his work in migrant settlement, he climbed the ranks from colonel to brigadier (*mirliva*) and then divisional general (*ferik*); he was appointed a member of the Council of the Ministry of War (Dar-ı Şura-yı Askeri) in 1862 and became its chair in 1872.[31]

Despite the commission's ongoing work in the mid-1860s, by 1865, budgetary concerns and the abatement of the immigration crisis contributed to the decision to dissolve the independent commission and split its responsibilities among the Ministry of Justice, the Police Ministry and the Supreme Council. The Migrant Commission was resurrected almost immediately once it became clear that unfinished settlement remained rampant. It was retitled the Migrant Administration (Muhacirin İdaresi).[32] During short stints as governor in Salonica and Ankara, Nusret remained active in procuring land for migrants; he rotated back into the Migrant Administration as an assistant director in 1873.[33] He later held brief governorships in two provinces of intense migrant arrival and settlement: Trabzon and Adana. In 1875, the independent Migrant Administration was subsumed into the Police Ministry. A new iteration of the institution, the General Migrant Administration (İdare-i Umumiye-i Muhacirin) emerged in July of 1878 in response to mass immigration following the 1877–8 Russo-Ottoman War. Sultan Abdülhamid II soon took the institution under his purview.[34] Nusret Pasha began serving as an aide-de-camp to Abdülhamid II in that year, a position from which he offered commentary on the course of migrant settlement.

PROVIDING AID AND INVESTING IN SETTLEMENT

What was the breadth of Nusret's position and the extent of the Migrant Commission's work in the 1860s? The reality officials confronted was one in which migrants, 'having fled their homelands and abandoned their property', necessarily required direct governmental assistance.[35] In its most expansive sense, migrant settlement began as soon as newcomers arrived in ports of embarkation to cross the Black Sea. It comprehensively covered their journeys to port cities and locations in the empire's interior.[36] As Settlement Director in Rumelia, Nusret's role extended to preparing for migrant arrival on the shores of modern-day Bulgaria and Romania. He coordinated temporary housing, transportation and aid, and contracted railroad and shipping companies to convey migrants and procure supplies.

Emergency aid covered rations and food allowances for migrants. Decrees in the late 1850s established daily rations of a half okka (roughly a pound and a half) of bread or an equivalent per diem.[37] Officials distinguished between younger and older migrants, offering a food stipend of two *kuruş* to those over fifteen years of age and one *kuruş* to those under fifteen. Food assistance for impoverished migrants was anticipated to last eight to ten months after their arrival.[38] Aside from food, the Ottoman state paid for coal, clothing and temporary housing, including in khans, merchant depots, mosques, stables, tents, warehouses and even homes in villages near sites of migrant arrival.[39]

There is not yet complete, comprehensive data regarding the Ottoman government's expenditures on migrants. The Migrant Commission saw transportation expenditures for Circassian migrants of 12,663,615 *kuruş* and three *para* over the nearly six-year period from January 1860 to December 1865.[40] From the final months of 1863 to March of 1864, the

Muhacir *as Problem*

central treasury spent 404,862 *kuruş* and 10 *para* on ferries, horses and carts to transfer migrants from Trabzon. It spent perhaps 60,000,000 *kuruş* on food assistance for migrants from 1856 to 1876.[41] Extrapolating from the figures that do exist, Abdullah Saydam proposes that the Ottoman state spent in the neighbourhood of 700 million *kuruş* (roughly 5.5 to 6 million British pounds) on migrant aid and settlement from 1856 to 1862, a number that accounts for 5 to 10 per cent of the state's expenditures in this period.[42] Migration continued to burden central and local treasuries in subsequent decades. During the 1877–8 War, the Istanbul Municipality put 6,750,000 *kuruş* towards migration expenses.[43]

Aside from responding to newcomers' most pressing needs, officials sought to facilitate migrants' rapid conversion into productive subjects. Settlement policy addressed issues of housing, food and work in the long term. Migrants who held trade skills were placed in urban areas and received shops and a stipend, and the commission attempted to find employment for educated migrants as imams and teachers.[44] Most migrants, however, were slated to join the agrarian workforce, and from 1856 onwards, they were to receive draft animals, tools and seed. To facilitate their integration and economic success, immigrants received exemptions from taxation and military conscription. Though vast amounts of money flowed into meeting migrants' immediate needs, officials anticipated they would eventually become tax-payers. In the 1856 instructions he sent to the governor of Silistre on settling Crimean Tatars, the grand vizier recognised the tremendous cost immigration entailed for the imperial treasury. Nonetheless, he anticipated relief in the future. Once migrants got back on their feet, they could slowly repay the treasury.[45] Other policies designated assistance to migrants as a loan to be paid back after migrants' tax exempt period expired, though such expenses were not always recouped.[46] Their taxes could also be used to cover the expenditures of new arrivals, as in the case of migrants previously placed near Mecidiye, who by 1864 had 'attained the degree' of self-sufficiency necessary to assist in paying for a new wave from the Caucasus.[47]

In the late 1850s, migrants could help determine their own settlement locations, much like the colonists invited by the *Muhacirin Nizamnamesi*. In its instructions to the Governor of Hüdavendigar Province in the summer of 1859, the Tanzimat Council described the situation of several groups of Circassian and Nogay migrants who were lodged temporarily in Istanbul. They refused to settle in Rumelia, despite the council's preference for placing them there. Instead, migrants 'insisted' on Anatolia. Moreover, they insisted on being settled in tribes and asked to inspect the land prior to settlement. To that end, an army captain (*yüzbaşı*) and a handful of migrant leaders scouted locations in the province and eventually found two available areas in the district of Kühtaya, one which could host twenty-nine households (328 people) and another for fifteen households (134 people).[48]

The question of cost influenced whether immigrants were settled in large groups. Though the grand vizier's instructions to the governor of Silistre in 1856 noted that there was no clear benefit, either to migrants or the state, to splitting up the newcomers, the expense of settlement began to shift statesmen's thinking.[49] In 1859, the Council of Ministers (Meclis-i Vükela) considered the question of whether to separate Circassian and Nogay tribes settling in Anatolia. Breaking up the tribes and scattering families throughout Anatolia allowed the state to defray costs by relying on the assistance of local communities. Although dispersing the migrants reduced expenses for the central treasury, the council decided that destroying the social fabric of the tribe undermined the traditional means of support it offered. Ultimately, the council decided that those who wished to be settled as a group could be accommodated in Adana and Kühtaya.[50]

Settling migrants in groups and allowing them some measure of autonomy to select settlement areas became less common in the 1860s. The number of arrivals made quick dispersal a paramount concern, especially given the state's reliance on local accommodation, transport and other assistance for migrants. From the 1850s onwards, officials mandated that local communities help migrants by building houses and preparing and sowing land. Officials attempted to encourage individuals and host communities to donate food and aid by referencing migrant's experiences as 'guests of the Muslim community' and 'prisoners of wretchedness and misery' and by advertising and celebrating the 'spirit of humanity' of those who did contribute.[51] Reliance on local communities remained an essential component of settlement into the Hamidian period, when officials called upon host communities, in particular local notables and wealthy and civically minded 'patriots', to employ migrants and to provide material to build their homes.[52] Still, many a 'donation' was the result of not reimbursing local communities for migrant expenditures.[53]

Given the cost to residents, officials were concerned with determining the ideal spatial relationship among migrants and other groups. Nusret's instructions in 1860, aside from discouraging the placement of *muhacirin* in Christian communities, stipulated only five to ten migrant households should be placed in each village; a note from Konya in the same year placed the number at three to five households per village.[54] Similarly, a directive in 1863 for settling migrants in districts within the central Black Sea Provinces of Trabzon, Kastamonu and Sivas stressed the ideal

Muhacir *as Problem*

ratio as one migrant household per five other families. The Council of Ministers countered concerns that this could be too heavy a burden for the region's villagers by referencing the successful dispersal and settlement of 30,000–40,000 members of several Kurdish tribes in the Central Anatolian district of Yozgat; experience thus showed that a twenty-household village could easily accommodate a handful of migrant families.[55]

Aid and settlement were intended to cultivate loyalty among newcomers and to ensure that they remained in the Ottoman state long term. Like those invited by the Migrant Regulations, Muslim migrants were to declare loyalty to the Ottoman sultan and sunder legal ties with the Russian Empire. Officials viewed migrant settlement as an opportunity to undertake the centralising reforms most needed in the Tanzimat state: to gain more administrative control and to develop the economy. Migrants were both targets of assimilation and agents of the extending power of the centralising state; settlement was intended to generate behavioural outcomes for newcomers and other Ottoman subjects. As a broad pattern, Cuthell has found that whereas Crimean Tatars, a landed peasantry before arrival, were settled in more agriculturally dense areas of Rumelia and West Anatolia, the Migrant Commission tended to funnel formerly nomadic pastoralists such as Nogay Tatars and Circassians into Central and Eastern Anatolia to compete with existing Kurdish and Turkmen tribes.[56] Settlement officials used migrants in the larger project of sedentarising nomads in Eastern Anatolia by placing migrants in internal frontier zones on lands confiscated from nomadic pastoralists.[57]

Creating migrant villages wholesale provided an opportunity to change migrants' behaviours. Following his success in urban development in Mecidiye, Nusret continued to approach settlement as an opportunity to design the layout of new villages and the structure of new housing. In 1862, he requested the assistance of Captain (*yüzbaşı*) Hasan Efendi, an engineer, to assist in the construction and arrangement of 300–400 houses and the repairing of roads in the town of Mankalya in Köstence.[58] Settlement decrees encouraged establishing mosques and schools, and officials honoured migrant requests for the same in order to spread religion and encourage 'civilisation' among the newcomers.[59]

While wholesale settlement could create the trappings of civilisation, so too could dispersing migrants. Officials interested in cultivating a loyal population questioned whether ties within migrant communities undermined newcomers' identification with the Ottoman state. The council viewed Nogay and Circassian tribes as similar to the nomadic tribes of Eastern Anatolia. In 1861, the Supreme Council (Meclis-i Vala) commented on the importance of scattering 10,000 Nogay Tatars in Konya. The council

Governing Migration in the Late Ottoman Empire

noted that dispersing the newly arrived encouraged their abandonment of particularistic tribal loyalties and 'ignorant customs'.[60] By 1870, draft regulations discouraged settling migrants, particularly Circassians in Anatolia, in groups. Splitting up migrants and encouraging them to intermarry with residents helped 'eliminate nomadism and ignorance' and produced the 'civilisational progress' that had so far eluded the newcomers.[61]

In general, as Nusret described his work in settlement, he emphasised the benefit that creating villages and placing migrants had for 'order and politics'; the grand vizier echoed that migrant settlement improved districts and benefitted the sultan's reign.[62] The Supreme Council's decision to award Nusret Bey the Order of Osmaniye (Nişan-ı Ali-i Osmaniye) for his work in Vidin Province in 1862 highlighted this thinking. Nusret's achievement in the districts of Lom, Belgradcik and Sahra revealed the role of migrant settlement beyond an end to itself. In 1851, the peasantry of Vidin revolted against oppressive taxation and land-holding practices. In response to the revolts, Sultan Abdülmecid approved a new mechanism for tax collection in the three districts, which bypassed the old landlords (*sipahis*) and Ottoman officials in favour of a chief headman (*kaza çorbası*) for each district. Peasants also received the right to purchase deeds to their land.[63] By 1862, the Supreme Council found that the new system meant that village and district headmen, rather than officials, oversaw the transfer of property deeds once people died or moved away. The situation needed to change, as it excluded the central state from an important revenue stream, and as the Council noted, 'the transferring of property is a right reserved to the government'. Thanks to Nusret Pasha's process of apportioning land and issuing deeds to *muhacirin*, the state had begun to reassert control over the process of land transfer in all three districts.[64]

The Supreme Council lauded Nusret's work on settlement and land reform in Lom, Belgradchik and Sahra because of the delicacy and strategic importance of districts that had seen widespread revolt over taxation and land use only ten years earlier. The council expected that the districts' residents would be frustrated by the imposition of a new system and the presence of the *muhacirin* on land previously used by locals. The districts bordered Serbia, which had become fully autonomous in 1838, and Ottoman officials suspected Serbian influence could lead to insurrection or emigration among the area's Christian inhabitants. Nusret had to reap the benefits of migrant settlement for the Ottoman treasury while making the prior inhabitants 'affectionate towards the Ottoman state' through just and judicious administration.[65]

Evidence of Nusret Pasha's success emerges not just with his elevation in rank and decoration, but within accounts of Circassian settlement in the

Muhacir *as Problem*

British press during the peak of their immigration to the Ottoman Empire in 1863–4. A letter to the editor of *The Times* encouraging readers to send aid for the Circassians described Nusret as 'a fine-looking Turkish General' who 'had already turned to account every available means of provision for the benefit of these poor emigrants, and had ordered all the carriages that could be found, including some hundreds of cattle trucks, to be applied to the conveyance of the crowds gathered at Kustendji [*sic*] to different places on the shores of the Danube'.[66]

One laudatory account of Nusret's work credited his efforts with bringing an 'above the average' harvest to Dobruca. The writer argued,

> Our general prosperity is in great measure due to the intelligence of Nusret Pasha ... New buildings are rising up on all sides. The commissioner has established a hospital at Medjidie [*sic*], in a highly salubrious situation, where the sick emigrants are received and carefully tended, and a normal school, on a large scale, and under admirable arrangements. He has further appointed a municipal council, under whose supervision the paving, lighting, and cleansing of the streets are carefully attended to. He has cut dykes for the drainage of the environs, heretofore extremely unhealthy, and thus turned the marshes into market gardens, and has planted more than 100,000 trees in front of the town.[67]

Nusret had also sent for 100,000 mulberry trees from Bursa, perhaps with an eye towards promoting silk manufacture Mecidiye's environs.[68] The listing of Nusret's many successes corresponds to the multifaceted projects Midhat Pasha famously undertook in the Danube Province beginning in 1864. Institutional reform, health and hygiene, urban development and beautification, education and economic development were all components of Nusret's capacious understanding of migrant settlement.

* * *

During the second half of the Tanzimat, the *muhacir* became a problem for the state to solve. From the legislative councils at the centre of Ottoman governance to provincial governors and Settlement Directors like Nusret, statesmen developed institutions and policies intended to provide emergency aid to migrants in crisis and to turn *muhacirin* into the colonists envisioned in the Migrant Regulations. Migrants were a problem to solve, but they were also an opportunity to extend the administrative power of the state. They could be placed strategically to sedentarise tribes, to shore up border areas, to contribute to changing patterns of landholding and to bring forth the many-faceted qualities of a 'civilised' society, from sanitation to economic development. In the early 1860s, as numbers became more overwhelming and as the make-up of the migrant population

Governing Migration in the Late Ottoman Empire

changed, the question of how to best integrate newcomers into the state changed as well.

Faced with 200,000 Tatars in 1860–1 and more than a million Circassians from 1861 to 1866, officials encountered financial and administrative obstacles to the vast settlement project. As M. Safa Saraçoğlu writes in his history of Ottoman governmentality in Bulgaria, the Ottoman state had 'to alleviate the suffering of the refugees and to alleviate the suffering caused by them'.[69] While the overarching project remained one of engineering a productive, loyal population, the state's limited capacity led to undue suffering on the part of migrants and residents, tied the distribution of resources to the meaning of the *muhacir* and contributed to the expansion of migration management as a field of social intervention for the Ottoman state. The chapter turns now to the challenges accompanying settlement in Rumelia and Anatolia.

The Challenges of Settlement

Though his role as settlement director was far-reaching, Nusret's tenure began in 1860 with the rather mundane questions that necessarily accompanied the establishment of a new bureaucratic position. Queries shuttled between the Interior Ministry, army, treasury and provincial government to determine his salary, his transportation costs, his retinue, his retinue's salary and his relationship to local officials.[70] Once the Ottoman bureaucracy resolved payment, housing and transport for one man, that man turned to the ever more urgent question of how to do the same for the rapidly increasing *muhacir* population. In considering the multiple entities involved in merely appointing Nusret, the Tanzimat Council's resolution to 'the migrant issue' appears fantastically optimistic. The council's detailed instructions to the colonel elided many links in a chain of Ottoman bureaucratic and non-bureaucratic entities involved in each aspect of migrant settlement. A slow down at any stage meant catastrophe for the process and for migrants themselves. Despite reports of Nusret's success, there were a myriad of challenges in the project that called into question the capacity of the Tanzimat state to live up to officials' ideals of good governance.

The logistics of moving supplies and people presented one such challenge. A few months into his tenure, Nusret urgently telegraphed Grand Vizier Kıbrıslı Mehmed Emin Pasha, describing a scenario in which migrants arrived more quickly than they could be sent inland. The port town of Köstence had run out of temporary housing for the newcomers, and migrants slept exposed to the elements. Nusret had coordinated the payment and delivery of 500 tents from Istanbul, using 5,000 *kuruş* from

Muhacir *as Problem*

the treasury to charter a ship from an English company. Still, a week had passed since the ship should have embarked, yet the tents failed to arrive.[71] Neither Nusret nor the *müdür* (subdistrict head) of Köstence commented on whether the tents were sufficient for the increasing *muhacir* population or able to protect migrants once the autumn rain turned to snow. The situation in Köstence was far from unique.

Costs and limited resources created further problems. The question of how to pay for migrant care met the reality of limited resources in the provinces. In the spring of 1857, Abdülveli Bey, the newly minted Kaymakam (district head) of Mecidiye and an immigrant from Crimea, explained that newcomers waited for seed, provisions and oxen. The area had seen not only Crimean Tatar migration but also the return of a Christian Bulgarian community that had emigrated to Russia a few years earlier. Provincial officials struggled to meet the needs of new arrivals. Officials in Silistre estimated that they needed 15,000–16,000 bushels of wheat and 700–800 pairs of oxen for migrants, all before the end of planting season. Existing stores and requisitions from locals were not sufficient, thus the central treasury had to assist in buying supplies from local merchants.[72]

Land disputes followed closely on the heels of migrant settlement. Migrants cleared land that was claimed by other communities and various groups argued over usufruct rights. Early in the course of seven decades of mass migration, officials encountered the problem of land filling more quickly than they had anticipated. Provincial officials emphasised the lack of cultivatable land in their districts and attempted to stem the flow of migrants into overburdened communities. In 1860, local administrators in Dobruca estimated that the region could support only 20,000 more settlers.[73] Similarly, the District Council of Bolu in Northwestern Anatolia worried about land availability around the town of Düzce in 1860. An official inquiry determined there was no space for the 200 Crimean migrants the town was supposed to accommodate. The only land available was near the seaside, too rocky and hilly for settlers. The District Council emphasised that the people of Düzce had assisted enough in migrant settlement.[74] The same issue was raised again in 1864.[75]

Conflict over land contributed to the widespread belief that migrants brought crime to their settlement areas. In Bulgaria, Circassians became notorious as cattle thieves in the 1860s and 1870s.[76] Banditry was so rampant that migrant villages in Dobruca signed attestations that they harboured no thieves in their midst, and special decrees instructed the Migrant Commission to avoid the settlement of large groups and to confiscate firearms.[77] In 1868, Circassian leaders in Anatolia pinned the charge of banditry on the carelessness of settlement officials, which left Circassians without homes for three to four years.[78] Vladimir Hamed-Troyansky's careful examination of tax records suggests the migrant leaders' observations held true in Rumelia, too: in 1873, tax assessments for Circassians were half the average rate paid by the rest of the population in Dobruca's Babadağ district.[79] Officials and migrants alike blamed corruption within and outside the Migrant Commission for settlement problems. Nusret himself was not immune to such charges. The British Vice Consul in Varna reported that 'it is very broadly hinted ... that [Nusret] causes useless delays in order to screw money out of the Tatars ... These reports may, very probably, not be true, however I heard them and certainly [the Tatars] do move off very slowly.'[80]

Migrants petitioned the state when it fell short of its promises of aid, hospitality and security. Their petitions and those of host communities relate stories of the financial, physical and emotional toll that the settlement process created. Migrants' and long-term residents' descriptions of delayed transfer and deleterious settlement locations revealed the limitations of administrators' attempts to remake Ottoman society. Locals petitioned for relief from the burden of caring for migrants, and the Migrant Commission responded to their plight. For example, the self-identified 'natives' (*ahali-i kadime*) of Divriği, a district in Sivas Province, petitioned the Migrant Commission in May of 1867. The residents had provided food and other assistance for migrant 'guests' placed in villages throughout the district since winter. The people of the district claimed that they could no longer bear such a load. Now that it was spring, they asked the commission to quickly find the migrants a permanent home. The commission asked the Governor of Sivas to assist in settling the migrants without delay, citing the suffering of the 'wretched' people of the district importuned by long-term hosting.[81]

In 1873–5 and 1879–81, the peasantry of Rumelia and Anatolia faced drought, harsh winters and ultimately widespread famine, leaving host communities with little to spare for newcomers.[82] The Ottoman state, which had defaulted on its loan payments in 1875, lacked resources to address the suffering of *muhacirin* and other Ottoman subjects. Into the 1880s and 1890s, migrants facing difficult winters and insufficient food supply ate their state-issued farming seed, delaying their ability to plant crops the following season. In 1890, Batumi immigrants who settled in Şile, north of Istanbul, vividly described the 'violence of their hunger' and the likelihood that they would 'perish beneath the weight of the snow'. The migrants begged for food and grain because local residents were unable to provide for them throughout the winter. The Interior Ministry organised shipments from Istanbul to meet the migrants' request for one bushel of corn per person per month.[83]

Muhacir *as Problem*

According to policy, migrants' 'temporary/visiting' (*hal-i misafiret*) status, that is, the period before they found permanent settlement locations, was to last no more than one year, but petitions from migrants across Rumelia and Anatolia attest to the fact that temporary arrangements persisted far longer.[84] In phrases describing immigrants' 'visiting and miserable state' or 'visiting and impoverished state', officials and migrants linked temporary status to general hardship. In 1862, Crimean and Circassian migrants sent petitions noting that their visitor status stretched for more than a year in sites around the Marmara and Aegean region.[85] Ömer bin Edhem, a Circassian migrant in Biga, near Çanakkale, noted that he and his family had fallen into difficult times after being stuck as 'visitors' for two years.[86] The Tanzimat Council observed in 1861 that most migrants had not yet been settled, and it described a group in Konya who had been left in temporary conditions for two years. The 'wretched migrants' desired to return to their former homes, a fate that Ottoman administrators hoped to avoid.[87]

Like other large-scale colonisation projects, ecological factors affected the creation of new homes, as settlers constructed new communities in unfamiliar ecological contexts.[88] Mortality rates, especially for migrants sent to the malarial lowlands of south-eastern Anatolia, were horrific. Chris Gratien has found evidence from multiple observers who estimated that some migrant villages lost 50 to 80 per cent of their inhabitants in the 1860s and 1880s.[89] Ostensibly available lands were often of poorer quality or located in lowland plains and marshes. Officials, migrants and doctors recognised wetlands and lakeshore environments as dangerous sources of disease. Migrants asked to be relocated from swampy areas or simply fled insalubrious locations.[90] When newcomers were placed in lowlands, they could not avoid exposure to malaria, which plagued Anatolia from July to October.[91] Immigrants in malarial areas, particularly those who lacked the knowledge or resources to avoid exposure by seeking refuge in elevated locations during the summer, could lose more than half of their communities to the disease in just a few years.[92] Rather than an accident, sacrificing settlers in malarial areas was an outcome of the developmentalist ethos of Tanzimat reformers and the 'silent violence' that accompanied it.[93]

Unsuitable settlement areas were no more tenable than those that exposed newcomers to disease. Migrants found other areas impracticable for farming, leaving them with few options for subsistence. In a petition submitted in the district of Canık in Samsun Province in 1866, a Circassian from the Ubykh tribe and his cohort of ten families described the hardships they faced because their settlement location was neither suitable for farming nor large enough to raise animals. He asked to be resettled with

Governing Migration in the Late Ottoman Empire

his brother in Düzce and offered to forgo financial assistance during the move. His bid for relocation to Düzce was unsuccessful due to land shortages, but the migrants were offered resettlement elsewhere in Canık.[94] In 1870, the rash of petitions led the Council of State (*Şurayı Devlet*) to allow for migrant relocation in cases of environmental difficulties, and officials adopted permanent transfer as a solution to migrant suffering.[95] Though migrant settlers continued to perish due to ecological factors, by 1878 Ottoman administrators recognised 'health and acclimation as key factors in determining the parameters of settlement and mobility'.[96]

Immigrants offered a variety of reasons when requesting transfers, complaining that settlement areas were not suitable for farming based on swampiness, stoniness, low-quality soil prone to flooding and insufficient allotment.[97] Alongside complaints regarding the quality of settlement locations, migrants in the 1860s cited acclimation as a key concern with the phrase, '*mahallenin ab ve havasıyla imtizac edememek*' or 'being unable to adapt to an area's climate'. This phrase, like many found in petitions, was not exclusive to the migrants. State officials used the same language to request transfers, and the Migrant Commission occasionally employed the phrase as a useful excuse to justify relocating troublemakers.[98] Though reliant on a recurring rhetorical device, the petitions provide insight into migrant desires. Migrants paired their criticism of settlement locations with specific resettlement requests. Just as much as migrants hoped to be removed from a particular location, they petitioned in hopes of being placed in a particular elsewhere.

In criticising their current location, petition writers across Anatolia emphasised those components they saw as most important to their community's well-being. For example, three Crimean Tatar leaders hoping to relocate 465 individuals from Bursa described an inability to acclimate. They also noted the difficulties caused by their wide dispersal in various districts and towns, which had undermined their ability to find 'tranquillity' (*asayış*) in their settlement locations and exacerbated their ongoing economic struggles.[99] Another pair of Tatar leaders travelled from the Aegean town of Manisa to Istanbul to request the relocation of thirty-two families to either Erzurum or Uzunyayla in Eastern Anatolia. They emphasised that the climate made it impossible to subsist. Women and children were struck ill by sickness and fevers, and no one retained the capacity to complete daily work, as 'at the moment of beginning any labour they were struck again with sickness'.[100]

The authors of these petitions, after noting the deficiencies of the areas where they had been placed, highlighted the benefits of resettlement. Those requesting relocation to nearby locations found new areas through

Muhacir *as Problem*

reconnaissance work or information from locals. For example, a petitioner in Erbaa District on the Black Sea requested permission to relocate to a location only ten minutes away. After describing the insufficiency of housing, the poor quality of the land and its tendency to cause illness, the petitioner noted the advantages of the lands surrounding a nearby abandoned granary. The new locale was elevated and had flowing water, and the wood from the abandoned granary facilitated the construction of new homes.[101] Requests for long-distance transfer relied on immigrant networks or time spent in temporary locations during the arrival and settlement process. In requests to move longer distances, migrants often sought reunification with family and other kin. For example, eighty-three migrants detained in Izmir explained that they had originally settled in Manisa. Some 100 of the 120 families they had originally settled with had fled to Varna, and the remaining eighty-three individuals sought to be reunited with their companions and relatives.[102]

Though environmental unsuitability is an unyielding constraint, migrant decisions to vacate settlement areas were complex. Immigrants' references to acclimation encompassed both physical and psychological reactions to settlement locations. Newcomers seeking to facilitate their economic transition and to maintain affective ties to their previous communities described difficulties stemming from differences between their homelands and settlement locales.[103] In one such case, a Circassian named Ibrahim who worked for the Ottoman state successfully petitioned to have his family and other relatives, a group of several hundred people, placed on the Black Sea in the district of Islimiye/Sliven. He explained that the tribe could not thrive in the interior, as they were a 'people born and raised' on the seashore. Nusret was instructed to find land close to the water for the well-connected newcomers.[104] The various origins of many migrants remain obscured within state sources. Even when ethnic or topographical markers (e.g. Caucasian, Circassian, Tatar, Chechen; Crimea, Caucasus, Dagestan, Thrace) reveal a general point of origin, variations within those areas makes it difficult to pinpoint the ecological milieu from which migrants hailed. Nevertheless, migrant petitions suggest challenges of acclimation stemmed from linguistic, cultural and ecological difficulties migrants faced vis-à-vis other Ottoman subjects, the Ottoman state and Ottoman territory.

Regardless of the level of hardship faced by migrants, state officials agreed that environmental factors played an important role in settlement situations. Though officials might confirm migrants' difficulties, they did not always honour migrants' choices for resettlement. The Migrant Commission moved the migrants in Erbaa District to the nearby site they had identified, but the Manisa-based migrants waylaid in Izmir were not allowed to continue to Varna to join their countrymen for fear the move might facilitate their return to Crimea. Rather than Varna, and instead of returning to the hardship of Manisa, the eighty-three migrants resettled in Izmir.[105] Their requests were only partially successful because officials likewise employed a hierarchy of settlement criteria and goals. Whether ecological or emotional, factors in migrant acclimation contributed to officials' sense that the *muhacir* might remain on the move, and that that mobility, too, was something that officials needed to solve.

The goals of *muhacir* settlement, and the vast project of colonisation in Rumelia and Anatolia, encountered infrastructural, economic and environmental stumbling blocks that held major implications for settlers and residents. The *muhacir* may have been a problem to solve and an opportunity to enact reform, but the process of providing direct aid, moving migrants quickly to settlement locations or facilitating their transition into self-sufficient subjects did not unfold easily. Administrators responded to challenges, failures and critiques by developing policies and techniques that contributed to the state's developing capacity to know and therefore manipulate its population.

Mapping the People and the Land

As officials sought to resolve the many problems associated with settlement, migrant management remained a site to enact Tanzimat officials' ideals of good governance. It is in the space between the vision of self-sufficient colonists and the problems endured by migrant and non-migrant populations that officials developed mechanisms for comprehending the population and the land. Faced with crisis, officials decided that what the state was lacking was the capacity to know the population, which was necessary for proper administration. More information would yield the wherewithal to influence the behaviours of Ottoman subjects, whether by directly prescribing and proscribing behaviours or in selling the promise of a modernising state to its subjects. The 'proper administration, good order, and classification paradigms' of modernising states 'required knowledge and information about the peoples, landscapes and ecologies' under their control, though 'this knowledge was illusory and hard to obtain'.[106] During the Tanzimat and Hamidian periods, Ottoman officials sought to gain the capacity to know and transform the population. Officials treated migrant settlement as a means for the state to 'grasp' its population by recording people, categorising their status and mapping where they existed in space.

Muhacir *as Problem*

MAPPING

If, as the Supreme Council proclaimed in its recognition of Nusret's work in Lom, 'the transferring of property is a right reserved to the government', then exercising that right required knowing the relationship between territory and people.[107] Investigating and recording land use was essential to distributing the migrant population. In August of 1860, as Nusret began his work, the grand vizier instructed the governors and subgovernors of Vidin, Edirne, Silistre, Varna, Şumnu, İslimiye, Silivri, Tekfurdağı, Filibe, Tulça and Tırnova to investigate all towns, abandoned homes and available farms in their regions. They were to record whether towns were all Muslim or mixed Muslim-non-Muslim and to count the number of houses that had been abandoned for twenty or more years, indicating where those houses were and in what condition they could be found.[108]

For Nusret, registers were not enough. Instead, he turned to a passion project: the precise and comprehensive mapping of Ottoman territory essential to his vision of good administration. Nusret returned to the question of mapping repeatedly in in his correspondence with the grand vizier and Supreme Council in 1861 and 1862. A progress report he sent in 1862 outlined Nusret's successes. In the span of a few months, he had overseen the shuttling of 10,000 migrants to temporary housing in Vidin and its environs, distributed the 'basics of settlement' to 34,344 migrant households and combated the spread of a devastating cattle plague. Each achievement was tied to careful planning and data collection, such as disseminating housing plans to local officials and recording distributed aid.[109] Despite these accomplishments, as Nusret set his sights on the spring and the possibility of placing migrants in permanent homes, he felt woefully uninformed about the province and the distribution of people within it. The governor of Vidin and the Supreme Council were convinced of the region's capacity, but the land registers and pre-existing surveys were simply not sufficient for Nusret's purposes. Instead, he commented, what was needed was an 'accurate map' of districts, subdistricts, towns and villages. His ideal map encompassed physical and human geography. It included descriptions of the demographic make-up of the population (Muslim and non-Muslim), sites of note such as monasteries, mountain passes and rivers, and the topography of each province. Unfortunately, he ruefully noted, such a map did not exist – neither in the Ottoman state nor 'even in foreign countries'.[110]

Given the absence of such a map, Nusret thought himself an ideal candidate to create one. Coupled with his years of formal training at the Military

83

Academy and in Paris was his own interest in cartography and science, which he had fostered since youth and 'undertaken at his own expense'.[111] Armed with this expertise, he had already taken it upon himself to draft a detailed map of the district of Lom. The map was in conformity with 'practical trigonometry'. 'Without missing one', it showed each existing town, appended villages and neighbourhoods, and numbers of houses for each migrant settlement. Given the size of the map, he included a numbered guide to make finding each village easy for other users.[112]

To Nusret, accurate maps could combat insecurity, upheaval and unrest. Nusret's years-long role in security and settlement in the region contributed to his desire and capacity to map entire provinces. His work on a comprehensive map of Plovdiv/Filibe, the first of its kind, began during his anti-banditry efforts in Islimiye. Whether addressing the countless 'cries and moans' of people suffering from highway robbers and other brigands in years prior, or in dealing with the disputes and accounts of wrongdoing that had emerged after migrant settlement, each visit was an opportunity to continue to plot the territory.[113] His tour of migrant settlements in Vidin, Sofia, Tirnova, Silistre and Tulça allowed him 'neither sleep nor comfort', but he drew his map in the time allotted during his village by village exploration of the region.[114]

Nusret needed maps, but making them was not a project he could complete on his own. His dispatches to Istanbul were also requests for more personnel. The map he drafted encompassed just one district, and it had not been easy to complete. Mapping the rest of the empire, or even just Rumelia, required more trained army officers than were available in the entirety of the empire, and likely, he added, more than were available in Europe. That being the case, he scaled back his vision to something more achievable: making and distributing copies of his map. To that end, Nusret had requested three capable captains (*yüzbaşi*) from the Minister of War. Instead, Nusret noted ruefully, the three officers (*zabit*) he had been sent failed to meet even the basic qualification of being literate.[115]

In making his request for help in mapping the province, Nusret emphasised the value such a project could bring. The map was useful not only for migrant settlement but also as an essential tool in administering the entire province. He argued a comprehensive map offered benefits in a thousand realms, chief among them travel, property, statecraft and military. Nodding to the ever-present threat of European intervention, Nusret promised that if Ottomans were to hold such a map for the entire territory, 'we would no longer need to learn about our land from foreigners'.[116] For Nusret, the dream of a well-mapped territory was one

Muhacir *as Problem*

in which cartographic knowledge brought about effective governance and the guarantee of full sovereignty. His point regarding the directionality of knowledge about Ottoman territory held true for his map of Filibe, completed in 1862/1863, which was translated by German geographer Heinrich Kiepert in 1876.[117]

PRODUCING CATEGORIES AND CUTTING COSTS

As officials responded to large-scale migrations in the late 1850s, they considered the successful settlement of previous years. Instructions to the governor of Hüdavendigar in 1857 on settling Circassians noted that every effort should be made to follow the patterns of migrant aid and settlement established in Dobruca and Mecidiye. A component of the success in Mecidiye had, apparently, been a register of all immigrants, and so the same was undertaken in Hüdavendigar. The register divided up the population according to household, and it recorded each migrant's name, age, gender and relationship to the head of household (e.g. wife, son, daughter, enslaved person).[118] As the difficulties of transporting, housing and feeding migrants became more apparent, officials turned again to careful record-keeping. Categorising and counting the population helped to resolve officials' gravest concern: the sheer cost of turning refugees into colonists.

The twin interests of cutting costs and creating a productive *muhacir* population influenced the knowledge officials produced about migrants and the categories they employed to do so. As the cost of settlement became too much for local populations and the central treasury, officials turned to the migrant population. Officials distinguished among migrants, evaluating how, as individuals, they might defray the cost of their own settlement. Instructions in 1856 required wealthy migrants to cover their housing and other expenses.[119] Likewise, instructions to Nusret in 1860 noted that the current arrivals tended to be better off than their predecessors and that many had managed to sell off property in their homelands prior to departure. Nusret was to distinguish among them; only those in dire need of assistance were eligible for aid. Otherwise, wealthy migrants were to purchase their own provisions and agricultural equipment. Those in between these two extremes were to work as hired labour for wealthy migrants or established populations.[120]

Using migrants to defray the cost of their own settlement remained a priority after Nusret's departure from Rumelia in January of 1865. In late fall of 1864, Midhat Pasha arrived as the governor of the newly created Danube Vilayet, comprised of the districts of Vidin, Niş and Silistre.

Governing Migration in the Late Ottoman Empire

The province was the site of a pilot project in administrative reorganisation, infrastructure, communications, economic development, urban beautification and judicial reform. The stakes of Midhat's work were heightened by statesmen's concerns about Bulgarian nationalism, and the pasha worked to sell the Ottoman state to the province's diverse population.[121] Soon after Midhat arrived, he and Nusret quarrelled, leading to the latter's resignation.[122] Following Nusret's departure, Midhat was left with the reality of the tremendous cost of migrant settlement.

Midhat wrote to the Supreme Council, explaining that poor and non-existent record-keeping plagued the endeavour and gave rise to disorder and potential wrongdoing. Hoping to gain a comprehensive understanding of the state of settlement in the Danube Vilayet, Midhat had gathered together all the migration officials in the province. None of them could produce satisfactory information regarding the number of migrants, the places unhoused migrants were to be sent and current expenditures. Though Nusret had presumably kept registers and documents, such records were nowhere to be found. Starting from scratch, Midhat put forth his method for *muhacir* management, one that relied on categorising migrants based on their wealth and projected productivity.

Midhat identified the essential issue within migrant management as one of cost to the local population. The 'sensitive' conditions of the region meant 'squeezing' residents could give rise to bad influences – presumably Bulgarian nationalism and general unrest – and migrant housing and stipends created too much of an imposition. To defray costs, migrants had to cover more of their expenditures, and for that to happen, officials needed more information about the *muhacir* population. According to Midhat, the migrant population could be divided into four types (*sınıf*) according to their resources and likelihood of self-sufficiency. The first two categories were the wealthy and already employed, neither of which needed aid at all. The third category comprised those who had the physical capacity to work, either as porters, watchmen and servants or as farmers, but who did not yet have sufficient funds. The fourth category referred to those who required long-term or perpetual assistance from the state, such as widows, the elderly, invalids and orphans. Orphans, while a potential drain on expenditures, could of course become productive members of society, either by adoption or after being sent to one of the orphanages Midhat had established in Niş and Rusçuk.[123]

Midhat wrote his instructions in early February; he hoped to cut the stipends of the first two groups by the end of March. To that end, he gave the province's migration officials a month to submit completed registers noting the head of household, family size, any extended family in the

Muhacir *as Problem*

same village, trade and the *sınıf* of each *muhacir* in their district.[124] To standardise the collection of that information, he included a sample register (Figure 2.2) in his instructions. Midhat's goal was retrievable data. Faced with the cost of settlement and concerned about provincial security, Midhat elevated categories of current and potential productivity in his management of the *muhacir*.

THE APPEAL OF PERSUASIVE DATA

While Tanzimat reformers' overall goal was to use *muhacir* settlement to create a more governable, productive and loyal population, the reality of the project was one in which short- and long-term security and economic factors determined how officials dealt with specific migrant populations as they weighed settlement priorities. In this centralising era, statesmen saw the appeal of Ottomanism as one in which legal fairness and just administration led people to be loyal, to consider themselves participants with shared patriotic duties and to behave in alignment with core 'civilised' values. While officials sought to change behaviours and create unmediated relationships between state and subject, they also employed conciliatory and localised policies of accommodation. The successful sedentarisation of some tribes, for example, often required granting expanded rights to others.[125] Elsewhere, the state's 'civilising mission', though a component of Ottoman governmentality, was balanced with strategic empowerment of local power brokers who could integrate peripheral regions.[126] This was true in the midst of the mass migrations of the early 1860s, as particular contexts gave rise to specific policies and outcomes in settlement. Assimilation and co-optation functioned within migration, settlement and aid regimes.

For officials, the benefit of data extended beyond merely knowing about the population. Maurus Reinkowski has argued that the Tanzimat era witnessed a shift in how officials imagined the functioning of order in Ottoman society. The pre-Tanzimat model had relied merely on disciplining subjects to reassert order. By the 1860s, officials wrote of civilising subjects. They identified ignorance and poverty as the sources of bad behaviour.[127] Officials could use information to 'teach' unruly subjects, and well-deployed data could sell Ottoman administration to Ottoman subjects, especially those who might be lured by alternate loyalties beyond Ottoman borders. The well-administered state endeared itself to its people, bringing about their desired behaviour and sentiments.

In 1863, the Kaymakam of Köstence hoped that carefully collected and disseminated information would win over populations 'accustomed to

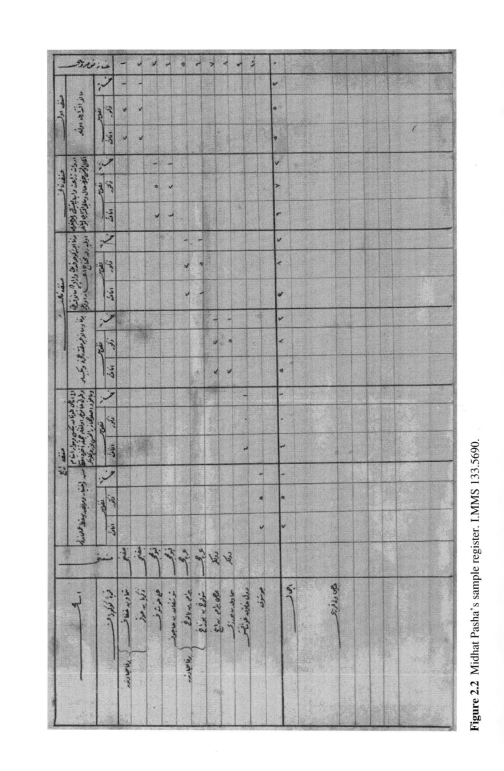

Figure 2.2 Midhat Pasha's sample register. I.MMS 133.5690.

Muhacir *as Problem*

using large swaths of land' and apprehensive about losing it to migrant settlement. Nusret was busy with his work in Rusçuk, leaving the Kaymakam to confront a 'migrant onslaught' of more than 37,000 on one hand and residents' 'incessant' concerns about the loss of land on the other. His solution was to deputise migrants and residents in the tasks of data collection and persuasion. The Kaymakam dispatched Hacı Ömer Ağa, a member of Köstence's Agriculture Office, and Ismail Efendi of Mecidiye to tour the area and create a register of migrants and migrant households. He instructed Ömer and Ismail to establish commissions in each village comprised of the imam, village head (*muhtar*), and 'reasonable people' from among the residents and the migrants who had already settled. The commissions were to register the boundaries of the village and the land within it.

The Kaymakam noted that the two ministers were likely to encounter protests from local residents, such as, 'we haven't much land, and if you settle migrants here we will be scattered'. Recognising that the migrants might be a burden on existing villages, he instructed Ömer and Ismail to investigate such claims and to evaluate whether available land could actually accommodate settlement. However, if their investigation revealed that there was enough land for some number of migrants, the Kaymakam believed the daily quarrels over land between migrants and residents would die down once the knowledgeable officials divided and apportioned territory. Registers, explanations and an appeal to facts would mollify the residents' concerns. To convince the residents to help aid the migrants 'as far as their means would allow', the Kaymakam recommended inciting their religious and patriotic zeal.

The Kaymakam's belief in the power of persuasive facts and participatory government applied to the migrants as well. He recommended making sure migrants recognised a leader as soon as they were settled. The leader could help the state keep tabs on the migrant population and help convince migrants to likewise conform to official decisions. Migrants were not interested in being separated during settlement. To resolve this issue, the Kaymakam encouraged the local commissions and migrant leadership to call together those who were to be sent elsewhere one by one and simply explain, 'this village cannot hold the existing number of families here. For the sake of the comfort of all, you are going to another village. Your village will have enough fields and pastures for you to successfully farm, and you will be comfortable there.'[128] The Kaymakam suggested that gentle appeals to reason from their own leaders would succeed in convincing intransigent migrants and residents alike, but there were limits to the appeal of facts, patriotism and common good, and representation.

The Kaymakam noted that officials could use force where explanation and encouragement failed to yield aid from residents or acquiescence from migrants.[129]

For officials, maps and records could resolve the delicate situations that emerged from *muhacir* settlement in Rumelia. In his detailed study of Midhat Pasha's tenure as governor of the Danube Province, Milen Petrov defines the Tanzimat discourse of 'Ottoman modernism' as one that 'sought to justify the claim that the *Tanzimat* reforms would bring (or were already bringing) – the benefits of progress and modernity to all their subjects'.[130] Ottoman modernism contended with the alternate loyalties and depictions of Ottoman backwardness lodged by orientalists and Bulgarian separatists. Tanzimat reformers' goals in Rumelia included demonstrating 'to the public that the *Tanzimat* and *Tanzimat* statesmen … could be bona fide agents of modernity and progress' through achieving the reforms officials envisioned.[131] Similarly, Tanzimat officials believed record-keeping and participation helped to mould the behaviours of the population and served as a route to cultivate among the people a belief in the justness and longevity of the Ottoman state.

Conclusion

The defining feature of *Deli* Nusret Pasha's life for those who work in the Ottoman archives has tended to be his long memoranda addressing major issues facing the state, from the failings of Ottoman bureaucratic personnel to the need for wide-ranging reform in Iraq. True to form, he wrote such a memorandum in 1883, in which he complained of the failures of the Migrant Administration and, in particular, the individuals who manned its office in Istanbul. He blamed officials for wasting money, delaying settlement and creating misery. He shared a conversation he had had with a Circassian he encountered in Istanbul. The Circassian stated that he and those with him had not received a bread ration for three days, and when they tried to petition the Sultan, the head of the Migrant Administration sent a group of thugs to threaten them into silence. The Circassian's story of injustice, suffering and cruelty would have been familiar to many Ottoman subjects facing the outcomes of mass movement and delayed settlement.[132]

Whether writing in 1863 or 1883, reporting on his own success or critiquing the flaws of others, Nusret's descriptions of the settlement process narrate the story of Ottoman mass migration as a story of the *muhacir* becoming a social problem to solve. At the same time, for Nusret the

Muhacir *as Problem*

muhacir remained an instrument to address the weaknesses of the Ottoman state and an opportunity to effect new behaviours and loyalties among the population. As officials confronted large-scale movements from the Crimean Peninsula and Caucasus in the 1860s, they consolidated policies and tools that persisted across the next several decades. Problematising the migrant and tapping into the resource the *muhacir* offered were exercises in extending the administrative breadth of the ideal state. As officials confronted the reality of these limitations, the settlement process was tied to the larger project of mapping the land and locating individuals.

Nusret Pasha shows up here and there as a footnote in histories of Ottoman migration and in the dramas unfolding for Midhat Pasha and the other great statesmen of the Tanzimat era. This chapter elevated Nusret Pasha from footnote to focus because his words and actions highlight the centrality of migration in the Ottoman state in the final decades of the nineteenth century. Though he does not show up among the pantheon of Tanzimat or Hamidian statesmen, he was just as invested in the broad concerns of Ottoman reform. In a career that spanned decades and stretched from the Danube to the Euphrates, Nusret sought to manage migration in order to change Ottoman governance and Ottoman society. Every facet of settling the *muhacir* provided opportunities to contribute to the myriad projects that made up Ottoman reform. The vastness of the settlement project – in terms of duration, territorial breadth and number of administrators, migrants, and local populations affected by the process – is clear in the relatively limited historiographical impact Nusret Pasha has made despite his influence over hundreds of thousands of individuals during his tenure in Rumelia.

This chapter has traced institutional and ideological elements of the Ottoman state's immigration and settlement regime from the late 1850s to the first half of the 1860s to demonstrate that, when faced with the challenges of mass migration, officials turned the *muhacir* into a realm of state intervention. Over that period, migration administration changed from ad hoc and local efforts to more institutionalised responses. The chapter considered as well the story of how the project of settlement encountered infrastructural, financial and ecological challenges. Nusret, Midhat and other administrators responded to failures in and critiques of migrant settlement by developing techniques and tools to generate granular, encompassing and retrievable information about Ottoman territory and the Ottoman population. The following chapter considers migrant disease and welfare as further facets of the problematisation of the *muhacir*. During the mass migrations of the 1860s and late 1870s, Ottoman officials' appeal to legitimacy through effective migration administration was intended for

Governing Migration in the Late Ottoman Empire

domestic and international audiences. The *muhacir* was a figure of international concern, and physicians, politicians and philanthropists navigated the dynamics of the Eastern Question by asserting their role in rescuing migrants from enemy hands, disease and financial ruin.

Notes

1. Mustafa Oğuz, 'Osmanlı Devleti'nde Devlet Adamı Kitliği (Kaht-ı Rical) Hakkında II. Abdülhamid'e Sunulan Bir Rapor', *Türklük Bilimi Araştırmaları* 24 (2008): 101; Gökhan Çetinkaya, *Ottoman Administration of Iraq, 1890–1908* (London: Routledge, 2006), 52.
2. Mehmed Süreyya, *Sicill-i Osmani, yahut, Tezkire-yi Meşahir-i Osmaniye*, vol. 4 (Istanbul: Matbaa-i Amire, 1308/1893), 554.
3. Süreyya, *Sicill-i Osmani*, IV, 554; Ali Adem Yörük, 'Introduction', in *Nusretü'l-Hamid Ala Siyaseti-l-Abid Mikyasü'l Ahlak: Sülükü'l-Malik Tercümleri* (Istanbul Bilnet Matbaacılık ve Yayıncılık, 2020), 28.
4. Oğuz, 'Osmanlı Devleti'nde.'
5. Çetinkaya, *Ottoman Administration of Iraq*, 31–2.
6. I.DH 346.22848, 8 Şevval 1272/12 June 1856; A.MKT.UM 243.88, 11 Zilkade 1272/13 August 1856.
7. *Journal de Constantinople*, 27 August 1860. Cited in Mark Pinson, 'Ottoman Colonization of Crimean Tatars in Bulgaria, 1854–1862', in *VII. Türk Tarih Kongresi (Ankara: 25–29 Eylül 1970). Kongreye Sunulan Bildiriler*, vol. 2 (Ankara: Türk Tarih Kurumu Basımevi, 1973), 1051.
8. As noted in Chapter 1, the population of Dobruca was estimated at 100,000 in 1830. I.DH 460.30579, 26, Muharrem 1277/14 August 1860. Cited in Saydam, *Kırım ve Kafkas Göçleri*, 100.
9. I.DH 460.30579.
10. Dobruca is a historical region bordered by the lower Danube River and the western Black Sea coast. It spans the eastern and north-eastern regions of contemporary Romania and Bulgaria.
11. I.DH 460.30579.
12. The Meclis-i Vala created the Danube Province from the districts of Vidin, Niş, and Silistre in 1864.
13. Gatrell, *Making of the Modern Refugee*, 5.
14. Scott, *Seeing Like a State*, 11.
15. Kasaba, *A Moveable Empire*, 58; David Moon, 'Peasant Migration and the Settlement of Russia's Frontiers, 1550–1897', *The Historical Journal* 40, no. 4 (1997): 859–93.
16. Pinson, 'Demographic Warfare', 1.
17. I.DH 438.28947, 22 Zilhicce, 1275/23 July 1859.
18. I.MMS 16.649, 8 October 1859, in *Belgelerinde* 1, no. 1, 24–9; A.MKT. MHM 209.85, 21 February 1861, in *Belgelerinde* 2, no. 8, 64–5.
19. I.DH 524.36128, 17 April, 1864, in *Belgelerinde* 1, no. 8, 66–73.

Muhacir *as Problem*

20. A.MKT.MHM 191.73, 27 Cemaziyülahır 1277, 10 January 1861.
21. Maurus Reinkowski, 'The State's Security and the Subject's Prosperity: Notions of Order in Ottoman Bureaucratic Correspondence (19th Century)', in *Legitimizing the Order: The Ottoman Rhetoric of State Power*, ed. Hakan T. Karateke and Maurus Reinkowski (Leiden: Brill, 2005), 201–2; Saydam, *Kırım ve Kafkas Göçleri*, 96–7.
22. I.MVL 454.20302, 11 Safer 1278/18 August 1861.
23. Faruk Kocacık, 'Balkanlar'dan Anadolu'ya Yönelik Göçler', *The Journal of Ottoman Studies*, 1 (1980): 157.
24. David Cameron Cuthell, 'The Muhacirin Komisyonu: An Agent in the Transformation of Ottoman Anatolia, 1860–1866' (PhD diss. Columbia University, 2005), 98.
25. Saydam, *Kırım ve Kafkas Göçleri*, 102–5.
26. Eren, *Türkiye'de Göç ve Göçmen Meseleleri*, 54–61; Saydam, *Kırım ve Kafkas Göçleri*, 105–6.
27. I.DH 479.32201, 4 Rebiyülahir 1278/9 October 1861.
28. Hafiz Pasha (1860–1), İzzet Pasha (1862–3), Vecihi Pasha (1863–4), and Osman Pasha (1864–5, who also headed the reorganised commission after 1865).
29. Cuthell, 'The Muhacirin Komisyonu', 110.
30. Saydam, *Kırım ve Kafkas Göçleri*, 116; A.MKT.MHM 332.72, 21 April 1865, in *Belgelerinde* 1, no. 13, 79–80.
31. I.DH 507.34551, 15 Cemaziyülevvel 1279/8 November 1862; Süreyya, *Sicill-i Osmani*, IV, 554.
32. Saydam, *Kırım ve Kafkas Göçleri*, 114–15.
33. ŞD 1334.16, 4 August 1873, in *Belgelerinde* 2, no. 74, 282–6.
34. Saydam, *Kırım ve Kafkas Göçleri*, 114–18.
35. I.MMS 16.649, 8 October 1859.
36. A.MKT.UM 365.56, 13 October 1859, in *Belgelerinde* 2, no. 1, 24–6.
37. A.MKT.UM 432.47, 19 October 1860, in *Belgelerinde* 2, no. 55, 217–21. This document references an amount from an *emirname* dated 1 October of the same year. An okka is 2.83 pounds.
38. A.MKT.UM 365.56, 13 October 1859. Saydam, *Kırım ve Kafkas Göçleri*, 157. Regulations issued in later years set the amount at 100 dirhem of bread for those under ten and a half okka of bread for those over ten. See Y.PRK. KOM 1.26, March/April 1878, in *Belgelerinde* 1, no. 17, 153.
39. Saydam, *Kırım ve Kafkas Göçleri*, 119.
40. MAD.d 9072, 6 May 1867, in *Belgelerinde* 2, no. 20, 96–9. See also Saydam, *Kırım ve Kafkas Göçleri*, 200.
41. Saydam, *Kırım ve Kafkas Göçleri*, 155–9.
42. Ibid., 203. The exchange rate for the Ottoman *kuruş* to the British pound ranged from 1:115.5 in 1855 to 1:128.5 in 1864. Denzel, *Handbook of World Exchange Rates*, 394. I calculated the figure of 5 to 10 per cent using data from Stanford Shaw, 'Ottoman Expenditures and Budgets in the Late

Governing Migration in the Late Ottoman Empire

Nineteenth and Early Twentieth Centuries', *IJMES* 9, no. 3 (1978): 373–8. Those budget sheets begin with financial year 1278 (1860) and do not account for every year in the 1860s. Yearly expenditures during the decade ranged from 1.475 to 1.7 billion *kuruş*.

43. İpek, *Rumeli'den Anadolu'ya*, 235. The central treasury put at least 1,020,000 *kuruş* towards migration; İpek notes that local entities covered much of the cost during the war (ibid., 234–5).

44. Saydam, *Kırım ve Kafkas Göçleri*, 134.

45. I.DH 343.22622, 27 Şevval 1272/1 July 1856. See also Saydam, *Kırım ve Kafkas Göçleri*, 120.

46. Milen V. Petrov, '*Tanzimat* for the Countryside: Midhat Paşa and the *Vilayet* of Danube, 1864–1868' (PhD diss., Princeton University, 2006), 360–1.

47. I.MMS 28.1220, 2 June 1864, in *Belgelerinde* 1, no. 12, 74–8. See also Margarita Dobreva, 'Circassian Colonization in the Danube Vilayet and Social Integration (Preliminary Notes)', *OTAM* 33 (2013): 18.

48. I.DH 438.28947, 22 Zilhicce, 1275/23 July, 1859.

49. I.DH 343.22622, 27 Şevval, 1272/1 July, 1856.

50. I.MMS 16.649, 8 October 1859.

51. A.MKT.UM 432.47, 19 October 1860, in *Belgelerinde* 2, no. 55, 217; I.MMS 27.1189, 1 Recep 1280/12 December 1863.

52. Y.PRK.DH 2.93, 1889, in *Belgelerinde* 1, no. 28, 155–6.

53. Dobreva, 'Circassian Colonization in the Danube Vilayet and Social Integration (Preliminary Notes)', *OTAM* 33 (2013): 12–14; Pinson, 'Ottoman Colonization', 1053–6.

54. I.DH 460.30579, 1860; A.MKT.UM 432.47, 19 October 1860, in *Belgelerinde* 2, no. 55, 217–21.

55. I.MMS 27.1189, 1863.

56. Cuthell, 'Muhacirin Komisyonu', 24–5, 147–50.

57. Ibid., 17, 175–6; Eugene Rogan, *Frontiers of the State in the Late Ottoman Empire: Transjordan, 1850–1921* (Cambridge: Cambridge University Press, 1999), 85; Kasaba, *A Moveable Empire*, 104, 108–9.

58. MVL 954.53, 9 Rebiülevvel 1279/4 September 1862.

59. I.MMS 38.1590, 26 Zilhicce 1286/29 March 1870. Document cited in Georgi Chochiev, 'XIX. Yüzyılın İkinci Yarısında Osmanlı İmparatorluğu'nda Kuzey Kafkas Göçmenlerin Toplumsal Uyarlanmasına Dair Bazı Görüşler', *Kebikeç* 23 (2007): 419–20; A.MKT.MHM 427.38, 7 Şaban 1286/23 November 1868.

60. Saydam, *Kırım ve Kafkas Göçleri*, 132.

61. I.MMS 38.1590, 1870.

62. I.MVL 454.20302, 1861.

63. Mark Pinson, 'Ottoman Bulgaria in the First Tanzimat Period: The Revolts in Nish (1841) and Vidin (1850)', *Middle Eastern Studies* 11, no. 2 (1975): 127–30.

64. I.DH 494.33544, 12 Safer, 1279/9 August 1862.

Muhacir *as Problem*

65. Ibid.
66. 'A letter to the Editor from the Vicar of Lydney', *The Times*, 17 June 1864. Cited in Sarah A. S. Isla Rosser-Own, 'The First "Circassian Exodus" to the Ottoman Empire (1858–1867), and the Ottoman response, Based on the Accounts of Contemporary British Observers' (MA thesis, School of Oriental and African Studies, University of London, 2007), 40.
67. 'The East', *The Times*, 31 December 1864.
68. Ibid.
69. M. Safa Saraçoğlu, *Nineteenth-Century Local Governance in Ottoman Bulgaria: Politics in Provincial Councils* (Edinburgh: Edinburgh University Press, 2018), 156.
70. C.DH 204.10152, 29 Safer 1277/16 September 1860; A.MKT.MHM 190.11, 13 Muharrem, 1277/1 August, 1860; A.MKT.MHM 192.39, 3 Safer, 1277/ 21 August, 1860; A.MKT.MHM 197.76, 28 Rebiyülahır, 1277/14 October 1860; A.MKT.MHM 198.93, 16 Recep, 1277/28 January 1861.
71. A.MKT.MHM 198.102, 4 Rebiyülevvel 1277/20 September 1860.
72. I.MVL 368.016159, 26 Recep 1273/22 March 1857.
73. Vladimir Hamed-Troyansky, 'Imperial Refugee: Resettlement of Muslims from Russia in the Ottoman Empire, 1860–1914' (PhD diss., Stanford University, 2018), 80.
74. A.MKT.NZD 324.65, 29 Safer 1277/16 September 1860.
75. A.MKT.MHM 305.65, 12 July 1864, in *Belgelerinde* 2, no. 65, 252–3.
76. Saraçoğlu, *Nineteenth-Century Local Governance*, 146–64.
77. Hamed-Troyansky, 'Imperial Refugee', 87–9.
78. Chochiev, 'XIX. Yüzyılın', 418–19.
79. Hamed-Troyansky, 'Imperial Refugee', 95.
80. Suter to Bulwer, 29 October 1860, NA, FO 195.644.
81. MVL 533.109, 23 Muharrem 1284/27 May 1867.
82. Özge Ertem, 'Eating the Last Seed: Famine, Empire, Survival and Order in Ottoman Anatolia in the Late Nineteenth Century' (PhD diss., European University Institute, 2012).
83. I.DH 1173.91704, 18 February 1890.
84. The effort to get migrants farming within a year remained a consistent goal across the decades. See I.MVL 505.22848, 9 Zilkade, 1280/16 April 1864; Y.A.RES 1.41, 2 Safer, 1295/5 February 1878.
85. MVL 388.3, 6 Zilkade 1278/5 May 1862; MVL 504.44, 13 Cemaziyülevvel 1283/23 September 1866.
86. MVL 511.127, 25 Cemaziyülahır 1283/25 4 November 1866.
87. I.MMS 22.962, 13 Zilkade, 1277/23 May 1861.
88. Thomas Barrett, *At the Edge of Empire: The Terek Cossacks and the North Caucasus Frontier, 1700–1860* (Boulder, CO: Westview Press, 1999).
89. Gratien, *Unsettled Plain*, 69–70.
90. DH.MKT 1016.26, 13 Şaban 1323/13 October 1905; MVL 527.75, 14 Muharrem 1284/18 May 1867.

91. Henry John Van Lennep, *Travels in Little-Known Parts of Asia Minor*, vol. 1. (London: John Murray: 1870), 41–2.
92. The case of Chechen migrants in the 'malarial outpost' of Resülayn, now the city of Ras al-Ayn in northeastern Syria is particularly sobering. One Chechen described burying fifty-seven relatives, including his own children, as a result of the disease. Chris Gratien, 'The Ottoman Quagmire: Malaria, Swamps, and Settlement in the Late Ottoman Mediterranean', *IJMES* 49, no. 4 (2017): 589.
93. Ibid., 584.
94. MVL 503.64, 17 Rebiyülahir 1283/29 August 1866.
95. I.MMS 38.1590, 16 Şevval 1286/20 January 1870.
96. Gratien, *Unsettled Plain*, 87.
97. MVL 527.75, 14 Muharrem 1284/18 May 1867; MVL 511.40, 22 Cemaziyülahır 1283/1 November 1866; MVL 503.64, 17 Rebiyülahir 1283/29 August 1866; DH.MKT 332.24, 17 Recep 1312/18 January 1895.
98. According to David Cuthell, the Migrant Commission employed the excuse of 'failure to adapt' to justify the removal of Nogay leaders Berakey Bey and his brother Haci Timur from Izmit to Samsun. Both had petitioned for permission to return to Crimea. Cuthell, 'Muhacirin Komisyonu', 182.
99. DH.MKT 1.3, 13 Ramazan 1277/25 March 1861.
100. A.MKT.UM 9.510, 21 Rebiyülahir 1278/26 October 1861.
101. A.MKT.NZD 429.92, 6 Muharrem 1279/4 July 1862.
102. A.MKT.UM 504.65, 8 Rebiyülahir 1278/8 October 1861.
103. A.MKT.UM 9.510, 21 Rebiyülahir 1278/26 October 1861. Environmental imagery and attachment to various landscapes persists in the oral traditions of descendants of migrant communities. See Dawn Chatty, *Displacement and Dispossession in the Modern Middle East* (Cambridge: Cambridge University Press, 2010), 110.
104. A.MKT.MHM 301.89, 31 May 1856, in *Belgelerinde* 1, no. 71, 356–9.
105. A.MKT.UM 504.65, 8 Rebiyülahir 1278/8 October 1861.
106. Breyfogle, 'Enduring Imperium', 107.
107. I.DH 494.33544, 1862.
108. A.MKT.MHM 191.73, 27 Muharrem 1277/15 August, 1860.
109. MVL 949.41, 5 Recep 1278/6 January 1862.
110. Ibid.
111. Ibid.
112. I.MVL 454.20302, 1861.
113. A.MKT.MHM 250.100, 19 Teşrinisani 1278/1 December 1862.
114. MVL 949.41, 1862.
115. I.MVL 454.020302, 1861.
116. Ibid.
117. Mehmet Hacısalioğlu, 'Bulgaristan'da Bağımsızlıktan Günümüze Yer İsimlerinin Değiştirilmeleri', in *Balkanlar'da Islam Medeniyeti II.*

Muhacir *as Problem*

Milletlerarası Sempozyumu Tebliğleri Tiran, Arnavutluk 4–7 Aralık 2003 (Istanbul: İslam Tarih, Sanat ve Kültür Araştırma Merkezi, 2006), 178.

118. I.DH 438.28947, 1859.
119. Saydam, *Kırım ve Kafkas Göçleri*, 119–20; document transliterated in Eren, *Türkiye'de Göç ve Göçmen Meseleleri*, 42–9.
120. I.DH 460.30579, 1860.
121. Petrov, 'Tanzimat for the Countryside', 317–21.
122. Dobreva, 'Circassian Colonization', 11.
123. I.MMS 133.5690, 16 Ramazan 1861/12 February 1865.
124. Ibid.
125. Kasaba, *A Moveable Empire*, 18, 109–10. For a discussion of the pragmatic bargains officials made with Kurdish tribes, see Janet Klein, *The Margins of Empire*.
126. Thomas Kuehn, *Empire, Islam, and the Politics of Difference: Ottoman Rule in Yemen, 1849–1919* (Leiden, Brill, 2011), 13. The distinctiveness of the Ottoman civilising mission has caught many scholars' attention. See, for example, Selim Deringil, '"They Live in a State of Nomadism and Savagery": The Late Ottoman Empire and the Post-Colonial Debate', *Comparative Studies in Society and History* 45, no. 2 (2003): 311–42, and Ussama Makdisi, 'Ottoman Orientalism', *The American Historical Review* 107, no. 3 (2002): 768–96.
127. Reinkowski, 'State's Security and the Subject's Prosperity', 195–212.
128. A.MKT.NZD 410.32, 9 Şevval 1278/9 April 1862.
129. Ibid.
130. Petrov, '*Tanzimat* for the Countryside', 320.
131. Ibid., 318.
132. Y.PRK.MYD 3.11, 13 December 1883, in *Belgelerinde* 2, no. 31, 138–46.

3

Muhacir as Victim

Elif, age 35, was positioned in profile. Disembodied hands steadied her torso and manipulated her yielding right arm, displaying her wounds to observers unknown. Her forearm and a section of her skull had been removed; the hands served not only to manipulate but also to support.

Elif was a member of several sets – a set of several dozen and a set of hundreds of thousands. Her image is one among the twenty-eight that comprise 'Victims of Russian Atrocities', a photo album commissioned by Sultan Abdülhamid II and distributed to ambassadors and heads of missions in Istanbul. Elif's wounds were photographed in Edirne and developed by the studios of Pascal Sebah on the Grande Rue de Pera in Istanbul. The photographer captured Elif and her cohort of fellow victims – mostly women and children, ranging in age from two to sixty – on film. He artfully arranged them in rags, alone or in small groups, seated or gathered in mourning around their lost children's funeral biers – a young woman, an infant girl, an elderly man holding two small boys in his arms. Most were positioned obliquely, their gazes directed away from the camera, though a few looked directly back at it. Those who gazed back pulled away their clothing to reveal their injuries to the camera's lens. Personal information about the subject of each portrait was limited to what easily fit on the back of the postcard-sized mementos to their suffering. Each individual was reduced to, at most, their image, name, age, village of origin and a brief description of their losses.[1]

The photographs are a way of knowing and fixing in space and time. The information on the back of each arrests their subjects in place and establishes their membership within a much larger set: refugees of the 1877–8 Russo-Ottoman War. The photographs subsume each individual under the category of 'victim' – an identity rendered via suffering, and a suffering rendered meaningful via consumption by those who could

Muhacir *as Victim*

intervene in the forces of their displacement. The album captures a handful of individuals among a vast number of persons displaced by August 1877. The war was fought in part through public opinion, with multiple sides seeking aid and foreign intervention on the basis of victimhood. With that in mind, Elif's name, age and image were recorded to trigger their audience's sympathy. The album is an early example of how photography elevated and consolidated the category of 'the refugee' while denying displaced individuals voice to describe the complexities of their experiences and needs.[2]

The photographs are also a signal that the Ottoman state's response to migrants and its engagement with population politics did not occur in a vacuum. Rather, populations displaced by war were a component in a global discourse linking civilisation and victimhood to governance and sovereignty. The 'fugitives' of the 1877–8 War moved through a world in which the concept of 'the international' provided a new vernacular with which to engage in state-building and state legitimacy. The concept emerged, Mark Mazower argues, as 'the shrinkage of time and space ... [and] an era of accelerated migration forged a culture increasingly attentive to the idea of the world as a unity'.[3] World's fairs, international meetings and scientific congresses, the adoption of global standards to measure weight and time, and a modern humanitarianism, based upon 'greater inclusivity of the category "humanity"', characterised the internationalism of the second half of the nineteenth century.[4]

The Ottoman Empire's participation in and appeals to international organisations, institutions and spheres of meaning-making influenced its responses to episodes of mass migration. This chapter analyses the internal and international dynamics of Ottoman migration governance from the 1860s to the 1880s from the perspectives of health, philanthropy and Ottoman self-representation. Public health and population welfare were arenas of Ottoman state-building and centralisation; they were also realms to participate in claiming the empire's status as a civilised state within the international sphere. Though public health was a field in which the Ottoman state fashioned its international image as a 'civilised' state, international protocols and institutions also provided pathways for Great Power influence over Ottoman territory. Diplomacy and concerns over domestic and international legitimacy contributed to Ottoman migration management.

By the time Elif arrived in Edirne, migrant health and welfare were familiar grounds on which to assert legitimacy and contest sovereignty. During the 1860–6 migrations of Crimean Tatars and migrants from the Caucasus, the Ottoman state and the Constantinople Superior Health

Council attempted to avert epidemics in Ottoman port cities around the Black Sea. Officials leveraged public health concerns to confine migrants to camps and to circumscribe their movement within the empire. As concern for health, sanitation and welfare extended beyond ports of arrival, managing health concerns became another route to know the population, facilitate productivity and assert control over space. Nusret Bey's hospitals in Mecidiye and Midhat Pasha's orphanage in Niş (Chapter 2) reflected officials' attempts to manage the qualitative as well as quantitative aspects of population. During and after the 1877–8 Russo-Ottoman War, increased anti-Ottoman and anti-Muslim sentiment among the Great Powers influenced how Ottoman administrators and philanthropists within and outside the empire crafted the *muhacir* as a deserving recipient of aid. In this light, the 'Victims of Russian Atrocities' album serves as a literal example of Hamidian-era 'image management', or Abdülhamid II's use of images and symbols to appeal to and cultivate legitimacy among international and internal audiences.[5]

The manipulation of images – actual and discursive – of the *muhacir* as migrant/refugee/fugitive/victim supported claims to expertise, civilisation and the right to rule and further expanded the Ottoman state's role in migrant and refugee management. Moments of crisis contributed to the development and expansion of a migrant aid regime; in response to mass immigration, Ottoman officials crafted ways of addressing migrant health and welfare that endured beyond the inflection points of epidemic disease and immigrant death. By the 1880s and 1890s, concern with refugee welfare, legibility and productivity contributed to administrators' programmes for orphans, widows and the ill. Before turning to the policies and institutions that emerged to administer refugee health, the chapter discusses the stark realities of death and disease that marked the mass migrations of the era.

Migrant Mortality

In the summer of 1864, newspapers ranging from *The Times* in London to *The Christian Advocate and Journal*, a Methodist newspaper based in New York City, published an account on the plight of Circassians in the Ottoman Black Sea port town of Samsun. A Monsieur Barozzi, the Ottoman Sanitary Inspector in Samsun, penned the report six days after his arrival in the city. He presented an excruciating depiction of migrant suffering:

> No words are adequate to describe the situation in which I found the town and the unfortunate immigrants … Everywhere you meet with the sick, the

Muhacir *as Victim*

dying, and the dead – on the threshold of gates, in front of shops, in the middle of streets, in the gardens, and the foot of trees. Every dwelling, every corner of the streets, every spot occupied by the immigrants has become a hotbed of infection.[6]

Barozzi described overcrowded warehouses in which the living cohabited with rotting bodies. Less fortunate migrants were left without shelter at all. Newcomers succumbed to disease and starvation; a large number of the 70,000–80,000 individuals in the city and surrounding encampments had not eaten for four or more days. Barozzi's description was one of many issued by observers in Ottoman coastal cities who responded to the realities of refugees' violent expulsions from their homes, their devastating travel conditions, and the limited housing and food they found as they moved across the empire.

From the migration of the Crimean Tatars following the Crimean War, to the mass exodus of the Circassians in the 1860s, to the eventual upheaval of the 1870s and 1880s, the health repercussions of mass migration to the Ottoman Empire were devastating. Sickness and death conditioned the experience of immigrating to Ottoman territory. As villages and tribes moved en masse, family members, friends, neighbours and close acquaintances were lost to disease, overcrowding, exposure, malnutrition and lack of access to clean water.

Issues of overcrowding contributed to disease and mortality among populations who arrived already weakened by difficult travel conditions. In the 1860s, the majority of migrants travelled over the Black Sea. Russian officials' eagerness to expel Caucasians led migrants to flee during the winter, a time when the Black Sea was notoriously difficult to travel and sailors faced frequent storms and fog.[7] Russian, Ottoman and British ships assisted in transporting migrants, but individuals departing from encampments on the northern Black Sea coast also crowded onto smaller, poorer-quality vessels, many of which sank during winter voyages.

The sheer number of individuals arriving in port cities overwhelmed the capacity of local officials to house and feed newcomers. In July of 1860, shortly before Nusret's appointment as Director of Migrant Settlement in Rumelia, some 25,000–35,000 Tatars arrived in Varna.[8] In October, the British Vice Consul estimated that 18,000 individuals had landed in Köstence within the previous twenty days, bringing the total number of arrivals to 140,000. Thousands of 'half dead, half starved' Tatars remained without shelter in the town.[9] The doctor for the Köstence railway company wrote of overcrowding and poor burial strategies and worried about the arrival of hundreds of thousands more over the winter.[10] In Mecidiye, the

Governing Migration in the Late Ottoman Empire

British Vice Consul estimated fifty to sixty migrants died per day.[11] Nusret Bey took public health and sanitation into account while settling migrants in Mecidiye. An 1864 article in *The Times* (quoted in Chapter 2) praised Nusret's establishment of a hospital for sick immigrants, his creation of a municipal council to oversee street cleaning, and his use of drainage projects to overcome the town's previously 'unhealthy' environs.[12]

Intense mortality likewise characterised the journeys of Circassians to Trabzon and Samsun in 1863–5. Harsh conditions contributed to the spread of epidemics in port cities. Arthur de Fonvielle, a Frenchman who fought alongside Circassians in 1864, described the shores of Circassia, where refugees 'huddled in the snow and wind', waiting for their turn to embark on boats filled six to eight times their capacity for the five-day journey to Trabzon. In de Fonvielle's boat, which carried 347 refugees packed so tightly 'on deck that the crew had to walk on the passengers' heads to get to their places', twenty-one passengers died in the first four days of the journey; the boat ran out of potable water after three days.[13] Upon arrival, migrants, already malnourished, could be left for several days without food, and local administrators did not have enough funds or workers to bury the rapidly rising number of bodies.[14]

Disease spread quickly through refugee encampments. In February 1864, Trabzon witnessed forty to fifty deaths daily. In May, as many as 120–150 migrants died per day. In June, British Consul Stevens estimated that 300 migrants died per day among the 60,000 migrants camped outside Trabzon, and among the population of more than 100,000 in Samsun, daily mortality climbed above 800.[15] In July and August of 1864, Edward Dickson, physician to the British Embassy at Constantinople and a member of the Constantinople Superior Health Council, calculated mortality of 200–300 per day in Trabzon and 350 per day in Samsun.[16] Overall, Stevens calculated a mortality rate of roughly 50 per cent in Samsun and Trabzon over a ten-month period: he believed that of the 220,000 migrants arriving between November 1863 and September 1864, 60,000 had perished in Samsun and 40,000 had died in Trabzon.[17] Migrants continued to suffer as the state moved them away from Black Sea port cities. In December of 1864, Dickson reported that of the 2,718 who sailed from Samsun, 202 died prior to reaching Istanbul. In February, he reported that on an overcrowded voyage from Sinop to Varna, 238 out of 600 passengers passed away.[18]

Environmental factors contributed to migrant suffering. Migrants housed in tents and other makeshift structures faced extreme hardship during winter months. Though the timing of winter was predictable, the availability of transportation was not. A group of 1,200 Circassian

Muhacir *as Victim*

migrants was stranded near Trabzon after their ships failed to arrive. Given the weather, it was not possible to send them to their permanent settlement locations in Köstence until the start of spring. Since officials had anticipated that the migrants would stay in the area only temporarily, they housed them in tents. Faced with rapidly dropping temperatures, officials endeavoured to improve the Circassians' circumstances through relocating the migrants to several khans, coffeehouses and similar buildings in a nearby town. The large group was to be cared for over the winter months via state and private coordination providing migrants with housing and food.[19]

During the mass migrations from the Balkans after the 1877–8 Russo-Ottoman War, potential passengers inundated railroad stations in Shumen/Şumnu, Plovdiv/Filibe, and Varna. Desperate to escape, some individuals fell to their deaths after clinging to the outside of trains or perished from the disease that spread through overcrowded carriages.[20] Many more travelled on foot, and hundreds of thousands found their way to mosques, hospitals and temporary holding areas in Istanbul. In March of 1878, after a particularly harsh winter, and at a time when Istanbul was besieged by epidemics of typhus, typhoid and smallpox, twenty-five to thirty migrants died per day in the Hagia Sophia mosque complex, which held more than 10,000 within its walls.[21] Migrants' weakened condition contributed to ongoing sickness, difficulty traveling and trouble surviving once Ottoman officials determined settlement locations. Removing migrants from port cities remained the preferred solution to the crisis, whether or not the decision to move migrants reflected refugees' interests.

Environmental factors affected the logistics of migrant arrival and settlement. Climate and weather conditions created complications and delays in migrants' original voyages and their journeys within the Ottoman Empire. Seasonal conditions determined the timing of settlement and influenced officials' decisions to keep migrants in provisional housing or to move them more quickly to their ultimate destination. Seasonal change affected the feasibility of overland routes into Eastern Anatolia and the ability of Ottoman officials to transport migrants from coastal towns. Randal Roberts, an observer of the 1877–8 War, noted the condition of the roads throughout the empire. Roberts described the Black Sea region as 'rugged mountainous ranges, crossed by difficult and sometimes impassable roads [and] rocky valleys, intersected by huge marshes and rivers, which are impossible to cross at certain seasons of the year'.[22] According to Roberts, of the three roads from Trabzon to Erzurum, only one was passable during the spring due to snowmelt. In Tokat, a district due south of Samsun, the roads were passable during summer but were nearly impossible to traverse during the rainy season and winter, while near Batum, snowmelt caused road flooding throughout the area.[23] The poor quality of the roads affected the rate and timing at which migrants were transferred from Black Sea ports to settlement locations, allowing temporary arrangements to drag on for months and even years and straining migrant and local populations.

Whether in the 1860s or 1870s, the threat of mortality characterised each stage of the *muhacir* journey. As migrants travelled across sea and land, they encountered Ottoman officials, foreign consuls, physicians and other observers whose tactics of assisting the fugitives stemmed from evolving understandings of disease and the state's role in preventing it. Upon arrival in the empire, migrants lacked food and housing. Ideas of disease, civilisation and public order directly and indirectly influenced their survival of those conditions. Descriptions of refugee mortality and suffering reveal aspects of migrants' experiences, but official reports and accounts published in newspapers were themselves generative of those experiences. Such accounts served to articulate claims to expertise, legitimacy and sovereignty, and put forth assumptions that altered migrants' lives.

Protecting Wellness in the 'Well-Protected Domains': The Constantinople Superior Health Council

The era when migrants entered the empire was one in which the welfare of the population had entered under the purview of the Ottoman state. The nineteenth-century Ottoman state-building effort included attempts to standardise medical practice and monitor public health. Sultan Mahmud II opened an Imperial Medical School in 1827, and the establishment of the Civilian Medical School followed in 1866. Certification of doctors, vaccination regulations, urban sanitary inspections and other components of health reform were essential in the developing apparatus of the modern state. Theories about sanitation and the spread of disease tied together the regulation of public health and the regulation of public space. Nusret's tactics in Mecidiye reflected officials' expectations of sanitation in urban environments; legislation throughout the second half of the nineteenth century elaborated guidelines for public cleanliness, such as new policies on butchery and street cleaning in Istanbul.[24]

Barozzi's depiction of 'the sick, the dying, and the dead' in 1864 reflected the tragedy that unfolded around the shores of the Black Sea. However, his presence in the city, and the measures he took to address the suffering he witnessed, were an outcome of changes in the Ottoman approach to public health, sanitation and quarantine. By the early nineteenth century,

Muhacir *as Victim*

Ottoman officials conceptually linked migration and the threat of epidemic disease. In response to an increasing density of trade and migration and the menace of plague and cholera, Ottoman officials established medical checkpoints around Istanbul in the 1810s and 1820s. Legislation in the 1830s checked 'the spread of disease in Istanbul through the imposition of social control mechanisms', by investigating and documenting newcomers, restricting movement and encouraging neighbourhood informants to report on disease.[25] Andrew Robarts argues that Ottoman officials' concerns with stemming disease by regulating space in the early nineteenth century served as the basis for the empire's later engagement with an international system of quarantine and sanitation.[26]

The creation of the Ottoman Quarantine Council (Meclis-i Tahaffuz) in 1838 was representative of the empire's effort to govern its population, assert control over its economy and stem the spread of disease within and outside the empire. Quarantine measures asserted Ottoman territorial sovereignty and protected internal commercial interests.[27] By the mid-nineteenth century, in response to the increased flow of people and commodities throughout the world and to outbreaks of plague and cholera, representatives of the Great Powers advocated for international cooperation to combat disease. Signing on to international health protocols offered a way for the Ottoman Empire, Persia and Russia to assert their status as 'hygienically trustworthy, reforming, and modern'.[28] Ottoman participation offered an opportunity for the empire to position itself as a modern Muslim state.

The Ottoman state's adoption of quarantine measures cohered with the centralising agenda of the nineteenth-century reforming state; nevertheless, the relationship between quarantine, sanitation and sovereignty was a complicated one. The British protested Ottoman quarantine regulations and argued that quarantine violated the Ottoman Empire's free trade commitments. Subsequently, the 1838 Anglo-Ottoman Treaty of Balta Liman allowed the British to create the Constantinople Superior Health Council to oversee and advise on quarantine implementation. The council's membership was comprised of Ottoman appointees and delegates from foreign legations.[29] Michael Christopher Low notes that while quarantine was a 'potential vehicle of imperial border control and sovereignty', the Board of Health eventually became 'an enduring symbol of the Capitulations'. In the second half of the nineteenth century, British and French doctors increasingly embraced an infectionist perspective on disease, portraying plague as an outcome of unsanitary conditions, which justified medical policing of certain populations. By the 1880s, European representatives dominated the council's membership.[30] In 1881, Dickson, physician to

Governing Migration in the Late Ottoman Empire

the British Embassy at Constantinople and long-time member of the council, asserted that 'all the foreign Governments represented at the Porte' necessarily held the right to comment on measures that applied to 'persons and ships of every nationality'.[31] Members of the board assumed oversight of Ottoman practices as their prerogative, and they prioritised protecting the commercial interests of their own subjects. While Ottoman officials adopted measures to police the poor and other marginal populations through the imposition of sanitary measures; the British and the French deployed infectionist perspectives to justify colonial practices in Egypt and Algeria. By the 1890s, Europeans read the presence of plague as a signal of 'decline and barbarism'.[32] Civilised countries had overcome the disease; from this basis, they were the only ones capable of creating sanitary spaces.

The international dimensions of quarantine rendered the Constantinople Superior Health Council an important influence in the Ottoman response to migrant sickness in port cities. In 1860, Ottomans retained control over the council, yet diplomats importuned the body to dispatch doctors in 1860 and 1863 to respond to epidemic disease in Varna and Trabzon.[33] The council's European representatives coordinated quarantine measures in areas of migrant settlement, questioned ship captains, collected data on mortality and sickness, determined locations for migrant temporary placement, and pressured local officials and representatives of the Migrant Commission to enact sanitation measures. Accounts of migrant health and disease shaped Ottoman policy alongside the unfolding intricacies of the Eastern Question; reports of migrant mortality represented and influenced the horrific outcomes of forced migration. Images of refugee sickness and public health techniques were used to leverage claims of civilisation and expertise, to generate knowledge about the incoming population and to control space.

DEPICTIONS OF THE DISEASED AND THE DISPLACED

In February of 1864, on the recommendation of its French delegate, Dr Sulpice-Antoine Fauvel, the Superior Health Council sent Dr Barozzi to enact quarantine and sanitation measures for migrants in Trabzon and Samsun.[34] Barozzi served as Sanitary Inspector in Trabzon for a total of two months. He performed the same role in Samsun for just twenty-two days.[35] Despite his brief tenure, his presence in the cities during the 1864 crisis and the publication of his report make him an enduring figure in accounts of the period. Newspapers in Europe and the United States published Barozzi's report and closely followed the status of the exiles.

Muhacir *as Victim*

European representatives were sceptical of the Ottoman capacity to deal effectively with the health crisis of migration. Barozzi and other European observers blamed local corruption and ignorance in describing an ongoing state of emergency in Trabzon. While in Trabzon and Samsun, Barozzi worked with and in opposition to local officials. Prior to Barozzi's arrival, Yaver Efendi, the Trabzon representative of the Migrant Commission, had established a hospital and attempted to quickly move migrants out of the cities. These efforts failed as the number of migrants rose exponentially. In dispatches to Istanbul, the French consul accused Yaver Efendi of profiting from speculation and breaking quarantine protocol. After Barozzi and Yaver Efendi clashed over the latter's decision to house migrants in the city, Yaver Efendi requested a Muslim physician replace Barozzi on the basis of cultural disagreements on issues such as burial practices for Muslim migrants.[36] In contrast, the British Consul suggested that the Ottoman government should organise a Medical Commission with 'full powers', for only a fully empowered Medical Commission could overcome 'certain prejudices' held by 'Turks' regarding burial practices and other measures.[37] The Sublime Porte responded to consular complaints, replacing Yaver Efendi with another official more amenable to Barozzi's plans.

Even when sympathetic to local officials, Barozzi remained frustrated with the lack of administrative action and control in an 'immigration thus left to itself'. According to Barozzi, Atta Bey, the governor of Samsun, was 'dismayed' and 'altogether at a loss how to act in such an emergency'. He had no money and no police force at his disposal. Barozzi believed funds from the central government were the only solution to alleviate the disaster, and wished the 'Grand Vizier could ... witness the spectacle which this ill-fated town and its encampments present'.[38] Over and again, observers repeated the need for more resources, commenting on migrants abandoned 'to themselves' in 'circumstances fraught with disastrous results' and others left with 'barely sufficient food to sustain life'.[39] Despite the difficulties any state would have found in coping with the rapid arrival of hundreds of thousands of impoverished, weakened migrants, Europeans could read in the refugees' illnesses the reflection of the 'Sick Man of Europe's' enfeebled administration.[40] The attenuated sovereignty of the Ottoman state and the discursive amalgamation of health, sanitation and civilisation framed the actions and words of European observers who cast the *muhacir* as the victim of Ottoman failings.

Depictions of the refugee as a threat to public health affected understanding of and responses to the crisis, influencing the tactics used to resolve migrant sickness and the casting of migrants as a problem unto themselves. Barozzi identified migrant suffering as a tragedy, but as Sanitary Inspector, his mandate to address the spread of disease took precedence in his discussion of the contours of the crisis and the measures that could alleviate it. In Barozzi's description, the migrants' lamentable state paled in importance to the threat that they posed to public order and public, non-immigrant health. He described a city besieged, in which migrants not only 'heaped up' in all the uninhabited buildings of the city but also 'penetrate[d] everywhere'. Outside the city, he wrote, encampments were 'hardly less revolting', hosting 'forty to fifty thousand individuals in the most absolute state of destitution, preyed upon by diseases, terminated by death ... cast there without bread, without shelter, without sepulchre'. He estimated that the population of 70,000–80,000 migrants the city hosted would double in days. Without a rapid influx of money, men and supplies from the central government, Barozzi predicted chaos, a situation 'pregnant with dangers' and 'a calamity, a catastrophe, a scourge'.[41]

Those who described the migrants' plight were moved by the devastating loss of life they witnessed around the Black Sea, but they were not immune to the implications of mass migration. They were concerned for native populations and themselves. Dickson described the effect of migration on the population of the district of Uşak, an important commercial centre in Hüdavendigar Province in Western Anatolia. According to Dickson's report, Uşak held 140 independent villages, a permanent population of 10,000 Muslims, 1,500 Greeks, 500 Armenians, and a new population of 2,000 Circassian immigrants, who brought with them 'diarrhoea' and typhus. Ottoman officials initially housed the newcomers in khans and houses in town before dispersing them among several villages. Over the course of six months, from June to November, 700 natives fell ill with typhus and 'bowel-complaints', and 220 died, an uptick in illness and mortality the doctor attributed directly to Circassian settlement.[42] Consular agents reported similar cases of Ottoman subjects falling victim to immigrant-borne typhus and smallpox in Trabzon in January, February and April of 1864, and Dickson reported that government officials and quarantine physicians died from exposure to immigrant populations.[43]

Representatives of the Great Powers assessed the commercial implications of crisis in Ottoman port cities, and weighed the outcome of extensive quarantine measures in Istanbul and the Dardanelles. In April, the British consul in Trabzon reported that fears of disease had 'paralyzed commerce', and forecasted that migrants' impending arrival would contribute to famine in the city.[44] By May, when Trabzon already hosted 25,000 migrants and Samsun 35,000–40,000, the number of anticipated arrivals climbed to 200,000. Aside from concerns about health, consular agents,

Muhacir *as Victim*

as commercial representatives of the British Empire, worried that the 'two important commercial cities [would] ... suffer considerably'.[45]

Experiences of contagion and disorder contributed to rumours about further suffering for migrants and townspeople. Such rumours had palpable effects; consuls wrote of panic and dread of 'invasion' within towns already besieged. They described fears of price inflation, food shortages and disease. Consul Stevens, writing in mid-February, estimated 3,000 migrants had arrived in town in the previous three days, leading to an uptick in the spread of disease amongst the Circassians and the 'natives'. Rumours of 40,000–50,000 on their way contributed to a 'great and general panic', in which 'everyone is making arrangements to quit the town'.[46] Likewise, in April of that year, an estimated 100,000 people waited to embark from the northern shores of the Black Sea; Stevens suggested Barozzi's attempts to clear the town of emigrants were no match for these types of numbers.[47]

As disgust and fear coded their encounters with the crisis, Barozzi and others broadened their frustrations from the Ottoman state to migrants themselves. The diseased bodies they encountered became proof of refugees' personal failings and ignorance of the basics of hygienic and civilised habits. In Consul Stevens's descriptions, migrants were 'indolent'. Their disregard for cleanliness meant they themselves contributed to the spread of disease, and he lumped their sicknesses in with his broader critique of their behaviours, which he claimed included trading rations, selling their children into slavery, disinterring and robbing corpses, and concealing deaths to receive provisions. For Stevens, this final act was one reflecting migrants' dishonesty and almost inhuman disregard for cleanliness. He described a group of emigrants who had lived with one such corpse in their tent for eleven days, 'without the slightest repugnance'.[48] A few months later, Stevens again described the migrants as ungrateful, 'unruly' and 'indifferent to their miserable condition, thus nourishing the distemper which daily thins their ranks'.[49]

After migrants passed from the world of the living to the world of the dead, their bodies continued to pose a threat, with improper burial or disposal rendering corpses 'matter out of place'.[50] Dickson described particularly wrenching scenes in Trabzon. After migrants had succumbed to typhus and smallpox they were 'buried in a disgraceful manner ... the bodies are merely covered over with snow; so that human limbs are seen peering above ground'. The physician predicted the spring thaw would eventually 'expose more of their persons, and thus infect the air with human effluvia'. Even before the thaw, inhabitants could see the 'slime fluid' of decomposing bodies 'trickling into' an open water source.[51]

Governing Migration in the Late Ottoman Empire

Stevens described a similar scene, in which neighbourhoods near the cemeteries were 'uninhabitable'. Improper disposal tainted water supplies, and a 'Circassian corpse' was found floating in the city's chief aqueduct.[52]

CONFINING THE *MUHACIR*

During the migration crisis of the 1860s, disease, hygiene and the fear of epidemics became primary elements in describing refugees, justifying intervention and leading to policies to surveil and isolate migrant populations. As observers tied mobility and refugees' bodies to concerns about the threat of disease, administrators sought to control access to public space through quarantine and cordon. In the winter of 1863, the Board of Health issued a report identifying key measures to take in the face of the growing immigrant population and an anticipated uptick in migrant sickness and death. The Board's recommendations included directing boats carrying migrants through quarantine, subjecting all migrants to examination by doctors and the separation of migrants exhibiting symptoms of sickness and disease. The Supreme Council (Meclis-i Vala) endorsed the Board's recommendations.[53] Barozzi described this effort in his report:

> Every dwelling, every corner of the streets, every spot occupied by the immigrants has become a hotbed of infection. A warehouse on the seaside, a few steps from the Quarantine-office, hardly affording space enough for 30 persons, inclosed [*sic*] till the day before yesterday 207 individuals, all sick or dying. I undertook to empty this pestilential place ... I then took steps for the evacuation of the town and the landing of the Circassians I had detained on board the eleven ships and seven cutters lying in the harbor. All the passengers were landed at Koomdjoogah [*sic*], a few miles distant from the town. It is to this locality I sent the 3,000 or 4,000 individuals I have during the last three days extracted from the dens they filled in the city.[54]

As well as directing migrants out of the immediate vicinity, Barozzi dispatched them to Varna and elsewhere. Stevens confirmed Barozzi's account, noting that the physician had sent some 4,000–5,000 to Varna by April of 1864.[55]

Alongside embracing the Board's quarantine recommendations, the Supreme Council reiterated several times the importance of moving migrants out of their ports of arrival and into settlement locations in the interior.[56] Removing refugees from crowded locations offered a potential solution to the spread of disease in congested temporary settlements. Transferring the newcomers from the cities also served to separate migrants from the watchful eye of local reporters, an international audience and

Muhacir *as Victim*

foreign consuls such as Henry Bulwer, who articulated his concern with disorder in urban spaces and his anxieties about the migrant menace.[57] In April of 1864, Bulwer estimated 25,000 migrants had arrived in Trabzon. In a letter to the British ambassador in Istanbul, the consul warned, 'the conglomeration of vast quantities of these people, who have no industrial habits, threatens the health and peace of any one locality'.[58] Migrant bodies polluted the urban environment; the route to solving both disorder and disease lay in removal. Ottoman officials' concerns about the visibility of impoverished migrants in Istanbul and other port cities influenced their attempts to quickly remove the newcomers to the interior.

The threat posed by immigrants to public order and health led Barozzi and Tanzimat officials to define and control access to space. The encampments for refugees were 'ringed with guards' to prevent escape and the spread of infection.[59] Demarcating alternative spaces outside towns as appropriate for migrants allowed for the removal of their bodies and the disorder caused by their presence. Correspondence within the Ottoman government after Barozzi's stint in Samsun reveals broad agreement with the doctor's tactics. In August of 1864, the Meclis-i Vala wrote to the office of the Grand Vizier and the *Mutasarrif* of Canık, a district within Samsun Province, to discuss migrant arrival in the province. The council deplored the logistical problems contributing to migrant suffering, describing a situation in which more than 100,000 migrants were located just outside the city proper. The migrants' 'distress increased daily'. There were neither sufficient food and medical supplies nor enough boats to transfer the migrants elsewhere. Though exact numbers were unknown, the writer suggested 250–350 migrants died daily, and a lack of proper burial had brought about putrefaction of the migrant corpses. Increasing numbers of migrants crowded one another as their numbers swelled, and the writer noted that these conditions encouraged the spread of sicknesses including typhus, bouts of diarrhoea, smallpox and malaria.[60]

While migrants suffered in encampments, officials' resolve to restrict their movement persisted. According to the report, migrants' entrance into the city and presence in the markets had spread typhus to the majority of shop owners. In order to aid the migrants and protect the town, the quarantine doctor at the time recommended the migrants' removal to higher ground and the prevention of their entrance into the city.[61] That these precautions were circulated between the council, the governor of the district and the office of the grand vizier suggests an official acceptance of the efficacy of the preventative measures. The effort to control contagion relied on spatial separation of the diseased migrant and the healthy city dweller and required imposing a boundary on migrant mobility.

Governing Migration in the Late Ottoman Empire

Physicians, the consular corps and Ottoman officials sought to move migrants from crowded cities and overwhelmed encampments. Contagion fears contributed to the effort to rapidly transfer migrants from urban centres and into provincial areas for temporary or permanent settlement, though migrant health was rarely the exclusive concern of those advocating for action. American missionary Henry John van Lennep described the exhaustive efforts of the governor attempting to move immigrants out of Samsun:

> The Pasha was doing all that lay in his power to scatter these poor exiles in every direction. Shiploads of them were sent to other ports. All the muleteers who came on business into town were seized by his police agents, and compelled to carry Circassians and their effects into the interior ... so great was the Pasha's anxiety to dispose of them as soon as possible, that he engaged every means of transportation at high prices, and paid cash down.[62]

According to Van Lennep, the governor's haste arose from the difficulties of maintaining the 'filthy' and diseased migrants. The city's infrastructure was pressed to the limit by the crisis, with little transportation, business at a standstill and bread increasingly difficult to find.[63]

The cramped conditions of temporary housing in Samsun did not facilitate the convalescence of the migrants. The Board of Health encouraged the central government to move migrants to Varna, where it could in turn dispatch doctors to assist new arrivals.[64] Adding a leg of the trip from Samsun to Varna prolonged migrants' journeys over sea, where the death toll could be horrific. Aside from Varna, ships transported migrants to locations around the Sea of Marmara and northern Aegean.

By October of 1864, Dickson estimated that nearly 75,000 Circassians had passed through the Dardanelles, 5,511 of whom landed at Istanbul. Roughly 1,400 passed away during the course of their voyages from Samsun to Istanbul and beyond.[65] In November, Dickson conveyed disturbing rumours of mutilated bodies, migrants thrown overboard and Circassians forced to drink seawater as they sailed from Samsun through Istanbul to Cyprus. Despite declaring the worst of the rumours false, the Board of Health confirmed that 637 out of 1,988 migrants had died during the voyage. In December, the quarantine doctor in the Dardanelles reported that 670 migrants out of 1,800 had died from 'disease, exhaustion, hunger, and above all from the "horrible crowding"' during a thirty-five-day journey from Samsun.[66]

Istanbul was potentially a crucial stop during immigrants' journeys into the Dardanelles, but not all were in favour of allowing immigrants into the city. In July of 1864, the grand vizier noted that migrants on postal boats

112

Muhacir *as Victim*

from Samsun or Trabzon should be forced to disembark and quarantined in the Istanbul's Haydarpaşa neighbourhood.[67] The Health Council strongly advised against the plan. The council warned that bringing the Circassians to Istanbul 'would create in [the city] the same evils which are deplored at Trebizond and Samsoon, whose sickness and loss of life are still very great'.[68] The decision to remove migrants and to prevent their entry into spaces was justified in terms of the strain the newcomers placed on cities. It was a decision that plunged migrants once more into voyages in which the odds of survival were breathtakingly low and the addition of a single day to the journey could determine a traveller's fate.

Journeying within the empire could be just as devastating as sailing around it. The effort to move individuals perpetuated refugee sickness. In 1864, the majority of migrants in transit from the coastal city of Amasya inland to Harput and Sivas fell gravely ill with infectious disease. Due to excessive hunger and sickness, some of the travellers could not continue their journey. As there was no doctor in the area, those who were sick had to be loaded on carts and transferred for care to Samsun. This taxed the already overwhelmed port town and required the shuffling of personnel, including the transfer of another pharmacist to the city.[69]

The Health Council's role in the Ottoman response to mass migration persisted with the arrival of Abkhazians in spring of 1867. So too did the tactics used to address migrant disease. Based on agreements with Russia, the Ottoman state estimated that 45,000 migrants would begin their journey to the empire on 1 April. The Porte and Council worked together to dispatch medical personnel to Trabzon, Samsun and Sinop.[70] Instructions to the physicians reflected the key lessons drawn from the Circassian migrations a few years prior. The medical officers, working in conjunction with the Migrant Commissioner and the Governor, were to place migrants temporarily in camps outside of towns, forward them speedily but methodically to their destinations and distribute provisions honestly. The council and Porte prohibited migrants from landing in Istanbul or the Dardanelles.[71] The council also sought to avoid the problem of overcrowding for those sailing from Trabzon to Varna, encouraging the Migration Director to reduce the number of migrants on each ship.[72]

* * *

States employ public health concerns as a component in 'fixing populations'.[73] Sanitation and the threat of epidemic are integral to the modern state's policing of migrant bodies. Public health and sanitation regimes during the Ottoman reform period informed efforts to control contagion through quarantine and other bounds on migrant mobility. Examples from Samsun and the surrounding Black Sea region highlight the initial ramifications of migrant disease and prevailing tactics in battling epidemics in the early stages of migration and settlement. Consular agents, observers and physicians on the Superior Health Council directly and indirectly influenced Ottoman tactics of quarantine and removal. Fears of contagion and portrayals of the diseased, unproductive migrant led to restricted movement and enforced evacuations of urban space. Environmental factors complicated efforts to transfer and establish newcomers.

State policies and environmental conditions placed newcomers at the fateful locus of life, sickness and death. Laid over the realities of the catastrophe and loss of life for migrants and those exposed to epidemic disease were the stories told by officials and foreign observers about the meaning of migrant sickness and migrant bodies. These images emerged from internal and international politics and from an ideology that tied sanitation to civilisation and that prioritised the protection of international trade. The portrayal of the *muhacir* as a victim and as a threat conditioned their movement, influenced their trajectories across the empire and affected their ongoing struggle to survive. When the Eastern Crisis of 1875–8 prompted another mass movement of refugees into the empire, concerns of contagion once more influenced migrant trajectories. As migrants, officials, diplomats, philanthropists and observers responded to the crisis, depictions of the *muhacir* as victim contributed to stories of civilisation, sovereignty, productivity and migrant welfare. For the Ottoman state, changing geopolitics raised the stakes of such depictions, which positioned Balkan Muslims variously as savage religious fanatics, vectors of disease and deserving recipients of aid. In this climate, the administration of migrant health and welfare remained a key element not only in crafting a productive population but also in Ottoman internal and international self-representation.

Philanthropy, Civilisation and the Eastern Question

During the 1877–8 Russo-Ottoman War, officials once more found themselves responding to epidemic disease and migrant death, though this time, the violence that initiated mass displacement emerged within the empire itself. The war was the culmination of several years of turmoil. The Eastern Crisis (1875–8) began with uprisings in Herzegovina and Bosnia in the spring and summer of 1875. Bulgarian nationalists led a revolt in April of 1876, and the ostensibly Ottoman territories of Serbia and Montenegro declared war against the empire that summer. The revolt in Bulgaria was put down with violence. Accounts of massacres of entire

Muhacir *as Victim*

villages by Ottoman irregulars (*başı bozuks*) encouraged anti-Ottoman sentiment in England and France and served as justification for Russian intervention. The turmoil in the Balkans contributed to upheaval at the upper echelons of the Ottoman state. A coup deposed Sultan Abdülaziz in May of 1876. His replacement, Murad V, was removed only three months later, and Abdülhamid II took the throne. The new sultan promulgated the first Ottoman constitution and established the Ottoman Parliament in December of 1876, as the Great Powers convened in Istanbul seeking to put an end to the crisis. Once the Ottoman state rejected the terms of their convention, Russia declared war and opened fronts in the Caucasus and the Balkans.

The war in the Balkans had a profound effect on civilian life there, shattering intercommunal relations as violent reprisals followed the movement of armies. The war uprooted more than one and a half million Balkan Muslims and 100,000 Balkan Christians, and its denouement had radical geopolitical repercussions. In January of 1878, the Russian Army reached the outskirts of Istanbul, forcing the Ottoman government to sign the Treaty of San Stefano in March. For the other European powers, San Stefano provided Russia with too much control over fledging states in the Balkans. In 1878, the Treaty of Berlin, an attempt to resolve the Eastern Question, revised the terms of San Stefano and redrew the map of the Balkans.

Migrant sickness and suffering were among the immediate implications of the displacement brought by the Eastern Crisis. Though in 1867 the Health Council and the Porte directed Abkhazian immigrants away from Istanbul, ten years later the capital city became home to hundreds of thousands of individuals fleeing the Russian Army. The concentration of immigrants in Istanbul augmented the sense of crisis. Building on the techniques of the 1860s, officials registered, surveilled and isolated newcomers in order to combat the spread of epidemic disease. In August of 1877, the Ottoman Health Ministry advertised for volunteer doctors and pharmacists to examine and write prescriptions for migrants, the cost of which the ministry planned to cover. In January of 1878, as the immigrant population in Istanbul rapidly increased, Ottoman statesmen passed temporary regulations, which appointed physicians to inoculate newcomers against smallpox, to conduct daily medical examinations of all registered immigrants and to ensure the immediate transfer of contagious individuals to newly established migrant-specific hospitals.[74]

Ottoman administration of migrant health and welfare remained linked to the empire's self-representation and Ottoman claims of legitimacy on the basis of effective governance. The stakes of such claims were high.

Governing Migration in the Late Ottoman Empire

In the lead-up to the Treaty of Berlin, Austro-Hungarian leaders used the plight of refugees to pave the way for Hapsburg occupation of Bosnia and Herzegovina. The treaty created the Autonomous Province of Eastern Rumelia, and after the conflict, Russian diplomats, Ottoman administrators and the provincial government used mobile populations to support their claims to civilised rule and effective administration.[75]

Public health and hygiene were crucial components of Ottoman image management beyond the immediate context of the Eastern Crisis and mass migration. For example, disease, epidemics and poor sanitation threatened Ottoman claims to authority over the hajj, where British officials undermined Ottoman sovereignty and caliphal authority by citing concerns about Indian pilgrims' exposure to disease.[76] As with hajj pilgrims, Ottoman competence in caring for Muslim migrants was important to the sultan's claim to act as a protector of the spiritual and material well-being of the international Muslim community. Care for immigrants was also a realm in which Abdülhamid II managed his legitimacy for a domestic audience. As Nadir Özbek describes, internally, the sultan positioned himself as a 'popular and paternalist figure' and the 'sole guardian' of the empire's poor, and he created a 'monarchical welfare system' to cultivate 'feelings of closeness' between himself and the population.[77] The sultan headed multiple commissions intended to address newcomers' long- and short-term welfare in the immediate aftermath of the crisis.

Claims to sovereignty, legitimacy and civilisation emerged not only from official institutions but also from semi-official and private initiatives. Nineteenth-century humanitarian organisations were a signal of the consolidation of the international. In his history of humanitarianism, Michael Barnett underscores how the industrial revolution, wars and colonialism 'destroyed a local sense of community' even as 'the forces of compassion encouraged individuals to widen their horizons and to imagine new obligations to one another'. Populations around the world were increasingly moved to address the suffering of those in distant lands, and the exercise of 'compassion ... moved from part of the private realm and into the public realm'.[78] Within this wider context, Adrian Ruprecht identifies the Eastern Crisis as a 'global humanitarian moment', one that incited interest and the creation of charitable funds and institutions from the Americas to South Asia.[79] Those moved by the suffering of distant people identified compassion as a key component of a moral foreign policy.

Alongside their significance in crisis management, self-representation and philanthropy, health and welfare emerged as key to the empire's unlocking of the productive potential of the *muhacir*. The toll of death and epidemic disease accompanying the migrations of the 1860s and the

Muhacir *as Victim*

decade of environmental difficulties witnessed by administrators such as Nusret Pasha and attested to by migrants themselves necessitated officials' recognition of the significance of health and sickness in immigration and settlement (Chapter 2). As with the aid regime developed in the 1860s, immigration and settlement policies of the 1870s were embedded within Ottoman centralising initiatives. Strategies developed to manage crises, such as Midhat Pasha's 1865 categorisation of migrants based on gender and presumed productivity, persisted in moments of less acute immigration. By the mid-1880s, Abdülhamid II established a migrant hospital, school and widow's asylum in Istanbul; officials recorded the numbers of those passing through those institutions and sent their daily tabulations to the Migrant Commission. Likewise, migrant settlement regulations issued in 1889 called for detecting, detaining and treating sick migrants prior to sending them to settlement locations.[80]

Response to crisis, appeals to legitimacy, competitive compassion and the goal of making the migrant productive figured in portrayals of those displaced by the war. For administrators, migrant welfare was a field to assert the role of the state in managing the population, yet their capacity to manage migration was also crucial to the empire's self-representation. Thus, portrayals of the Muslim *muhacir* reflected the domestic politics and foreign policies of multiple states; an emergent humanitarianism; ideas of health, contagion and sanitation; ideologies of victimhood, savagery and civilisation, and expectations of economic development and productivity. Portrayals of the *muhacir* and the *muhacir*'s health, disease and welfare contributed to the extension of ways of tabulating, categorising and administering that underpinned Ottoman social engineering. In the late 1870s, those portrayals emerged within a rapid realignment of alliances and approaches to the Eastern Question.

FROM NOBLE SAVAGES TO BAŞI BOZUKS

Images and accounts of violence influenced international and domestic politics during and after the Eastern Crisis. The conflict was cast in racialised terms of Muslim vs Christian, defying political expediency in an era when empires ruled over religiously diverse populations. The crisis promoted a new interest within Europe in intervention on behalf of Christians in the Ottoman Empire. In Britain, the public responded with outcry when the *Daily News* published accounts of 'Muslim Atrocities' in June and August of 1876.[81] Domestic politics and the racialised terms of the crisis in turn shaped images of the forcibly displaced. The English-language press's shift in its portrayal of Circassians from the Crimean War to the Eastern Crisis provides a striking example.

117

In the 1830s, '"Circassia" became a household word in many parts of Europe and North America'.[82] The British government considered the mountaineers a welcome obstacle to Russian expansion into Persia, and British consuls and parliamentarians celebrated the Circassians as noble savages. In the 1860s, journalists described the Muslim mountaineers as 'inflexible in their determination to live as freemen' in the face of Russian expansion.[83] Convinced of the amity of the British government, the 'people of Circassia' sent a petition to the queen to 'invoke the mediation and precious assistance of the British Government and people' to intervene against Russian attacks or to provide 'a place of safety' for the helpless of their country.[84]

By the mid-1870s, however, British public opinion and the English-language press redrew the lines of tyranny and freedom. Whereas the 1856 Treaty of Paris that ended the Crimean War positioned the Ottoman Empire within the 'family of nations', by the 1870s, Europeans had begun to criticise the Ottoman government as unable or unwilling to carry out reform for its Christian subjects. In a context in which the Ottoman Empire no longer met this 'standard of civilisation', Russia shifted from geopolitical threat to fellow defender of Christian minorities against Muslim oppression.[85] The Eastern Crisis likewise shifted the portrayal of Circassians. The Circassian migrants who had settled in Rumelia after 1864 and other Balkan Muslims became notorious as the irregular troops, or *başı bozuks*, responsible for pillaging villages and massacring Christians. As the British public responded to the news of massacre, William Gladstone published 'The Bulgarian Horrors and the Question of the East', in which he referred to 'the Turkish race' as 'the one great anti-human specimen of humanity'.[86] The pamphlet captured a widespread public critique of the British government's relationship to the Ottoman Empire. Gladstone leveraged his role as the voice of the public conscience to electoral victory in 1880. As public opinion engaged with foreign policy debate, the Circassian shifted from freedom-loving underdog to fanatical *başı bozuk*.

As they had in the 1860s, outside observers in the 1870s utilised portrayals of the refugees to cast both the Ottoman Empire and the newcomers as uncivilised and ultimately deserving of their fate. A *New York Times* article from 1878, after lamenting the inconvenience of living close to the refugee population, coupled a description of disease with a statement on Ottoman ignorance:

> Every khan and mosque is crowded with filthy men and women and children, many of them suffering from typhus and small-pox. The authorities are without a notion of the most elementary hygienic principles ... The refugees

Muhacir *as Victim*

are apparently as numerous as ever, and support their sufferings with so much resignation that people are beginning to think that they are rather glad of an excuse to be idle.[87]

For the writer, the ignorance and impotence of Ottoman officials was as much a source of disgust as refugee 'filth'. The crisis reflected the empire's lack of technological and scientific expertise necessary to solve problems and prevent disease. If governmental inefficacy undermined Ottoman legitimacy, refugees' own plight reduced their humanity. Their poverty and illness elicited revulsion. Resigned, idle refugees passed 'the day basking in the sun like so many dogs!'[88] With action, efficiency and productivity tied to the civilisational ideal, the moribund refugee symbolised the moribund state. Addressing the suffering of the *muhacir* was crucial to the Ottoman argument for the perpetuation of the empire's sovereignty. In the midst of the global humanitarian moment of the Eastern Crisis, Abdülhamid II and members of the short-lived first Ottoman Parliament embraced philanthropy not only to reduce *muhacir* suffering but also to make this argument to international and domestic audiences.

IMPERIAL HUMANITARIANISM AND PATRIARCHAL PHILANTHROPY

Ottoman efforts to respond to mass migration in 1877–8 emerged within the ecosystem of an 'imperial humanitarianism' 'fueled by new ideologies of humanity' and 'new kinds of compassion'.[89] Though humanitarianism and the demand for compassion provided a perspective from which to critique domestic and foreign policy, humane interventions also aligned with strategies of imperial governance. In their analysis of the British Empire, Alan Lester and Fae Dussart argue that rather than the sole preserve of missionaries and abolitionists, the principles and vernacular of humanitarianism were intrinsic to colonial administrators' rationales and strategies of rule. Given its emergence within colonial conquest, 'humanitarianism has always been imbricated with Western state projects', and the efforts to effect 'a particular kind of change' for a specific population aligned with the governmental rationality of 'reshaping society'.[90] Similarly, Nadir Özbek locates compassion, and a 'monarchical welfare regime', within Hamidian-era governance. The sultan and the Ottoman elite used philanthropy to cultivate legitimacy and to develop programmes of state intervention. Abdülhamid cast himself as an appealing, popular and paternalist figure at the centre of the state; his use of poor relief and migration management thus extended the state into the realm of population welfare.[91] Comparisons among European, especially British, and Ottoman

Governing Migration in the Late Ottoman Empire

philanthropic efforts to care for Muslims displaced by the 1877–8 War reveal shared expectations about the politics of aid, population productivity and civilised administration, and underline how the context of the Eastern Question shaped governance and the framing of the *muhacir* as victim.

On 12 August 1877, English philanthropist Angela Burdett-Coutts appealed to the humanity and Christian charity of readers of the *Daily Telegraph*, beseeching them to send relief to Muslim women and children displaced by the war unfolding in the Balkans. In Burdett-Coutts's response to the Eastern Crisis, the so-called 'Queen of the Poor' appealed to 'that real Christianity, which is still, in God's providence, the appointed means by which hunger and thirst are assuaged, sickness alleviated, and consolation given'. Imploring her readers to remember those suffering in a 'far-away country, of another creed', she counselled that money, prayer and sympathy could render their hands 'free of [the] stain' of universal culpability emerging from the war. Readers of the *Daily Telegraph*, which was largely pro-Ottoman in its reporting of the conflict, responded quickly. On 15 August, Burdett-Coutts announced the formation of the Turkish Compassionate Fund (TCF), an organisation intended to aid non-combatants.[92]

A week after the formation of the fund, British Ambassador Austen Henry Layard forwarded Sultan Abdülhamid II's photo album of wounded Muslims to London. Layard cautioned that the sultan was convinced Europe held no compassion for Muslim suffering; the ambassador hoped the TCF would persuade the sultan that 'England' did.[93] Over the next two years, the TCF channelled money through Layard and the British consular corps and provided food, clothing and housing for 'fugitives' throughout Rumelia and Western Anatolia. The fund's soup kitchens fed nearly 17,000 in Istanbul in mid-February of 1878, and an offshoot of the fund employed refugee women into the 1890s. In recognition of the baroness's work, Abdülhamid II awarded Burdett-Coutts the First Class and Star of the Order of Mecidiye.

During and after the 1877–8 War, refugees were characters in stories officials and observers told about the conflict. Those who mobilised on behalf of the migrants were moved by human suffering they encountered first-hand or through newspaper accounts. Nonetheless, administrators and key contributors to such organisations often held official and semi-official roles within their respective governments. As such, their aims extended beyond mitigating human misery. For example, the TCF's humanitarianism was a deliberate form of diplomacy in the midst of a sea change in British and Ottoman relations. Ambassador Layard's warning that Abdülhamid II wished 'to afford proof of those atrocities to Europe, as he is induced to think that they are not believed in, or, that having been committed by Christians upon Mussulmans, they are not worthy of compassion or notice' reflected the Sultan's awareness of the anti-Muslim press within Great Britain and elsewhere, his sophisticated efforts to use 'image management' to shift sympathies at home and abroad, and Layard's own reservations about Gladstone's anti-Muslim rhetoric.[94] The fund's contributors addressed the suffering of non-combatants and promoted such work as important for England as a nation and Britain as an empire. Layard and Burdett-Coutts both emphasised the fund's capacity to promote positive feelings among 'the fugitives', among Ottoman subjects and among Muslims generally.[95] Portrayals of the *muhacirin* and their suffering were refracted through the prism of the Eastern Question.

Britain's role in the war and in relief efforts was of concern to publics from London to Lahore. The prevailing political discussion of British foreign policy played out in critiques of Stafford House, Lady Strangford's Hospitals, the International Relief Committee and the British Red Cross, as public figures took to the press to critique philanthropists for neutrality or for exhibiting variously Turcophobia or Turcophilia.[96] The violence of the conflict inspired interest and aid globally. In British India, vernacular presses carried accounts of the war, calling upon the 'nobleness of sentiment' and 'universal sympathy' of their readers to encourage Indian donations on behalf of Ottoman soldiers and Balkan Muslims.[97] Indian Muslims responded with anger to Gladstone's anti-Muslim rhetoric and warned of Muslim alienation from the British Empire. Robert Bulwer-Lytton, the viceroy of India, shared the same fear. Indians petitioned the British government to ally with the Ottomans before and during the war, and offered financial support for the Ottoman War and relief effort. By March of 1878, organisations such as the 'Society of Aid to Turkey' and 'The Assembly of Islamic Aid' had sent some 1,052,003 Indian rupees to Istanbul.[98]

Subjects of the British Empire were not the only individuals moved by accounts of the war's victims. In January of 1878, as tens of thousands of Balkan migrants arrived in Istanbul, the Austro-Hungarian Ambassador in Istanbul established the International Aid Committee for Refugees from the Provinces (Comité International de Secours aux Refugies des Provinces), which opened nine hospitals and fourteen bakeries and distributed aid across several cities.[99] Non-Ottoman subjects within and outside the empire donated to and worked with displaced Muslims. Among those Abdülhamid II officially recognised for their work and donations on behalf of the displaced included a woman 'from one of the

Governing Migration in the Late Ottoman Empire

wealthiest American families', the matriarchs of the wealthy Levantine Jewish Fernandez and Camondo families, and seventeen women of the International Committee.[100]

In mid-January, deputies within the Ottoman General Assembly, the parliamentary body established by the Ottoman constitution in 1876, described being moved to tears by the horrors of individuals' flights from Edirne. Noting that mere words and petitions were insufficient in the face of such suffering, Agob Efendi (Istanbul) and other deputies called upon their colleagues to establish an aid committee.[101] In advocating for the committee, Mustafa Bey (Salonica) referenced the Turkish Compassionate Fund. He was grateful to Layard, yet, he added, it was 'Europe' that had brought the empire to this point. Therefore, he argued, 'we ourselves ought to manage these individuals', and a commission was the best way to do so.[102] The chamber agreed and voted to create the İane-i Muhacirin Encumeni (Migrant Aid Committee), comprised of twenty deputies. Committee members raised and distributed money and aid in kind. Each day, four of them volunteered to serve migrants in Istanbul's Sirkeci neighbourhood, the point of disembarkation for migrants arriving by rail. Within a month of its founding, the İane-i Muhacirin Encumeni raised 1,747,625 *kuruş*.[103]

The personnel and contributors to the Migrant Aid Committee, like those of the TCF and the International Aid Committee, inhabited official and semi-official spheres. Among the first to contribute was a member of the General Assembly's upper chamber (Meclis-i Ayan), Altunizade Ismail Zühdü Efendi, who pledged 100,000 *kuruş* in the days before the Chamber of Deputies officially voted to establish the committee. Altunizade Ismail had made his fortune in trade, shipping and architecture. His professional trajectory reflected an overlap between upper-ranking civil servants and wealthy Ottomans in Istanbul. At the age of twenty-four, he acquired a fleet of sixty-four ships, and, upon graduating from the Palace School two years later, he became the construction official (*bina emini*) for the Imperial Medical School and Galatasaray High School. For holding the same position at such sites as Dolmabahçe Palace and the Imperial Cartridge Factory in Zeytinburnu, Altunizade Ismail received official recognition from Sultan Abdülmecid I, and he awarded himself the title of 'Agha of the Architects' (*Mimar Ağası*/Master Architect).[104] Like the TCF's 'Queen of the Poor', the 'Agha of the Architects' became well known for his philanthropy. In 1865, he paid for the restoration of sixteen mosques in Istanbul destroyed by a large fire. In the same year, he commissioned a *külliye* and mosque in Üsküdar, Istanbul, in a neighbourhood now named for him. During the 1877–8 War, he funded three battalions of

Muhacir *as Victim*

volunteers and opened his house to refugees. Upon hearing of his pledge of 100,000 *kuruş* to the Migrant Aid Committee, a deputy from Aydın noted 'it was rare to find such a man as Altunizade Ismail in a nation of forty million'.[105]

While Altunizade Ismail may have been 'one in a million', other officials and civil servants, including the entire chamber of deputies, senators, Istanbul's chief municipal officer (*Şehremini*) and the head of the Council of State likewise contributed significant funds to the İane Committee. Abdülhamid II himself offered refuge in the palace to the 150 'neediest' newcomers and later donated 500,000 *kuruş* to the committee. Altunizade Ismail contributed in other ways to migrant welfare, including serving briefly as vice head of the Society for Migrant Aid (İane-i Muhacirin Cemiyeti), another semi-official voluntary association under the sultan's purview.[106] Some accounts of Altunizade Ismail's life note that he headed the Migrant Commission from 1880 until his death in 1887, though there is no record of that in Ottoman state almanacs.[107]

Much like those of the TCF, proponents and contributors to the İane Committee coupled their humanitarian and philanthropic aims with concerns for governance and politics. Members of parliament in Istanbul experienced the immediacy of the migrant crisis and personally attended to the displaced, but they also viewed the committee as an opportunity to inspire patriotism and to cultivate bonds among Ottoman subjects. The committee advertised its efforts, publishing the generous donations of the sultan and those at the centre of the state with the hope of inspiring all Ottoman citizens to similar acts of kindness.[108]

PRODUCTIVE VICTIMS: FRAMING THE DESERVING MUHACIR

When the Great Powers gathered in Berlin in 1878 to revise the treaty of San Stefano, their representatives questioned the Ottoman Empire's status as a civilised state, and thus its right to exercise sovereignty over its population and territory. Muslims displaced by the war became part of the calculation of whether the empire could protect its subjects. Images of refugees served in the making of claims about who might deserve aid and who held the expertise to distribute it. While those who sought to undermine Ottoman sovereignty and legitimacy in Western Europe, the Balkans, and Istanbul racialised Muslim migrants and emphasised the failures of Ottoman governance, Abdülhamid II and pro-Ottoman philanthropists emphasised the humanity, efficiency, and expertise that emerged in their efforts to care for the displaced in Istanbul. To do so, they considered migrant sickness and mortality and activated prevailing ideologies of gender, productivity, and poverty to construct the *muhacir* as a victim and as a worthy object of aid.

Those in favour of assisting Balkan Muslims sought repertoires to 'unstranger' the migrants, rendering them 'knowable, similar, and deserving'.[109] They disseminated detailed descriptions and images of migrant suffering that were intended to spur their audience to action. In 1883, three years into Gladstone's government, H. Mainwaring Dunstan published an account of the TCF. His account sought to justify the fund's actions by casting Balkan Christians and Russian forces as savage villains in contrast to the innocent victims the fund served during and after the conflict.[110] He asserted that the fund's methods of collecting information and distributing money ensured that only the neediest received support from the TCF.[111] Gendered and age-based expectations were employed to further the portrayal of victimhood. The twenty-eight photographs in Abdülhamid II's 'Victims of Russian Atrocities' contained only images of non-combatants: innocent women, children and elderly men. Similarly, though charitable organisations in India and England provided aid to wounded soldiers, their calls for assistance focused on suffering women and children. Hospitals and orphanages catered to women and children as the especial and unambiguous casualties of the conflict.

Philanthropic work, in alignment with the Ottoman government's interest in turning mass migration to the state's economic advantage, approached employment as essential to migrants' long-term survival. Burdett-Coutts's charitable endeavours rested on the principle that 'gratuitous distribution' of aid was itself 'demoralising'.[112] The TCF drew upon this prevailing expectation of labour for aid and coordinated its efforts with the municipality of Istanbul. Over a roughly six-month period from December 1878 to June 1879, the fund employed some 20,000–45,000 individuals per month in road repair and other public works.[113] Additionally, the TCF's Ladies Committee founded the Women's Work Establishment (WWE) to address long-term displacement by employing female 'fugitives' in embroidery work. The Turkish Compassionate Fund's mantra, 'Work for the able-bodied, alms only for the sick, the aged, and infirm', aligned with the mentality of Ottoman officials' aid efforts.[114]

Identifying populations of concern is crucial to states' development and deployment of social engineering techniques. Just as age and gender influenced the rhetoric of victimhood, so too did these categories affect the identification of populations of concern and the emergence of policies, techniques and institutions related to short- and long-term care. Health, sanitation and welfare were intertwined with the larger goal of turning the *muhacir* into a productive subject. Officials' prioritisation of productivity

Muhacir *as Victim*

emerged in their response to health crises and the distribution of aid. Productivity-oriented categories and strategies emerged from and persisted after moments of mass migration; policies made special note of those incapable of manual labour. For instance, 1889 regulations identified men who lacked the strength for manual labour as in need of special assistance, yet noted some might be employed in light work within the Ottoman bureaucracy. Bureaucratic offices were to inform the Migrant Commission of any openings in order to facilitate the employment of those individuals.[115]

Like men incapable of agricultural or heavy labour, women and children remained populations of concern for their relationships to productivity. Addressing women and children's welfare cohered with ongoing efforts to police, register and institutionalise urban and mobile populations. Nazan Maksudyan argues that moments of intensive migration and the emergence of an urban population of unhoused *muhacir* children contributed to the development of vocational orphanages (*ıslahhane*). Midhat Pasha began this trend in Niş in 1861. The presence of orphaned children in Istanbul after the 1877–8 War agitated reformers' anxieties about the threats 'dangerous' and 'delinquent' children posed to the public order, and regulations in 1881 led to the 'collecting' and institutionalising of several hundred refugee orphans in the city.[116] In a similar fashion, providing aid to single women reduced the likelihood of ongoing mobility, prostitution and begging. In 1878 and 1889, policies affirmed the state's role in caring for orphans and unaccompanied women and in employing such women to sew army uniforms.[117]

To care for women and children, administrators created new institutions. No later than 1884, officials converted the Kırmızı Kışla, an army barracks, into a widow's asylum for migrant women. The broader complex included a hospital, school and orphanage.[118] As with sanitary cordons used in Trabzon and Samsun in the 1860s, orphanages and widow asylums spatially organised and confined marginal populations. The orphanage and the asylum were sites to manage and bring about productivity. The creation of new institutions generated new opportunities to account for migrants and to identify characteristics and behaviours officials sought to promote. The Hamidian state's comprehensive approach to women and children as populations of concern emerged not only in the spatial arrangement of the Kırmızı Kışla but also in the conceptual coupling of these groups within daily registers. The Migrant Commission collected data recording the ailments and status of migrants in the *Muhacirin* Hospital; another register recorded the daily population of the widow asylum, orphanage and school. The earliest such registers date from fall of 1885.[119] Rather than suggesting

Governing Migration in the Late Ottoman Empire

a crisis beyond the means of the state, the records of the Migrant Hospital from 1885 to 1895 show that the entity housed a population hovering between fifteen and forty, with little daily fluctuation, and that Kırmızı Kışla housed several hundred individuals.

* * *

Some, though not all, of the organisations created to respond to the crisis continued their work in the years after the 1877–8 war. The WWE employed several thousand women into the 1890s, using earnings generated from the women's embroidery to support former migrants 'stricken down by age or illness'.[120] The İane Committee outlived Abdülhamid II's suspension of parliament in February of 1878, yet the committee was incorporated into the Migrant Commission in 1879, tipping its status from semi-official to official. The fate of the İane Committee was in keeping with the Hamidian approach of 'tolerating', supervising and 'integrating such initiatives into the regime's power strategies', as the sultan centred himself and Yildiz palace in the state's oversight of population welfare.[121]

The 'organised compassion' of the Eastern Crisis addressed human suffering while seeking to achieve domestic and foreign political goals. The Ottoman response to migrant health and welfare emerged from internationally shared repertoires of aid, governance, civilisation, victimhood and productivity. For Abdülhamid and the Ottoman elite, the context of the Eastern Question and internal approaches to legitimacy and population management raised the stakes of their engagement with those repertoires.

Conclusion

Given the scale of migrant suffering, historians recounting the health consequences of the mass migrations of the 1860s and 1870s have focused on the devastating epidemics marking newcomers' arrival. They have noted the failures of the Ottoman response and tabulated the horrific loss of life. These histories are essential to considering how sickness and health conditioned the outcomes of migration. Migrants' tenuous conditions during their flight from the Caucasus, Crimea and Balkans bled into experiences after arrival, including their journeys to temporary holding areas and designated settlement regions. Sickness and mortality were integral components of the mass migrations of the period; however, depictions of migrant health also reveal how diplomacy and domestic politics influenced the management of migrant welfare.

Whether via participation in international sanitary conferences or through acts of philanthropy, the international arena was one in which

126

Muhacir *as Victim*

the Ottoman state sought to claim its sovereignty. The very same arena, however, was one in which the empire found itself positioned outside European-endorsed standards of civilisation. Migrants were a part of this bargain. In the 1860s, the Constantinople Superior Health Council contributed to the logistical outcomes of *muhacir* arrival and settlement, pressuring Ottoman officials and coordinating quarantine and containment within the Ottoman state. Barozzi's depiction of refugees in Samsun revealed the struggle to respond to the sudden influx of hundreds of thousands of newcomers; his words also endorsed the modern state's purview over public health. Laying claim to civilisation via administrative ability, Europeans within the Health Council both questioned and endorsed the Ottoman state's right to control, assess and cordon off space in order to promote public health and public order. Following the 1877–8 Russo-Ottoman War, philanthropic organisations such as the TCF and the İane Committee likewise identified the migrant as a site of imperial and state intervention. Their approaches to the *muhacir*, qualified by ideologies of gender, empire, nation and philanthropy, conditioned immigrants' material outcomes, including, and especially, life and death.

The immigrants conjured a range of responses. They were portrayed as threats to health and order: diseased, contagious, revolting, out of place. En masse, they were the source of rumour and fear. Expelled from the social order as much as their homes, they were rendered outside humanity: lazy, indolent, dogs. They were also the victims of fate and human atrocity: uprooted, wounded, impoverished and forsaken. Ultimately, they were a problem in need of resolving. Diagnosing the *muhacir* as a public health issue created justifications for intervention in Ottoman society and Ottoman sovereignty. These interventions were enacted within a much larger drama, placing the lives of individuals within the balance of the Eastern Question. Ottoman 'obsession' with imagery in this era emerged from statesmen's realisation of the growing role of public opinion and the press in resolving internal and international crises. Migrants served as inflection points in diplomatic manoeuvres, as routes to claim a moral position for individuals and states who wielded the power of philanthropy, and as repositories for the label of civilisation. Techniques of managing migrant health and sickness adopted during moments of mass migration in the 1860s and 1870s persisted after these moments of crisis, contributing to officials' use of spatial organisation, population oversight and tabulation to administer the population. Like the broader aid regime described in Chapter 2, the effort to address migrant health and welfare meant that the category of '*muhacir*' evoked not just mobility but also the state's

Governing Migration in the Late Ottoman Empire

dispensation of resources. The attachment of resources to the category of the *muhacir* became crucial in illuminating the limits of inclusion and exclusion of the Hamidian (Chapter 5) and Second Constitutional Eras (Chapter 6).

The question of migrant health and welfare persisted beyond the *muhacir*'s arrival in the empire's port cities. Environmental factors, malnutrition and ongoing exposure to the elements and disease affected migrant settlement. Health concerns perpetuated the state-migrant relationship and contributed to state officials' efforts to control migrant mobility. Those concerns also influenced officials' attempts to integrate migrants into Ottoman society. I turn now to considering Ottoman migrant settlement projects during the Hamidian era, when officials' ideas of science, the environment, productivity, the use of space and administrative efficacy continued to shape settlement plans and provided language migrants and non-migrants used to contest settlement outcomes. In the depiction of the *muhacir* and his or her welfare, productivity continued to serve as both a basis of the refugee problem and the key to its resolution.

Notes

1. Layard to Stanley, 23 August 1877, NA FO 78.2583.
2. See Gatrell, *The Making of the Modern Refugee.*
3. Mark Mazower, *Governing the World: The History of an Idea* (New York: The Penguin Press, 2012), 25. The term international was invented by Jeremy Bentham in 1775. Mazower, *Governing the World*, 18–20.
4. Alan Lester and Fae Dussart, *Colonization and the Origins of Humanitarian Governance: Protecting Aborigines across the Nineteenth-Century British Empire* (Cambridge: Cambridge University Press, 2014), 9. See also Valeska Huber, 'The Unification of the Globe by Disease? The International Sanitary Conferences on Cholera, 1851–1894', *The Historical Journal* 49, no. 2 (2006): 453–76.
5. Selim Deringil, *The Well-Protected Domains: Ideology and the Legitimation of Power in the Ottoman Empire, 1876–1909* (London: I. B. Tauris, 1998).
6. 'The Circassian Exodus', *Christian Advocate and Journal*, 7 July 1864.
7. Saydam, *Kırım ve Kafkas Göçleri*, 87–8; Charles King, *The Black Sea: A History* (Oxford: Oxford University Press, 2004), 17.
8. Suter to Bulwer, 23 July 1860, NA, FO 195.644.
9. Suter to Bulwer, 29 October 1860, NA, FO 195.644.
10. Callem, 19 October 1860, NA, FO 195.644.
11. Sankey to Suter, 22 October 1860, NA, FO 195.644.
12. 'The East', *The Times*, 31 December 1864.

Muhacir *as Victim*

13. Oliver Bullough, *Let Our Fame Be Great: Journeys among the Defiant People of the Caucasus* (London: Penguin Books, 2012), 107.
14. Mark Pinson, 'Ottoman Colonization of the Circassions in Rumeli after the Crimean War', *Etudes Balkaniques* 3 (1972): 74.
15. Stevens to Erskine, 26 February 1864, NA, FO 195.812; Stevens to Bulwer, 19 May 1864, NA, FO 195.812; Stevens to Bulwer, 18 June 1864, NA, FO 195.812.
16. Dickson to Bulwer, 26 July 1864, NA, FO 195.869; Dickson to Bulwer, 10 August 1864, NA, FO 195.869.
17. Stevens to Bulwer, 24 September 1864, NA, FO 195.812.
18. Dickson to Stuart, 5 December 1864, NA, FO 195.869; Dickson to Erskine, 12 February 1864, NA, FO 195.869.
19. A.MKT.MHM 324.3, 29 Şaban 1281/27 January 1865.
20. Milena Methodieva, *Between Empire and Nation: Muslim Reform in the Balkans* (Stanford, CA: Stanford University Press, 2021), 26.
21. İpek, *Rumeli'den Anadolu'ya Türk Göçleri*, 46–9, 90.
22. Randal Roberts, *Asia Minor and the Caucasus* (Boston: James R. Osgood and Company, 1877), 35.
23. Ibid., 25, 37, 57.
24. See Anne Marie Moulin and Yeşim Işıl Ulman, eds, *Perilous Modernity: History of Medicine in the Ottoman Empire and the Middle East from the 19th century Onwards* (Istanbul: Gorgias Press and The Isis Press, 2010); Mehmet Mazak and Fatih Gürdal, *Osmanlı'dan Günümüze Temizlik Tarihi: Tanzifat-ı İstanbul* (Istanbul: Yeditepe Yayınevi, 2011).
25. Robarts, *Migration and Disease*, 117–19.
26. Ibid., 137.
27. See Huber, 'Unification of the Globe', 453–76; Birsen Bulmuş, *Plague, Quarantines, and Geopolitics in the Ottoman Empire* (Edinburgh: Edinburgh University Press, 2012).
28. Huber, 'Unification of the Globe', 463.
29. Bulmuş, *Plague, Quarantine, and Geopolitics*, 98–111.
30. Low, *Imperial Mecca*, 131.
31. Dickson, quoted in *Ninth Annual Report of The Local Government Board, 1879–1880 Supplement Containing Report and Papers Submitted by the Medical Officer ...* (London: Eyre and Spottiswoode, 1881), vol. 9, 142.
32. Bulmuş, *Plague, Quarantine, and Geopolitics*, 135.
33. Bulwer to Russell, 3 May 1864, in Great Britain, *Papers Respecting*, 4–5; Suter to Bulwer, 7 November 1860, NA FO 195.644.
34. Dickson to Erskine, 12 February 1864, NA FO 195.869.
35. Özgür Yılmaz, 'An Italian Physician in the Caucasian Migration of 1864: The Mission of Dr. Barozzi in Trabzon and Samsun', *Journal of Modern Turkish History Studies* 9, no. 28 (2014): 37.
36. Ibid., 36–8.
37. Stevens to Erskine, 26 February 1864, NA FO 195.812.

38. 'The Circassian Exodus'.
39. Dickson to Erskine, 12 February 1864, NA FO 195.869.
40. Cuthell, 'Muhacirin Komisyonu', 167.
41. 'The Circassian Exodus'.
42. Dickson to Stuart, 14 December 1864, NA FO 195.869.
43. Dickson to Erskine, 12 February 1864, NA FO 195.869; Dickson to Bulwer, 26 July 1864, 195.869.
44. Stevens to Bulwer, 15 April 1864, NA FO 195.812.
45. Stevens to Bulwer, 19 May 1864, NA FO 195.812.
46. Stevens to Erskine, 17 February 1864, NA FO 195.812; Stevens to Erskine, 13 February 1864, NA FO 195.812.
47. Stevens to Bulwer, 7 April 1864, NA FO 195.812.
48. Stevens to Bulwer, 19 May 1864, NA FO 195.812.
49. Stevens to Bulwer, 4 August 1864, NA FO 195.812.
50. Mary Douglas, *Purity and Danger: An Analysis of Concepts of Pollution and Taboo*, Routledge Classics ed. (London: Routledge, 2005).
51. Dickson to Erskine, 12 February 1864, NA FO 195.869.
52. Stevens to Erskine, 17 February 1864, NA FO 195.812.
53. MVL 858.53, 18 Recep 1280/29 December 1863.
54. 'The Circassian Exodus'.
55. Stevens to Bulwer, 7 April 1864, NA FO 195.812.
56. MVL 858.53, 18 Recep 1280/29 December 1863.
57. Cuthell, 'Muhacirin Komisyonu', 169–70.
58. Bulwer to Russell, 12 April 1864, in Great Britain, *Papers Respecting*, 2.
59. Bullough, *Let Our Fame*, 111.
60. MVL 685.30, 27 Rebiyülevvel 1281/30 August 1864.
61. Ibid.
62. Van Lennep, *Travels in Little-Known Parts*, 46–7.
63. Ibid., 44–7.
64. Dickson to Stuart, 11 October 1864, NA FO 195.869.
65. Dickson to Stuart, 9 October 1864, NA FO 195.869.
66. Dickson to Stuart, 4 November 1864, NA FO 195.869; Dickson to Stuart, 5 December 1864, NA FO 195.869.
67. A.MKT.MHM 306.78, 22 July 1864, in *Belgelerinde* 2, no. 66, 254–5.
68. Dickson to Bulwer, 26 July 1864, NA FO 195.869.
69. A.MKT.MHM 312.41, 21 Rebiyülevvel 1281/24 August 1864.
70. A.MKT.MHM 380.57, 11 April 1867, in *Belgelerinde* 1, no. 14, 81–7; Dickson to Lyons, 23 March 1867, NA FO 195.844.
71. Dickson to Lyons, 2 April 1867, NA FO 195.894.
72. Palgrave to Lyons, 29 May 1867, NA FO 195.812.
73. Tomas Balkelis, 'In Search of a Native Realm: The Return of World War One Refugees to Lithuania, 1918–24', in *Homelands: War, Population, and Statehood in Eastern Europe and Russia 1918–1924*, ed. Nick Baron and Peter Gatrell (London: Anthem Press, 2004), 85.

Muhacir *as Victim*

74. İpek, *Rumeli'den Anadolu'ya Türk Göçleri*, 93–6.
75. Jared Manasek, 'Refugee Return and State Legitimization: Habsburgs, Ottomans, and the Case of Bosnia and Herzegovina, 1875–1878', *Journal of Modern European History* 19, no. 1 (2021): 63–79; Anna Mirkova, '"Population Politics" at the End of Empire: Migration and Sovereignty in Ottoman Eastern Rumelia, 1877–1886', *Comparative Studies in Society and History* 55, no. 4 (2013): 955–85.
76. Low, *Imperial Mecca*.
77. Nadir Özbek, *Osmanlı İmporatorluğu'nda Sosyal Devlet: Siyaset, İktidar, ve Meşrutiyet 1876–1914* (Istanbul: İletişim Yayıncılık, 2002), 31.
78. Michael Barnett, *Empire of Humanity: A History of Humanitarianism* (Ithaca, NY: Cornell University Press, 2011), 30; 49. See also, Michelle Tusan, *Smyrna's Ashes: Humanitarianism, Genocide, and the Birth of the Middle East* (Berkeley: University of California Press, 2012).
79. Adrian Ruprecht, 'The Great Eastern Crisis (1875–1878) as a Global Humanitarian Moment', *Journal of Global History* 16, no. 2 (2021): 159–84.
80. Y.PRK.DH 2.93, 1889, in *Belgelerinde* 1, no. 28, 148–70.
81. Tetsuya Sahara, 'Two Different Images: Bulgarian and English Sources on the Batak Massacre', in *War and Diplomacy: The Russo-Turkish War of 1877–1878 and the Treaty of Berlin*, ed. M. Hakan Yavuz and Peter Sluglett (Salt Lake City: University of Utah Press, 2011), 479–510.
82. Charles King, *The Ghost of Freedom: A History of the Caucasus* (Oxford: Oxford University Press, 2008), 93.
83. 'The War in Circassia', *The Charleston Mercury*, 27 February 1862.
84. 'Petition', 9 April 1864, in Great Britain, *Papers Respecting*, 2–3.
85. Davide Rodogno, *Against Massacre: Humanitarian Interventions in the Ottoman Empire, 1815–1914* (Princeton, NJ: Princeton University Press, 2012), 45–7; Tusan, *Smyrna's Ashes*, 22.
86. William E. Gladstone, *Bulgarian Horrors and the Question of the East* (London: John Murray, 1876), 9.
87. 'Giaours in Constantinople', *The New York Times*, 6 May 1878.
88. Ibid.
89. Barnett, *Empire of Humanity*, 30.
90. Lester and Dussart, *Colonization and the Origins*, 16; 18–19.
91. Özbek, *Osmanlı İmporatorluğu'nda Sosyal Devlet*, 19, 31.
92. H. Mainwaring Dunstan, *The Turkish Compassionate Fund: An Account of Its Origin, Working, and Results* (London: Remington and Co., 1883), 21–2.
93. Layard to Stanley, 23 August 1877, NA FO 78.2583.
94. Ibid.
95. Dunstan, *Turkish Compassionate Fund*, 24.
96. Dorothy Anderson, *The Balkan Volunteers* (London: Hutchinson, 1968).
97. Ruprecht, 'Great Eastern Crisis', 159.

Governing Migration in the Late Ottoman Empire

98. Azmi Özcan, *Pan-Islamism: Indian Muslims, the Ottomans and Britain (1877–1924)* (Leiden: Brill, 1997), 64–78; Ruprecht, 'Great Eastern Crisis', 175.

99. İpek, 76–7. For information on the emergence of aid societies in an Austro-Hungarian context, see Manasek, 'Empire Displaced', 126–37.

100. I.HR 279.17207, 7 Recep 1296/27 June 1879; I.HR 281.17341, 7 Safer 1297/20 January 1880; I.HR 33521545, 22 Rebiyülevvel 1297/4 March 1880.

101. Hakkı Tarik Us, comp., *Meclis-i Meb'usan, 1293 = 1877; Zabıt Ceridesi*, vol. 2 (Istanbul: Vakit Gazete Matbaa-Kütüphane, 1954), 134–5.

102. Ibid., 141.

103. Ibid., 397.

104. Hamit Küşükbatır, 'Altunizade İsmail Zühdü Paşa', *TDV İslam Ansiklopedisi*, accessed 17 March 2023, https://islamansiklopedisi.org.tr/altunizade-ismail-zuhdu-pasa; İbrahim Alaettin Gövsa, *Türk Meşhurları Ansiklopedisi: Edebiyatta, Sanatta, İlimde, Harpte, Politikada ve her Sahada Şöhret Kazanmış Olan Türklerin Hayat Eserleri* (Istanbul: Yedigün Neşriyatı, 1946), 416; Süreyya, *Sicill-i Osmani*, IV, 387.

105. Us, *Meclis-i Meb'usan*, 139.

106. Health problems led him to step down in October 1879. Y.MTV 2.22, 9 Zilkade 1296/25 October 1879.

107. *Salname*s identify Rıza Pasha as Head of the Migrant Commission across the years in question.

108. Us, *Meclis-i Meb'usan*, 154.

109. Watenpaugh, *Bread from Stones*, 19; Ruprecht, 'Great Eastern Crisis', 165.

110. Dunstan, *Turkish Compassionate Fund*, 10.

111. Sena Hatip Dinçyürek, *A 'Compassionate' Episode in Anglo-Ottoman History: British Relief to the '93 Refugees (1877–1878)* (Istanbul: Libra Kitapçılık ve Yayıncılık, 2013), 102–3.

112. Edna Healey, *Lady Unknown: The Life of Angela Buredett-Coutts*, 1st American ed. (New York: Coward, McCann & Geoghegan, 1978), 147.

113. Dunstan, *The Turkish Compassionate Fund*, 222–3.

114. Cariclee Zacaroff, 'The "Turkish Compassionate Fund"', in *The Congress of Women: Held in the Woman's Building, World's Columbian Exposition, Chicago, U.S.A., 1893*, ed. Mary Kavanaugh Oldham (Chicago: Monarch Book Company, 1894), 619.

115. Y.PRK.DH 2.93.

116. Nazan Maksudyan, *Orphans and Destitute Children in the Late Ottoman Empire* (Syracuse, NY: Syracuse University Press, 2014), 81–8.

117. I.MMS 58.2786.3, 17 Cemaziyülahır 1295/18 June 1878.

118. Gülhan Balsoy, 'The Solitary Female Refugees and the Widows' Asylum (Kırmızı Kışla) in Late-Nineteenth Century Istanbul', *JOTSA* 6, no. 2 (2019): 73–90.

Muhacir *as Victim*

119. I have not found a complete, systematic collection of the registers. Examples are available in the records of the Migrant Commission (DH.MHC) and the Y.PRK.KOM collection.
120. Angela Burdett-Coutts, 'Woman the Missionary of Industry', in *Woman's Mission: A Series of Congress Papers on the Philanthropic Work of Women by Eminent Writers*, ed. Angela Burdett-Coutts (New York: Scribner's Sons, 1893), 295.
121. Nadir Özbek, 'Philanthropic Activity, Ottoman Patriotism, and the Hamidian Regime, 1876–1909', *IJMES* 37, no. 1 (2005): 64.

4

Muhacir as Failure

In the summer of 1887, Reşid Bey, a resident of Sarıyer, one of the Bosporus fishing villages on Istanbul's European side, petitioned the Ministry of Endowments (Evkaf-ı Hümayun Nezareti) on behalf of the Garipler Cemetery. He directed his grievance at a group of fifty migrant families who had lived in the area for nearly ten years, and the administrative branches that had facilitated the migrants' settlement in the neighbourhood (also known as Garipler Mezarlığı/Cemetery). According to Reşid, the migrants' huts and latrines had breached the cemetery's walls and threatened to damage it. He filed his petition upon learning that the Ministry of Education planned to assist the migrants in building a new school, a school that would further encroach on the cemetery and render the newcomers' status in the neighbourhood ever more permanent. The migrants' request to build a school in the neighbourhood previously had been denied. Reşid asked that the government reject the school again, expel the migrants from the neighbourhood, and demolish their houses. Mustafa Nuri Pasha, Minister of Endowments, took up the issue with Istanbul's Municipality (*Şehremaneti*), calling for an investigation of Reşid Bey's claims.[1]

Sarıyer, like many of the Bosporus villages, changed rapidly during the second half of the nineteenth century. The village and its surrounding district had long been home to the Istanbul elite's summer homes. The creation of the Şirket-i Hayriye ferry line in 1851 and its regular steamboat service from Eminönü rendered permanent residence feasible for those wishing to live in villages along the water while commuting to Istanbul's centre. Over the course of fifty years, as access changed, so too did the village's demographic and infrastructural make-up. Alongside serene Bosporus mansions and fishing communities, the Migrant Commission placed migrants there following the 1877–8 war. Population pressure and

Muhacir *as Failure*

infrastructural change rendered space in the district more valuable, while new building codes, the extension of roads and the regularisation of the city's fabric became legal tools to displace individuals and appropriate common space.

Reşid's petition set off a flurry of responses among the Migrant Commission, the Şehremaneti, the Seventh District Municipality, the Interior Ministry, the Ministry of Education and the Ministry of Endowments. The Migrant Commission and District Municipality remained on the side of the migrants, casting the issue as a long-running dispute in which Reşid and other residents of Sarıyer wanted the migrants' land for their own gain. The Şehremaneti seemed to agree, implying that locals cared less about the sanctity of the cemetery and more about the loss of a place they had previously used to dry and cure fish. Aside from questioning Reşid's motives, sympathetic officials argued that the migrants' permanent settlement was the most important outcome, one that the government should not sacrifice solely to preserve a cemetery that had not seen a burial in ages. In a plea to consider the living over the long since passed, they argued against disrupting the migrant's lives. Though it was illegal to destroy a cemetery, it was more problematic to cause the immigrants undue suffering. The municipality also defended the legality of the settlement on the basis of city ordinances. A local committee had approved the location of each house and registered each family; the housing itself met Istanbul's most recent building regulations. The Ministry of Education weighed in as well. If the migrant community was allowed to remain in Sarıyer, then by law it was necessary to provide a school for the fifty-family neighbourhood.[2]

The Şehremaneti further considered the issue. Its council sketched out the disputed territory, providing a map confirming that roughly half of the migrants' houses 'had spread' beyond the retaining wall and 'into the area that used to be the cemetery' (Figure 4.1). Unmoved by the plea to consider immigrants' needs, Mustafa Nuri Pasha remained uncompromising in his response. Siding with Reşid, the Minister of Endowments dismissed the migrants' settlement as unlawful and demanded their immediate removal. The Şehremaneti confirmed the order to remove the migrants and their homes.

The ruling was a definitive setback for the migrants, but they proved persistent. In the two years following their expulsion from the contested land, some moved back within the cemetery's boundaries, leading to renewed complaints from the local imam, *muhtar* (headman) and other 'reputable people' (*mu'teberan*). The Şehremaneti responded with the same arguments it had referenced two years prior, noting that the cemetery

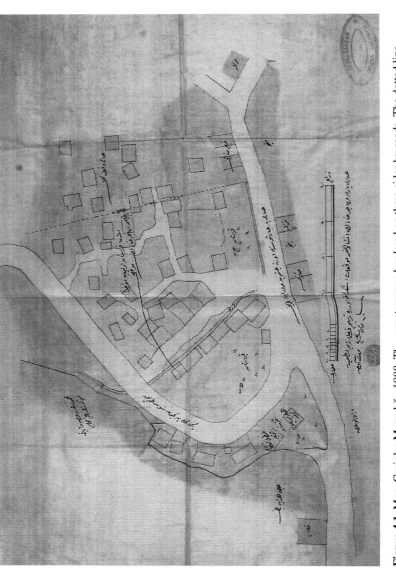

Figure 4.1 Map, Garipler Mezarlığı, 1888. The cemetery was bordered on three sides by roads. The dotted line corresponds to the old retaining wall, over which was written, 'The space that used to be a cemetery and into which migrants' houses have spread.' ŞD 750.14.

Muhacir *as Failure*

had long fallen into disuse, that the houses met building codes, that the migrants had been there twelve years and intended to remain permanently, and that they held official deeds to the land. Summarising these arguments, the Interior Ministry asked the police to prevent residents from harassing the migrant community.[3]

The fight over the cemetery persisted for nearly a decade. In October of 1891, the grand vizier's office issued a delay on all migrant construction in the neighbourhood to allow the Ministry of Endowments to demarcate definitively the cemetery's boundaries.[4] By June of 1892, the migrants who had been unable to complete their homes lodged complaints, while non-migrant residents raised concerns about sanitation and the threat to public health resulting from the migrants' incomplete latrines, particularly in the heat of an Istanbul summer. Despite repeated calls for urgency, the issue remained unresolved.[5] The 1894 Istanbul Earthquake further undermined the integrity of the migrants' housing and sewage system and renewed calls for the Şehremaneti to respond. It answered by allowing only repair on structures directly damaged in the event.[6] Sanitation concerns and threats of contagious disease in the village, reiterated in 1898, again failed to finalise the status of the Ministry of Endowments' report. The District Municipality brought up the issue once more in October of 1903. Due to the long delays in construction and repair, the municipality found that migrants' housing no longer met local ordinances. It was too irregular and too close to the avenue running along the southwest border of the old cemetery, giving rise to sewage problems and ruining the look of the neighbourhood. The Şehremaneti endorsed the need to remove some of the migrants' housing, but called once again for a resolution to the Ministry of Endowments' investigation and an end to the delay on migrant construction.[7]

Laced throughout the saga of migrant housing in Garipler Mezarlığı was the question of who had the right to a contested space. The participants in this long-running dispute, including the officials who oversaw the case, navigated a changing regulatory and administrative framework, blending a series of assumptions about documentation and land use as they awaited the outcome of a more than ten-year cycle of investigation, delay and reiterated calls for clarification. The migrants' success in establishing houses, building a school and acting as a unified community, in short in forming permanent ties to the neighbourhood, emerged through their persistent and legally documented presence. Despite their precarious experience in Sarıyer and their 'small, ugly, and irregular' houses, the migrants carved out 'something akin to a neighbourhood'.[8] All the while, locals stubbornly maintained their resistance to migrant sprawl. For residents, the presence of the migrants threatened their own economic claims and, if Reşid's concern about the cemetery is taken at face value, their affective response to their own community's sense of place.

Garipler Mezarlığı reveals as well that rather than a simple act of placing migrants in empty space and waiting for them to become taxpayers, settlement was a process riddled with obstacles and contestations that both reinforced and challenged documentary regimes and ideologies of land use in the 1880s and 1890s. Throughout the empire, as migrants arrived in 'empty land' set aside for their use, they faced potential hostility to their presence within that territory. In Sarıyer and elsewhere, those involved in disputes over land invoked the conceptual framework of governmental regulation and responsibility – the state's right to intervene in health, sanitation, building codes and infrastructure; to organise public and private space; and to arbitrate through documents such as deeds, registers and maps.

Migrant settlement was a territorialising process of naming, bounding and designating space for certain persons or purposes.[9] It was also an act of social engineering; officials sought to organise space in order to create a more ideal population. Migrants served as targets and agents of a larger attempt to develop the empire's land and to establish direct relationships between a centralising state and its population. This chapter considers how settlement unfolded via spatial claims and describes the tools, institutions and projects officials deployed to render visible the population and its distribution in space. It also examines the obstacles officials encountered and the critiques officials, migrants, peasants, notables and others presented as plans unfolded. Rather than taking these critiques as merely descriptive of the central state's failure to achieve its plans, the chapter considers how the space between plan and outcome was essential to Ottoman state-building during the Hamidian era. Failure is inherent to governmental projects. Within migrant settlement, contestation and critique contributed to the disciplining of officials and to shifting assumptions about the population, environment, development, productivity, rational bureaucracy and civilisation. Critiques and proposed solutions contributed to the hegemony of the state's documentary regime among officials, migrants and non-migrant residents, a hegemony that disciplined not only the population but also officials themselves.

Laying Claim to Land and Expertise

In May of 1891, *Ferik* (General) Muzaffer Pasha, Chief Inspector of the Imperial Stud Farms (Hara-yı Hümayun), reported that more than 150,000

Muhacir *as Failure*

donums of available land lay near the Sultansuyu Stud Farm in Malatya, a subprovince (*sancak*) of Mamuretülaziz Province in Eastern Anatolia. Muzaffer Pasha's report was the result of an ongoing land discovery project he conducted across Anatolia in his capacity as Chief Inspector. In Malatya, the pasha promised that irrigation would easily improve vacant state lands. The project he had in mind cost an estimated 20,000 lira, but it would open up a half million lira worth of territory. According to Muzaffer Pasha, the vast quantity of unused, fertile land lay sandwiched between two tributaries of the Euphrates near the district (*nahiye*) of Yazıhan. Unlike the farmers of West Anatolia, who had already harnessed the power of irrigation, Malatya's peasants remained dependent on the rivers to water their crops. Thus, aside from the areas surrounding running water, 'no one profited from the abundant land'. After preliminary discussions with provincial engineers, the pasha fastidiously drew a map of where the six irrigation canals would flow (Figure 4.2).[10]

Settling migrants was a project dependent on finding land and constrained by logistics. In the immediate aftermath of the 1877–8 Russo-Ottoman War, officials estimated that there were roughly ten million donums of available land in the empire; however, four fifths of this was located in East Anatolia and Mesopotamia, too far to make possible intensive settlement for Balkan migrants. As they considered where to place newcomers arriving from the west, officials wrote off the entirety of Diyarbakir Province as too distant for mass transport, too arid and too politically unstable to render settlement feasible. Given these constraints, in the immediate aftermath of the Eastern Crisis, migrants from the Balkans instead settled intensively in Thrace and West Anatolia, especially Bursa, Izmir and Izmid.[11]

Political change contributed to statesmen's renewed interest in placing migrants in central and eastern Anatolia. The 1878 Congress of Berlin elevated the international dimension of the Armenian Question by calling upon the Ottoman Empire to undertake reforms on behalf of the Armenian populations in the 'six provinces' of Eastern Anatolian. The demographic justification for the reforms meant that settling and registering Muslim migrants and nomadic tribes offered the Ottoman state a route to undermine the claims of non-Muslim minorities in Anatolia (Chapter 5).[12] As a result of the war, the empire lost some of its most densely populated districts in the Balkans, which increased the importance of developing Anatolia. Finally, by the mid-1880s, after decades of intensive immigration, finding land had become more difficult in those areas closest to the ports and hubs at which newcomers had arrived in previous decades.

The question of where to place migrants revolved as well around issues of reform, productivity and economic development. In 1875, the empire

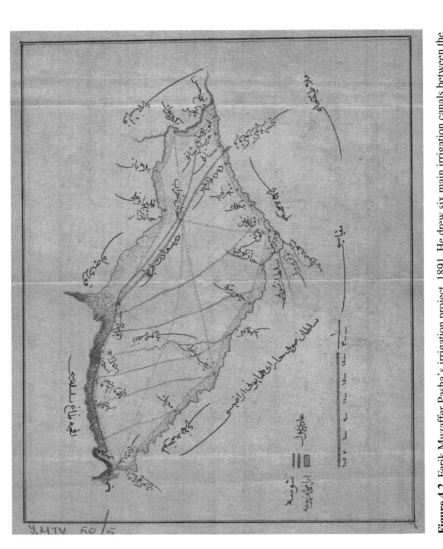

Figure 4.2 Ferik Muzaffer Pasha's irrigation project, 1891. He drew six main irrigation canals between the Tohma (south boundary) and Kuru Çay (north boundary) streams. Both streams are tributaries of the Euphrates River, visible on the eastern boundary. Y.MTV 50.5.

Muhacir *as Failure*

defaulted on its foreign loan payments, threatening the empire's very viability as the Eastern Crisis began. In 1881, in accordance with the Treaty of Berlin, the sultan established the Ottoman Public Debt Administration (OPDA), an entity comprised of representatives from European states and the empire. The OPDA administered the revenues of several monopolies and taxes and eventually controlled nearly a third of state revenues. The era was one in which visions of reform echoed throughout the upper echelons of Ottoman administration and within the OPDA. Abdülhamid II conceived of wide-scale reform as early as 1879, describing the need for a range of projects, including military reorganisation, clarification of administrative responsibilities at all levels of bureaucracy, reform of judicial procedure, mapping and statistical programmes, and more.[13] Soon after, the Minister of Public Works provided a comprehensive report on roads, railways, harbours and irrigation on all of Ottoman Asia.[14] The OPDA encouraged foreign lending and facilitated direct foreign investment, and by the late 1880s it helped to secure foreign investment in infrastructure, in particular railways, irrigation works, ports and bridges.[15] Though different provinces had different needs, running through the language of migrant settlement and economic development was a common refrain: a modular vision of security, education, agriculture, industry and trade that could rescue the empire from bankruptcy and instability. Muzaffer Pasha's vision for Malatya and Eastern Anatolian captured this mood, one in which transformative projects were a matter of technological improvement and capacious vision.

ENVISIONING CHANGE

A member of the elite, forty-member Military Inspection Commission, Muzaffer Pasha personally tied together the projects of military reform, land reform, settlement and economic development. The Inspection Commission, created after the disaster of the 1877–8 war, investigated and proposed military-related reforms.[16] As a cavalryman, Muzaffer Pasha was determined to address the military's need for high-quality livestock. In 1879, he called for the state to take a more active role in improving the quality and supply of cavalry horses. By the mid-1880s, the government opened state-managed stud farms to breed horses, supply livestock to the military and modernise animal husbandry. The empire created imperial stud farms from existing state estates in the *sancak* of Malatya (Sultansuyu) and the *kaza*s of Eskişehir (Çifteler) and Bursa (Mihaliç/Karacabey). Muzaffer became the first chief inspector of the farms, adding to his existing responsibilities as chair of the Standing Veterinary Committee.[17]

Governing Migration in the Late Ottoman Empire

As chief inspector, Muzaffer embraced migrant settlement to populate the large estates. Determined to uncover more land for newcomers, the Migrant Commission and grand vizier dispatched officials to work in coordination with Muzaffer, the Ministry of Imperial Registry (Defter-i Hakani Nezareti), and local officials to assess availability.

The expertise of military men such as Muzaffer Pasha played a tremendous role in making possible the formerly impossible – finding space in regions that had already seen intensive settlement, and making Eastern Anatolian provinces such as Diyarbakir and Mamuretülaziz appear more feasible as settlement locations. Over the course of his surveying, the pasha uncovered over 900,000 donums of land in Hüdavendigar and Ankara Provinces, both of which had seen intensive migrant settlement in previous decades.[18] Deployed throughout Anatolia to comb through land records and map terrain, the pasha was well positioned to consider the big picture. Over the course of a few months in 1891, his reports locate him on opposite ends of provinces 600 miles apart. His reference to irrigation in West Anatolia likely emerged from first-hand observations made during his work at the Mihaliç farm in Bursa. A year later in 1892, he travelled east to Adana, where he established Anavarza Imperial Farm. His experiences lent themselves to an Anatolia-wide scale of problem-solving.

The pasha's work on the farms and in land discovery reflected the relationship between migrant settlement and comprehensive reform. Muzaffer Pasha's confident assertion that the Malatya project could be managed with 'little effort' echoed the era's ethos of development and signalled his own belief in the capacity of engineering, science and technology to make possible large-scale change. A few months after his trip to Malatya, the pasha shifted from envisioning arterial canals and irrigation trenches in Yazıhan to imagining how the steel track of the Anatolian Railway would channel new life into Ankara Province.

In 1889, the Anatolian Railway Company (CFOA – Chemins de fer Ottoman d'Anatolie) was awarded a concession to build the Anatolian Railroad. By 1892, the company had extended the railroad from Istanbul to Eskişehir, a town in Kütahya, one of the eastern districts of Hüdavendigar Province. The company then extended the rail from Eskişehir to Ankara (Figure 4.3), and in 1896 it added a branch from Eskişehir to Konya.[19] The rail lines were intended to increase exports and to resolve Istanbul's dependence on grain shipments from the empire's European provinces and politically unstable regions. The Ankara route initially transported 34,000 tonnes of grain per year, a figure that increased to 187,000 tonnes per year within the first decade of the twentieth century. The Ankara station

Muhacir *as Failure*

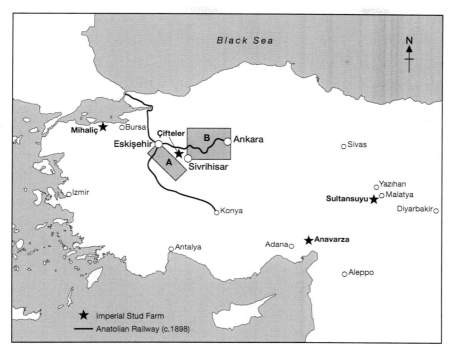

Figure 4.3 Ankara–Eskişehir branch of the Anatolian Railway and Imperial Stud Farms. Shaded rectangles correspond to settlement maps in Figure 4.4 (Area A) and Figure 4.5 (Area B).

became responsible for nearly 40 per cent of all merchandise shipped to Istanbul on the railway.[20] The railway and its capacity to contribute to Anatolia's economic development converged with the ongoing phenomenon of migration from Rumelia. The Anatolian Railroad became a key conduit in conveying migrants from the Balkans eastward, easing the time and cost of transportation, making possible intensive migrant settlement, and connecting new settlers to new markets.

As the CFOA's plans emerged, Muzaffer Pasha and the Migrant Commision recommended adding immigrants to the project as manual laborers and agricultural settlers. To that end, in March of 1891, the Migrant Commission and Muzaffer Pasha devised a land speculation scheme. In a memorandum to the Council of Ministers (Meclis-i Mahsus), the General Migrant Commission noted that local landowners did not realise that land prices would rise along the proposed Eskişehir line. By buying low and selling high, the state could ensure that it made enough money to pay for migrant settlement fees. At the very least, the commission noted, the Council of Ministers should not approve any sales of state land in the area

Governing Migration in the Late Ottoman Empire

until after Muzaffer Pasha had surveyed it for settlement. Though the council shot down the land-grab scheme, it did endorse sending Muzaffer Pasha, as someone already familiar with the area given his work on the Imperial Stud Farm, to survey state lands.[21] Thus, after finishing his work in Malatya, Muzaffer headed west.

In fall of 1891, Muzaffer Pasha undertook a twelve-day trip with a group of surveyors to tour the area around the Çifteler Stud Farm, southwest of Eskişehir. His cohort, comprised of several lower-ranking military officers, determined that state lands supported the settlement of 2,525 households, or some 12,000–13,000 migrants from Bosnia, Bulgaria and Eastern Rumelia.[22] The results of Muzaffer Pasha's survey of the area tied reform to data collection, land categorisation and mapping. The pasha produced a map (Figure 4.4) outlining the surveyors' route, the rough location of each farm and the terrain. The twenty-three state farms designated by the pasha's team encircled a large area off limits to migrant settlement based on prior residents' claims, unviable land and the location of the stud farm. Alongside the map, the surveyors provided a register recording the amount of arable land in each plotted state (*miri*) farm, its projected capacity and its environmental characteristics (Table 4.1).

Together, the Pasha's register and map present in visual shorthand claims to expertise based on measurement, calculation and labelling, revealing how categories became 'actionable' in the mind of an Ottoman reformer. Designating space as available and viable was the first step in tying people to land. As officials considered how to change the economy, the landscape and the population, the categories they developed to assess each were flexible and adapted from the information they could collect. In the register and elsewhere, the most important characteristics were those that increased the likelihood of stable, permanent and economically productive settlement. As Muzaffer Pasha toured the area, the land's ecological attributes, such as altitude, vegetation and water sources, became information easily observed and recorded. The question then became how to use that knowledge to enact settlement. The answer was to reduce the incoming migrant population to another set of categories, one that rendered scientific the process of matching migrants to land.

CATEGORIES AND CLAIMS

Environmental viability had been a consideration in settlement since the 1850s and 1860s, when instructions for Nusret Pasha and other settlement agents in Rumelia outlined the importance of evaluating land arability and proximity to fresh water.[23] The many petitions migrants had

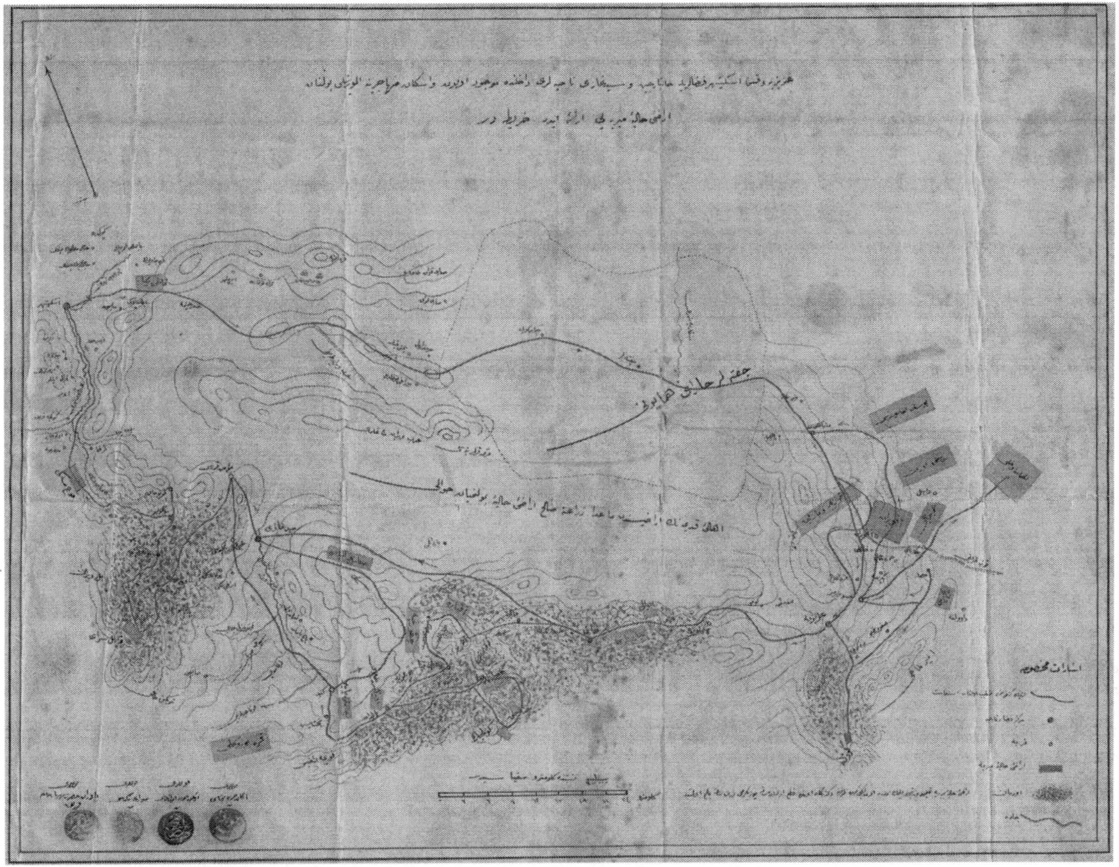

Figure 4.4 Muzaffer Pasha's map of *miri* farms along projected railroad, 1891. Y.PRK.KOM 8.14.

Table 4.1 Register: available *miri* land along projected railroad, 1891.

Plot	Area	Towns	Households	Water source	Distance to forest	Landscape	Migrant origin
1	2,000	1	20		Forested	High altitude	Balkans
2	10,000	1	100	Well water	1–2 hours		Dobruca
3	20,000	3	250	Flowing and well water	Distant		Filibe
4	15,000	4	200	Well water	Few hours		Dobruca
5	15,000	2	200	Fountains and well water	Few hours		Dobruca, Deliorman
6	35,000	2	250	Flowing and well water	3 hours		Kuban
7	7,000	1	100	Fountains and well water	2 hours		Dobruca
8	12,000	1	80	Fountains and well water	2 hours		Dobruca
9	25,000	1	150	Well water	2–4 hours		Dobruca, Deliorman
10	2,000	1	40	Springs and fountains	Forested		Bosnia, Bulgaria
11	12,000	1	50	Springs and fountains	Forested		Bosnia, Bulgaria
12	13,000	1	45	Springs and fountains	Forested		Bosnia, Bulgaria
13	3,000	1	50	Springs	Forested	High altitude	High mountains
14	3,500	1	60	Springs	Forested	High altitude	High mountains
15	8,000	1	50	Fountains	Forested		Bosnia, Bulgaria
16	9,000	1	120	Fountains	Forested		Bosnia, Bulgaria
17	10,000	1	120	Fountains	Forested		Bosnia, Bulgaria
18	9,500	1	40	Springs	Forested	High altitude	Balkans
19	15,000	1	100	Fountains	Forested		Bosnia, Bulgaria
20	7,000	2	200	1.5 hours to flowing water	Forested		Eastern Rumelia
21	7,000	1	200	Flowing water	Forested		Rumelia
22	2,000	1	50	Fountains	3 hours		Bulgaria
23	3,000	1	50	Fountains	3 hours		Bulgaria
	234,000	**31**	**2,525**				

Note: Numbers correspond to farms mapped in Figure 4.4. 'Area' refers to amount of arable land in donums. 'Towns' and 'households' indicate each farm's projected capacity.

Muhacir *as Failure*

sent requesting resettlement based on environmental issues (Chapter 2) reinforced the importance of environmental compatibility in settlement, as did the astounding loss of life that had accompanied settlement in East Anatolia.[24] Aside from sustenance and economic self-sufficiency, officials accounted for natural resources, such as state forestland, which could be threatened by intensive migrant settlement.[25] Land distribution became a component in viability, and officials developed ratios of people to area to determine the size of parcels best suited to agricultural production. In 1879, the Council of State, in keeping with the definition of a farm (*çiftlik*) established in the 1858 Land Code, determined that each migrant family should receive seventy-to-one hundred thirty donums of land. Anything smaller was insufficient for farming.[26] Another set of instructions in 1879 reiterated this standard, mandating that each household, defined as containing one-to-five adult male individuals, receive a farm comprised of seventy-to-one hundred donums of arable land. The entirety of this land allotment included both tillable land and newly opened pastureland.[27]

Officials thus recognised the environment as a chief factor in determining the likelihood that settlers would thrive, and when Muzaffer Pasha set out across Ankara, the relationship between migrants and the terrain they would inhabit was at the forefront of his mind. His team assumed migrants' economic success could emerge through matching settlers' previous and future environments. Based on their assessment of each plot's ecology, the pasha and his retinue identified the point of origin of migrant groups best suited to inhabit the area. For example, surveyors designated Area One as appropriate for migrants from the Balkans *because* it was an elevated and forested region.[28] Migrants' origins became shorthand to determine the easiest realisation of their economic potential.

In the case of environmental shorthand and the capacity to match people to land, diagnosing problems and designing solutions required categorising and producing corresponding 'knowledge' about the population. As the settlement project unfolded, other officials took up the language of improvement and linked ecological observations about the province to its inhabitants. The extension of the railway east towards Ankara encouraged ongoing demarcation of land for migrant settlement. Soon after Muzaffer Pasha's evaluation, Ahmet, a commissioner from the Ankara Province Migrant Settlement Committee (Ankara Vilayeti İskan-i Muhacir Heyeti), toured the district of Sivrihisar. Alongside describing the geographic characteristics of the district, the commissioner's report took on an ethnographic tone, and he emphasised his familiarity with the conditions and mentality of the people there.

Governing Migration in the Late Ottoman Empire

In terms of physical features, the commissioner emphasised the region's abundance of natural resources. Like the 1891 assessment, his report began by evaluating the quality of land intended for settlement. However, far more so than Muzaffer Pasha's report, the commissioner's 1893 assessment explored issues of human ecology. Ahmet reported the rail line traversed several valley locations, where the air quality was inferior to that of elevated areas. According to the commissioner, this state of affairs was the result of poor management. Locals never dredged the low-lying riverbeds surrounding the rail line, and their use of the land and water had exacerbated the issue. They had dammed the rivers for rice cultivation and other purposes, altering the course of the riverbeds, encouraging overflow and giving rise to wetlands, all of which undermined the quality of the climate. Because the wetlands and climatic issues were the result of poor stewardship, Ahmet declared that a little management and minimal expense could improve the situation. Overall, the region contained a wealth of underutilised natural resources.

Ahmet's confident assertion of the transformative power of proper land management extended to his assessment of social conditions in Ankara Province. The province's population was 88 per cent Muslim. Based on his tour, he observed that the people in the villages were generally hospitable and diligent in their religious duties. Inhabitants grew wheat, barley and poppy, and raised a variety of animals, particularly Angora goats and sheep. In terms of available land, the commissioner stressed the thin distribution of people and the existence of many abandoned or ruined villages. Large districts throughout the province frequently had 30,000–40,000, or at most 80,000 individuals, a population density Ahmet characterised as extremely low. His observations ranged from merely optimistic to hyperbolic, as he boldly suggested millions of individuals could be settled within the province with 'minimal expense and complete ease' so long as officials proceeded in accordance with the settlement regulations.[29]

While the settlement regulations afforded a clear protocol to ensure successful settlement, according to Ahmet, upon his arrival in the province he realised officials did not have a copy of the regulations on hand. He had to go to lengths to find one, so once he did, he immediately requested the provincial press print copies. In classic technocratic fashion, Ahmet's elevation of the plan as an entity imbued with the might of science meant that he blamed failure on human error rather than on plans themselves. Problems, whether the climatic complications posed by the wetlands or broader issues of exorbitant cost, inefficiency, delay and migrant suffering, resulted from a failure of proper management. Upon his return to Ankara,

Muhacir *as Failure*

the commissioner disseminated the freshly printed settlement regulations and established Sivrihisar as a model area to apply them.

Given Ahmet's belief in the power of sound management, it is no surprise that he portrayed his model application as a significant success. Within just one and a half months, he had constructed 700 houses. Whereas previous housing projects were wasteful and sloppily constructed, the houses the commissioner oversaw were solid, regularly placed and nearly ready for use. In fact, he saw fit to suggest the migrant houses were superior to many existing non-migrant houses in the district. Moreover, through his careful method and efficient planning, he had saved the state several thousand gold liras.[30] For Ahmet, exposure to the expertise embedded in settlement plans and the logic of careful administration would rescue officials from their ignorance, save the state undue expense, and deliver migrants from the clutches of poverty and suffering.

Migrant settlement was essential to reformers' vision of Anatolia because it promoted a new, optimised relationship between people and land. The correct relationship between people and land was one of environmental mastery and profitability. Sound management encompassed residents' land use and settlement officials' decisions. In promising economic development easily obtained, Muzaffer Pasha and Ahmet's critique of the status quo was one that centred people and their ignorance. As he planned the irrigation canals near Yazıhan, Muzaffer Pasha portrayed a population dependent on the environment, which meant that they underutilised land. Whereas Commissioner Ahmet could easily correct the ignorance of officials by disseminating instructions and regulations, the reformers addressed that of the wider population through science, example, tutelage and, in some cases, displacement. Knowing how best to use land was an expertise that lent itself to determining who should access it.

THE CLAIM OF EMPTY LAND

Empty land is a familiar concept across multiple sites of imperial expansion; the terms empty, uninhabited and unused were frequent rhetorical devices used to appropriate land from indigenous populations in settler colonial societies.[31] Nora Barakat draws an important distinction between the Ottoman use of the term and that of other imperial formations. The Ottoman priority was one of cultivation; the 1858 Land Code prioritised cultivation in the establishment of usufruct rights and the 'bundle of rights' that constituted ownership, such that empty (*hali*) could be legally conflated with uncultivated (*mahlul*) land. Population expulsion was not a necessary component of the Hamidian drive towards agricultural

Governing Migration in the Late Ottoman Empire

production, and in some cases changing land use could accommodate existing populations.[32] Despite the specificities of the Ottoman context, as in other empires, the designation of land as empty was an assertion that could radically change access to it.

Muzaffer Pasha and Commissioner Ahmet used maps and plans to promote and solidify new claims on territory. Their reports positioned officials as experts on geography and population. Their plans elevated them as authorities on the correct use of land, and their categories became mechanisms to undermine alternative claims to space. In determining the ideal migrant to place in available state lands, Muzaffer Pasha's emphasis on the environmental compatibility of settlers and land presented an argument about who should inhabit the areas he had uncovered. Muzaffer Pasha and Ahmet extrapolated from this basic idea of environmental compatibility, positing an intimate relationship between land and people in which mismanagement or misuse reflected the fundamental failings of its inhabitants and undermined their right to the land.

By the time empty lands were designated as such in settlement plans or recorded in disputes, administrators had already engaged in an act of (re)categorisation. Even when researchers are sceptical of the sudden emergence of large amounts of 'empty land', such as the 900,000 donums Muzaffer 'discovered' in Hüdavendigar and Ankara Provinces, the route through which surveyors found land is difficult to uncover. For instance, in Muzaffer Pasha's report, he and his team marked spaces as off limits for migrant settlement but also designated twenty-three areas of available state lands. Though the report is relatively rich in data about each plot's area and geographic characteristics, the surveyors give no indication as to whether other individuals or groups made use of the land for activities such as summer pasturage.

While Muzaffer Pasha's 1891 report on the area east of Eskişehir reveals only that he categorised land as available, Ahmet's 1893 report on Sivrihisar reveals that claiming land as underutilised – not just empty – was an essential route in finding room for migrants. Rather than just exploring land and marking boundaries, Ahmet observed the people of the province. The commissioner gained expertise on social conditions through touring villages and spending time among residents. This experience allowed him to endorse paternalistically the potential of the region's inhabitants while emphasising their lack of productive economic behaviour. Populations gained and lost access to land through administrators' evaluation of their economic activity. Put another way, officials determined the 'emptiness' of land according to the economic activity performed on it.

Muhacir *as Failure*

In describing the climate of the region, Ahmet faulted the local population for failing to clean the rivers and for growing rice. Though these activities promoted 'personal gain' (*menafi-i zatiye*), they contributed to climatic problems in the region. In general, the commissioner evaluated the inhabitants as well meaning but inept. Their economic inefficiencies extended into all areas of production. According to Ahmet,

> The people are kind, but they do not know how to properly farm. They cannot properly profit from their sheep or goats ... Since they are not inclined toward trade and do not farm, it as if the Christians have a monopoly over commercial matters. There are just a few shops manufacturing and selling the famous Angora wool and camlets. Consequently, the people of the province cannot be described as particularly poor or rich. They are happy with their lot. However, agricultural and commercial transactions following the extension of the railroad have generated a readiness to progress.[33]

The inhabitants' inefficiency and ignorance contributed to the overall impression of land availability and economic potential within the province, and completion of the railroad offered the ideal moment to intervene. Migrant settlement assisted not only in increasing the number of cultivators in the province, but also in improving the quality of agriculture. According to Ahmet, migrants from the European provinces were more knowledgeable and technologically advanced than Anatolian peasants. As such, Balkan migrants contributed to the improvement of agriculture, industry and trade in the region. The newcomers' cart horses and heavy ploughs were three-to-four times as efficient as the wooden ploughs and oxen used by the local population, and the migrants could use their horses to move goods and participate in trade after the sowing season. The commissioner concluded that the people of the province, recognising all the benefits migrants would bring, were happy and exceptionally helpful since the newcomers' arrival.[34]

Muzaffer Pasha and Commissioner Ahmet employed the environment to understand and cultivate the population they most wished to see in the Anatolian countryside. When Ferik Muzaffer Pasha matched migrants to land based on their ecological origins, he assumed that familiar environments would help migrants acclimate to their new homes, an expectation that aligned migrant and state interest in the long-term viability of settlement. As officials wielded population categories, they extrapolated from the categories applied to the groups in question. Beyond familiarity with a type of terrain or climate, they assigned groups attributes such as technological knowhow on the one hand and ignorance on the other, traits that could influence whose claims to contested land prevailed. The relationship between land and people and the truths each seemed to reflect about the other influenced officials' application of this ecological shorthand. For Ahmet, the very climate of Sivrihisar reflected the ignorance of its inhabitants and their failure to harness the land's potential. Even as ecology revealed the shortcomings of the people, the environment offered a path to their development. The entanglement of culture, cultivation, productivity and progress meant that enhancing one enhanced the other.[35] The railroad and the migrants offered the chance to create 'the right disposition of things', such that the population became industrious, knowledgeable and wealthy and the land became productive.[36]

Not all Ottoman subjects were equally eligible for the improvements promised by reform. The Treaty of Berlin's call for reform on behalf of specific groups, such as Armenians, affected officials' migrant settlement strategies. During the Hamidian era, settlement policies were intended to bolster the economic development of the Muslim peasantry and to dispossess non-Muslims (Chapter 5).[37] As they surveyed vast swaths of land and devised schemes for placing tens of thousands of migrants, officials conceived of the population as raw material through which to remake Anatolia. Useful populations were entitled to land, but utility was a context-driven category. The categories officials used to understand the population justified the very nature of policy. Whereas ignorance and poverty were changeable attributes ameliorated through exposure to new technologies and new ideas, officials increasingly understood religion as an immutable characteristic. Whether undertaken as a project of improving or neutralising sections of the population, development proceeded through claims to land and expertise. Registering and furnishing documents for new migrant villages played an essential role in the perpetuation of those claims.

POWERFUL PAPERS AND INCENTIVISED PARTICIPATION

Whether Muzaffer Pasha's map and register or Commissioner Ahmet's report, officials initiated a paper trail. The map, the register and the plan conferred expert status on their producer. Other powerful papers were likewise alchemical, generating claims to space and then rendering those claims increasingly intractable. Once migrants established communities, officials' next task was to register their villages' names, locations and defining features with the Interior Ministry and local administrative entities. By the 1880s and 1890s, provincial officials described the location of the new villages, at times writing a brief explanation of a village's cardinal direction and distance from town and provincial centres and at

Muhacir *as Failure*

others providing rough diagrams of the same.[38] In other cases, officials provided meticulous maps showing natural features and other settlements in the area.[39] Along with location, officials communicated demographic information, noting the number of immigrant households and their points of origin. In areas of intensive migrant placement, officials registered villages in clusters, alerting the central state of the layout of areas encompassing dozens of new settlements.[40] Cataloguing the new settlements of Anatolia was a component in a comprehensive attempt to define and know the population by matching people to land; the same laws governed the registration of settled tribes. Reformers across the empire saw registration as fundamental to strengthening the army and levying taxes; whether migrant or nomadic pastoralist, new villages were places where people would be settled, recorded and then improved.

Accompanying registration were a series of papers that rendered migrants permanent fixtures. Recording village names changed the status of migrants and their communities, bringing them under the purview of multiple branches of local administration. Once a village was registered, officials recorded its inhabitants in population registers (*nüfus sicilleri*) and documented their newly issued deeds in the Office of Imperial Registers. Deed and register ended migrants' guest or temporary status and clarified their timeline for tax exemptions and conscription eligibility.[41] Administrators so valued this change that they at times invited migrants who had settled without permission to register in order to shift them from illegal and potentially impermanent residents to taxable entities subject to regulation.[42] Registering villages expanded local administration, an essential component in efforts to surveil migrant populations.

The state benefitted from registering villages, and so too did migrants, who received deeds and new access to resources and administrative power. As individuals and as community members, migrants operated within a matrix of incentivised participation. For example, in selecting the names of their new villages, migrants were expected to choose 'suitable' names, a suitability verified by the central administration. Migrants choose names based on the existing names of their settlement location, their community leaders, local officials who had been helpful during settlement and their former villages.[43] One popular set of names were those of the sultans, a signal of gratitude towards the Ottoman state and the Sultan himself. The Anatolian countryside is dotted with Hamidiyes, Aziziyes, Mecidiyes, Osmaniyes and Orhaniyes. This 'suitable' set of names never seemed to go out of style – at least not until the 1908 constitutional revolution, when some immigrants changed village names from Hamidiye to *Meşrutiyet* (Constitutionalism) or *Hurriyet* (Independence).[44]

The stakes of registration were such that migrants themselves petitioned for recognition. Participation in district and provincial politics was one incentive for registering villages. Administrative reorganisation during the Tanzimat created more opportunities for local, elected representation in government. Elected *muhtar*s, or village heads, and local councils (*ihtiyar meclisi*) took on administrative tasks. The councils were a route to participate in the broader politics of the provinces, as the vetting process for candidates to the more central councils went through village councils. Registration also entitled villages to officially recognise an imam.

The language of registration indicates that some migrants submitted registration requests in order to establish local administration. In 1868, Circassian migrant leaders in Sivas viewed the muhtar as a stabilising entity and explicitly emphasised the importance of appointing a *muhtar* in all migrant neighbourhoods and villages to prevent banditry.[45] When groups of migrants in Izmir and Kırk Kilise signed petitions requesting permission to appoint a *muhtar* and imam in their newly named villages, they signalled their interest in establishing offices that facilitated their political access and legitimised local religious practice.[46] The *muhtar* was a liaison with provincial administrators and communicated individual and community grievances. The position included responsibilities intended to curb unanticipated movement within the countryside, including collecting information for the issuing of travel passes and verifying travel papers for visitors, vouching for newcomers and registering all inhabitants.[47]

Registration offered proof of an ideal repeatedly obtained: groups of migrants were settled, catalogued and sought recognition through official routes to conduct daily business and receive resources. Naming and registering new neighbourhoods and villages was an important component in realising official recognition and an essential first step in migrant incorporation at both the community and individual family levels. The mere existence of something on paper imbued claims with legitimacy. In the anecdote that began this chapter, when residents challenged migrants' use of space in Sarıyer, the Migrant Commission's defence of the settlement repeatedly referenced the fact that the municipality had registered and approved the building of immigrant homes. The Commission's insistence that the houses, even if initially built illegally on cemetery grounds, had been registered, indicated the power that accrued by documentation. Registering houses and villages became a way for both migrant communities and the state to bolster the new spatial arrangements brought about by settlement. Documents rendered claims more intractable and migrants' status more permanent. Papers became a powerful tool in influencing the outcomes of contested land claims.

Muhacir *as Failure*

Contesting Settlement

In 1898, a few years after the CFOA opened a rail line to Konya, the British Vice Consul, Keun, sent a lengthy report to the consul in Ankara on the status of the district. Keun had lived in Konya for over a decade, first as a representative of the Ottoman Bank and later as an agent for an Istanbul mercantile firm, under whose auspices he established a network of carpet manufacturers across the province.[48] In his report, Keun discussed the possibility of settling a few thousand German colonists in Konya. He observed that the government needed to proceed cautiously with any colonisation plan to avoid resistance on the part of local inhabitants. He noted, 'when ... the Government wished to find lands for Rumelian and Circassian refugees, every small plot of ground thus set aside was at once claimed by the nearest villagers as their property notwithstanding the fact that the country is very thinly populated'. Despite forecasting difficulty related to a German colonisation plan, he emphasised the benefits of settlement, describing success in Konya much along the lines that Commissioner Ahmet had predicted in Sivrihisar a few years prior. The Vice Consul wrote, 'Wherever refugees from Rumelia have settled, ease and progress reign. They are good workers. Their agricultural implements are better than those used here, consequently, the yield of their crops is higher than that of the natives. Their cattle are not at risk of starving; they have managed to stock up on dry grass for the winter.' He predicted that thanks to the migrants and with the addition of the 'enlightened methods' brought by foreign capital, the province 'might pass from poverty to prosperity' within ten years.[49]

Two years later, the Anatolian Railway carried a group of Bosnian immigrants to Ankara. The French Vice Consul reported that the city housed 3,000 refugees and officials anticipated 12,000 more. Far from the 'happy' and 'helpful' occupants the ever-optimistic Ahmet had described in 1893, among the Muslim and Christian inhabitants of the city 'a great emotion reigns ... spirits are very pessimistic', and all feared they would have to 'defend themselves against all kinds of abuse' if migrants were given insufficient aid by the government.[50] A commission comprised of a general of engineering, an army captain and a doctor had surveyed several locations for the migrants and then returned to Istanbul. The Vice Consul predicted their plans would be ignored, as the population was 'determined to oppose' further migrant settlement.[51] He agreed with the opposition, suggesting that if immigration to the city were stopped, its inhabitants would witness an improvement in material interests, health and public safety.[52]

Alongside the local population, migrants presented their own opposition to the committee's settlement plans, refusing to be separated and 'demanding' their own village. As their population reached the thousands, the Bosnian migrants became a powerful block. Faced with 800 migrants due to arrive in Ankara by train, the governor attempted to divert them to a nearby village, ordering that the wagons carrying the newcomers be detached 27 km away from the city and dispatching a posse of gendarmerie to manage the situation. Upon learning the governor's orders, the immigrants protested, refusing to exit the wagons and demanding to be transported the rest of the way to Ankara. Once Bosnians in the city heard of their brethren's plight, they marched to the village to lend assistance. Faced with the two groups, the governor yielded, ultimately allowing the migrants to disembark at the Ankara station.[53]

The Vice Consuls' descriptions of local opposition and unyielding migrant demands in Konya and Ankara offer an image of settlement far more chaotic than the tidy tables presented in Muzaffer Pasha's report. No matter the surveying committees and settlement regulations nor the handsomeness of Commissioner Ahmet's model housing, the plans officials generated met moving masses of people, each navigating new possibilities and challenges posed by migration. Moments of cooperation, like prior residents contributing housing, labour and capital to temporary and permanent migrant placement, could also become points of conflict in response to undue burdens. Years of famine, fears of banditry, and precarity exacerbated by temporary placement affected migrant and non-migrant alike. The gap between policy and outcome was inevitable, and so too was critique of failures and of consequences intended and unintended. Critiques were themselves consequential, evidence of a coalescing set of ideas about population, territory and state, about the documentary regime, and about who was entitled to inhabit, use and own land within the empire.

PLANS MEET PEOPLE

Land, the heart of the settlement project, became one of its most contentious aspects. Placing migrants was an act of territorialisation, a way of carving up imperial space to improve governance, affect economic change and influence the population. Rumours of impending migrant settlement hastened the pace of registration; nomads and others who had expanded holdings by reclaiming abandoned land codified their claims and began to pay taxes.[54] Migrants also engaged in claiming and clearing land beyond that demarcated in settlement surveys. Land contestation was an obvious

Muhacir *as Failure*

by-product of a project intended to affect the movement of people through Ottoman space. Contestation and officials' responses to contested land consolidated changes in land usage and access.

There were two unshakeable premises in the minds of administrators like Muzaffer Pasha and Commissioner Ahmet: that immigration was necessarily positive for the Ottoman state and that there was enough land in Anatolia to accommodate virtually unlimited settlement. While land was plentiful, its proper distribution was essential to success. Proper distribution of land would overcome issues of undue expenses to the state, avoid burdening the local population, and prevent poverty and suffering among migrants. Thus, rather than land, people – officials, migrants or non-migrant residents – were the limiting factor.

Settlement officials were not the only individuals to view land distribution as the key to the entire project. Decades prior to Muzaffer Pasha and Commissioner Ahmet's surveys in Ankara, over 300 Circassian communal leaders led by *Mirliva* Musa Pasha, a migrant and former officer in the Russian Army, gathered to address the problem of Circassian banditry near Sivas. In 1868, they proposed a plan to reduce lawless behaviour through empowering local headmen and establishing prohibitive punishments for various crimes. While the leaders' solution acknowledged migrants' internal politics, they also blamed Circassian banditry on officials' failures to properly carry out settlement goals.[55] They argued that carelessness and negligence on the part of officials had left many newcomers in temporary settlement conditions for over three years, and dire economic circumstances forced migrants into theft and other illegal activities.[56] The Circassians requested that the Ottoman state dispatch more conscientious and honest settlement directors and incorporate migrant leaders into settlement commissions and local councils.[57]

Musa Pasha continued to serve as a go-between for the Circassian migrants in Sivas and the central state. A year and a half later, he submitted another petition emphasising the importance of careful settlement and recommending completely redoing land distribution in the province. The Council of State (Şura-yı Devlet) drafted a directive in response to his petition. The council attempted to address settlement failures with a familiar set of tools – surveying, assessment and registration. Whereas Musa Pasha emphasised inequality, the council redirected the question to one of agricultural productivity and the proper use of land. Its directive called for correctly registering the existing migrant population and assessing whether migrants had allowed some areas to remain fallow, a signal that they had received unnecessarily large allotments. The Şura-yı Devlet recommended that local councils work with trusted migrant leaders to redistribute abandoned land and that the land office issue migrants deeds to further solidify their claims.[58]

Issues of local influence and official corruption persisted across the decades, emerging once more after the 1878–9 war pushed migrants from Rumelia and Eastern Anatolia into Ankara and Sivas. In 1880, the British Consul General in Anatolia, Charles William Wilson, described migrant illness, death and delayed settlement throughout Anatolia, noting that as the central government stopped its supply of rations to migrants, they had no choice but 'starvation or robbery'.[59] The fault lay not with migrants, who 'make good colonists, and, if properly cared for, will soon settle down and become a well-ordered peasantry'.[60] Instead, the fault lay once again with poor administration and efforts stymied by local interests. In language echoing that of the Ottoman officials he criticised, Wilson noted that 'the resettlement of the refugees might be effected with no great difficulty by the Porte were it in earnest. All that is necessary is a well-considered scheme to be rigidly carried out in the provinces, however unpleasant it may be to local notables and individual refugees.'[61]

The question of just how much land was available confronted the representatives of the central Ottoman state, who relied on local actors to carry out nearly every aspect of settlement. District councils and deed offices responded to Muzaffer Pasha's railroad settlement plan with their own estimates of land availability. Though commissioners, settlement officials, governors and consuls described central Anatolia as thinly populated, officials were frequently frustrated with the mechanisms of local land politics, crediting the influence of notables in obstructing the dispersal of land.[62] A telegram circulated among the *mutasarrifs* and *kaymakams* (district heads) in Sivas admonished the officials, noting 'though inquiries made here show that there is plenty of waste land everywhere, replies, dictated by the jealousy and influence of local people, have been received that there were no waste lands available for the settlement of refugees'.[63]

The lines between the categories of migrants, representatives of the central state, local officials, residents and other 'people of influence' were not always cleanly drawn. The migrant leaders in Musa Pasha's Circassian delegation suggested that appointing migrants to settlement commissions would reduce corruption in land distribution; yet migrants who became administers were equally capable of seeking personal gain. As Oktay Özel has shown, Çürüksulu Ali Pasha, a Georgian migrant settled in the Black Sea town of Ordu, used his status as regional Commissioner for Migrant Settlement to solidify his bid to become governor of Trabzon, to facilitate Georgian migrants' appropriation of land in opposition to other groups and to maintain the material well-being of the Georgian community and

Muhacir *as Failure*

his place within it.[64] Musa Pasha eventually played a similar role in Sivas. In 1868, Musa Pasha and his cohort had written to resolve the issue of banditry, an attribute so attached to the image of the Circassian migrant that other outlaws adapted their dress.[65] By 1880, Musa Pasha served as a lieutenant general in Sivas, from which position he determined settlement areas for refugees arriving from Kars after the 1877–8 war. Rather than a paragon of conscientious officialdom, Consul Wilson described the pasha as ambitious and scheming, quick to prioritise Circassian concerns, guilty of stoking religious animosity among Christians and Muslims, and under the sway of those Circassians whose connections to the palace protected them from punishment.[66]

Though Wilson questioned Musa Pasha's interest in bringing peace to the district, he shared the pasha's critique of corrupt settlement officials and overly influential provincial notables. In January of 1880, a skirmish broke out among a group of Circassian refugees and several Greek villages. The Circassians had been living in dire conditions in temporary settlement locations since their arrival in Sivas Province two years prior. Musa Pasha allocated permanent settlement locations to them, but as soon as the Circassians began constructing houses, the inhabitants of two nearby Greek villages drove the migrants off the land. The villagers, who had suffered repeatedly from Circassian banditry in previous years, accused the migrants of building on cultivated land belonging to the village. They were so frightened by the thought of a migrant village near theirs that they vowed to emigrate if the Circassians were settled near them.

When Wilson visited the district, he found sufficient 'waste land' for 500 families. He noted that the Greek villagers had hastily burnt, cleared and sown the fields they claimed to have cultivated, and they presented him with clearly doctored deeds to the land. Wilson blamed the situation on the local land official. According to Wilson, the official had made no effort to clarify the boundary between the Greek villages and the Circassian settlement. Furthermore, he had been influenced by a Turkish notable to place the migrants too close to the Greek villagers and outside the area designated by Musa Pasha. While Wilson acknowledged that the villagers had suffered from Circassian banditry over the years, he blamed the Turkish notables of the district for pushing them into the dispute, as the notables 'are opposed to the settlement of the Circassians but do not like to say so openly'.[67]

Settlement problems extended across Anatolia. In 1884, *Miralay* Suleyman Bey, an honorary aide-de-camp to the Sultan sent to observe migrant settlement in West Anatolia, put forth two resolutions on migrant settlement. In both, he blamed the twin issues of official corruption and influential notables. According to the reports, in 'most provinces', migrant settlement was neither successful nor complete. Wealthy notables used their influence to remove migrants who had already settled, preventing the state from realising the benefits of settlement.[68] The central state's primary role remained transferring migrants to suitable land, but Suleyman recommended other strategies to overcome corruption. Alongside the standard calls to more rapidly investigate land and move migrants from temporary to permanent settlement locations, he recommended eliminating any legal possibility under which officials or notables could remove settled migrants and preventing migrant settlers from being charged as plaintiffs in land cases emerging from their placement in designated areas. Dependent on local entities to place migrants, and cognisant that these were entities beholden to 'local influences', Suleyman sought to increase the power of the documents associated with settlement. Once officials placed migrants, they should immediately issue deeds to the settlers, bolstering their documentary claims to the land.[69] His plan to overcome corruption, much like that of other officials sent to resolve settlement issues, elevated the mechanisms of documentation and registration to better control migrants, residents, notables and even agents of the Ottoman state.

Critiques of the settlement process were revealing in what they left unquestioned. Despite migrant suffering and locals' fears, certain assumptions remained uncontested. Officials approached outcomes like temporary settlement and legal contestation from the perspective that flaws in the system arose from human behaviour, such as corruption among officials or interference on the part of notables. Better plans, better follow-through and thorough documentation would improve settlement outcomes. Among those who supported settlement, the stability of those underlying premises created paths through which to assert expertise, to discipline officials, to cast notables as obstacles to reform, to retain the right to govern 'simple' peasants and to create space for representation among migrant leaders.

CONTESTATION AND CONSOLIDATION

Much like Keun's depiction of a sudden rush on 'thinly populated land', Suleyman's memorandum asserted official scepticism of locals' claims to migrant-designated land. Increased population pressure contributed to a growing number of territorial disputes, such that a land inspector in Sivas in the 1890s estimated that migrant-related issues comprised 90 per cent of land disputes in the province.[70] In demarcating territory for migrant settlement based on their vision for a transformed Anatolia, officials ignored alternative claims to space, and in doing so opened up terrain for contes-

Muhacir *as Failure*

tation. The 'formation and maintenance' of a territory's meanings and boundaries is a political process.[71] Promoting an ideology of productivity and blaming individuals for the difficulties of settlement became elements in asserting Ottoman territoriality.

Given officials' suspicion of the local interests that prevented migrant settlement, administrators tended to favour migrants' claims when resolving disputes. For example, a petition from a Dagestani sheik and fifteen households of his followers in Trabzon Province alleged that people from a nearby village took over the migrants' designated land. Though the sheik had received permission from the local council to settle his group in the area, the two-month dispute with the other villagers had left his group in 'pitiable conditions'. The neighbouring villagers countered with a claim that the migrants appropriated land that had been under common use. The Meclis-i Vala reaffirmed the original decision designating the land as empty and available for migrant settlement.[72]

Even under circumstances when the relationship between migrants and locals grew violent, officials attempted to establish and maintain migrant placement. In a case from 1868, Circassians in Düzce petitioned to be reinstated in their homes following a dispute. According to an official, the group had been settled with sufficient land, seeds and housing. Nonetheless, the migrants were dissatisfied with their land apportionment, and they appropriated roughly 360 donums of the sown fields of a neighbouring non-migrant group. Düzce's *müdür* and neighbourhood council attempted to resolve the dispute through returning fifty-to-sixty donums of land to the wronged villagers. In response, a gang of migrants attacked and stabbed a member of the council and a villager. The instigators of the attack were transferred to another district, but the Meclis-i Vala found the rest of the Circassians innocent based on their petition. After the migrants apologised and accepted their wrongdoing, they were reinstated in the village and allowed to continue to use the land they had appropriated. Though local and imperial officials recognised that migrants had unjustly stolen land, their solution was to return just one sixth of it to its original users.[73]

Officials also compensated legitimate non-migrant claims in order to maintain migrants' presence on land they had appropriated. In 1901, Cafer Bey, a landowner in Hüdavendigar Province, petitioned for restitution after migrants took over an area larger than what was originally agreed between him and the state twenty years prior. The original settlement included forty-one migrant households on 3,670 donums of land. The community had grown in both population and size to 130 households and 4,850 donums. Officials agreed that Cafer was entitled to the land, but they hesitated to remove a migrant community that had been there for nearly two decades, especially since the migrants had dutifully worked and paid taxes. Thus, their solution was to purchase the land, especially since once it was purchased, more migrants could be placed on it.[74] In a similar case from 1909, Dagestani migrants near Pazarköy (Hüdavendigar) appropriated extra land including mulberry orchards from a neighbouring village. The people of the neighbouring village submitted a petition and successfully established their legitimate claim to the trees. The matter was resolved by purchasing the land for the migrants.[75] In both of these cases, migrants benefitted from officials' tendency to award them land regardless of its original availability.

Officials' tendency to override claims that could delay settlement or uproot settled migrants meant the original designation of land as available was a powerful route to effect land transfer. This designation became even more significant as directives closed other doors to legally disputing migrant settlement. The Land Code established a ten-year time period for disputing claims to land that was held by absentee owners or had passed to public auction due to lack of heir.[76] The Council of State reduced this ten-year period to two years for migrants in 1888, determining that once migrants had used land designated as vacant (*mahlul*) for farming or building for two years, they were immune to suits. Aside from establishing migrant immunity, the council went on to dismiss any disputes brought against migrants in Sharia courts, a decision that addressed an ongoing reason for delayed migrant settlement.[77]

When officials designated an area as 'empty' and located migrants on it, they initiated a process that retroactively legitimated their initial assessment. Faced with complaints that migrants had been wrongly placed, officials preferred to leave migrants where they were. James Scott has observed that administrative categories are 'partly fictional shorthand', but 'backed by state power through records, courts, and ultimately coercion, these state fictions transformed the reality they presumed to observe'.[78] Issuing deeds and court rulings offered a paper reality officials could employ to render migrant settlement legitimate. Disputes resulting from migrant settlement provided the impetus to enact the power of records and courts in determining legitimate claims.

Fictional shorthand also becomes reality as individuals adopt state language and administrative practices to articulate their claims. Yücel Terzibaşoğlu's research on land disputes in Western Anatolia reveals that economic and religious characteristics became components in how individuals and groups navigated disputes. 'Empty land' was conflated with uncultivated land, and productivity became tied to right to use. Thus,

Muhacir *as Failure*

aside from registering land, migrants and others asserted claims on land by working it.[79] The Greek villagers Consul Wilson described as falsifying deeds and quickly cultivating land in Sivas suggests Terzibasoglu's observations apply outside of Western Anatolia. Alongside productivity, the attachment of ethno-religious characteristics to the qualities of the ideal landholder came to the fore. As inter-communal relations worsened in the early twentieth century, when Muslim refugees disputed Christian land claims, they increasingly did so in ethno-religious terms. By the 1910s, land conflict still revolved around the issue of ownership, 'but the ethnic and religious identity of the title holder had become a criterion for the determination of the rightful owner'.[80]

Settlement and land reform contributed to the 'contested, dialectical, and social (not merely technical) processes by which explorers, surveyors, and cartographers attempted to define, codify, and naturalize space in cooperation and struggle with the people they encountered in the field'.[81] Rather than a strict enforcement of settlement or the land law, participation in and contestations over migrant placement contributed to the ordering of space. Increased demographic pressure emerging from migrant settlement increased the prevalence of land disputes. Categories used to divide the population and Ottoman territory became more socially meaningful as individuals and groups began to employ them to articulate claims.

* * *

The distance between plan and outcome is generative. In the case of migrant settlement, it contributed to the embrace of a certain mode of governance; to shared understandings of the correct relationship between people, land and property; to the disciplining of officials and development of a rational, standardised bureaucracy; and to claims of expertise. Officials, migrants, notables, consular agents and peasants amplified the distinction between policy and outcome with contestation, critique and calls for improvement. Across time, the solutions officials generated to address settlement failure left unquestioned their belief in the inherent benefit of immigration, the availability of land and the correctness of the plans underlying the project.

Organising Space

Ferik Muzaffer Pasha and Commissioner Ahmet agreed on the principles of settlement, believing in its transformative potential to reorganise space and remake the relationship between human and land in Central Anatolia.

Governing Migration in the Late Ottoman Empire

Migrant settlement was one aspect of a changing mode of Ottoman governance, the reorganisation of 'power over persons' as 'a power over space'.[82] The migrants from the Balkans brought with them a promise to introduce new modes of cultivation and new attitudes towards work, commerce and the state itself, so long as their settlement was orchestrated by expert officials. Organising space was essential in situating migrants within a 'cycle of social control' comprised of 'observation, judgement, and enforcement' that rendered individuals visible and their behaviour manipulatable.[83] The audacity of Commissioner Ahmet's visions of migrant settlement is measured not just in his promise that millions of people could settle in Ankara Province, nor only in his confident guarantee of 'easy' success in a project that had failed multiple times, but in the even more stunning assertion that the millions of people he hoped to place in the province could be managed at the level of the individual and the individual household. For Ahmet and other officials, organising the very space migrants inhabited was fundamental to the settlement project.

Ten years after Muzaffer Pasha surveyed Ankara, and eight years after Ahmet extolled the potential of his model village in Sivrihisar, Ferik Hasan Saidi Pasha, head of the Ankara Settlement Committee and, like Muzaffer Pasha, a member of the Military Inspection Commission, evaluated the progress of settlement in Sivrihisar and Haymana for Bosnian Muslim migrants who had been arriving in Ankara Province since the 1877–8 war. After surveying the area, he submitted a map, housing blueprints and a register to Yıldız Palace (Figure 4.5). The map and register detailed the varying level of completion of housing for some 6,802 individuals or 1,407 families across twenty-five neighbourhoods and villages proximate to the railroad.[84] The Pasha's report included blueprints for rural and urban houses (Figure 4.6). The design for the rural house was similar to those Commissioner Ahmet described in Sivrihisar in 1893; each structure included a main room, kitchen and stable. The design called for the rooves to be made from clay, wood or reeds, and walls were constructed from a blend of stone and sun-dried brick. 'Urban' houses, which were constructed only in one settlement to the southeast of Ankara, had space allotted for two main rooms and were made with brick rooves, sun-dried brick walls and a stone foundation.

Beyond registering individual ownership via deed, officials like Hasan Saidi Pasha constructed and arranged private and public spaces. This is not to say that migrants did not modify their homes just as they modified and expanded the fields they received, but by including a diagram of the houses alongside a register and map, the Pasha created a sense of organised placement. When officials in the provincial centre or Istanbul read

Muhacir *as Failure*

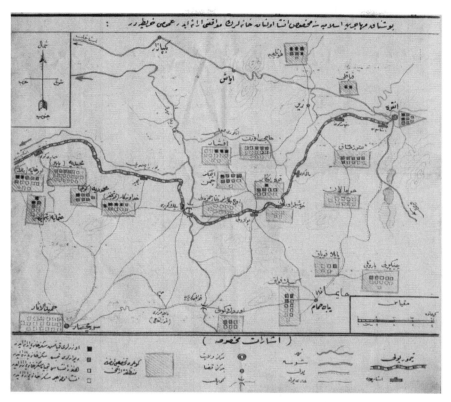

Figure 4.5 Map of immigrant housing, Ankara, 1901. Hasan Saidi Pasha's map shows the completion of migrant houses along the railway. Each small box represents eight houses. Boxes with black and grey shading indicate completed and nearly completed housing. Y.MTV 218.79.

the Pasha's report, they could not only consider the data in its raw form but also envision the physical structure of the village and each migrant's home. With the blueprint came the promise that a five-person family from Mostar or Novi Pazar would reside in their two-room house in complete loyalty to the sultan, cultivating their land with their two state-granted oxen and sufficient grain seed, rendering their sons for military service and paying taxes. The diagram, map and register also promised improvement. Hasan Saidi Pasha's emphasis on housing emerged from an ongoing problem. The Bosnian migrants sent to Ankara remained without permanent domicile for at least a year; the end of the construction season halted progress on their housing. The pasha's register recorded that failure on the part of Ankara's migrant commission but assured eventual progress through adopting standardised projects across the villages.

Governing Migration in the Late Ottoman Empire

In the railway-adjacent settlements and beyond, officials engaged with migrants and other populations within an ever-expanding project of spatial reorganisation, one that unfolded across Anatolia as a route to promote development and to ensure political stability. Following the Balkan Wars (1912–13), the Migrant Commission published blueprints establishing what migrant settlements should look like and once more distributed guidelines for founding migrant settlements to the provinces.[85] The map, the register and the plan were tools to integrate migrants into officials' vision of Anatolia and its population. Faced with the challenges of putting migrants in place, officials nevertheless moved beyond merely locating migrants within the empire to organising space at the level of the family, in ways that influenced the intimate settings of their daily lives. Reformers' belief that it was possible to achieve such a level of oversight emerged from their trust in the efficiency of standardisation and sound management. Registering, recording and designing migrant villages and houses were acts that made 'real' the planned outcomes of officials.

When Muzaffer Pasha, Commissioner Ahmet and Hasan Saidi Pasha drew and described ideal villages, they conjured the standardised, regularly distributed housing in vogue in Ottoman urban planning. Regularity in itself was a value to be lauded, such that the Migrant Commission

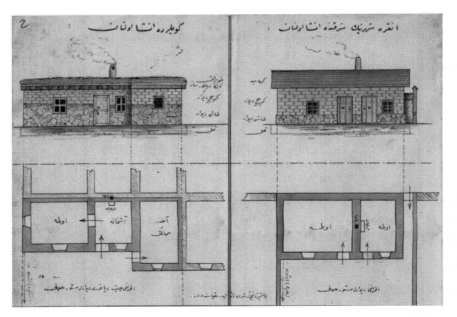

Figure 4.6 Blueprints for migrant housing, Ankara, 1901. Blueprint shows Hasan Saidi Pasha's rural (left) and urban (right) housing designs.

Muhacir *as Failure*

could advocate for migrants in Sarıyer based on the fact that their houses comported with the regularity and structural expectations of Istanbul's building codes. Concerns about contagion, fire and lawlessness led to the planning of wider streets. New sewage systems, model neighbourhoods and street lighting in Istanbul, Salonica, Izmir and elsewhere aligned with an aesthetic of the modern, civilised city.[86] Executing large-scale urban planning in Istanbul and other Ottoman city centres meant waiting on fires to clear parts of the urban fabric, but building new villages in the suburbs and the provinces allowed more freedom to envision new developments from scratch.[87]

Officials responded to the calls for efficiency with detailed maps and blueprints that attempted to match each migrant household with a house and a plot of land. Circa 1902, a village plan for Cretan migrants in Tripoli established a gridded settlement covering 56,448 square metres. The blueprint plotted 208 houses, ten shops, a mosque, a school, a police station and five wells.[88] Houses were designed to share walls in clusters of four (Figure 4.7). Planning of this kind promised efficient use of both money and space. Plans for migrant villages stemmed from reformers' visions rather than representing an existing reality, but cadastral maps from villages established following 1878 indicate at least short-term success in

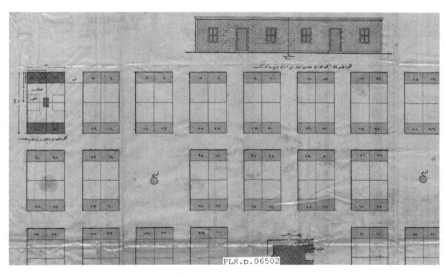

Figure 4.7 Blueprint for migrant village, Tripoli, c. 1902. Image corresponds to upper-right quadrant of a gridded plan for the entire village. Upper-left corner shows standard housing unit. Each rectangular block includes four houses. Each block of four houses is separated from the next by an eight-metre walking path. The dark square at the bottom is the mosque, located in the village's centre. PLK.P 6502.

Governing Migration in the Late Ottoman Empire

distributing regular, gridded land parcels and housing to migrants, suggesting the plans for regularity at times achieved their intended purpose.[89]

Regularity was not just an aesthetic choice driven by the beauty of straight lines or the appeal of the modern façade. Indeed, regularity and design were most important in their presumed capacity to engineer the behaviours of those who would inhabit the cheap, secure, attractive houses lining the streets of the new villages. Placing migrants conceptually made them knowable, and in turn made them objects upon which officials could act. The housing grid located migrants in space, putting each family in a numbered, standardised structure. In planning the distribution of homes, schools, mosques and police stations, migrant villages became sites to enact the spatial ordering necessary for surveillance.[90] Like the individual migrant, the family was rendered an abstraction with standardised and categorisable features.

In calling for regularity and attractiveness, however, reformers also drew upon an understanding about humans, their environments and civilisation. It was because of their greater mastery over their environments, their superior technology and their agricultural expertise that the Balkan migrants changed not only the landscape of the area around the railroad but also the social practices of those among whom they were settled. Nevertheless, migrants themselves were targets of a type of planning meant to engineer behaviour. Plans for villages told a story of how officials hoped to organise space and, in so doing, promote behaviours. Designing villages was a way to facilitate rule, to establish commercial centres, to increase state revenue and to signal the reach of Ottoman civilisation with secondary schools, hospitals, courts and administrative offices.

The grid also held officials accountable, for aside from local notables, local officials were the main perpetrator in many a report on migrant mismanagement. Regularity made visible officials' actions, requiring them to adapt standardised modes of organisation and communication. Solutions offered by Ahmet and Suleyman emphasised the importance of printing and disseminating regulations and increasing the power of documents such that officials and notables could not remove migrants after settlement. The regulation establishing the Commission for Muslim Migrants in 1897 made clear the relationship between plan, oversight and outcome.[91] The commission intended to collect 'the required drawings and plans ... so that the village streets will be regular and the installed housing will be secure, suitable, cheap, and attractive'.[92] Gridded knowledge reinforced the fiction of oversight for officials.

Muhacir *as Failure*

Conclusion

At the turn of the twentieth century, officials like Muzaffer Pasha, Commissioner Ahmet and Hasan Saidi Pasha saw in migrant settlement the opportunity to remake Anatolia, to redesign the relationship between land and people, and to shape the future of the Ottoman Empire. The settlement process was one that unfolded spatially, as officials carved up land, designated it for migrants and determined ideal distributions within and across villages. The remaking of the relationship between population and territory was one that required a series of claims to space, laden with the science of settlement and the goal of productivity. The *muhacir* in this capacity was a quantifiable abstraction, human material useful in articulating and enacting spatial claims. Muzaffer Pasha's register and Ahmet's report conceived of an interdependent relationship between environment and individual in which each reflected the other's flaws and adjusting one regulated the other. Migrant settlement was an essential tool in imagining the central state's capacity to 'landscape' the population.

This chapter has traced Ottoman officials' beliefs in the right distribution of things and the importance of sound management. Failure is one more pillar of officials' mentality. Visions of reform are laden with critique; diagnosis of failures and flaws and faith in capacity to find solutions are a part of how states shape populations and manage economies. The 'will to improve' is not separate from the identification of flaws. Indeed, reform projects 'identify deficiencies' within populations and government itself, reflecting the inevitable gap between 'what is attempted and what is accomplished'.[93] The act of governing relies on isolating and describing social problems and their solutions, while 'the "will to govern" ... [is] fueled by the constant registration of "failure", the discrepancy between ambition and outcome, and the constant injunction to do better next time'.[94] Thus, rather than external to the process of reform, failure is inherent to the project of governance, including in an Ottoman context.

Failure is thus worth investigating for what it reveals about how problems are articulated and solved, be it by officials, migrants, consular representatives or local residents. Officials approached outcomes like migrants' temporary settlement and legal contestation over land from the perspective that flaws in the system arose from human behaviour, such as corruption among officials or interference on the part of local notables. Thus, better plans, better follow-through and more thorough documentation promised to improve settlement outcomes. Despite repeated assurances about the power of the 'well-considered scheme' from Ottoman officials and European consuls, Ottoman migrant settlement was never a story of 'minimal expense and complete ease'. Nevertheless, the stability of officials' belief in plans allowed them to assert expertise, discipline other officials, cast notables as obstacles to reform and retain the right to govern.

The story of failure within Ottoman settlement is not one of administrators engaging in reform and migrants or locals resisting a modern vision for change. Officials contributed to the messy realities of settlement; plans do not always hold sway even over those who create them. Despite taking up the role of managers of people and territory, administrators were not the only participants capable of affecting change within the evolving project of developing Anatolia. The boundaries between officials and local residents or migrants were porous. As they aggregated data, surveyors remained dependent on provincial actors operating within their own matrix of interests to generate knowledge about each village and district. Migrants participated in the administration of their villages and districts, becoming intermediaries with other entities within the state apparatus and contributing to settlement decisions. They sought to regularise their status and advocated to fulfil their needs. Local residents, provincial notables and absentee landholders likewise articulated claims, employing the language of productivity, safety and stability. The development and enactment of policy in turn created ongoing displacement, intercommunal tension and, at times, chaos rather than the extension of Ottoman control.

Nonetheless, it is insufficient to leave analysis at the level of failure. Failure is generative. The distance between plan and outcome contributed to the embrace of a certain mode of governance; to shared understandings of the correct relationship between people, land and property; to the disciplining of officials and development of a (supposedly) rational, standardised bureaucracy; to claims of expertise. In assessing failures to plan, failures to conceive of major change and failures to execute, officials reinforced their claims to expertise about the science and technology of sound settlement and asserted their personal capacity to serve the state. The diagnosis and response to failure contributed to a larger process: the positioning of the state, and officials as its representatives – as outside of and acting upon society, elevated by regularity, standardisation, and the binding qualities of legal codes and documentary evidence.

The power of diagnosis and response to create new techniques of rule and to generate claims to expertise was embedded in Ottoman migration administration in the 1860s, when Nusret and Midhat Pasha met the rising cost of settlement with registers and maps intended to count, locate and categorise the *muhacir* based on their potential productivity. By 1870, migrant death, disease and departure from insalubrious environments increased the significance of ecology within officials' approach to

Muhacir *as Failure*

settlement. Faced with the uneven 'civilisation' of groups he identified within Ottoman society, Muzaffer Pasha used environmental shorthand to unlock the productive potential of migrants and other Ottoman subjects. Officials continued to develop techniques to know the population, to assert claims over space and to manipulate the behaviours of Ottoman subjects. As statesmen and administrators responded to further threats to Ottoman sovereignty, they began to apply those techniques to identify, exclude and expel those whom they thought threatened the Ottoman state. The next chapter turns to why, how and to what effect Hamidian-era officials added 'Muslim' to their vision of the ideal *muhacir*.

Notes

1. ŞD 750.14, 17 Muharrem 1306/23 September 1888.
2. Ibid.
3. DH.MKT 1814.147, 22 Recep 1308/3 March 1891; DH.MKT 1828.1115, 2 Ramazan 1308/11 April 1891.
4. DH.MKT 1876.81, 7 Rebiülevvel 1307/11 October 1891.
5. DH.MKT 1955.106, 5 Zilkade 1309/1 June 1892.
6. DH.MKT 116.43, 17 Zilhicce 1311/21 June 1894.
7. DH.MKT 772.40, 11 Recep 1321/3 October 1903.
8. Ibid.
9. Territorialisation is essential to generating legible spaces and populations. It is crucial to territoriality, that is, 'the attempt by an individual or group to affect, influence, or control people, phenomena, and relationships, by delimiting and asserting control over a geographic area'. Robert Sack, *Human Territoriality: Its Theory and History* (Cambridge: Cambridge University Press, 1986), 19.
10. Y.MTV 50.5, 4 Şevval 1308/13 May 1891.
11. İpek, *Rumeli'den Anadolu'ya*, 165.
12. Fuat Dündar, *Crime of Numbers: The Role of Statistics in the Armenian Question (1878–1918)* (New Brunswick, NJ: Transaction Publishers, 2010), 25–31.
13. Stanford Shaw, 'A Promise of Reform: Two Complimentary Documents', *IJMES* 4, no. 3 (1973): 359–65.
14. Çetinsaya, *Ottoman Administration of Iraq*, 27.
15. Murat Birdal, *The Political Economy of Ottoman Public Debt: Insolvency and European Financial Control in the Late Nineteenth Century* (London: I. B. Tauris, 2010), 92–7.
16. Stanford Shaw and Ezel Kural Shaw, *History of the Ottoman Empire and Modern Turkey*, vol. 2: *Reform Revolution, and Republic: The Rise of Modern Turkey, 1808–1875* (Cambridge: Cambridge University Press, 1977), 245.
17. Seda Tan, 'Osmanlı Devleti'nde At Yetiştiriciliği (1842–1918)' (PhD diss., Akdeniz Üniversitesi, 2015), 34–5.

Governing Migration in the Late Ottoman Empire

18. Y.A.HUS 255.64, 23 Cemaziyülahır 1309/24 January 1892. Register Transcribed in İpek, *Rümeli'den Anadolu'ya*, 165–7.
19. Alexander Schweig, 'Tracking Technology and Society along the Ottoman Anatolian Railroad, 1890–1914' (PhD diss., University of Arizona, 2019), 73.
20. Donald Quataert, 'Limited Revolution: The Impact of the Anatolian Railway on Turkish Transportation and the Provisioning of Istanbul, 1890–1908', *The Business History Review* 51, no. 2 (1977): 139–60.
21. Y.A.RES 54.15, 7 Şevval 1308/16 May 1891.
22. Y.PRK.KOM 8.14, 16 Rebiyülevvel 1309/20 October 1891.
23. I.DH 460.30579.
24. See Gratien, *Unsettled Plain*.
25. Y.PRK.OMZ 3.2, 18 Cemaziyülahır 1319/2 October 1901; DH.MKT 2587.22, 11 February 1902, in *Belgerlerinde* 1, no. 35, 194–6.
26. Y.A.RES 4.42, 12 Ramazan 1293/10 September 1879. According to the Land Code, a farm (*çiftlik*) was an area that was 'cultivated by means of a pair of bullocks', gave produce every year, and consisted 'of about 70 to 80 donums of superior, 100 donums of middling, and 130 *donum*s of inferior land'. Ongley, *Ottoman Land Code*, 68–9.
27. Y.PRK.KOM 2.13, 4 Muharrem 1297/18 December 1879.
28. Y.PRK.KOM 8.14.
29. Y.PRK.UM 27.104, 30 Zilhicce 1310/14 July 1893.
30. Y.PRK.UM 27.104.
31. For comparative approaches, see Banner, *Possessing the Pacific*; Tracey Banivanua-Mar and Penelope Edmonds, eds, *Making Settler Colonial Space: Perspectives on Race, Place, and Identity* (Basingstoke: Palgrave Macmillan, 2010); Steven Sabol, *'The Touch of Civilization': Comparing American and Russian Internal Colonization* (Boulder: University Press of Colorado, 2017).
32. Nora Barakat, 'An Empty Land? Nomads and Property Administration in Hamidian Syria' (PhD diss., University of California, Berkeley, 2015), 53.
33. Y.PRK.UM 27.104.
34. Ibid.
35. In his work history of Cukurova, Chris Gratien shows how Tanzimat reformer Ahmet Cevdet Pasha's civilising mission in Adana drew a similarly reciprocal relationship between the reform of the environment and the reform of its inhabitants. Gratien, *Unsettled Plain*, 75–83.
36. Michel Foucault, 'Governmentality', 93.
37. Stephen Astourian, 'The Silence of the Land: Agrarian Relations, Ethnicity, and Power', in *A Question of Genocide: Armenians and Turks at the End of the Ottoman Empire*, ed. Ronald Suny, Fatma Müge Göçek, and Norman Naimark (New York: Oxford University Press, 2011), 55–81.
38. I.DH 1321.39, 21 Şevval 1312/17 April 1895; I.DH 1336.29, 23 Safer 1314/3 August 1896; I.DH 1336.33, 27 Safer 1314/7 August 1896; I.DH 1356.48, 27 Rebiyülahir 1316/14 September 1898.

Muhacir *as Failure*

39. I.DH 1355.54, 10 Safer 1316/30 June 1898; I.DH 1362.33 5 Zilkade 1316; 17 March 1899; I.DH 1393.25 4 Zilkade 1319/12 February 1902; I.DH 1414.20 23 Rebiyülevvel 1321/19 June 1903; I.DH 1411.33 19 Rebiyülahir 1321/15 July 1903; I.DH 1416.26, 9 Ramazan 1321/29 November 1903; I.DH 1408.24, 24 Muharrem 1324/20 March 1906.
40. Y.A.RES 156.69, 22 Rebiyülahir 1326/24 May 1908; Y.MTV 283.46, 7 Zilhicce 1323/February 1906; I.DH 1330.45, 20 Recep 1313/January 1896.
41. I.DH 1003.79235, 26 Zilhicce 1303/25 September 1886; Y.A.RES 121.26 19 Zilhicce 1320/19 March 1903; I.DH 1298.33, 3 Rebiyülevvel 1310/ September 1892; I.DH 1300.11, December 1892; I.DH 1032.81278 7 Şaban 1304/1 May 1887; I.DH 1423.16, 9 Rebiyülahir 1322/23 June 1904.
42. I.DH 1300.11, 14 Cemaziyülevvel 1310/4 December 1892.
43. For example, the village of Akyeri retained its name after being settled and incorporated by Georgian migrants, and the village of Hayriye was named for the *kaymakam* Mamud Hayri Bey. I.DH 1044.82058, 6 Zilkade 1304/27 July 1887; I.DH 1230.96327, 21 Zilkade 1308/28 June 1891.
44. Nedim İpek, 'Göçmen Köylerine Dair', *Tarih ve Toplum* 25, no. 150 (1996): 20.
45. I.MMS 36.1481.
46. I.DH 1035.81483, 28 Ramazan 1304/20 June 1887; I.DH 1039.81719, 4 Şevval 1304/26 June 1887.
47. Musa Çadırcı, 'Türkiye'de Muhtarlık Teşkilatının Kurulması Üzerine bir İnceleme', *Belleten* 34.135 (1970): 413–14.
48. Donald Quataert, *Ottoman Manufacturing in the Age of the Industrial Revolution* (Cambridge: Cambridge University Press, 1993), 153.
49. Keun to Shipley, 20 May 1898, NA, FO 195.2019.
50. Pous, 20 November 1900, NA, FO 195.2073.
51. Pous, 9 December 1900, NA, FO 195/2073.
52. Pous, 20 November 1900, NA, FO 195/2073.
53. Pous, 9 December 1900, NA, FO 195.2073.
54. Yucel Terzibaşoğlu, 'Landlords, Nomads, and Refugees: Struggles over Land and Population Movement in North-Western Anatolia, 1877–1914' (PhD diss., University of London, 2003), 135–7.
55. Chochiev, 'XIX. Yüzyılın', 418–19.
56. I.MMS 36.1481, 12 Cemaziyülevvel 1285/31 August 1868.
57. Chochiev, 'XIX. Yüzyılın', 419.
58. I.MMS 38.1590, 26 Zilhicce 1286/29 March 1870.
59. Wilson to Layard, 12 April 1880, NA, FO 78.3129.
60. Wilson to Layard, 23 January 1880, NA, FO 78.3129.
61. Wilson to Goschen, 28 May 1880, NA, FO 78.3129.
62. Y.PRK.KOM 8.14.
63. Wilson to Layard, 23 January 1880, NA FO 78.3129.
64. Oktay Özel, 'Migration and Power Politics: The Settlement of Georgian Immigrants in Turkey (1878–1908)', *Middle Eastern Studies* 46.4 (2010): 480–2.

Governing Migration in the Late Ottoman Empire

65. Wilson to Layard, 23 January 1880, NA, FO 78.3129.
66. Wilson to Layard, 6 January 1880, NA, FO 78.3129; Wilson to Layard, 10 January 1880, NA, FO 78.3129.
67. Wilson to Layard, 23 January 1880, NA FO 78.1329.
68. Y.PRK.KOM 4.54.
69. Ibid.; Y.PRK.KOM 4.43, 7 Cemaziyülahır 1301/4 April 1884.
70. Terzibaşoğlu, 'Landlords, Nomads, and Refugees', 149.
71. David Delaney, *Territory: A Short Introduction* (Oxford: Blackwell Publishing, 2005), 11.
72. MVL 493.25, 10 Zilkade 1282/27 March 1866.
73. MVL 700.49, 24 Şevval 1281/22 March 1865.
74. BEO 1676.125669, 1 Rebiyülevvel 1319/18 June 1901.
75. DH.MKT 2705.96, 20 Zilhicce 1326/13 January 1909.
76. Ongley, *The Ottoman Land Code*, 11–12.
77. Y.PRK.ŞD 3.11, 11 Cemaziyülevvel 1305/25 January 1888.
78. Scott, *Seeing Like a State*, 24.
79. Terzibaşoğlu, 'Landlords, Nomads, and Refugees', 116.
80. Yucel Terzibaşoğlu, 'Land-Disputes and Ethno-Politics: Northwestern Anatolia, 1877–1912', in *Land Rights, Ethno-Nationality and Sovereignty in History*, ed. Stanley Engerman and Jacob Metzer (London: Routledge, 2004), 176.
81. Raymond B. Craib, *Cartographic Mexico: A History of State Fixations and Fugitive Landscapes* (Durham, NC: Duke University Press, 2004), 2.
82. Timothy Mitchell, *Rule of Experts*, 90.
83. Matthew C. Hannah, 'Space and Social Control in the Administration of the Oglala Lakota ('Sioux'), 1871–1879', *Journal of Historical Geography* 19, no. 4 (1993): 413.
84. Y.MTV 218.79, 3 Rebiyülahir 1319/20 July 1901.
85. Fuat Dündar, 'Balkan Savaşı Sonrasında Kurulmaya Çalışılan Muhacir Köyleri', *Toplumsal Tarih* 14, no. 82 (2000): 52–4.
86. Sotirios Dimitriadis, 'Transforming a Late-Ottoman Port-City: Salonica, 1876–1912', in *Well-Connected Domains: Towards an Entangled Ottoman History*, ed. Pascal Firges, Tobias P. Graf, Christian Roth, and Gülay Tulasoğlu (Leiden: Brill, 2014), 207–21; Sibel Zandi-Sayek, *Ottoman Izmir: The Rise of a Cosmopolitan Port, 1840–1880* (Minneapolis: University of Minnesota Press, 2012).
87. Zeynep Çelik, *The Remaking of Istanbul: Portrait of an Ottoman City in the Nineteenth Century* (Berkeley: University of California Press, 1986); Murat Gül and Richard Lamb, 'Mapping, Regularizing and Modernizing Ottoman Istanbul: Aspects of the Genesis of the 1839 Development Policy', *Urban History* 31, no. 3 (2004): 420–36.
88. PLK.P 6502, 1319/1901. See also İpek, 'Göçmen Köylerine Dair'; Faruk Kocacık, 'XIX. Yüzyılda Göçmen Köylerine İlişkin Bazı Yapı Planları', *Istanbul Üniversitesi Edebiyat Fakültesi Tarih Dergisi* 32 (1979): 415–26; Dündar, *İttihat ve Terakki'nin*, 201–13.

Muhacir *as Failure*

89. Wolf-Dieter Hütteroth, 'The Influence of Social Structure on Land Division and Settlement in Inner Anatolia', in *Turkey: Geographic and Social Perspectives*, ed. Peter Bendict, Erol Tümerlekin, and Fatma Mansur (Leiden: Brill, 1974), 33–5.
90. Michel Foucault, *Discipline and Punish: The Birth of the Prison*, 2nd ed., trans. Alan Sheridan (New York: Vintage, 1995), 196–8.
91. The Muhacirin Komisyon-ı Alisi was a short-lived entity. It was established in 1897, in part to manage migrants from the Ottoman-Greek War. The commission was closed in 1898.
92. Y.A.RES 90.5, 2 Recep 1315/27 November 1897.
93. Li, *The Will to Improve*, 1, 6–7. See also, Scott, *Seeing Like a State*; Miller and Rose, *Governing the Present*.
94. Nikolas Rose and Peter Miller, 'Political Power beyond the State: Problematics of Government', *The British Journal of Sociology* 43, no. 2 (1992): 190–1.

5

Muhacir as **Muslim**

In March 1904, Grand Vizier Mehmet Ferid Pasha sent a brief note to the Commission for Muslim Migrants (Muhacirin-i İslamiye Komisyonu), an entity created in 1897 to facilitate Muslim migration and settlement.[1] The grand vizier wrote in regard to some fifteen hundred families who wished to migrate from Soğutlu district in Kars, an area in Eastern Anatolia ceded after the 1877–8 Russo-Ottoman War. Ongoing conflict and territorial change meant migrants continued to arrive in the empire from the east, north and west. The fifteen hundred families from Kars were to be sent to Hüdavendigar, Konya and Adana Provinces, regions that were also sites of ongoing settlement for immigrants from Eastern Rumelia. Yet Ferid Pasha wrote not only out of concern for several thousand repatriates. By the turn of the twentieth century, Ottoman statesmen cited their fear of Armenian revolutionary ideas imported from abroad to enact policies restricting Armenian return migration from the United States.[2] In February 1904, a mere month prior to the grand vizier's note, Armenian revolutionaries staged an insurrection in Bitlis Province. Ferid Pasha had no qualms about the Muslim families from Soğutlu. However, it was known, he noted, that some Armenians changed their names and their clothing to cross into Ottoman territory. Thus, to prevent Armenian arrival and the undermining of settlement in Anatolia, a local representative of the Commission for Muslim Migrants had to verify 'with their own eyes' that the Soğutlu families and anyone else wishing to immigrate from Kars were 'truly Muslim'.[3] For the grand vizier, the border served as a site to determine who was allowed into the empire, who was to be assisted by the commission and who was to be offered land. Though brief, Ferid Pasha's note captures a reality of the Hamidian Period (1876–1908): for Ottoman statesmen, increasingly, the ideal *muhacir* was explicitly a Muslim *muhacir*.

Muhacir *as Muslim*

Changing demographic, territorial and geopolitical realities contributed to Ottoman statesmen's evolving conception of the ideal Ottoman immigrant. Some historians have cast the mass movement of Muslims into the empire as a key catalyst in a decades-long swing from the intercommunal promise of Tanzimat-era Ottomanism to narrow, religiously inflected ethno-nationalism epitomised by massacre, deportation and genocide in the empire's final years. Several decades ago, Kemal Karpat argued that Muslim migration created 'the most significant change in social identity in the last decades of the Ottoman Empire'. Migration 'not only changed the original communal Muslim identity of the migrants but also helped to politicise the identity of Muslims in the areas to which they went'. Muslim migration ultimately 'forced' Sultan Abdülhamid II to shift from promoting intercommunal Ottomanism to embracing Ottoman Islamism, an appeal to a Muslim community within and beyond the empire's borders.[4] A more indirect explanation for immigrants' role in Abdülhamid II's adoption of Ottoman Islamism merely gestures to the demographic changes brought by territorial loss and mass immigration, especially during and after the 1877–8 war.[5]

Religion was a factor in Muslim and non-Muslim migration in the nineteenth and twentieth centuries. Religious categories contributed to Muslim movement and displacement directly, as in the case of the Russian Empire's purposeful ethnic cleansing of the Caucasus in 1864, and indirectly, as in the case of exclusionary property regimes in Bulgaria and Eastern Rumelia in the 1880s.[6] The pull of an Islamic homeland in the Ottoman Empire and existing cross-border ties influenced the direction of *muhacir* paths and framed petitions they sent to the Ottoman state.[7] Nevertheless, evidence of return migration, dynamic cross-border mobility and legal forum shopping exercised by some individuals supports the notion that religious identity was neither the exclusive determinant of movement nor the overarching impetus for successful integration.[8]

This chapter analyses religion as a component of the meaning of *muhacir* within the Hamidian era's migration and settlement regimes. The Hamidian government's adoption of Ottoman Islamism led to the official promotion of Muslim immigration and influenced administrators' use of settlement as a means to increase Muslims' control over the economy. Hamidian immigration policies relied on a 'logic of facilitation' and a 'logic of constraint'.[9] While statesmen developed policies, laws and institutions intended to enable Muslim immigration, their concerns over Armenian revolutionaries contributed to their efforts to enact a stricter documentary regime at the border. Stricter border controls had repercussions for potential Muslim immigrants; without passports, they summoned border agents' fears of Armenians in disguise. In the face of such constraints, officials referenced the *hijra*, religiously obligated migration, to argue that some Muslim migrants were particularly deserving of assistance in crossing the border. Thus, as I explore below, statesmen and officials' use of the *hijra* reveals the countervailing yet entwined interests of facilitating Muslim immigration on the one hand and strengthening the mechanisms of border control on the other.

Ottomanism and Islamism at the Fin de Siècle

The tumultuous second half of the 1870s witnessed multiple turning points in the political fate of the Ottoman Empire. A list of just a few of the major events that occurred in the three-year period from 1875 to 1878 includes the empire's default on its sovereign debt in 1875, the Eastern Crisis, the 1877–8 Russo-Ottoman War, the Treaty of Berlin, an 1876 coup that dethroned Sultan Abdülaziz, the three-month reign and deposition of Murad V, Abdülhamid II's ascension to the throne, the promulgation of the Ottoman Constitution in 1876, the convening of parliament, and Abdülhamid's suspension of the parliament in 1878.

The 1877–8 war, mass migration and the territorial changes brought by the Treaty of Berlin significantly altered the demographics of the Ottoman population. As a result of the war, the Ottoman Empire ceded Kars, Batum and Ardahan to Russia. Romania, Serbia and Montenegro became independent states. The Principality of Bulgaria exercised de facto independence, and the treaty established the new autonomous province of Eastern Rumelia (Figure 5.1). The empire's proportion of Christians fell from one third to one fifth of the population, and Muslims accounted for two thirds to three quarters of the population in the late 1870s and early 1880s.[10] In the decade after the Treaty of Berlin, the Ottoman state continued to lose territory. The French invasion of Tunis in 1881 and Britain's occupation of Egypt in 1882 limited Ottoman rule in North Africa, while the unification of Bulgaria and Eastern Rumelia in 1885 and the creation of autonomous Crete in 1898 contributed to large-scale cross-border movement.

The terms of the Treaty of Berlin signalled how, in the nineteenth and early twentieth centuries, religion and ethnicity became ever more important markers of political belonging and state sovereignty. Eric Weitz describes the era as one characterised by a 'tectonic shift' in European diplomacy premised on 'an entirely new' view of 'politics focused on discrete populations and the ideal of national homogeneity'. Diplomacy encompassed not just 'territorial adjustments' but 'the handling of entire population groups categorized by ethnicity, nationality, or race, or some

Figure 5.1 Territorial changes following the Treaty of Berlin.

combination thereof'.[11] To that end, one sixth of the articles of the Treaty of Berlin addressed the rights and freedoms of minority population groups in Bulgaria, Eastern Rumelia, Serbia, Montenegro, Romania and the Ottoman Empire.[12]

Abdülhamid II and Ottoman statesmen responded to the rapid political changes of the period with new measures intended to promote internal cohesion within the empire and to achieve diplomatic power in the empire's foreign relations. In the face of demographic shifts brought about by the loss of territory in the Balkans, persistent European intervention on behalf of Ottoman non-Muslims and the competitive international arena of imperial citizenship, Abdülhamid II emphasised Islamic symbols to appeal to Muslims within and outside the empire.[13] In the era of high imperialism of 1880 to 1920, European racialisation of Muslims encouraged the emergence of a global, transnational Muslim consciousness marked by a new sense of 'the Muslim world', a new attachment to the Ottoman sultan as the caliph and a new meaning of the caliphate as a 'polity representing all Muslims'.[14] Hamidian policies are sometimes dubbed 'pan-Islamism' to reflect this global shift. Nevertheless, as Adeeb Khalid notes, 'pan-Islamism' was a term 'coined in Europe in the 1870s'. It 'conventionally carried negative connotations of regressive anti-modernism rooted in the fanaticism of Islam and its followers'.[15] In contrast to pan-Islamism, a more neutral terminology of 'Islamic Ottomanism' and 'Hamidian Islamism' avoids framing Islam as a necessarily unifying force.

Recent treatments of the Hamidian era evaluate the significance of Islamism within Hamidian domestic and international politics, recognising these as separate and at times contradictory political projects. On the domestic front, studies of Islamic Ottomanism recognise Hamidian-era policies as continuing the effort to clarify nationality within the empire and to craft a viable Ottoman nationalism. Abdülhamid intended to thwart the emergence of ethno-nationalism among the empire's Muslim communities by emphasising the caliphate, mobilising religious patronage, participating in religious festivals and improving Ottoman Muslims' economic and educational status. Despite the use of new symbols, in many ways Abdülhamid promoted the same centralising agenda embraced by Tanzimat statesmen to assert Ottoman sovereignty. The empire's 1869 Nationality Law, which asserted a secular definition of the Ottoman national, remained in force across the period and allowed for migrant naturalisation regardless of religion.[16] Internal aspects of Islamic Ottomanism reveal the extent to which sovereignty and nationality were primary in statesmen's strategic considerations.

Attention to Hamidian Islamism's trans-imperial ramifications reveals the complex challenges encountered by the Hamidian state. The sultan emphasised his 'spiritual sovereignty' over Muslim subjects of European powers, utilising a strategy akin to that of the Russian, French and British Empires' interventions on Ottoman Christians' behalf.[17] The simultaneous promotion of Ottomanism as a secular nationality project and elevation of the sultan's spiritual sovereignty over non-Ottoman Muslims revealed contradictions within Ottoman policy. For example, as Lale Can has shown, while non-Ottoman Muslims petitioned the caliph as a patron of the hajj, they were legal subjects of other states. Thus, the

Muhacir *as Muslim*

empire had to balance its role in facilitating the hajj with concerns for its lack of jurisdiction over non-Ottoman Muslims. The legal status and strategic use of nationality by such 'spiritual subjects', whose pilgrimage experiences could last for years, reveal the limitations of pan-Islamism as an analytical device to explain policies or outcomes for Muslims on the move.[18]

Pan-Islamism is likewise analytically insufficient to understand the relationship between the Hamidian state and Muslim *muhacirin*. Despite the adoption of formal elements of Islamism within Ottoman immigration and settlement policies – for instance, the creation of the Commission for Muslim Migrants – the empire prioritised its sovereignty. Another Islamic form of mobility – the *hijra*, or the religious obligation to move into Islamic territory – was, like the hajj, embedded within Hamidian-era governing practices and statesmen's concerns over subjecthood. Officials' use of the concept of the *hijra* in migration administration shows that *muhacir* subjecthood remained paramount for the sultan, statesmen and officials in the era of Ottoman Islamism.

Facilitation and Restriction in the Hamidian Migration Regime

Islamic Ottomanism found its way into the language, institutions and policies of Ottoman immigration and settlement in the years following the Treaty of Berlin. In 1884, for example, Colonel (*Miralay*) Suleyman, referenced in Chapter 4, conducted a detailed investigation of the conditions of migrant settlement in West Anatolia. In his reports, his estimates of the capacity of Ottoman territory aligned with the grandiose estimates common among settlement officials of the era. He noted that over two million immigrants had arrived in the empire, and he suggested another ten million individuals could be settled on available lands.[19] In offering the number ten million, Suleyman forecasted a 50 per cent increase in the empire's population.[20] Strikingly, rather than concerns about the potential for social upheaval accompanying a large and rapid increase in population density, Suleyman's report offered a rosy projection of potential profit from such a turn of events:

> Muslim migrants are emigrating to and taking refuge under the protection of the exalted Caliph. Accordingly, the people of Islam are drawn under the royal wings, garnering innumerable benefits for the empire within a brief period of time, such as naturally augmenting the prosperity, industry, agriculture, and trade of the imperial lands and enriching the royal army with increased revenues for the imperial treasury and a [more] abundant population.[21]

Governing Migration in the Late Ottoman Empire

At first glance, Suleyman's words are a redux of the 1857 Migrant Regulations: one more iteration of the unshakable belief that migration, and the population increase it brought, 'naturally' enriched the empire. As in 1857, more people meant more farmers, taxpayers and soldiers. Despite the familiar formula, there was a difference: the benefits immigrants offered depended on their status as Muslims. Suleyman's report tied the empire's economic future to migrants' religious identity.

Suleyman was not the only Hamidian-era official to recast the 'ideal' *muhacir* as a Muslim *muhacir*. In mid-July of 1893, Commissioner Ahmet from the Ankara Province Migrant Settlement Committee submitted a report on land availability and settlement following the extension of the Anatolian Railway from Eskişehir to Ankara the year prior (see Chapter 4). In it, the commissioner, like Suleyman, argued that migrant settlement brought progress and economic development. Ahmet estimated the population of the area was 88 per cent Muslim, yet by and large, Ahmet's descriptions of 'the people' of the province, and particularly 'the people' who benefitted from migration, exclusively referred to the Muslim population. The commissioner argued that placing migrants in the area undermined the 'Christian monopoly' on trade. According to Ahmet, Balkan Muslim migrants were more productive and efficient farmers than the peasants in the region, and so they could participate to a greater extent in local trade. Thus, migrant settlement guaranteed that Muslims benefitted from the economic development brought by the railway.[22] Though Ahmet explicitly endorsed migrant settlement to undermine Christian economic dominance, he noted that the 'people of the province' were pleased by the migrants' arrival – presumably another conflation of 'the people' with the Muslim population.[23] Reflective of a broad trend embedded in Hamidian Islamism, Ahmet's vision of social change was one premised on promoting the economic well-being of Anatolia's Muslim population.

Despite Suleyman and Ahmet's emphasis on Muslim migrants, Hamidian-era settlement policies were neither entirely new nor entirely driven by a non-Muslim vs Muslim framework. In the 1860s and 1870s, Tanzimat officials referenced the Ottoman Empire's significance as a religious refuge for Muslims, and they participated in a long history of population exchanges and colonisation for strategic purposes; 'demographic warfare' was carried out by the Ottoman and Russian Empires in Bulgaria and Bessarabia beginning by the late eighteenth century.[24] Likewise, Hamidian-era officials did not treat all Muslims as equally loyal, productive subjects. Like their Tanzimat counterparts, they continued to use Muslim migrants to colonise Muslim-majority areas and to settle frontiers, as at the turn of the twentieth century, when administrators deployed

Muhacir *as Muslim*

Muslim Cretan refugees on the coast of Libya to expand the state's reach, to develop agriculture and to provide security against local tribes, Sanusi Sufis and European imperial encroachment.[25]

Nor did Hamidian-era officials' prioritisation of Muslim migration preclude assistance for non-Muslims. The Migrant Aid Commission (Muhacirin İane Komisyonu), founded in the midst of the 1877–8 war, explicitly extended its purview to 'Muslims and Christians' fleeing conditions in the Balkans.[26] Likewise, Ottoman administrators attempted to accommodate displaced Albanian Catholics who arrived in western Kosovo at that time.[27] For the most part, the regulations establishing migration commissions, committees and governmental offices immediately after the Eastern Crisis referenced migrants' religion only obliquely, for instance by mandating the building of mosques in migrant villages.[28] Into the 1890s and 1900s, migrant commission records occasionally referenced Jewish migrants (*Musevi muhacirleri*).[29] Despite these continuities from the Tanzimat era, the same political, territorial and economic factors that encouraged Islamic Ottomanism during the Hamidian period influenced immigration policy and the official rhetoric describing migrants.

FACILITATING MUSLIM MIGRATION

Suleyman and Ahmet's reports are but two examples of how officials in the 1880s and 1890s prioritised Muslim migrants in internal memos and directives. The terms of the Treaty of Berlin contributed to a changing calculus of the ideal *muhacir*. The treaty's protection of minority rights elevated the international dimensions of the Armenian and Macedonian Questions, providing yet more proof to Ottoman statesmen of the dangers of separatism among the empire's non-Muslim subjects. Article 61 of the treaty, which encouraged the Ottoman Empire to undertake reforms in provinces inhabited by Armenians and to protect them against Kurds and Circassians, contributed to changing intercommunal relations in the six Eastern Anatolian provinces of Sivas, Van, Erzurum, Diyarbakir, Bitlis and Mamuretülaziz. The demographic justification embedded in the treaty's call for reform in the six provinces encouraged officials to use the settlement of Muslim migrants and nomadic tribes to undermine the claims of non-Muslim minorities in Eastern Anatolia and elsewhere.[30]

Dispossessing Armenian peasants in Eastern Anatolia was a means to undermine a potential Armenian nationalist base.[31] Officials' shift in language sharpened after a group of revolutionaries announced the unification of Eastern Rumelia with Bulgaria in 1885 and with the emergence of other revolutionary groups, most notably the Armenian Hnchak, founded

Governing Migration in the Late Ottoman Empire

in Geneva in 1887, the Armenian Revolutionary Federation (Dashnak/ the ARF), founded in Tiblisi in 1890, and the Internal Macedonian Revolutionary Organization, founded in Salonica in 1893. On 11 May 1895, the British, French and Russian Empires issued a joint memorandum calling for another reform project in the six vilayets. The memorandum once more prioritised demographic ratios and called for the redrawing of Ottoman internal administrative boundaries according to ethnic categories. The memorandum further demanded administrative reform, requesting that the principle of representation based on population ratios be applied to all levels of administration, from the village to the province.[32]

After 1878, the demographic and economic development of Anatolia became more important to the empire's future, given the loss of developed and densely populated districts in the Balkans. As administrators changed their calculus about who might threaten the empire's sovereignty, they tied the Muslim *muhacir* to overcoming those threats in Anatolia. Whereas Ahmet considered the benefits for Muslim economic development arising from placing Balkan Muslim migrants within a province that he estimated was already 88 per cent Muslim, Ottoman officials also adopted migrant settlement as a strategy to demographically neutralise non-Muslim populations. For example, in the village of Gemlik, near Bursa, in 1881, officials from Hüdavendigar Province noted that the Muslim population had fallen in response to the banditry and predations of the Greek population, leaving just eight to ten impoverished families. They suggested one hundred fifty orderly, 'well-mannered' migrant households should be settled in the town.[33] In 1890, on the other side of Anatolia, officials in Bitlis Province noted the primary reason for settling migrants in the district of Muş was to equalise the distribution of Christians and Muslims, as there were many more of the former.[34] Similarly, in 1891 the grand vizier observed that settling Muslims from the North Caucasus in Sivas, Samsun and Sinop had the benefit of increasing the Muslim population in those provinces.[35] That this goal remained incomplete was a subsequent point of critique, as in an 1894 memorandum reiterating the importance of increasing the Muslim population in Erzurum and Van, two of the six vilayets designated by the Treaty of Berlin, with migrants from the Caucasus.[36]

At the same time that Anatolia became increasingly vital to the empire's economic and political future, the Russian Empire's expansion in Eastern Anatolia, the local power exercised by Kurdish tribes and clans, and Armenian revolutionaries threatened Ottoman state control over the region. In 1891, Abdülhamid II created the Hamidiye Regiments, light cavalry units comprised mostly of Kurds, in order to defend the border, quell the threat of Armenian separatism and integrate Kurdish tribes

Muhacir *as Muslim*

and clans into the central state. Instead, the militias soon contributed to increased insecurity in the region by exacerbating struggles over resources and disempowering local officials.[37]

The threat of externally imposed reform, the power vacuum in Eastern Anatolia following Ottoman centralisation during the Tanzimat, the Hamidiye regiments, years of famine and conflict, and the emergence of Armenian political organisations came to a head in Anatolia in the 1890s. In 1893 and 1894, Ottoman officials cast small-scale unrest in Yozgat and Sasun as wide-scale rebellion by Armenian revolutionaries, allowing police, the army and the Hamidiye regiments to indiscriminately massacre Armenians there. Violence spread across Anatolia, to Zeytun, Trabzon, Erzurum, Arapgir, Bayburt, Bitlis, Urfa and Diyarbakir; an estimated 100,000 to 300,000 Armenians lost their lives.[38] Rumours of Armenian bids for autonomy and imposed reforms by the Great Powers underlay widespread looting and violence undertaken by Kurds, Circassians, Turks and other Muslims, in what Ronald Suny describes as an 'unbalanced, unequal, uncivil war that degenerated into indiscriminate and brutal massacres of largely unarmed, unprotected Armenians'.[39] The massacres prompted a massive transfer of land from Armenians to the Kurdish chiefs of the Hamidiye regiments.[40]

Commissioner Ahmet's promotion of Muslim migrant settlement in Ankara occurred mere weeks after the eruption of violence in Sasun. His words suggest that remaking demographic realities was as much a component of the Hamidian state-building effort as the 'exemplary repression' levied against the Armenians of Eastern Anatolia.[41] Officials like Suleyman and Ahmet believed Muslim migrants could more easily be assimilated into a productive, prosperous and stable empire. Their emphasis on crafting a productive population was decades in the making and built from settlement policies articulated in the 1850s. However, by the 1890s, religion and ethnicity were factors in their determination of how populations could serve their visions of reform.

Alignment between migrant settlement, the economic future of the empire and the specific well-being and development of its Muslim population led to the emergence of other migration institutions. Months after the Ottoman-Greek War of 1897, the Council of Ministers created a High Commission for Migrants (Muhacirin Komisyon-ı Alisi). As the Council of Ministers described the rationale and duties of the new commission, it tied the religion of the migrants to the Ottoman state's spiritual and material well-being. The new commission served as 'a means to increase, protect the preponderance of, and expand the capital and resources of the Muslim population in the empire'. In describing the commission's

Governing Migration in the Late Ottoman Empire

purview, the Council placed increasing the Muslim population alongside expanding land cultivation, advancing the state's revenues and strengthening the army.[42] That is, the demographic changes promised by the policy were as self-evidently advantageous as economic development and military security. Two years later, the Council made the connection explicit; it established the Commission for Muslim Migrants (Muhacirin-i İslamiye Komisyonu) to set aside land and to assure the welfare of Muslims arriving in the Empire.[43]

Migration regimes encompass attempts to facilitate and to limit the movement of individuals across borders (Chapter 1). The goal of encouraging Muslim immigration in the 1880s and 1890s – a facilitation that ranged from coordinating travel documents with the Russian state to the typical assistance for immigrants – emerged at the same time that the Ottoman state actively discouraged migration for some non-Muslim populations. The development of Zionism as a political movement contributed to restrictions on non-Ottoman Jewish immigration from 1880 to 1914. As Jewish refugees fled from state-initiated pogroms in Russia, some began to turn to Palestine. Abdülhamid II and Ottoman statesmen saw in Zionism and Jewish colonisation an attempt to create a state within a state. In 1881, Ottoman authorities passed legislation allowing Jewish immigration to any part of the empire aside from Palestine so long as Jewish immigrants became Ottoman subjects. The 1881 law and other legislation had a limited effect on Jewish immigration and landownership in Palestine. Indeed, Palestinians lamented that Ottoman authorities did not do more to protect them from potential displacement.[44]

In 1888, the Ottoman state banned Armenian emigration to North America. Officials, concerned that Armenian emigres imported dangerous and subversive ideas upon their return to Ottoman territory, issued a subsequent ban on Armenian return migration beginning in 1893.[45] In 1896, Ottoman law mandated that in order to travel abroad, Armenians had to renounce their nationality. This 'bureaucratic process of exclusion' included photographing and recording Armenian emigrants. The 'expatriation portraits', intended to foreclose the possibility of their return to Ottoman territory, were sent to the police, Ministry of Interior and Foreign Ministry.[46] The Ottoman state was not alone in passing legislation to curb the emigration of certain groups. The Russian Empire sporadically banned Muslim pilgrimage to the Ottoman Empire, while British administrators passed statues regulating movement into and out of Fiji nearly every year in the 1880s and 1890s.[47] As with other states, the Ottoman Empire's selection and organisation of border crossers added new significance to the categories it used to govern subjects.

Muhacir *as Muslim*

Ahmet and Suleyman believed migrant settlement contributed to the economic development of a Muslim Anatolian population in competition with Ottoman Christians. Whereas the *muhacir* of 1857 contributed to social transformation regardless of their religion, in the context of the demographic competition conjured in Ahmet and Suleyman's reports, the *muhacir*'s Muslim status was essential. The role of demographics in asserting legitimacy after the Treaty of Berlin and the 1895 reform memorandum, Ottoman subjects' calls for reform and armed action against the state, and the ongoing reality of Great Power influence contributed to Ottoman restrictions on Armenian and Jewish migration. As an ideology of internal and external cohesion, of state-building and state preservation, Ottoman Islamism influenced the parameters of social engineering during settlement and shifted the nature of officials' ideal Ottoman subject. Nevertheless, as discussed below, facilitating Muslim migration did not undermine the goal of ensuring all who settled in Ottoman domains were unambiguously Ottoman subjects.

HIJRA: THE OBLIGATION TO MIGRATE

Migration regimes and border policies create distinctions within migrant populations: distinctions between those who sojourn and those who intend to stay long term; between documented and undocumented immigrants; between desirable populations and undesirable ones; between deserving and undeserving migrants; and, relatedly, between those who conjure a sense of moral obligation among host communities (e.g. refugees/forced migrants) and those who do not (e.g. economic/labour migrants). Hamidian Islamism contributed to the contours of those border-based distinctions in the Ottoman Empire. The Commission for Muslim Migrants and its settlement policies became a route to ensure Muslims prevailed in the demographic and economic competition for Anatolia. Despite facilitating Muslim immigration, the Ottoman state also distinguished among Muslim border-crossers, particularly in terms of those who intended to stay permanently and those who arrived as sojourners, such as hajj pilgrims.

As officials weighed who to welcome to the Ottoman state, the *hijra* became a component in how they distinguished among potential Muslim immigrants. Officials questioned whether Muslims living subject to non-Islamic governments were religiously obligated to migrate, for if they were, the Ottoman sultan as caliph had a responsibility to provide them refuge. Nevertheless, the *hijra* did not undermine the development of Ottoman border control. Indeed, rather than external or contrary to the consolidation of Ottoman migration management, the question of the *hijra*

Governing Migration in the Late Ottoman Empire

was one more facet in its development. Bringing the *hijra* directly into the question of which Muslims the state was obligated to welcome reinforced the principle that the Ottoman state had the right and capacity to deny entry to others.

The conditions under which *hijra* becomes a religious obligation have remained a persistent question among Islamic jurists since Islam's first centuries. The duty of the *hijra* emerges from the migration (*hijra*) of Muhammad and his followers from Mecca to Medina in the year 622. Those who accompanied the prophet became known as the *muhajirun*, a title reflecting the permanence of their move, their abandonment of property and connections in order to follow Islam, and the new community they formed with the inhabitants of Medina (*ansar*). Though the term *hijra* does not appear in the Quran, within accounts of the Prophet Muhammad's life (*hadith*) the meaning of the *hijra* occurs as a 'physical movement away from unbelief' and 'towards self-definition in the nascent Muslim community'.[48] Jurists consider the necessity of the *hijra* in light of the designation of territory as, variously *dar al-Islam* (territory of Islam), *dar al-ahd* (territory of treaty) and *dar al-harb* (territory of war), the last of which may necessitate *hijra*. In their categorisations of territory and evaluation of the obligation to migrate, jurists consider Muslims' relationship to governance, the legal systems in a particular territory, personal and communal security, and freedom to practise religion.

In the nineteenth and twentieth centuries, these evaluations shifted. Ottoman territorial loss and European colonial rule created large populations of Muslims inhabiting territories less easily designated as *dar al-Islam*. Jurists, community leaders and individual Muslims had to reconcile religious practice with territorial and political change brought by European colonisation and the emergence of the modern state system. Had their homelands become *dar al-harb*? Could they continue to practise their religion? Could they do so while adhering to the laws of a non-Muslim polity or serving in its army? To what extent could or should they identify with a non-Muslim sovereign or national identity?[49] In short, were they religiously obligated to emigrate?

Investigating the role of *hijra* as a factor causing migration requires that historians balance cognisance of faith as an element in the lives of pious Muslims with an awareness that colonial administrators interpreted the *hijra* as one more element of 'Muslim fanaticism'.[50] Brian Glyn Williams's work on the Crimean Tatars is instructive. In the nineteenth century, Tsarist Russian administrators portrayed the Crimean Tatar peasantry as easily swayed by calls for migration. Some Crimean Tatars believed that Russian expansion converted the Crimean Peninsula

Muhacir *as Muslim*

to *dar al-harb*. For village leaders (*mullahs*) in support of the *hijra*, the Ottoman Empire offered refuge as *dar al-Islam*.

Nevertheless, Williams emphasises that Crimean Tatar emigration was equally an outcome of land dispossession and displacement throughout the eighteenth and nineteenth centuries. In the late 1850s and 1860s, Crimean Tatar peasants described the cruelty of Tatar and Russian landowners. Some Tsarist officials directly encouraged Tatars to flee in 1860, only to then discourage their emigration when faced with the economic devastation caused by the peasantry's exodus.[51] Williams concludes that the *hijra* of the Crimean Tatars 'combined both the hope of preserving their community's religious identity and finding salvation in socio-economic terms in the *ak toprak* – the white lands of the sultan'.[52] In the wake of the 1860 exodus, Russian officials instituted a measure to prevent Tatar emigration: Muslims had to obtain a foreign travel passport, oftentimes at great expense and personal difficulty.[53]

Some individuals and communities embraced the *hijra* as necessary to religious practice and as a result of trauma stemming from war, persecution, upheaval and changing borders. Nonetheless, discussion of the *hijra* extended beyond matters of personal belief or communal practice, and Muslims were not the only ones who discussed its implications. For modernising empires, the changing calculus of who was an insider and who was an outsider was tempered by other aspects of statecraft: the imperial competition for population and legitimacy drawn from civilised treatment of minority groups.[54] For officials in Russia and in new political entities created by the Treaty of Berlin, the benefit of having a population at all outweighed the need for that population to be religiously or ethnically homogenous. Officials in areas that initially encouraged Muslim displacement in the wake of the 1877–8 war, such as Serbia, Bulgaria and Eastern Rumelia, eventually wielded the concept of the *hijra* to discourage the mass departure of Muslim populations.[55]

Other colonial enterprises similarly relied on local spiritual authorities to stem emigration. British and French administrators sought and received legal opinions from *muftis* in Mecca discouraging armed resistance and migration from India and Algeria.[56] Similarly, in the Caucasus, Volga Region and Crimea, Tsarist officials called upon the leaders of the Russian Empire's Muslim Spiritual Assemblies to discourage emigration in the 1880s and 1890s. These legal experts emphasised that Muslims in Russia were free to practise their religion and faced no danger of conversion.[57]

In the late nineteenth century, Muslim reformers seeking to strengthen Muslim communities changed their views of the relationship between Muslim communities and their homelands. At times they advocated accommodation with new governments in order to preserve the culture and coherence of the community. When the Treaty of Berlin allowed for the Austro-Hungarian occupation of Bosnia, some members of the Bosnian *ulema* cast *hijra* to the Ottoman Empire as religious duty. Others argued that large-scale emigration destroyed the Bosnian community. In 1882, the *mufti* Mehmed Teufik Azab Azapagic published an anti-*hijra* treatise. The *mufti* opined that Bosnian Muslims could freely and publicly observe Islamic rites and practices despite Austro-Hungarian occupation, and he cautioned that the *hijra* further weakened the Muslim community. Azapagic's views aligned with the Austro-Hungarian government's desire to stem Muslim out-migration, and the *mufti* eventually occupied the top position in Bosnian religious hierarchy.[58]

The *hijra* featured in political discussions among Crimean Tatars as well. The well-known Crimean Tatar reformer Ismail Gasprinskii advocated for cultural reform among Tatars and all Russian Turkic Muslims. He encouraged some borrowing and adaptation of Russian language and culture and endorsed educational reform, notably by establishing 'new method' (*Usul-i Jadid*) schools in the Crimean Peninsula. For Gasprinskii, whereas a new style of education strengthened the community, emigration further weakened it. The *hijra* was a symptom of the conservative Islam he sought to overcome. Gasprinskii edited the Tatar/Russian newspaper *Tercüman* (Translator), and he penned an anti-emigration article in 1883 in the newspaper's first year of publication.[59] In 1890, he addressed the issue again, writing, 'what need do you have to leave Russia? Nobody prevents us from confessing our religion. Our religious practices are not constrained.'[60] Gasprinksii and others discouraging *hijra* balanced their appeal to religious freedom with a plea that deprioritised the *dar al-harb/ dar al-Islam* divide. Among the Tatar intelligentsia, the turn of the twentieth century marked a new embrace of the community's territorial tie to the peninsula, which precluded the *hijra* in favour of retainment of the homeland (*vatan*).[61]

Like Azapagic and Gasprinksii, when Ottoman officials evaluated the question of the *hijra*, they did so not just in terms of religious expression but also in terms of the benefit migration offered to a wider Muslim community. In the aftermath of Bulgaria's annexation of Eastern Rumelia, an 'initial rush' of emigrants to Istanbul led Yildiz Palace to call for quick resettlement of the newcomers.[62] In 1887, the grand vizier and the Council of Ministers recommended establishing another migration commission under the purview of the Sultan to 'facilitate the emigration and settlement of Muslims from Bulgaria and Eastern Rumelia'. Before enumerating the personnel, channels of communication and other prosaic facets of the new

Muhacir *as Muslim*

commission, the council set forth its justification for the new institution – that the potential migrants felt a religious obligation to leave their homes in the Balkans, and that the Ottoman state, in turn, had a religious obligation to welcome them. The council wrote,

> The Muslims of Bulgaria and Eastern Rumelia can no longer endure the oppression and aggression they have experienced of late. They petition continuously for permission to migrate to the empire. Though their lives and property are protected [in the region], since they declare that it is absolutely impossible to meet the requirements of Islam under a Bulgarian government, it is a sacred duty to carefully regard their statements.

As they established the commission, the council weighed whether the 700,000 Muslims of Bulgaria and Eastern Rumelia were religiously required to flee from lands now ruled by non-Islamic governments and laws. Influenced by the reports from the Superintendent of Muslims in Eastern Rumelia and the endorsement of the Şeyhülislam, the council concluded that they were. If they stayed, the 'courageous' Muslims of the Balkans would be 'destroyed and annihilated'.[63]

While Azapagic considered the benefits and detriments of the *hijra* with reference to the fate of Bosnian Muslims, the Ottoman Council of Ministers did so with reference to the preservation of the empire. Prior to creating the commission, members of the upper echelons of the Ottoman state met thirty-nine times to debate whether it was more advantageous to maintain the Muslim population in Bulgaria and Eastern Rumelia or to have them settle in Anatolia.[64] If it were the former, then the correct course of action for the Ottoman state was to discourage or even forbid (*men' etmek*) their emigration; however, the memorandum concluded, emigration was more beneficial. Perhaps the destruction and annihilation of an estimated 700,000 individuals was in itself compelling to members of the council, but so too was the strategic advantage attached to the mass movement. The departure of that many Muslims promised to severely undermine the economies of Bulgaria and Eastern Rumelia and to increase the revenue and population of Anatolia. Thus, the council concluded, every step should be taken to facilitate the Balkan Muslims' arrival and successful settlement.[65] The sultan's sacred duty as Caliph aligned with the empire's geopolitical interests.

THE LIMITS OF THE *HIJRA*

How salient was religion and religious obligation in the council's assessment of the issue? By 1887, there may have been a certain conceptual redundancy in the label of 'Muslim *muhacir*'. Many, though not all, of the empire's immigrants since the 1850s had been Muslim. Nevertheless, by evaluating the Balkan Muslims in terms of their strategic value as a population, the council signalled that though being Muslim was necessary to be an ideal *muhacir*, it was not sufficient. Facilitating Muslim migration was one strategy among many as Ottoman officials sought to strengthen the empire, preserve its sovereignty, and develop its economy. A mini-exodus from the Crimean Peninsula in 1901–2 reveals that, despite the creation of the Commission for Muslim Migrants a few years prior, migration was subsumed within larger concerns about border control, security and subjecthood.

Historians have not traced the start of Tatar emigration in 1901 to a specific event or single cause. While Brian Glyn Williams notes the 'perennial' issue of land ownership as a factor, Crimean Tatars may have also been alarmed by the Russian Interior Ministry's announcement of a ban on the hajj each year from 1897 to 1900.[66] Additionally, changes to Russian military policies bred discontent. Crimean Tatars, along with other Muslims in the Volga-Ural region, had been subject to universal conscription and served in mixed-confession regiments since 1874. The Russian Army observed Muslim religious holidays and installed Muslim chaplains, a policy it abandoned in 1896. Tatars resented this change, as indicated by petitions they sent during the Russian Revolution of 1905, which 'often mentioned' military service and the need to reinstate the former religious accommodations.[67] Aside from these general grievances, Williams notes that at least one individual, a Sheikh Haci Bekir Effendi from Bahcesaray, encouraged the *hijra*.

Though the precise cause of the 1902 emigration is unknown, the Russian state's response is not. Concerned about the possibility of a substantial emigration, Tsarist officials once more sought to prevent the departure of too many Crimean Tatar peasants. The governor of the province asked Ismail Gasprinskii to publish a statement warning Tatars not to sell off their property until they had received permission to emigrate. Gasprinskii obliged by publishing a series of articles in *Tercüman*. He noted that those choosing to depart had no reason to do so. Emigration promised only suffering and poverty, as many who had travelled previously to the Ottoman Empire endured illness and ruin. Seyit Abdullah Ozenbashli, a friend of Gasprinskii and a fellow contributor to *Tercüman*, published an article arguing that emigration was 'not courageous'. It was 'without merit' and 'opposed to religious creed'. In contrast to Tatars' religious ties to the Ottoman Empire, Ozenbashli tied Tatars to their homeland in the peninsula. Those who left the Crimean homeland, he argued, betrayed their nation (*millet*).[68]

Muhacir *as Muslim*

In contrast to Gasprinskii and Ozenbashli's stance, the Ottoman consul in Akmescit/Simferopol endorsed the necessity of the *hijra*. He wrote to the Foreign Ministry in June of 1902 to advocate on behalf of Crimean Tatars seeking permission to immigrate. According to the consul, their religious obligation to move stemmed from the conditions of army service. Due to the 1896 policy changes, Tatars could no longer serve in the army and practise Islam. Rather than posts in Crimea or Bessarabia, Tatar soldiers were transferred to the interior of Russia, Siberia and Manchuria. They were sent there without imams, muezzins or Muslim cooks. Thus, they were forced to eat pork and other non-Halal meat, and, if they died, an Orthodox priest conducted their funereal rites. The consul concluded that 150,000 Crimean Tatars should be allowed to enter the Ottoman Empire. In response to the consul's statement, the grand vizier agreed that the Tatars were allowed to immigrate, so long as they renounced Russian subjecthood and never returned to the Crimea.[69]

Whereas the consul's appeal and the grand vizier's response seem a straightforward enactment of the rationale for the Commission for Muslim Migrants, the consul's claim of the applicability of the *hijra* emerged because the Ottoman state had closed other paths to Crimean Tatar entry. In December of 1901, the Council of Ministers called for clarification on how the empire could respond to the number of Russian immigrants from Dagestan and elsewhere who arrived without passports. The council noted that such migrations posed multiple issues. First, immigrants' arrival 'of their own accord' or without papers was unacceptable and unlawful, because migration was to be controlled by the states. That is, before an individual migrated from one country to another, the 'two countries' had to agree upon the terms of that migration. Second, irregular migration prevented the Ottoman state from organising settlement, which contributed to migrant suffering, undermined stability in crucial provinces such as Erzurum and depleted the state's funds. Third, since the immigrants did not formally renounce their ties to the Russian state, they could invoke Russian subjecthood long after their arrival and settlement. Finally, individuals who arrived without passports or visas might be Armenians posing as Muslims in order to gain entry.[70]

Following the Council of Minister's call, early in 1902, three lawyers in the Foreign Ministry's Office of Legal Counsel drafted legislation to clarify entry conditions for migrant settlers. The 1857 Migrant Regulations, discussed in Chapter 1, served as the only relevant law governing *muhacir* entry, and the office's attorneys noted that the previous law no longer met the empire's needs. Whereas the Tanzimat Council had issued the 1857 regulations in order to draw Europeans to the empire, the Hamidian

193

Governing Migration in the Late Ottoman Empire

state only accepted Muslim migrants. Furthermore, rather than following the application protocol set forth fifty-five years earlier, current migrants arrived 'suddenly and without notice'. Thus, the office drafted new regulations articulating the steps for preparing and processing *muhacir* applications.

The new regulations, finalised in the spring of 1902, reflected the state's changing expectations of the *muhacir* and its formal shift away from a law originally 'intended for non-Muslims'. Article Three of the 1857 *Muhacirin Nizamnamesi* evoked the 1856 Reform Edict by promising colonists freedom of religious practice and the right to construct houses of worship. In 1902, the Office of Legal Counsel deemed Article Three 'superfluous' and excised it. Further, the office's attorneys did away with the 1857 regulation's capital requirement. Unlike the Tanzimat Council, which had envisioned self-sufficient colonists, the Hamidian state accepted its role in providing long-term assistance to newcomers. To that end, and in keeping with decades of practice, the 1902 law retained migrants' period of tax and military exemptions and required settlers to fulfil a twenty-year term on their allocated land.

The 1902 regulations added identity documents to various stages of the immigration process. According to the new regulation, migrants were to identify themselves and submit paperwork to an Ottoman consular representative in their home countries six months in advance of their anticipated arrival. Consuls were responsible for verifying that applicants were of good moral quality and that the applicants planned to renounce their nationality. Foreign ambassadors in Istanbul were to coordinate with Ottoman officials. As soon as migrants arrived at Istanbul or another port of entry, they surrendered their foreign passports to the relevant embassy and received Ottoman identity documents. If migrants came from places that had no formal diplomatic ties with the Ottoman state, such as China, Afghanistan, Baluchistan or Morocco, then the Migrant Commission had to thoroughly investigate their status.[71] Implicitly, aside from those exceptions, those without formal paperwork or permission from their sending state were denied entry.

Thus, at the same moment that the Ottoman state drafted regulations to deny entry to migrants who did not have formal documentation, Tsarist officials sought to prevent Crimean Tatar emigration by refusing to grant Tatars exit visas. Indeed, rather than reflecting the Ottoman state's categorical facilitation of Muslim migration, the consul's comments on the relevance of the *hijra* reflected the effective closure of Ottoman borders to Crimean Tatars. Despite the grand vizier's decision to allow Crimean Tatar immigration, the state seems to have quickly backtracked. In 1903,

Muhacir *as Muslim*

the grand vizier reminded the Foreign Ministry and the consul in Akmescit that Russian Muslims could not be given permission to immigrate or receive *muhacir* status prior to renouncing their Russian subjecthood.[72] The denial of entry and settlement for undocumented Muslim migrants was never uniformly applied, but migrants from Russia could be turned away if they arrived without permission (*rühsatsız*). Others without passports awaited the results of investigations into their subjecthood as 'guests' (*misafir*) rather than as *muhacirin*.[73] Perhaps due to the myriad legal obstacles or perhaps due to the success of Gasprinskii's anti-*hijra* advocacy, the 1901–2 migration never amounted to more than a few thousand people, and of those who emigrated, many returned to the Crimean Peninsula after the 1908 Constitutional Revolution.[74]

THE INTERSECTION OF OBLIGATION AND ADVANTAGE

The question of the empire's responsibilities towards potential refugees was filtered through geopolitical concerns. Abdülhamid II sought to maintain and increase Ottoman sovereignty over all Ottoman subjects. For this reason, he endorsed a system of international law and norms that supported the empire's claims over its own non-Muslim subjects. The Sultan asserted that Muslims could live peacefully under non-Muslim rule so long as their religion was respected. He instructed Indonesian Muslims to be loyal to the Dutch Queen Wilhelmina, and he encouraged Muslims in the Philippines not to revolt against newly established American colonial rule in 1898. Encouraging the loyalty of colonised Muslims to European rulers promoted the Ottoman Empire as a partner to other European states and supported the concomitant right of the Ottoman state to rule over its non-Muslim subjects.[75]

In terms of Ottoman sovereignty, the most important attributes of the *muhacir* remained their adoption of Ottoman subjecthood and their permanent settlement in the empire. Facilitating some Muslim migration did not preclude increased attempts to ensure the identity of border-crossers. Muslim immigration, even from traditional 'sending areas' like the Caucasus, was not a free for all. The brief note from the grand vizier that started this chapter suggests that prioritising Muslim migration could necessitate extending greater oversight to those who petitioned for arrival. As the Ottoman state attempted to limit Armenian migration – especially of potential revolutionaries from across the Russian border – Ottoman consuls, the Commission for Muslim Migrants and the Police Ministry were tasked with taking every precaution to clarify the identity of those who sought to enter Ottoman territory.[76] Whereas the grand vizier emphasised checking that the migrants from Kars were Muslims, the more typical assessments and investigations carried out by Ottoman consuls and the police focused on the question of subjecthood. The state flexed its regulatory muscle to determine that migrants changed subjecthood, lending as much weight to the question of whether migrants had cut ties to their former homelands as to their religious identity.

In migration regimes, categories of desirable and undesirable emerge alongside questions of obligatory and non-obligatory migration. Migration causes and their meaning for state's engagement with immigrants are embedded in and occur alongside the development of border control. For example, the Aliens Act of 1905, the first law to define and restrict unwanted immigration to Britain, was also the first law to establish moral and legal criteria for claiming asylum.[77] The conceptual and legal separation of refugees from immigrants is an inherent characteristic of the modern international refugee regime, but the two categories remain interrelated: states maintain this conceptual separation to restrict the entry of some immigrants by privileging the rights of others. In doing so, they establish their prerogative to exercise control over the border and to reinforce their capacity to determine the basis of legal belonging and citizenship.

The Hamidian-era immigration regime did not formally or legally distinguish among forcibly displaced populations and 'voluntary' *muhacirin*, but religious obligation contributed to the enactment of a border regime through an analogous gesture of separation. Embedded in the justification of the *hijra* were implicit limits on the state's duty to welcome all Muslims. For Ottoman officials, Muslims from the Caucasus, Crimea or Balkans were not inherently forced to migrate just because they lived under non-Ottoman/non-Islamic governments. The limits of the *hijra* are one more signal of how sovereignty, subjecthood and legal jurisdiction remained primary concerns in the Hamidian-era border regime.[78]

The Ottoman state was not unique in crafting laws to restrict movement or police borders, but it was unique in doing so as an Islamic Empire that claimed spiritual sovereignty over a global Muslim population. The Commission for Muslim Migrants' mission influenced officials' emphasis on migrants' religious status; documents repeatedly referred to 'Muslim people' when discussing financial issues or the need to finalise migrant settlement.[79] Nevertheless, anti-*hijra* positions persisted within the Ottoman state, as, for example, administrators grew concerned that the departure of the Muslim population in Bulgaria and Eastern Rumelia reduced Ottoman political sway there.[80] As Lale Can argues, though religion may have been essential to migrants and to Ottoman officials, 'pan-Islamic unity was an aspiration, not a model or paradigm for historical analysis of how

Muhacir *as Muslim*

states or people behaved'.[81] A series of considerations – the nature of the caliphate, sovereignty and subjecthood – contributed to the exclusions and inclusions statesmen identified and officials enacted in the Ottoman migration regime. Though religion became a component in defining the ideal Ottoman subject and thus the ideal *muhacir*, the empire did not abandon its interest in evaluating potential settlers. Officials' elevation of the *hijra* reflects both the significance and the limits of Ottoman Islamism in explaining Ottoman immigration policies.

Conclusion

The Ottoman history of border regulation, though tied to its specific history as a land-based, multi-religious Islamic empire in the nineteenth century, fits a global pattern. The 1860s–1880s were an era of 'limited border controls', but these decades also saw institutional consolidation and a new acceptance of states' right to exercise sovereignty through controlling immigration.[82] In the 1880s, at the same moment that the Ottoman state began facilitating and restricting mobility with reference to religion, states like the United States and Canada issued immigration restrictions based on race, ethnicity and profession. These restrictions gave rise to new modes of identity creation and made borders newly meaningful, not least for those excluded from entry. Globally, border regulations following the 1880s sought to generate individuals with standardised, categorisable and bureaucratically retrievable identities.[83] Requiring individuals or individual families to petition for entry into Ottoman territory likewise elevated the central state as the mediator of movement.

As Hamidian-era officials envisioned the ideal *muhacir*, the question of religiously motivated movement featured in the depiction of the state's responsibility towards potential Muslim migrants. 'Gardening' states classify and categorise their populations, and the labels states use produce knowledge about the population. Labels that are invested with material and political meaning contribute to transforming the population. Migrants and the state officials advocating on their behalf at times underlined the *muhacir*'s unique history of being forced from one's homeland to seek refuge in the empire as Muslims. For example, in 1887, the governor of Hüdavendigar sent a general description of migrant conditions in the district of Adapazarı. He summarised the perspectives of the Abkhaz, Circassian and Rumelian migrant leaders, noting they had all sought the protection of the Sultan after migrating from their homelands. Though they were settled and received housing, they were deprived of a mosque for their prayers and a school for their children's education, leaving their people in

Governing Migration in the Late Ottoman Empire

a state of 'ignorance and misery'.[84] By juxtaposing the ongoing injustice of migrants' spiritual deprivation with their gratitude for the Sultan's previous religious protection, the governor highlighted the sultan's responsibility for the material and spiritual well-being of the *muhacir*.[85]

The meaning of *muhacir* retained, across several periods of late Ottoman history, its importance as a population category tied to subjecthood and productivity, yet changes in statesmen's rationale of who was the ideal Ottoman subject created different assimilative policies and possibilities within Ottoman social engineering. In the Hamidian era, Ottoman Islamism promoted the facilitation of Muslim immigration. Nonetheless, the Hamidian state retained its prioritisation of migrant subjecthood and state sovereignty, and thus new border regulations and an extended documentary regime elevated the *hijra* as a component in evaluating who deserved to be a *muhacir*. As I show in the next chapter, migrants themselves engaged with the concept of the *hijra* and their experiences of displacement. During the first years of the Young Turk period, one group of migrants did so to consider their future in post-revolutionary Ottoman society. In the same moment, Ottoman politicians likewise embraced the *muhacir*'s possibilities for positive change, yet as they sought to reverse trends begun by the *ancien régime*, they debated the meaning of the *muhacir* to consider whether the revolutionary-era government sufficiently embraced or betrayed the principles of Ottomanism.

Notes

1. The Commission for Muslim Migrants (Muhacirin-i İslamiye Komisyonu) was also referred to as the High Commission for Muslim Migrants (Muhacirin-ı İslamiye Komisyon-ı Alisi).
2. Gutman, *Politics of Armenian Migration*.
3. DH.MHC 61.6, 7 Muharrem 1322/24 March 1904.
4. Kemal Karpat, 'The *Hijra* from Russia and the Balkans: The Process of Self-definition in the Late Ottoman State', in *Muslim Travellers: Pilgrimage, Migration, and the Religious Imagination*, ed. Dale F. Eickelman and James Piscatori (Los Angeles: University of California Press, 1990), 131–2, 138.
5. M. Şükrü Hanioğlu, *A Brief History of the Late Ottoman Empire* (Princeton, NJ: Princeton University Press, 2008), 130.
6. Anna Mirkova, *Muslim Land: Christian Labor: Transforming Ottoman Imperial Subjects into Bulgarian National Citizens, c. 1878–1939* (New York: Central European University Press, 2017).
7. Kemal Karpat, 'The Status of the Muslim under European Rule: The Eviction and Settlement of the Cerkes', *Journal of Muslim Minority Affairs* 1, no. 2 (1979): 7–27; Williams, 'Hijra and Forced Migration', 79–108.

Muhacir *as Muslim*

8. Meyer, *Turks across Empires*, 21–47.
9. Mongia, *Indian Migration and Empire*.
10. Hanioğlu, *A Brief History*, 130.
11. Eric D. Weitz, 'From the Vienna to the Paris System: International Politics and the Entangled Histories of Human Rights, Forced Deportations, and Civilizing Missions', *The American Historical Review* 113, no. 5 (2008): 1313, 1314.
12. Methodieva, *Between Empire and Nation*, 30–1.
13. Kemal Karpat, *The Politicization of Islam: Reconstructing Identity, State, Faith and Community in the Late Ottoman Empire* (Oxford: Oxford University Press, 2001), 223–40.
14. Cemil Aydın, *The Idea of the Muslim World: A Global Intellectual History* (Cambridge, MA: Harvard University Press, 2017), 67.
15. Adeeb Khalid, 'Pan-Islamism in Practice: The Rhetoric of Muslim Unity and Its Uses', in *Late Ottoman Society: The Intellectual Legacy*, ed. Elisabeth Özdalga (London: Routledge, 2005), 201.
16. Ebru Akcasu, 'Migrants to Citizens: An Evaluation of the Expansionist Features of Hamidian Ottomanism, 1876–1909', *Die Welt des Islams* 56, no. 3/4 (2015): 395.
17. Aydin, *Idea of the Muslim World*, 91.
18. Can, *Spiritual Subjects*.
19. Y.PRK.KOM 4.54, 15 Teşrinisani 1300/27 November 1884.
20. See Karpat, *Ottoman Population*, 151. According to the 1881/82–93 Census, the population of the Balkans, Anatolia, Syria, and Iraq was roughly twenty million. The population of the entire empire, including its special administrative and autonomous areas, was in the neighbourhood of forty million.
21. Y.PRK.KOM 4.54.
22. Y.PRK.UM 27.104, 30 Zilhicce 1310/15 June 1893.
23. Ibid.
24. Pinson, 'Demographic Warfare', and Cuthell, 'Muhacirin Komisyonu'.
25. Fredrick Walter Lorenz, 'The "Second Egypt": Cretan Refugees, Agricultural Development, and Frontier Expansion in Ottoman Cyrenaica, 1897–1904', *IJMES* 53, no. 1 (2021): 89–105.
26. I.DH 751.61326, 17 Recep 1294/28 July 1877
27. Blumi, *Ottoman Refugees*, 51.
28. Y.PRK.DH 2.93, 1889, in *Belgelerinde* 1, no. 28, 148–70. This is a reprint of the 1879 regulations.
29. DH.MHC 13.1, 8 Muharrem 1310/2 August 1892; DH.MHC 24.91 25 Şevval 1317, 26 February 1900. During World War I a brief memorandum from the Interior Minister noted that Jewish migrants from 'lost territories' could be registered in the same way as Muslim migrants. DH.MHC 76.49, 26 Mayıs 1331/8 June 1915.
30. Dündar, *Crime of Numbers*, 25–31.
31. Astourian, 'The Silence of the Land', 65.

Governing Migration in the Late Ottoman Empire

32. Dündar, *Crime of Numbers*, 36–7.
33. I.DH 876.69927, 29 Rebiyülevvel 1300/7 February 1883. See also İpek, *Rumeli'den Anadolu'ya*, 158.
34. I.DH 1185.92756, 4 Zilkade 1307/22 June 1890.
35. DH.MKT 1920.106, 21 November 1891, in *Belgelerinde* 1, no. 104, 470–3.
36. Y.A.HUS 314.14, 2 Cemaziyülahır 1312/1 August 1894.
37. See Klein, *Margins of Empire*.
38. Ronald Suny, *They Can Live in the Desert but Nowhere Else* (Princeton, NJ: Princeton University Press, 2015), 113–29.
39. Ibid., 123.
40. Astourian, 'Silence of the Land', 62–5; Klein, *Margins of Empire*, 143–5. Klein notes Hamidiye regiments and chiefs also dispossessed many Muslim and Kurdish villagers throughout the region during the same era.
41. Suny, *They Can Live in the Desert*, 131.
42. Y.A.RES 90.5, 2 Recep 1315/27 November 1897.
43. Y.A.RES 98.29, 11 Şevval 1316/22 February 1899.
44. Louis A. Fishman, *Jews and Palestinians in the Late Ottoman Era, 1908–1914: Claiming the Homeland* (Edinburgh: Edinburgh University Press, 2020); Mim Kemal Öke, 'The Ottoman Empire, Zionism, and the Question of Palestine (1880–1908)', *IJMES* 14, no. 3 (1982): 329–41.
45. See Gutman, *Politics of Armenian Migration*.
46. Zeynep Devrim Gürsel, 'Classifying the Cartozians: Rethinking the Politics of Visibility Alongside Ottoman Subjecthood and American Citizenship', *photographies* 15, no. 3 (2022): 353.
47. Bashford, 'Immigration Restriction', 37.
48. *Hijra* in its verbal noun form does not occur in the Quran, though related parts of speech from the same Arabic root (*hajara, muhajir, hajaru*) do. Muhammad Khalid Masud, 'The Obligation to Migrate: The Doctrine of *Hijra* in Islamic Law', in *Muslim Travellers*, 29; 32.
49. See Sarah Albrecht, *Dar al-Islam Revisited: Territoriality in Contemporary Islamic Legal Discourse on Muslims in the West* (Leiden: Brill, 2018).
50. Karpat, 'Status of the Muslim', 13.
51. Brian Glyn Williams, *The Crimean Tatars: From Soviet Union to Putin's Conquest* (Oxford: Oxford University Press, 2016), 9–31.
52. Ibid., 28.
53. Meyer, *Turks across Empires*, 25.
54. Manesek, 'Refugee Return'; Mirkova, '"Population Politics"'.
55. Mirkova, *Muslim Land, Christian Labor*; Methodieva, *Between Empire and Nation*, 47, 59; Blumi, *Ottoman Refugees*, 53–5.
56. Sara Albrecht, 'Dar al-Islam and Dar al-Harb', in *Encyclopaedia of Islam*, Three, ed. Kate Fleet et al. (Brill Online, 2016), http://dx.doi.org/10.1163/1573-3912_ei3_COM_25867.
57. Meyer, *Turks across Empires*, 26–8.

Muhacir *as Muslim*

58. Muhamed Mufaku al-Arnaut, 'Islam and Muslims in Bosnia, 1878–1918: Two "Hijras" and Two "Fatwas"', *Journal of Islamic Studies* 5, no.2 (1994): 242–53.
59. Williams, *Crimean Tatars*, 34–46.
60. Meyer, 'Immigration', 18.
61. Williams, *Crimean Tatars*, 45.
62. Mirkova, *Muslim Land, Christian Labor*, 125.
63. Y.A.HUS 198.69, 26 Rebiyülahir 1304/22 January 1887.
64. Karpat, 'Status of the Muslim', 15–16.
65. Ibid.
66. Williams, *Crimean Tatars*, 44; Eileen Kane, *Russian Hajj: Empire and the Pilgrimage to Mecca* (Ithaca, NY: Cornell University Press, 2015), 100. Though the Interior Ministry announced bans on the hajj, Kane's research by and large reveals Russian patronage and facilitation of pilgrimage.
67. Norihiro Naganwa, 'Tatars and Imperialist Wars: From the Tsars' Servitors to the Red Warriors', *Ab Imperio* 1 (2020): 177.
68. Williams, *Crimean Tatars*, 42–6, 45.
69. Y.A.HUS 431.72, 30 Rebiyülevvel, 1902/7 July 1902.
70. MV 103.27, 5 December 1901, in *Belgelerinde* 1, no. 33, 183–7; Y.A.RES 114.102.1–2, 11 December 1901, in *Belgelerinde* 1, no. 34, 188–93; Y.A.RES 115.57, 26 March 1902, in *Beleglerinde* 1, no. 36, 198–219.
71. Y.A.RES 115.57.
72. I.HUS 73.120, 17 Zilkade 1316/29 March 1899; HR.ID 9.11, p. 1, 3 Zilhicce 1320/3 March 1903.
73. DH.MHC 6.11, 25 March 1320/7 April 1904; DH.MHC, 73.65 28 Temmuz 1323/10 August 1907.
74. Williams, *Crimean Tatars*, 45; Meyer, *Turks across Empires*, 33. At least 541 such families who had used their Ottoman passports to return were given the option to stay in Russia if they reverted to their Russian subjecthood.
75. Aydin, *Idea of the Muslim World*, 94–7.
76. A.MKT.MHM 524.29, 4 April 1904, in *Belgelerinde* 1, no. 38, 222–33.
77. See Alison Bashford and Jane McAdam, 'The Right to Asylum: Britain's 1905 Aliens Act and the Evolution of Refugee Law', *Law and History Review* 32, no. 2 (2014): 309–50; Lynne Ann Hartnett, 'Alien or Refugee? The Politics of Russian Émigré Claims to British Asylum at the Turn of the Twentieth Century', *Journal of Migration History* 3, no. 2 (2017): 229–53.
78. Michelle Campos, *Ottoman Brothers: Muslims, Christians, and Jews in Early Twentieth-Century Palestine* (Stanford, CA: Stanford University Press, 2011), 62.
79. Y.MTV 291.137, 7 Zilkade 1324/23 December 1906; Y.MTV 296.193, 27 Safer 1325/11 April 1907.
80. DH.MHC 60.20, p. 14, 10 Zilhicce 1321/27 February 1904.
81. Can, *Spiritual Subjects*, 23.
82. McKeown, *Melancholy Order*, 42.

Governing Migration in the Late Ottoman Empire

83. Ibid., 12.
84. I.DH 1043.82014, 26 Zilkade 1304/16 August 1887.
85. For a discussion of how communities' requests for institutional funding framed in religious or civilisational terms reflected both religious sentiment and the strategic mobilisation of Ottoman officials' concerns, see Evered, *Empire and Education*.

6

Muhacir as Possibility

In January of 1910, Hacı Ömer Fevzi, a representative of Bursa serving in the Ottoman General Assembly, published a 'A Call to Migrants' in *Muhacir*, the recently established gazette of the Society for Rumelian Muslim Migrants (Rumeli Muhacirin-i Islamiye Cemiyeti – RMIC). Ömer Fevzi began his article noting the sacred history of the term *muhacir* and its ties to those who accompanied the prophet to Medina. The example of the *muhajirun* revealed that a believer showed their gratitude for God's blessings not merely through words of praise but rather through acts that protected their community. At the turn of the twentieth century, it was no longer the case that protecting the community required taking up arms. Instead, Ömer Fevzi argued, 'the fundamental duty of migrants like us, who flee their homes and endure all manner of disaster, is to serve the religion and nation of Islam and to inspect and protect our nation and government as others do'.[1] He and other *muhacirin* had done much to teach the people of Anatolia, and he argued that their experience gave them a special role in the ongoing improvement of Ottoman society and the future of the Ottoman state.

Ömer Fevzi's status as a parliamentarian and his publication venue were signs of the momentous changes constitutional revolution had brought to Ottoman society just two years earlier. In early July 1908, 200 soldiers from the Ottoman Third Army took to the hills of Macedonia and called for the reinstatement of the Ottoman Constitution of 1876. Their revolt spread throughout Macedonia through the network of the Committee of Union and Progress (CUP), a secret political society that connected many within the Young Turk movement. On 23 July, Sultan Abdülhamid II acquiesced to the revolutionaries' demands to reinstate the constitution and to reopen the Ottoman parliament. Ömer Fevzi stood for election as a member of the CUP in the fall, and in December he sat

Governing Migration in the Late Ottoman Empire

among his fellow deputies as the Ottoman General Assembly convened for the first time in thirty years. The empire's ethnic and religious groups met the news of the reinstated constitution with joy and celebration. Broadly, participants in the Young Turk movement – a coalition of many groups, ranging from the CUP's officer corps to Armenian revolutionaries – endorsed the liberty and equality of all Ottoman subjects regardless of religion.

Issues of migration and mobility were among the revolutionary government's initial concerns. In August 1908, the new government lifted the Hamidian-era ban on Armenian return migration and dissolved the Commission for Muslim Migrants.[2] In parliament, after abolishing internal passports in 1910, deputies deliberated the need for external passports, a debate David Gutman characterises as a disagreement over whether 'constitutionalism [was] first and foremost about protecting the liberty of the individual or [was] primarily concerned with guaranteeing the security and prosperity of society as a whole'.[3] As with their debates on passports and mobility restrictions, MP's discussions of immigration and settlement reflected broader questions about the individual, society and the contours of democratic governance.

The revolution ushered in a brief era of freedom of press and association, which contributed to the emergence of mass politics, including public demonstrations, boycotts and new civil societies. The RMIC, founded in 1909, was one such political organisation.[4] The RMIC was headquartered in Istanbul, and members established provincial branch organisations. The RMIC's membership was restricted to well-educated individuals over twenty years of age. Its charter specified that the majority of members were to be Muslim migrants from Rumelia. Ömer Fevzi's call for migrants to contribute to Ottoman society was in keeping with the goals of the organisation. According to its charter, the RMIC's purpose was twofold: to protect the religious and civilisational rights of Rumelian Muslims in the Ottoman Empire and the Balkans and to promote the economic progress and well-being of every Ottoman subject.[5]

The *Muhacir* newspaper was a short-lived endeavour. During its one-year lifespan (December 1909–December 1910) it ran a total of 90 issues. It was a twice-weekly publication under the management of Lofçalı Mehmet Hulusi and later Ahmed Şukri, who also served as chief of the organisation's headquarters in Istanbul and the newspaper's head writer.[6] To fulfil the society's expansive goals, the gazette included articles ranging from domestic and international current events, minutes of the Ottoman Chamber of Deputies, injunctions to contribute to the navy, descriptions of

Muhacir *as Possibility*

RMIC events, and didactic pieces on agriculture and industry. The paper advocated for immigrant communities in Western Anatolia and gave voice to migrants themselves: its main contributors were migrants or descendants of migrants, and it published letters from migrant readers.

The immediate post-revolutionary context reveals how the ideology, techniques and infrastructures of social engineering had coalesced prior to the wide-scale violence and genocide of World War I. The question of 'who is a *muhacir*' echoed in the Chamber of Deputies and in the pages of the RMIC's newspaper. In the years immediately following the 1908 revolution, Ottoman subjects considered possibilities for unity and progress within Ottoman society and the Ottoman state. In this context, debates about the meaning of *muhacir* were equally debates about the meaning of Ottomanism, Ottoman subjecthood and the future of the Ottoman state. The meaning of *muhacir* was contested precisely because lines of inclusion and exclusion were not fully drawn and the nature of belonging in Ottoman society was under debate.

The revolution offered new possibilities for organising society, yet durable assumptions circumscribed how parliamentarians and writers in the *Muhacir* newspaper considered migrants, the Ottoman state and the Ottoman population. Of those durable assumptions, this chapter focuses on two. First, that *muhacir* was a forward-looking term. That is, though movement and displacement were fundamental in defining the *muhacir*, conceptually, the category was significant for what it offered. As it had for decades, the significance of 'the *muhacir*' emerged primarily from its status as an instrument to achieve the fundamental goals of Ottoman sovereignty and economic development. The second durable assumption was that careful planning and information-driven administration could unlock the innate potential of immigration and the *muhacir*. For the most part, critiques framed failure and challenges as emerging not from immigration but rather from poor planning, detrimental policies, mismanagement and corruption. The longer history of identifying and responding to failure in migration management had established seemingly apolitical, 'scientific' principles of population management, and the previous decades of settlement and failure had rendered the fundamental rationale of governance resilient in the face of critique. In order to understand the significance of those durable assumptions and their influence on how members of the RMIC and Ottoman parliamentarians considered the question of 'who is a *muhacir*', I turn first to a discussion of the Second Constitutional Era and historians' approaches to its possibilities of unity and episodes of violence.

Inclusion and Exclusion in the Second Constitutional Period

There is a jarring contrast between the language of equality and brotherhood characterising the immediate aftermath of 1908 and the mass violence and genocide that unfolded in the empire less than a decade later. Though those affiliated with the Young Turks embraced *ittihad-ı anasır* ('unity of elements'), a vision of shared contributions and causes among Muslim and non-Ottoman Muslims, they approached the question of what that unity entailed from different, at times opposing, perspectives. In the years immediately following the revolution, members of the CUP sought to establish a 'political system in which individuals would participate as citizens of empire rather than as members of disparate ethnic blocs'. The CUP sought administrative centralisation, and their vision of Ottomanism 'entailed the assimilation of ethnic difference, Ottoman Turkish as the main language, a centralized administrative system, and the abandonment of ethno-religious privileges'.[7] In contrast to the CUP's assimilating drive, many Ottoman subjects encouraged decentralised rule in the empire. Armenians, Arabs, Jews, Bulgarians, Albanians and others continued to identify with specific ethnic and religious groups to navigate the public sphere and to make political claims.

Internal political upheaval, territorial loss and war challenged the expectation of unity. Not all welcomed the revolution. In 1909, a coalition of opponents to the CUP and loyalists of the *ancien régime* staged a counter-revolution. The empire's immigrant groups did not respond uniformly to the revolution or the counter-revolution, and 'Albanian/Bosnian/Chechen/Muhacir Ottomans were heavily represented on both sides of the struggle for power' in Istanbul.[8] The counter-revolution was quickly quelled, and the General Assembly voted to depose Abdülhamid II. Reinstated after the counter-revolution, the CUP dissolved the main opposition party and sought ever greater control over the Ottoman state. Despite the reassertion of order in Istanbul, the upheaval of the counter-revolution shook the province of Adana, leading to the massacre of 20,000 mostly Armenian Christians over a two-week period.[9]

Like other constitutional revolutions of the era, the Young Turk movement was self-preservationist and motivated by the belief that constitutional rule could strengthen the empire. Nonetheless, in the weeks and months after the revolution, Bulgaria declared independence, the Austro-Hungarian Empire annexed Bosnia, and Crete announced its unification with Greece. The emergence of a more robust public sphere influenced the government's response to territorial loss. Thousands responded to the loss of Bulgaria and Bosnia-Herzegovina by marching in the streets

Muhacir *as Possibility*

and joining economic boycotts. In 1908 and 1909, Young Turk leaders encouraged boycotts against foreign states in order to unite communities within the empire in common cause, though it sought to avoid a boycott of Greece and the alienation of Ottoman Greeks. Conversely, in 1910–11, boycotters portrayed Ottoman Greeks as potential advocates of Greek expansion. Over time, the boycotts became a component in advancing Muslim/Turkish economic development at the expense of non-Muslims, a policy eventually adopted by the CUP in favour of unity across ethnic and religious communities.[10]

War necessitated the Ottoman state's management of mass migration throughout the Second Constitutional Era. The Kingdom of Italy invaded Tripoli in October of 1911. In December of that year, the Migrant Administration created a Special Commission for Tripoli and Benghazi Refugees (Trablusgarb ve Bingazi Mültecilerine Mahsus Komisyonu) fleeing from the conflict.[11] In October of 1912, prior to the end of the Italo-Turkish War (1911–12), the Balkan League – the Kingdoms of Serbia, Bulgaria, Greece and Montenegro – declared war against the Ottoman Empire. The First (October 1912–May 1913) and Second (June–August 1913) Balkan Wars witnessed mass population transfer, atrocities and reprisals from all parties. As armies advanced and retreated, religious and ethnic minorities faced repeated expulsions, including several hundred thousand Greeks from Eastern Thrace and some 640,000 individuals from the Balkans to the Ottoman Empire.[12]

The Balkan Wars changed the empire's internal political dynamics. In response to the CUP's authoritarian practices, a coalition of its opponents established the Liberal Entente in November of 1911. The Liberal Entente drew support among parliamentarians, including Ömer Fevzi, and succeeded in ousting the CUP from the prime ministry in 1912. Fearing the Liberal Entente government would cede Edirne to Bulgaria at the end of the First Balkan War, the CUP led a *coup d'état* in January of 1913, and established dictatorial control over the Ottoman state. Under the leadership of Talat, Cemal and Enver Pashas, the CUP government adopted increasingly radical social engineering policies. After the First Balkan War, the Ottoman Empire and Bulgaria agreed to a formal population exchange, and the empire signed similar accords with Serbia and Greece. The CUP government established a new entity, the Directorate for the Settlement of Tribes and Migrants (İskan-ı Aşair ve Muhacirin Müdüriyeti – IAMM). The IAMM combined the work of settling migrants displaced by the Balkan Wars with that of sedentarising nomadic tribes. In the summer of 1913, the CUP began its Turkification project in earnest, mandating that schools and other state institutions use only Turkish, Turkifying place

207

Governing Migration in the Late Ottoman Empire

names and promoting a national economy (*Milli İktisat*) through boycotts and expropriations of non-Muslim businesses.[13]

Historians identify the Balkan Wars (1912–13) as the juncture at which ethno-nationalism became 'the most important factor in the ... demographic catastrophes around the First World War', and credit Muslim migrants as a factor in the emergence of the more exclusive Turkism of the empire's final years.[14] Several hundred thousand Muslims displaced by the wars brought stories of atrocities committed by Christians, and many among the Young Turk leadership counted their own families among the displaced.[15] In this framing, CUP leaders, emotionally devastated by the war and threatened by nationalist separatism and Great Power intervention, embraced Turkish nationalism as the only viable route to secure the empire's remaining territory.[16] The RMIC's efforts during the Balkan Wars offers support for such an interpretation. In 1912 and 1913, the society became the primary civil organisation involved in publishing propaganda on Bulgarian and Greek atrocities. By describing death and torture endured by Muslims, the society aimed to encourage solidarity among Ottoman Muslims and to incite feelings of revenge against the Balkan states and non-Muslim Ottomans. The society's photographs, posters, paintings, postcards, pamphlets and books made their way into magazines, textbooks and classrooms. One pamphlet instructed children to 'heighten their feelings of hate and revenge by looking at the images again and again'; a poem asked children 'not to forget' the Bulgarian atrocities it described.[17] The propaganda played an important role in articulating and encouraging the embrace of a Muslim/Turkish nationalism among Muslim Ottoman subjects on the eve of World War I.

Scholars' recent evaluations of Ottomanism in the Second Constitutional Era dismiss the teleology of an inevitable path to ethnic division and nationalist violence, showing instead the widespread adoption and resonance of Ottoman imperial citizenship among Muslim and non-Muslim, Turkish and non-Turkish groups within the empire.[18] Historians have decoupled group identity and violence, emphasising how 'rogues' and 'ethnic entrepreneurs' employed national and sectarian identities as one among a range of strategies to make political claims during the period. Ethnic entrepreneurs used ethnic categories to navigate new circumstances, articulating identity with the practice of power in ways that both unified and divided existing and emerging communities.[19] These revisions reorient the chronology of the end of empire. For example, Ramazan Öztan argues that scholars' identification of the Balkan Wars as the 'point of no return' in Ottoman leaders' adoption of Turkish nationalism is an outcome of the Turkish Republic's official origin story rather than an accurate portrayal of a unified political

Muhacir *as Possibility*

stance among the Young Turks.[20] Similarly, Ronald Suny notes that the Armenian Genocide was an uncertain eventuality rather than an inevitable outcome even in the years immediately preceding it.[21]

Recent scholarship on Ottomanism, Ottoman Islamism and nationalism thus reveals a complex and circuitous path from empire to nation states. Those insights are worth applying to the diverse experiences of Ottoman immigrants. Like other Ottoman subjects, those who experienced displacement and identified as *muhacir* were not automatic catalysts in the hardening of ethnic/religious/linguistic social boundaries. The question of 'who is a *muhacir*' was always a question of 'who is an Ottoman'. It was so not only for Ottoman officials and politicians, but for migrants themselves. The ways in which Ottoman subjects, including the self-identified migrants of the RMIC, wielded the concept of the *muhacir* captures not only precursors of exclusion but also possibilities of belonging in the years immediately following the revolution.

The Muhacir *in Visions of a Post-Hamidian Future*

Within the pages of the *Muhacir* newspaper and within the Chamber of Deputies, the *muhacir* was a category that defined the nature of subjecthood, citizenship and the relationship between the state and its population. As it had for five decades, the significance of the category lay beyond movement and displacement and encompassed the potential to improve, reform and strengthen the empire. As Ottoman subjects navigated the post-revolutionary moment, the *muhacir* was a figure of metaphorical and material importance through which Ottoman subjects considered their future. The figure of the *muhacir* provided a lens for members of the RMIC to consider a new government, a renewed empire and the contributions of those who inhabited it. Though contributors to the society's newspaper considered a range of topics, they discussed 'the migrant' and 'migration', particularly the *hijra*, in order to comment on individuals' roles in society, and they argued that the immigrant's belonging, like that of other citizens, emerged from his or her willingness to sacrifice for and contribute to society. Thus, self-identified migrants, even those who recalled the tremendous suffering they had endured, understood migration and migrants in instrumental terms.

RUPTURE AND RESPONSIBILITY: WHAT CAN THE *MUHACIR* TEACH US?

On 22 January 1910, an individual by the name of Bezci Edhem published a short piece in *Muhacir* entitled 'A Father and Child's Conversation'.

Governing Migration in the Late Ottoman Empire

His imagined dialogue began with a young son's complaint of feeling left out when his classmates described trips they took to their families' orchards. His father explained that while the son's classmates were visiting orchards handed down across generations, he and his son were migrants (*biz muhaciriz, ya*). To this, the son replied, 'Papa, what is "migrant" supposed to mean? Didn't our grandfathers and fathers have a home? Why didn't you all plant orchards like everyone else?' In responding to this and several more of his son's questions, the father revealed the anger, grief and longing he felt for his 'homeland' (*vatan*). As he recalled the tree his own mother had planted for him, he was moved to tears. Though the family's orchards existed, they were 'as distant as the seat of final judgement', for he had been driven from his homeland. It was there that he 'buried [his] hopes along with the bodies of [his] mother and father'.

For the young, innocent son, the meaning of *muhacir* was loss, a loss made clear by the realisation that even in an era when 'man can traverse the world in a few years', a place could be out of reach, a family could lose access to their patrimony and parents could be cruelly killed by forces unknown. In asking, 'why didn't you plant a tree for me? It must mean you don't love me, papa', the son identified the *muhacir*'s multigenerational pain. The migrant, and especially the forced migrant, suffered the loss of the connections that tied him or her to the homeland and of a future once dreamed of – a future that had been 'buried' like so many bodies.

For Edhem, however, as palpable as that pain was for the migrant, '*muhacir*' was not just a past-oriented term. The dialogue did not end with the father's bleak depiction of lost hope and home. Instead, the conversation turned to the value of sacrificing oneself for one's new homeland. To comfort his father, the son asserted that he did not need orchards; their small house was enough. At school, one of his classmates had begun collecting funds for a warship that could withstand the enemy, and the son had donated his allowance. He recounted the similar contributions of migrant women in a nearby village and an olive oil factory owner, who donated to both the naval fund and the boy's school despite not knowing the students there. His father conceded that such acts were intended to make a new world for their descendants and affirmed that such sacrifices tied one to one's homeland. In the article's closing lines, the son vowed to donate his allowance once more, an act that connected him to future generations.[22]

By ending his piece with hope for a future to be built and with reference to belonging created by sacrifice, Edhem located the meaning of *muhacir* beyond an initial rupture between past and present. His writings reflected intellectual and emotional currents of the Young Turk Era, and

Muhacir *as Possibility*

his use of the term *vatan* echoed that of the Ottoman intellectual, writer and reformer Namık Kemal (1840–88). Kemal's writings 'transformed the meaning of *vatan* from a feeling of belonging to a birthplace into a feeling of loyalty toward a sacred territory'. The Young Turks inherited Kemal's notion of 'saving the *vatan*' as a sacred duty and the cornerstone of Ottoman belonging.[23] For Edhem, sacrifice was a path for those who had previously lost their homes to create connection to a new *vatan*. The *muhacir*'s experiences made clear the significance of the responsibility one held towards one's homeland. This commitment entailed more than the personal sacrifice of a mother and father planting a tree for their child; it required serving a *vatan* more broadly conceived, accessible to all willing to sacrifice on its behalf.

Writers in the pages of *Muhacir* defined their community and the meaning of the term *muhacir* in several ways. In their advocacy for migrants, members of the RMIC established the parameters of a community defined by shared experiences of suffering and displacement. As with Edhem, however, it was in combining and layering several identities – Muslim, migrant, Rumelian and Ottoman – that writers activated *muhacir* as a term to critique and improve society itself. The migrant, and the migrant's suffering, served as a rhetorical device from which to articulate the vision of social change described in the RMIC's charter. In the pages of the newspaper, the *muhacir*'s pain allowed writers to identify and correct faults within Ottoman society and to identify the responsibilities of individuals to the Ottoman state and to the Muslim *umma*.

The pivot from pain to possibility appeared from the newspaper's first issue, in an address penned by one Varnalı Ahmed Hilmi to his 'countrymen'. Ahmed Hilmi poetically described migrants' ongoing sorrow for their lost homeland, noting that to them, 'living is an enduring disaster and everything – life, family, children – awakens misery'. However, misery did not have to remain the migrant's fate. Instead, Ahmed Hilmi deployed the *muhacir*'s grief to advocate for improving the Ottoman nation. Despite their suffering, immigrants had to recognise an ongoing fight worth fighting – a fight to spread industry, agriculture and commerce within their new homeland. The true threats to a nation emerged from the ignorance and idleness (*cehalet ile atalet*) of its people. Education was the way to battle these threats.[24] For Ahmed Hilmi, migrants' suffering attuned them to the urgency of the problems facing Ottoman society. Their experiences served as a warning to Ottoman subjects, who needed to awaken to the necessity of education and economic progress in order to save themselves from the fate immigrants had endured in the Balkans.

Their personal histories of displacement and loss were fundamental to how Bezci Edhem and Ahmed Hilmi understood the *muhacir*; nonetheless, they utilised the term to consider the future and to contemplate the immigrants' role within Ottoman society. They instrumentalised the *muhacir*'s experiences, arguing that those experiences allowed immigrants to become ideal Ottoman citizens: individuals who were educated, connected to causes outside themselves, productive and willing to fight for the future of the *vatan*. The individual's responsibilities and potential and an instrumentalised understanding of immigration featured as well in how the newspaper's contributors approached the possibility of emigration for those who had not yet left the Balkans.

THE OBLIGATION TO STAY

The stated purpose of the RMIC included the protection of Muslims in Rumelia. In using the term Rumelia, the society and newspaper referred primarily to the areas ceded in the 1877–8 War. Writers' names referenced their origins in cities and regions in Bulgaria and Romania, such as Varna, Lofça/Lovech, Dobruca and Filibe/Plovdiv. Dispatches and articles on the conditions of Muslims in Bosnia, Bulgaria, Romania and Macedonia promoted a sense of shared community among those who left and those who stayed. Despite their ongoing connection to and sympathy for those who remained in the Balkans, the newspaper's contributors maintained an instrumental stance towards that population, a stance that emerges clearly in their arguments against the applicability of *hijra* for their Balkan coreligionists.

The question of the *hijra* was not new in 1909. The religious obligation of the *hijra* had been a factor in Muslim immigration prior to the Young Turk Revolution, and members of the RMIC referred to the *hijra* when recalling their flights from the Balkans decades earlier. Within and outside the empire, economic and geopolitical goals had influenced how statesmen, officials, jurists, reformers and intellectuals evaluated the applicability of the *hijra* for potential Muslim migrants during the Hamidian Era (Chapter 5). The political changes of 1908, in particular Bulgarian independence and the Austro-Hungarian annexation of Bosnia, renewed interest in the *hijra*. Still, contributors to *Muhacir* argued against the *hijra*'s applicability to Muslims in Bulgaria and Bosnia. Their approach to the *hijra* elevated the concerns of the community over those of the individual, and endorsed a fundamental premise of Ottomanism – that states could and would protect religious minorities. Concerns about politics and the organisation of society influenced how writers in the *Muhacir* newspaper assessed the religious obligation of *hijra*.

Muhacir *as Possibility*

In 1909–10, writers in *Muhacir* were not alone in re-evaluating the applicability of the *hijra* for Muslims living under non-Muslim rule. Their approach echoed that of Rashid Rida, a major intellectual figure and Sunni scholar of the late nineteenth and early twentieth centuries. Rida wrote extensively on the issue of Muslim minority jurisprudence in *al-Manar*, the journal he edited in Cairo. Though he acknowledged that there were limits to what Muslims could accommodate as subjects of non-Muslim states, Rida's writing reflected his pragmatic acceptance that some Muslims, including himself, necessarily lived under non-Muslim rule.

One of Rida's key formulations of the *hijra* and minority jurisprudence emerged in a response he wrote to a letter sent from Muhammad Zahir al-Din Tarabar, a medrese student in Bosnia, in July 1909. In his letter, Tarabar explained that a visiting scholar had claimed that Islamic practice and marriage were not legally valid after Austria's annexation of Bosnia in 1908, and Tarabar wondered whether the scholar was correct in calling for *hijra*. In a forceful response, Rida suggested that such claims 'could not issue except from an ignoramus'. He emphasised that living under non-Islamic government did not undermine the legality of Muslim practice, prayer and marriage. On the matter of *hijra*, Rida concluded that there were only two reasons for obligatory migration: if someone was incapable of practising his religion, or if someone were called to *jihad*. While *jihad* did not apply to Bosnian Muslims, Rida noted that Bosnian Muslims would 'know it for themselves' if Islam was corrupted by Austro-Hungarian rule.[25]

Writers for *Muhacir* echoed and expanded upon Rida's stance. They approached the *hijra* as an issue of population politics rather than individual conscience, and they determined its applicability from the perspective of political possibilities for the Ottoman state, Rumelian Muslims and communities within Ottoman society. Ahmed Şukri, head writer for *Muhacir*, outlined the parameters of the *hijra* in one of his first pieces in the newspaper, acknowledging that, 'in recent history, Muslims who fell under the misrule of Christian governments had to leave their homes and relocate to Islamic lands. Because it is forbidden to remain in a place where one is unable to perform publicly the requirements of Islam, their migration was required.' However, he continued, while the obligation to migrate had applied to those individuals, it did not apply to every situation in which Muslims were governed by non-Muslims. Indeed, it was permissible to remain, so long as Muslims held the right to practise Islam.[26]

Ahmed Şukri went further than merely asserting that Muslims could remain in Rumelia. Instead, he argued that they should: staying was the spiritually superior act. In an era when 'all civilized countries accepted

Governing Migration in the Late Ottoman Empire

the principle of freedom of religion' and when faith was spread through 'manner and word' rather than the sword, Muslims could better follow the path set forward in the Quran by maintaining communities in locations like Bulgaria and Romania. In the following issue, Ahmed Şukri reaffirmed that the principle of freedom of religion precluded the obligation to migrate. Subjecthood corresponded to a secular tie to a government separate from the realm of worship, thus Muslims could remain in the Balkans despite the loss of Ottoman sovereignty there.[27] In another piece, Ahmed Şukri emphasised that the Austro-Hungarian Empire's protection of minority religions meant that Bosnian Muslim migration was unacceptable.[28] Implicitly, Ahmed Şukri's affirmation of minority rights for Muslims in Rumelia and his distinction between one's religious practice and one's subjecthood endorsed the secular promise of Ottoman citizenship. By guaranteeing rights for all, Ottomanism could resolve issues of nationalist or ethnic separatism in the empire.

Alongside approaching the *hijra* from the perspective of Ottomanism and minority rights, Ahmed Şukri and other writers considered how *hijra* could undermine Islam. They worried that mass emigration from Bulgaria, Romania and Bosnia-Herzegovina would diminish Islam; conversely, encouraging people to remain ensured the maintenance of a Muslim community throughout the Balkans. Here, Ahmed Şukri offered a doctrine of anti-*hijra* – a moment when migration was not religiously permissible. Islam, he noted, requires steadfastness and resolution. Since 'emigrating would impoverish the state of Islam in those locations', it was an unconscionable act.[29] An anonymous article published several months later reasserted the obligation to stay in religious and national terms. The writer declared that migration was not canonically required from states governed by non-Muslims, reasoning that if it were, '180,000,000 Indian Muslims, nearly 100,000,000 Muslims in China and 40,000,000–50,000,000 more in Russia, the Caucasus, Egypt, Tunis and Algeria' would at least consider emigrating. In language similar to that used by Crimean Tatar intellectuals several years prior (see Chapter 5), the writer added the issue of national obligation to his religious rationale. The result of mass emigration would be not only the loss of Islam in Bosnia but also the loss of Bosnianness itself, as 'the name Bosniak would be likely lost to history'. The writer acknowledged the dangers and difficulties faced by Muslims in Bosnia, but maintained that 'migration hullabaloo' (*hicret velvelesi*) threatened 'to scatter the children of the *vatan*' across the world.[30] In his view, under conditions where one could continue to practise Islam, the obligation to stay was a nation-based responsibility that took precedence over a Muslim's connection to the Ottoman Empire.

Muhacir *as Possibility*

While Ahmed Şukri and the anonymous writer argued that emigration from the Balkans undermined the regional and global Muslim community, *Muhacir* also offered space to articulate the relationship between migration, administration and the Ottoman Empire's economic development. In a letter to the newspaper, Şukri from Dobruca identified three main outcomes of Ottoman immigration. The first outcome, quite frequent in Dobruca, was return. Return migrants tended to be religious emigrants, who had left 'the comfort of their homes' to go to the Ottoman Empire. Thanks to poor administration and the wretched conditions they faced after their arrival in the empire, they eventually returned, impoverished, to their homelands. The second outcome was immigrant success. Appropriate settlement and effective administration allowed these individuals to establish themselves in the empire. The third outcome was a state of confusion and doubt among those drawn to the empire by religious feeling but aware of the difficulties that accompanied migration. Given these three outcomes, the second was clearly optimal. Thus, Şukri argued, it was far better to urge his Balkan coreligionists to remain in their homelands rather than enduring the difficulties that could accompany leaving. There was no need to incite migration, he noted, because administrative success, once obtained, was encouragement enough for those considering relocation.[31] Careful migration administration improved the lives of Muslims in Rumelia and ultimately contributed to the Ottoman Empire's economic progress.

OTTOMANISM AND THE *MUHACIR* IN SOCIETY

The RMIC emphasised the religious significance of the term *muhacir*; nonetheless, the newspapers' contributors activated multiple communal identities (Muslim, migrant, Rumelian and Ottoman) and maintained the principle that the promotion of one did not undermine the promotion of another. The newspaper's main writers identified progress and patriotism as the way forward for Muslims in Rumelia and the empire, *muhacirin* and all Ottomans. In its first issue, Lofçalı Mehmet Hulusi identified the newspaper's purpose: 'to awaken the idea of progress' among 'our migrant brothers' and, in so doing, lead all Ottomans towards trade, agriculture and industry.[32] Like Arabs, Armenians, Albanians, Greeks and other minorities, writers as 'Rumelians' and 'migrants' weighed the relationship between advocating for their community and contributing to a unified Ottoman future in the Second Constitutional Period.

Though the RMIC's political advocacy identified *muhacirin* as a discrete group, contributors to the newspaper endorsed the primacy of the Ottoman political project over the concerns of their community and argued

Governing Migration in the Late Ottoman Empire

that full participation in a strengthened Ottoman state best protected the *muhacirin*. An individual writing under the penname 'Osmancık' asserted this perspective in frequent contributions to the newspaper. In an 'Address to Our Migrant Compatriots', Osmancık argued that the division between *muhacir* and 'local' (*yerli*) was a vestige of the 'duplicity' of the Hamidian period. Suffering, rather than a unique characteristic of the *muhacir*, was the shared heritage of all Ottomans who had experienced the wounds of the 1877–8 Russo-Ottoman War. Osmancık called upon his fellow migrants to remember that shared experience and to leave behind '*muhacir*-ness' (*muhacirlik*), because the future of the empire required locals and migrants to work together to withstand the threat of foreign invasion and control.[33]

Reflection on the religious context of the *muhacir* and the *hijra* was another route to comment on the obligations owed by individuals to their communities in the Constitutional Era. In a follow-up article to his 'Call to Migrants', Ömer Fevzi took this tack. In 'True Emigration', Ömer Fevzi noted the common definition of '*muhacir*': one who 'left one's home and took refuge under the protection of the Caliph in order to secure one's life, livelihood, religion, and honor'. This popular understanding, he argued, did not capture the true meaning of '*muhacir*'. The term's true meaning, as revealed by the life of the Prophet Muhammad, was 'one who leaves behind the things that God has prohibited'. Thus, he argued, the status of *muhacir* was not limited to those who physically fled their countries, but rather emerged through spiritual change, regardless of whether or not one lived within 'foreign countries'.[34]

In reality, he continued, both migrant and non-migrant Ottomans were failing to abstain from God's prohibitions, in particular the Quranic injunction against bringing about one's own death.[35] In this case, death referred to the potential loss of people, tribe, nation and race, and its threat emerged from idleness and a loss of relative power vis-à-vis Islam's enemies. Once again, the underlying issues were education, wealth and productivity, as 'the happiness and power of a group of people ... depends on education, trade, industry, possessions, and capital'. Ömer Fevzi concluded that only by striving to address those needs could one align oneself with Muhammad's *hijra* and become a 'true' *muhacir*.[36] In emphasising that the true *muhacir* was forged by a migration of the mind and heart, Ömer Fevzi both promoted and undermined *muhacir* as a discrete identity within Ottoman society.

Ömer Fevzi's commentary on the 'true' *muhacir* aligned with other members of the RMIC. *Muhacir* was a forward-looking category that framed the ideal Ottoman subject as one whose productivity contributed

Muhacir *as Possibility*

to the overall well-being of the empire. In keeping with the promise of Ottomanism, the *muhacir* forged their connection to the empire through sacrifice and a willingness to participate in the general good. Aspects of Ömer Fevzi's thinking aligned as well with that of his colleagues in the General Assembly, who, even as they debated policy, affirmed the economic promise of migration and likewise portrayed Ottomanism as essential to the empire's future.

'The Migration Issue is Fundamentally an Economic Issue'

Parliamentarians' approach to immigration during the Second Constitutional Period was influenced by the revolution's immediate context and the longer history of Ottoman migration management. Tanzimat and Hamidian-era officials' prior use of the *muhacir* in social engineering projects rendered the concept one through which Ottoman politicians considered inclusion and exclusion in the aftermath of the 1908 Revolution. Decades of responding to mass migration had tied the meaning of *muhacir* to the distribution of land, aid and rights; deputies wondered why immigrants received such resources while other subjects did not. Parliamentarians leveraged the question of 'who is a *muhacir*' to identify whether the revolutionary government fell short of its promises of equality and unity and to criticise policies that seemed to incite, encourage or prioritise Muslim immigration. Though the history of migration management framed how politicians employed 'the *muhacir*' to diagnose problems of governance, that history also determined the limits and effectiveness of their criticism. Parliamentarians debated the meaning of the *muhacir* and the implications of settlement, yet they left nearly unquestioned the relationship between migration and the economy and the expectation that well-planned, information-driven administration could unlock immigration's innate benefits.

In May of 1909, Mehmet Cavit Bey (Salonica), a founding member of the CUP and the soon to be appointed Minister of Finance, requested that the Chamber of Deputies refuse an Interior Ministry request for additional funds for migrant settlement. Such a refusal was reasonable, he noted, because parliament had not had time to fully assess how the money was to be spent. How, he wondered, could parliament understand what they were approving without more information? How could they allocate large amounts of money without carefully examining the nature of the proposed expenditures?[37] While Cavit sought to strengthen parliament's role through recourse to procedure and new precedent, another MP, Muharrem Hasbi Efendi (Karesi), cast the debate in terms of the fundamental identity of the state. Muharrem Hasbi supported the immediate allocation of funds. In principle he agreed with the wisdom of a more detailed budget, but the urgent need to assist immigrants overrode the need for parliamentary oversight. Their ongoing suffering was unacceptable to the fundamental magnanimity of the Ottoman character. Despite Muharrem Hasbi's argument, other MPs agreed that the Interior Ministry's request was ambiguous. Deputies wondered whether the allocation was to be used for settlement or to purchase seeds and tools for those already settled. They also noted that the request was poorly timed. The chamber was scheduled to consider, prepare and approve the following year's general budget in a few weeks' time. Thus, there was little to gain by adding emergency expenditures. The chamber endorsed Cavit's call for procedure and voted to address the allocation in June.[38]

A year later, Cavit Bey approached the Chamber of Deputies as Minister of Finance. This time, he advocated on behalf of the Interior Ministry, which once more required additional funds. The Interior Ministry requested 5,000,000 *kuruş* to meet its budget shortage. Of that, the ministry had earmarked 1,500,000 *kuruş* to resolve problems of migrant settlement.[39] Despite Cavit's suggestion that 'there [was] no need to debate the migrant settlement issue', MPs once again bristled at the lack of details embedded in the budget request. Why had the Interior Ministry delayed in asking for the budget allocation? Why had the Finance Ministry once again deprived the chamber of necessary information regarding how allocations were to be spent?[40]

When the General Assembly opened for the first time in thirty years, MPs took on the task of not only developing legislation but also of establishing the role of the legislature itself. They considered how Parliament might exercise oversight and contribute to decision-making, and deliberated its role in a society administered by constitution and rule of law. Debates over expenditures and the state's annual budgets, particularly funds dedicated to migrant settlement, provided opportunities for MPs to question who received government aid and whether such policies purposefully encouraged the immigration of some and not others. In raising and responding to such questions, deputies and other members of the Ottoman state commented on the nature of governance and the meaning of inclusion in the Second Constitutional Era.

IMMIGRATION VS RETURN: 'TO WHOM DOES THIS LAND BELONG?'

In February 1910, Keygam Efendi (Der Garabedian, Muş), an Armenian MP, responded to Cavit Bey's request for funds for migrant settlement

Muhacir *as Possibility*

expenses by asking 'which *muhacir*' the allocation covered. Cavit answered that the immigrants indicated in the budget were 'whichever migrants happened to come' to the empire. Keygam proposed that Armenian *muhacirin* should receive some of the aid allocation. Cavit affirmed that Armenian *muhacirin*, in fact, 'all kinds' of *muhacirin*, were of course included. If that were the case, Keygam wondered, then why were Armenians not provided aid, houses or land? Instead, they 'wandered the streets'. Yorgo Boşo Efendi, a Greek parliamentarian from Manastır (Serfiçe/Servia), offered a distinction: the Armenians were not *muhacirin*. Instead, they were 'returnees' (*avdeti*).[41]

The February 1910 session was neither the first time Keygam Efendi asked whom the term *muhacir* encompassed nor the first time the chamber considered the relationship between *muhacirin* and return migrants. Though the revolutionary government had lifted Hamidian-era restrictions on Armenian return migration in 1908, the status of the returners and their right to land and financial support remained contentious. Were all former Ottoman subjects who had left during the Hamidian era to be welcomed back into Ottoman territory? Would their needs take priority over non-Ottoman immigrants? Armenian and Bulgarian Deputies, including Keygam, Krikor Zohrab (Istanbul), Ohannes Varteks/Varteks Serengülian (Erzurum), Hristo Dalchef (Siroz/Serrres) and Pancho Dorev (Manastır), voiced concerns. The revolutionary government had seen to it that the Migrant Commission was no longer called the 'Commission for Muslim Migrants', yet did a change in name truly signify a change in policy?

For some non-Muslim MPs who had witnessed extensive emigration in previous decades, it was not enough to merely open Ottoman borders to returning subjects. Instead, the state's response to return migration had to redress the material outcomes of the previous regime's discriminatory and oppressive policies. In early March 1909, on the eve of the counter-revolution, an Armenian deputy, Stephan/Istepan Ispartalıyan (Izmir), presented a brief nine-point plan for reform in Anatolia. His plan, which the chamber did not pass on to the prime minister for consideration, pointedly called for returning the stolen (*magsube*) property and land of emigrants who were now returning to the empire.[42]

Redress encompassed not just returning land but also seeking to ensure that the new government did not perpetuate the selective immigration policies and discriminatory tactics of 'the autocratic period'. A week after Ispartalıyan's proposed programme, Sulayman al-Bustani Efendi (Beirut) called for creating a special commission for those who had emigrated 'by necessity' under the previous regime. In his proposal, al-Bustani noted the proclamation of the constitution had awakened the patriotic fervour

Governing Migration in the Late Ottoman Empire

of Ottoman subjects abroad. Nevertheless, emigration continued to contribute to the empire's population loss. His proposed commission would mitigate the 'problem of emigration' while also encouraging returnees. Future Interior Minister Talat Pasha (Edirne), noted that such a committee was in the state's economic interest.[43] Ohannes Varteks (Erzurum) asked for clarification: Would the proposed committee focus on Muslim migrants? Talat and al-Bustani, a Maronite Catholic, assured Varteks that the proposal made no special dispensation for Muslims, and that it in fact covered 'all Ottomans', including, according to Talat, 'Bulgarians, Serbians, Romanians, etc.'.[44] The proposal to create the new committee passed.

Following the spring 1909 counter-revolution and Adana massacres, Armenian MPs' concerns about the recurrence of pro-Muslim immigration policies increased. In August, the Chamber of Deputies considered a report from the Migrant Commission regarding Muslim immigrant settlement in Edirne Province. The commission sought executive power to purchase farms for settlement in order to increase population and to 'bring an end to the suffering' of those Muslims who had sought refuge in the empire. Krikor Zohrapb Efendi (Istanbul) was the first to respond to the proposal. Emphasising that he had no hesitation regarding aiding immigrants, he nonetheless rejected the committee's use of the label 'Muslim migrants' (*Muhacirin-i İslamiye*). 'Migration', he noted, 'is not unique to Muslims', and such a distinction based on religion should be rejected as contrary to the spirit of Ottomanism. Further, if migrants from elsewhere could become 'children of the homeland' (*vatanın evladı*), the same opportunity had to be extended to those who had been forced to flee the country prior to the 1908 revolution.

Ignoring the question of return migrants, Mehmet Vehbi Efendi (Çelik, Konya) dismissed Krikor as overly suspicious. Identifying immigrants as 'Muslim migrants', he argued, was not inherently 'anti-other migrants'. Since nearly all the migrants in Edirne were Muslims, it was appropriate to call them such. The President of the Chamber, Ahmet Rıza, agreed that the designation was merely a description of conditions rather than a signal of discriminatory policy. 'If nearly all of the migrants had been Jewish', Ahmet Rıza suggested, the Committee would have referred to them as 'Jewish migrants'.[45]

Though Krikor's second point did not receive attention in August 1909, the status of returners resurfaced in subsequent budget discussions. In May 1910, the Interior Ministry's proposed budget allocated 20,000,000 *kuruş* for an estimated 30,000 migrants. Keygam again advocated for Armenians returning to the empire. Like Krikor, he was quick to emphasise that he

Muhacir *as Possibility*

was not anti-immigration. Nonetheless, he asked parliament to consider why the state offered aid to newcomers while the 'local poor', who 'were poorer than migrants', were 'forgotten'. Since there should be no discrimination among Ottoman 'elements' (*unsur*), why not allocate money to immigrants *and* to the poor? For two years, Keygam continued, he had sought aid on behalf of Armenians who had returned to the empire. It was not merely a question of aid, he asserted, but a question of rights. Despite the government's language of equality, which dictated that aid be offered without discrimination, no aid had been offered to returners. In fact, those who had been displaced returned to find their land given away to immigrants. Rather than accepting the budget as it was, he offered an alternative proposal: to give to Armenians the land that legally should be theirs.[46]

Rıza Tevfik Bey (Bölükbaşi, Edirne), a self-identified *muhacir*, agreed with Keygam's commentary. Rıza Tevfik noted that so many individuals, himself included, had left their countries, homes and households due to oppression, and that the question of 'who is a migrant' was essential to answer prior to allocating aid. What might the label designate? How much time had to pass before an emigrant lost claim to their land? Should not *muhacir* encompass anyone who had been forced to abandon their homes? Was it right to import and aid foreigners from 'Bulgaria, India, and China' when the country's 'original inhabitants' (*asıl ahalisi*) were deprived of the state's protection? Who, he repeated, was a migrant? Rıza Tevfik called upon his fellow parliamentarians to protect 'the people of our country', who had left due to oppression. The issue of land was crucial. Ottoman subjects' rights were tenuous if the state could appropriate their land for newcomers. 'Today', he asked, 'to whom does that land belong?'[47]

Long before 1910, officials had tied the category of *muhacir* to the distribution of land and the dispensation of aid. Consequently, the discussion of 'who is a *muhacir*' was ultimately a discussion of to whom the state was beholden – those who were legal subjects of the Ottoman Empire or those who were 'spiritual subjects' seeking refuge in the caliphate.[48] As an immigrant himself, Rıza Tevfik approached the question as one of resources, land and legal belonging. The protection of the individual and his or her property was fundamental to the relationship between state and subject. By elevating some as *muhacir* and denying that status to Ottoman returners, the government undermined the nature of secular subjecthood and foreclosed some subjects' access to rights and protections guaranteed in the Ottoman constitution.

Governing Migration in the Late Ottoman Empire

DISPLACEMENT: WHO ARE THE CHILDREN OF THE HOMELAND?

The issues of land ownership, displacement, subjecthood and belonging were as pertinent in Rumelia as they were in Eastern Anatolia. Whereas Armenian MPs considered the question of return in regards to decades of Hamidian policy and in the wake of the 1909 massacres, Bulgarian MPs spoke in the context of the Macedonian Question – the political status of the provinces of Manastır, Salonica and Kosovo. In August 1903, the Internal Macedonian Revolutionary Organization (IMRO) led an uprising in Manastır. European powers decided against intervention, and within a month the Ottoman Army violently suppressed the unrest. The Young Turk revolution brought a brief period of peace to the region, but the three provinces remained volatile and home to a number of competing Bulgarian, Greek, Albanian and Serbian committees and militias.[49] As the euphoria of 1908 faded, the Macedonian Question, immigration and the fate of returners collided in proposals and budget discussions regarding *muhacir* settlement. Durable assumptions bounded the terms of the debate: deputies critical of the government's policies endorsed the benefit of immigration in general even as they sought to reduce migrant settlement in Rumelia.

By 1910, Bulgarian MPs weighing the Interior Ministry's budgets openly alleged that, like the Hamidian regime before it, the CUP-led government used Muslim migrant settlement to modify demographics. In May, Hristo Dalchef Efendi (Siroz), an MP affiliated with the IMRO (renamed the Internal Macedonian-Adrianople Revolutionary Organization), argued that allocating money for Muslim migrant settlement in Rumelia undermined the empire and contradicted the constitution by damaging the economies of the 'original inhabitants'. According to Dalchef, there was no empty land in the region. Instead, the government purchased agricultural estates at inflated prices 'in order to harm the local people and settle migrants'. When local Christians sought justice by petitioning the state, the government searched among them for 'provocateurs'. Aside from these practices, Dalchef criticised a policy that prevented the return migration of individuals in Bulgaria who had left the empire during the Hamidian era. He concluded that the two policies offered no benefit and contradicted the principles of Ottomanism. Despite his critique, Dalchef denied that he was anti-*muhacir*. He had no objection to using state money to settle Muslim migrants on empty land. In fact, if the land had indeed been empty, he agreed that it was beneficial and even necessary to increase the Muslim population through immigration. To affirm his pro-*muhacir* stance, Dalchef, like Krikor and Keygam, proposed aiding some immigrants while also redirecting funds

Muhacir *as Possibility*

to those 'forced to flee the previous regime' and to those whose 'land was extorted by the government'.[50]

In November of 1910, parliament considered an Interior Ministry request for an additional 1,000,000 *kuruş* for immigrant settlement. Pancho Dorev (Manastır), a Macedo-Bulgarian jurist, politician and intellectual, called upon his fellow deputies to consider whether the allocation was in the state's interest. Dorev noted that just a year prior, 'not a single Ottoman would have countenanced not accepting the migrants'; however, the government's settlement policies necessitated reconsidering this position. Any benefit that may have emerged had been sacrificed by the Interior Ministry's purposeful use of immigrants to undermine Christians. Dorev described several episodes in Tirnova and elsewhere in which the government had displaced locals in favour of migrants. He predicted that the settlement of 'penniless' immigrants from Bosnia and Bulgaria would destroy local economies in Rumelia, and he argued that Christians forced from their homes by the Ministry's tactics were more likely to become brigands and revolutionaries – what else could transpire 'if the government treat[ed] some groups like step children?' Though the goal of increasing the population was 'one of the oldest principles of statecraft', it was no longer implementable in the 'civilised' era.[51] Rather than increasing the state's power, authority and security, the government's actions alienated Ottoman subjects. Dorev's commentary placed Ottomanism at the centre of the empire's political future in Rumelia.[52]

Six months later, Dalchef repeated the charge that the government's immigration policies and its treatment of returners from Bulgaria betrayed Ottomanism. According to Dalchef, in September 1909 the government had issued a policy that prohibited the entry of former Ottoman subjects who had fled to Bulgaria prior to the 1903 uprising and that mandated that those who had left the empire after 1903 apply to Ottoman consuls for permission to re-enter Ottoman territory. Moreover, the Interior Ministry had begun to expel those who had returned from Bulgaria prior to the passage of the 1909 law. Those the Interior Ministry expelled had paid their taxes and the armed service fee to the Ottoman state even while in Bulgaria, held property in the Ottoman Empire and in some cases left children behind after their forced departure. For Dalchef, the expulsion of those who were 'Ottomans just like us' betrayed the promise of equality. There was no logical or legal basis to drive away tax-paying subjects, and thus the government's discrimination was a clear sign of the persistence of despotic policies developed in the Hamidian era.[53]

Though Krikor, Keygam, Dalchef and Dorev identified discrimination in the Interior Ministry's immigration and settlement policies, they were careful to note their belief that, if done correctly, immigration and population increase necessarily improved the economy. Deputies' discussions of Zionism and Zionist immigration to Palestine in 1911 reflected a similar stance. The question was not whether immigration was beneficial in general, but instead whether immigration of certain populations to certain areas was a mistake.

'POVERTY IS THE NATION'S TRUE ENEMY'

In debates on Zionism, the economic benefits of immigration were a fundamental assumption articulated by those in favour and those opposed to Zionist immigration to the Ottoman Empire. Anti-Zionist MPs acknowledged the economic benefits of Jewish immigration, and Louis Fishman's work has shown that doing so allowed MPs to oppose immigration to Palestine while denying the charge of anti-Semitism. For instance, in May 1911, two Arab MPs from Jerusalem, Said al-Husayni and Ruhi al-Khalidi, argued that the state should curb Zionist immigration because Zionists did not adopt Ottoman citizenship and because Jews would soon constitute a majority in Jerusalem. Nevertheless, al-Husayni endorsed Jewish settlement in other parts of the empire. He described 'the Jewish nation' as 'hard-working, intelligent, and economical' and agriculturally and industrially 'progressive'. Furthermore, the 'local population' around Jerusalem had 'benefitted from the scientific, agricultural, and industrial offices ... established' by the Jewish immigrants.[54] Al-Husayni endorsed the positive economic benefits of immigration to the empire, yet argued the state should direct it away from Palestine and ensure that immigrants accepted unequivocal Ottoman nationality.[55]

The following day, Dimitar Vlahov, a socialist deputy from Salonica, spoke in favour of Zionist immigration.[56] He began by remarking that an estimated 23,000,000–25,000,000 people had arrived in the United States over the previous five decades. Thanks to those migrants, from 1850 to 1900 the number and value of farms, the amount of cultivated land, and the value of farm animals and machinery each had increased by 370 to 600 per cent. Overall agricultural production had increased 130 per cent in the forty years between 1866 and 1907. Thus, he concluded, 'migrant settlement, rather than damaging a country, contributed to its advancement'.[57]

Vlahov asserted that though the chamber's debate on Zionism had been focused on politics, 'the migration issue is fundamentally an economic issue'. Deputies' fixation on the political ramifications of Zionism distracted attention from the true threat facing the empire: its incapacity to withstand pressure from other powerful states. Zionist settlement helped

Muhacir *as Possibility*

the state to become economically strong and to move against the country's 'real enemies' (*hakiki duşmanlar*).[58] Prior to the debate, Vlahov met with Zionist advocates in Salonica. According to his sources, Zionist immigration had been a tremendous success and had contributed to the overall economic development of the Arab peasantry.[59] Vlahov underscored his support of Zionist immigration by emphasising the relationship between immigration, emigration and the empire's economic development. Ottomans who had migrated to Bulgaria, Romania, America and other places did so in search of work. Zionist immigration allowed the state to curb such emigration by developing the empire's industry and trade.[60]

In the midst of their criticisms of immigration and settlement policies, Krikor, Keygam, Dalchef and al-Husayni were careful to deny that they were anti-immigration and to affirm that, in general, population increase created social progress and economic growth. As they identified the colonising impulse underpinning settlement in Rumelia and Palestine, Dalchef and Husayni held analogous positions. Dalchef endorsed as 'necessary' a policy of increasing the Muslim population, though only if there were available land, while al-Husayni espoused the benefit of Jewish immigration, as long as it was outside of Palestine. Their endorsement of immigration was an endorsement of migration-driven social engineering. Their critique centred on how and where the government undertook the effort to transform the population, rather than a critique of that phenomenon itself. Immigration was beneficial; it was up to policymakers and administrators to unlock the benefits of immigration.

Expertise and the Weight of History

In the spring 1910 budget discussions, Dalchef's comments on migration charged the government with damaging the local economy, with directing migrants to areas without available land in order to displace locals and ultimately with betraying Ottomanism. These critiques were not ones the government ignored. Instead, Prime Minister Ibrahim Hakkı spoke at length to the Chamber of Deputies to rebut Dalchef's remarks. To do so, he framed Muslim migration as an issue beyond internal politics. Accepting Muslims was not 'a constitutional requirement'. Rather, it was fundamental to the Ottoman state. It was simply not possible for the caliph to reject Muslim immigrants.[61]

Ibrahim Hakkı further portrayed immigration and settlement as beyond politics through reference to economic benefit, state-generated information and administrative expertise. He dismissed Dalchef's charges of economic ruin and lack of land in Rumelia as factually incorrect. Administrators had access to land surveys and censuses, which demonstrated that Rumelia was underpopulated. The government's goal was not displacement. Instead, it was to bring hard-working individuals to the area, whose contributions ultimately assisted the local inhabitants. Furthermore, by adding more labourers to the population, the Interior Ministry encouraged large projects that opened even more land to development. Finally, he noted that migration management, rather than a threat to Ottomanism, provided a path to Ottoman unity. Since migrant settlement required apportioning land and encouraged landownership, it produced uniformity among subjects. Ibrahim Hakkı suggested that the Interior Ministry's methods were an example of how European states plagued by land issues and unrest might themselves create social stability. Uniformity of land ownership, he asserted, eradicated intercommunal conflicts and differences; in places where the Interior Ministry had adopted these principles, social divisions were resolving themselves.[62] Though Ibrahim Hakkı asserted that the government's intentions were pro-Ottoman rather than anti-Christian, the prime minister did not endorse migration policies free from exclusion. When Dalchef described the injustice of preventing the entry of Bulgarian returners, Ibrahim Hakkı interjected that 'obviously committees (revolutionary groups) should not come'.[63] His reference to the committees conflated the security threat of the Bulgarian revolutionary with the immigration of the Bulgarian returner.

Ibrahim Hakkı's defence of the government's settlement policies and his portrayal of Bulgarian returners fit a pattern. Within debates on settlement, unquestioned assumptions about the economics of immigration and the power of sound management reflected hegemonic expectations about the relationship between the state and its population. Those assumptions had been rendered sacrosanct and seemingly apolitical by five decades of migrant management. Ministers and MPs used those assumptions to deflect accusations of discriminatory social engineering even in the midst of their open endorsement of pro-Muslim policies.

OTTOMAN FRATERNITY AND BROTHERS FROM ABROAD

As it did among those who critiqued the government, the language and ideal of Ottomanism featured in the rhetoric of those who endorsed the Interior Ministry's settlement policies. The relationship between the state and its subjects was complementary. The state protected and cared for its subjects, and its subjects contributed to the perpetuation and strength of the state. Whereas Krikor, Keygam, Dalchef and Rıza Tevfik emphasised the first half of this relationship, those who defended the Interior Ministry

Muhacir *as Possibility*

emphasised the second half. Belonging was created through sacrifice and contribution, thus many potential Ottoman subjects lived beyond the empire's borders. They too fit within the bounds of Ottoman fraternity.

Histories of oppression, the language of humanity and refuge, and Ottomanism were wielded by those who endorsed Muslim migration as well as by those who argued on behalf of returners. For those in favour of the government's policies, the history of the Hamidian era was as much a story of Muslim suffering as of Christian flight. The empire's loss of territory in the Balkans during the Hamidian period meant that those who immigrated from the region were former Ottoman subjects, just like the Armenians and Bulgarians who had fled from the empire. In May 1910, after Pancho Dorev spoke, some deputies asked why he supposed that supporting Ottoman fraternity precluded welcoming 'brothers from abroad', and wondered whether Dorev advocated for 'shutting the door' on 'true Ottoman subjects'.[64] Likewise, in his response to Dalchef in November, Ibrahim Hakkı wondered how anyone, especially one who did not own the land in the first place, could complain when they saw a 'brother, or a compatriot' – 'not a stranger, but a child of the homeland' – seeking refuge.[65] Deputy Abdullah Azmi (Torun, Kütahya) mobilised history as he argued that Ottoman subjects had a responsibility to welcome those who had suffered at the hands of the empire's enemies. He argued that the people of Anatolia had borne the brunt of mass immigration after the 1877–8 Russo-Ottoman War. 'Though our fathers', he stated, 'had opened their homes to migrants, now our Rumelian compatriots form gangs and seek to drive them away. How does this befit fraternity?' In this light, it was Rumelian Christians, rather than the Interior Ministry, who betrayed Ottoman brotherhood.[66]

MPs employed the language of Ottomanism even as they endorsed pro-Muslim immigration policies. They contended that pro-returner policies betrayed Ottomanism. In the May debate, Talat Pasha and several MPs suggested that the state's policies were actually discriminatory against Muslim subjects. Talat asserted that when the Interior Ministry acquired land for settlement, it was careful to distribute land equally to immigrants and local Christians, yet it did not offer land to local Muslims. This was unjust.[67] In response to Talat, Ibrahim Efendi (İpek) noted that the policy was a mistake not only because it was discriminatory but also because it did not promote state security. Regardless of the ministry's effort to provide Christians with land, Christians raised 'baseless complaints'. Strong government, rather than mitigation policies, was necessary for peace in Rumelia.[68] Mehmed Talat Bey (Ankara) went further. The Interior Ministry did not incite Muslim migration, he noted, but it should.

Governing Migration in the Late Ottoman Empire

Increasing the Muslim population was sound policy and the best route to resist brigandage and uprisings.[69]

The meaning of Ottomanism and the path to an Ottoman future were contested concepts. As MPs debated immigration, they considered the issue in terms of who might contribute to the state and who might threaten it. The power of durable assumptions and the summoning of expertise allowed Mehmed Talat Bey to simultaneously endorse a pro-Muslim immigration policy and to deny that the government pursued discriminatory strategies.

THE WILL TO IMPROVE AND THE EVOCATION OF EXPERTISE

The expectation that plans and procedure could solve the problems of settlement was a legacy of fifty years of migration management; the possibility of effective administration framed debates over the Interior Ministry's actions. In February 1910, İlyas Sami Efendi (Muş) described 'migrant settlement' as 'a very basic issue', yet 'though something is added to the budget every year, there is no benefit'. Administrative failure caused migrant suffering and myriad other social issues, and it was necessary to finally find a 'definitive solution'.[70] Embedded in İlyas Sami's call to find a solution was his expectation that such a solution existed. For the Young Turks, it was no wonder that thirty years of Hamidian absolutism had neither addressed migrant suffering nor realised all the benefits that immigration promised. The constitutional regime could surely overcome the mistakes of its predecessor.

Before the new government could find such a solution, it first had to surmount the problems created by the *ancien régime*. Ibrahim Hakkı cast displacement and the suffering of returners as legacies of Hamidian autocracy. He acknowledged that the upheaval of the previous era had encouraged some subjects to flee the empire and that the Hamidian state had prevented their return and stolen their land. In contrast, his government 'happily' welcomed back those subjects. Nevertheless, the previous regime had left a complicated situation and hasty decision-making could only make things worse. Conditions called for careful investigation and detailed planning. Whereas his government did seek to resolve land disputes and assist returners, finding settlement locations for immigrants in temporary housing was, he asserted, a more pressing issue.[71] By blaming the Hamidian regime, Ibrahim Hakkı absolved the constitutional government for existing migration issues. Like many statesmen and administrators before him, Ibrahim Hakkı emphasised that the problem was not immigration but rather poorly conceived and executed policies.

Muhacir *as Possibility*

By framing the issue as one requiring judiciousness and carefully developed policy, he sought an extended grace period from criticism. He argued that his government's careful approach could ensure tranquillity, secure the well-being of migrants and foster feelings of brotherhood among migrants and non-migrants.

As was the case during the Tanzimat and Hamidian periods, moments of critique were opportunities to affirm the potential for improvement. For example, in his statements in favour of Zionist immigration in 1911, Dimitar Vlahov coupled his endorsement of immigration-driven economic growth with a critique of mismanagement. Immigration and emigration were fundamentally economic issues; people immigrated in search of economic security. Thus, the Ottoman state could stem emigration by improving the economy. Like administrators and statesmen before him, Vlahov understood the problem as one of poor planning and poor follow-through on the part of the administrators and settlement officials. Despite receiving significant numbers of immigrants since 1783, Vlahov asserted that the empire had never created a clear, overarching settlement policy. The disease, death and lives of poverty encountered by those who came to the empire stemmed from the failures of provincial administrators, who placed migrants in swamps and on insufficient land plots.[72] Far from a break from the assumptions of the previous generation of statesmen and administrators, however, Vlahov's suggestions would have been familiar to those he criticised. Vlahov identified three fundamental principles to guide the creation of a successful policy: first, that immigrants contributed to the country's economic progress; second, that since migrants arrived in hopes of improving their lives, they required resources and support to ensure that they fared better in the empire than they had in their homelands; and third, that immigration should not undermine the rights and well-being of local populations. If the state followed these principles, he concluded, it would improve the economy, overcome issues in immigrant settlement and resolve the problem of emigration.[73]

The day after Vlahov's statements on migration policy, the Chamber of Deputies considered the Interior Ministry's apportionment for migrant settlement. Though the body quickly passed the allocation without debate, Dr Rıza Nur (Sinope), well known for his opposition to the CUP, asked to speak further on the matter. The allocation of 200,000 lira, he argued, was not sufficient to resolve the troubles stemming from immigration. Immigrants struggled to acclimate, fell ill and passed away. Particularly 'humiliating' was that some Bosnians had petitioned the Austro-Hungarian Consulate for money to return to their former homes. Rıza Nur's commentary identified resolvable problems, such as following 'hygienic'

Governing Migration in the Late Ottoman Empire

principles in migrant settlement. Nevertheless, he also cast migration as inherently dangerous. Migration 'nibbled away at' more than half of those who undertook it. He estimated that of those who had emigrated from Europe to the United States, some 70 per cent perished from hardship, malnourishment, a lack of acclimation and the difficulties of travel. Rıza Nur concluded that the Ottoman state should not seek or encourage immigration of any kind, for it was often a terrible thing.[74]

Despite Rıza Nur's emphasis on the inherently devastating effects of migration for those who undertook it, Halil Bey, the Interior Minister (February 1911 to May 1912), responded with the familiar assertion that policy changes and better administration could resolve the issues Rıza Nur identified. According to Halil, the government did not incite immigration, and a forthcoming policy change clarified that for potential immigrants. After settling the current migrant population of 4,500 households, in the future the state would offer only land and no other assistance to immigrants. Further, Halil noted, a key factor in the problems Rıza Nur described was administrative: there was no 'regular committee' devoted to migration. The 200,000-lira allocation could not resolve every settlement issue in every district, but it did include 1,800 lira to create a regular committee and eradicate corruption by properly compensating administrators.[75] The promise of improvement embedded in statesmen's understanding of governance sufficed as a rejoinder to the MPs' criticism. The mistakes of settlement were to be resolved through improved planning and improved administration.

The weight of fifty years of migration management emerged as accumulated expertise. The policies and procedures generated across decades of responding to failure and critique served to rebut the charge of discrimination in settlement policies. In 1910, alongside deferring blame to the Hamidian regime and adopting the 'will to improve', Ibrahim Hakkı invoked the science of settlement: the government's decisions were determined by ecology, not politics. Administrators knew from previous experience that environmental factors were crucial to settlement. Whereas in the past, migrants from mountainous, forested regions had been sent to their deaths in Syria, he promised that the new administration, with the help of oversight from parliament, intended to follow a more logical approach. After all, he assumed deputies would object if 'we were to kill eighty per cent' of Balkan immigrants by sending them to catch 'malaria in the lowlands of Adana'.[76] Settling immigrants in regions similar to their places of origin was a fundamental principle. Ibrahim Hakkı asserted that Rumelia was 'unique' not only for its political attributes but for its geography; consequently, it was 'quite natural' that the government settle migrants from the Balkans there.[77]

Muhacir *as Possibility*

Several months later, when Dorev and Dalchef once more argued that the government's settlement policies used Muslims to displace locals, Talat Pasha maintained that settlement decisions were dictated by environmental constraints rather than anti-Christian policies. In his role as Interior Minister, Talat denied that the government 'was following some organized emigration policy or inciting immigration'. If anything, the ministry struggled to gain control over migrant settlement. The ministry's only reason for settling migrants in Rumelia, he asserted, was its concern with immigrants' environmental acclimation.[78] As the debate continued, Ibrahim Efendi (İpek) combined his pro-Muslim stance, noted above, with this ecological argument. He described the ache he felt upon seeing the suffering of children and other innocents who entered the empire. Certainly, such individuals needed to be cared for by the government rather than being sent to their deaths in Anatolia. Consequently, newcomers from the Balkans belonged in Rumelia, where they could live in the climate to which they were accustomed.[79]

* * *

Despite the earth-shattering language of revolution and their desire to reject Hamidian-era policies, many MPs retained a stance towards migration aligned with the past. For them, carefully administered immigration offered a route to economically strengthen the state. The *muhacir* as a productive, permanent settler soon to take on Ottoman nationality remained an ideal through which MPs considered policy, though their stance was tempered by the suffering that had accompanied population movement in previous decades and the contexts of their own districts. Discussions of the *muhacir* in parliament offered a venue to air concerns about the new government's population politics. Such critique, however, was met with assurances that proper planning would resolve any problems. Descriptions of emergency, the state's responsibility for displaced Muslims, the assumption of the positive aspects of population growth and even attention to environmental acclimation provided well-trodden arguments to dismiss concerns about the pace, timing, geography and outcomes of migrant settlement.

Debates on migration administration were personal for those whose own lives had followed the trajectories of hundreds of thousands of others. Rather than the most vociferous voices in favour of immigration, some parliamentarians with *muhacir* backgrounds criticised the government and asked for greater caution in migration management. In November 1910, Ömer Fevzi emphasised that it was essential to investigate how the Interior Ministry had spent previous funds before allocating more for migrant settlement. The problem was not just one of oversight. Without a comprehensive law governing migration and migrant settlement, it was pointless to offer 'four thousand lira here or five thousand lira there'. Only statistics, official investigation and a comprehensive law could resolve rampant upheaval and land disputes related to settlement.[80]

When Rıza Tevfik (Edirne) came to a similar conclusion, he framed his perspective as one informed by his past. In the same November debate, he asked his fellow parliamentarians a question: 'Can a bucket with a hole be filled by adding water?' The same principle, he suggested, applied to the population. As long as the Ottoman state continued to lose people, its population could not increase. Thus, rather than encouraging immigration, the government should focus on addressing security and justice, the necessary conditions for population growth. The goals of increasing the population and welcoming Muslims to the empire were admirable, yet inviting them to the empire without a careful plan was not in migrants' best interest. He knew this from experience, as he recalled living as a child in 'a wretched neighbourhood' at a time when eight hundred migrant bodies 'were tossed in Bülbülderesi Cemetery' each day. If Ottoman subjects already perished from poverty and lack of resources, immigrants would suffer the same fate. Since, he continued, 'we are helpless to resolve poverty if we fill the country with poor people', the government should consider laws like those in Britain or the United States, which prevented impoverished and sick individuals from entering the state. In the meantime, until the state compiled statistics, developed careful policies and passed the necessary laws, he did not support a budget allocation for migrant settlement.[81]

Conclusion

The Second Constitutional Period was an era of contested terms, when multiple groups sought to determine the bounds and meaning of Ottoman subjecthood. In parliament and in the RMIC's newspaper, the figure of the *muhacir* raised fundamental questions about the relationship between the state and its subjects during the Constitutional Era. What did the state owe to its subjects? Where lay the bounds of Ottomanism? Could the constitutional government solve the persistent problems of poverty, land disputes and upheaval that accompanied migrant settlement while creating a new, stronger and more economically sound Ottoman state? Those who identified as and with Rumelian Muslim migrants drew upon multiple meanings of the term *muhacir* to articulate their visions for the future of the Ottoman state.

The contributors to *Muhacir*, individuals whose lives had been directly affected by displacement, were acutely aware of the dangers confronting

Muhacir *as Possibility*

the empire. Still, in seeking a secure future for the Ottoman state, the small, literate subsection of migrants who contributed to *Muhacir* advocated for the Muslims of their former homelands to remain in place. In doing so, they endorsed a vision of international law and citizenship in which states protected the rights of their religious minorities. Forced migration was not inherently radicalising; writers in *Muhacir* envisioned paths outside of a strict Islamist or Turkish nationalist vision in the years immediately following the revolution of 1908. Nevertheless, the stance of the RMIC shifted with the start of the Balkan Wars. Society members' perspectives changed, like so many others in the period, as events unfolded, yet based on their discussions in 1909 and 1910, radicalisation and hatred of non-Muslim Ottomans was neither an immediate or automatic outcome of forced movement nor of identifying oneself as a *muhacir*.

In Ottoman state documents, parliamentary debates and the newspaper, the *muhacir* was important not just for their experience of displacement but also for the change they themselves could bring to Ottoman society. Coerced movement and rupture did not constitute the entirety of the term's meaning. Instead, the significance of *muhacir* came from its promise of new possibilities for the Ottoman state and Ottoman subjects. As they endorsed and critiqued the Ottoman government's settlement policies, MPs in the Chamber of Deputies did not question whether the state should engage in social engineering nor whether migration had a role in projects to improve the Ottoman population and Ottoman society. They worked within a hegemonic understanding of the population and governance, itself an outcome of more than fifty years of experimentation, critique and consolidation of techniques and principles within migration management. The decades-long history of Ottoman migration administration thus reveals the creation of durable, seemingly apolitical assumptions about the state and its relationship to the population. The ideology, infrastructure and practices of social engineering that eventually featured in the mass violence of World War I emerged within a logic of facilitated immigration and along non-ethnic and non-national lines of exclusion; rendering a certain understanding of the state outside the field of critique in the Second Constitutional Era.

Notes

1. Ömer Fevzi, 'Muhacirine bir Nida', *Muhacir* no. 11, 26 January 1910.
2. Gutman, *Politics of Armenian Migration*, 161; Ufuk Erdem, *Osmanlı'dan Cumhuriyet'e Muhacir Komisyonları (1860–1923)* (Ankara: Türk Tarih Kurumu Yayınları, 2018), 151.

Governing Migration in the Late Ottoman Empire

3. Gutman, *Politics of Armenian Migration*, 164.
4. Other such entities included the Circassian Unity and Mutual Aid Society and the Himaye-i Muhacirin Cemiyeti (Society for the Protection of Migrants), founded in Salonica in the spring of 1909. ŞD 2784.52, 24 Rebiyülahir 1327/15 April 1909.
5. '1326 Mart Senesinde Birinci Defa Olarak İçtima Eden Rumeli Muhahcirin-i İslamiye Cemiyeti Nizamnamesi', Atatürk Kitaplığı, İstanbul Belediyesi, Belediye K.816, 86–92.
6. Züriye Çelik, 'Osmanlının Zor Yıllarında Göçmenlerinin Türk Basınındaki Sesi: "Muhacir" Gazetesi (1909–1910)', *Türkiyat Araştırmaları Dergisi* 2010, no. 28 (2010): 405–12.
7. Bedross Der Matossian, *Shattered Dreams of Revolution: From Liberty to Violence in the Late Ottoman Empire* (Stanford, CA: Stanford University Press, 2014), 7.
8. Blumi, *Ottoman Refugees*, 61.
9. See Bedross Der Matossian, *The Horrors of Adana: Revolution and Violence in the Early Twentieth Century* (Stanford, CA: Stanford University Press, 2022).
10. See Y. Doğan Çetinkaya, *The Young Turks and the Boycott Movement: Nationalism, Protest, and the Working Class in the Formation of Modern Turkey* (London: I. B. Tauris, 2014).
11. Nedim İpek, 'Trablusgarb ve Bingazi Mültecileri (1911–1912)', *19 Mayıs Üniversitesi Eğitim Fakültesi Dergisi* 9 (1994): 96.
12. Akçam, *The Young Turks' Crime*, 88–9.
13. Uğur Ümit Üngör, '"Turkey for the Turks": Demographic Engineering in Eastern Anatolia, 1914–1945', in *A Question of Genocide*, 295–7.
14. Donald Bloxham, 'Internal Colonization, Inter-Imperial Conflict and the Armenian Genocide', in *Empire, Colony, Genocide: Conquest, Occupation, and Subaltern Resistance in World History*, ed. A. Dirk Moses (New York: Berghahn Books, 2008), 325.
15. Erik Jan Zurcher, 'The Balkan Wars and the Refugee Leadership of the Early Turkish Republic', in *War and Nationalism: The Balkan Wars, 1912–1913, and the Sociopolitical Implications*, ed. M. Hakan Yavuz and Isa Blumi (Salt Lake City: University of Utah Press, 2013), 665–78; Üngör, *Making of Modern Turkey*, 42–6.
16. Şeker, 'Demographic Engineering', 462.
17. Y. Doğan Çetinkaya, 'Illustrated Atrocity: The Stigmatisation of Non-Muslims through Images in the Ottoman Empire during the Balkan Wars', *Journal of Modern European History* 12, no. 4 (2014): 469; Eyal Ginio, *The Ottoman Culture of Defeat: The Balkan Wars and Their Aftermath* (New York: Oxford University Press, 2016), 99.
18. See Campos, *Ottoman Brothers*; Julia Cohen, *Becoming Ottomans: Sephardi Jews and Imperial Citizenship in the Modern Era* (New York: Oxford University Press, 2014).

Muhacir *as Possibility*

19. See Isa Blumi, *Ottoman Refugees*; Ramazan Hakkı Öztan and Alp Yenen, eds, *Age of Rogues: Rebels, Revolutionaries and Racketeers at the Frontiers of Empires* (Edinburgh: Edinburgh University Press, 2021); Ussama Makdisi, *The Culture of Sectarianism: Community, History, and Violence in Nineteenth Century Lebanon* (Berkeley: University of California Press, 2000); Ryan Gingeras, *Sorrowful Shores: Violence, Ethnicity, and the End of the Ottoman Empire 1912–1923* (New York: Oxford University Press, 2011); İpek Yosmaoğlu, *Blood Ties: Religion, Violence, and the Politics of Nationhood in Ottoman Macedonia, 1878–1908* (Ithaca, NY: Cornell University Press, 2014).

20. Ramazan Hakkı Öztan, 'Point of No Return? Prospects of Empire after the Ottoman Defeat in the Balkan Wars (1912–1913)', *IJMES* 50, no. 1(2018): 65–84.

21. Suny, *They Can Live in the Desert*.

22. Bezci Edhem, 'Evlad Baba Müsahabasi', *Muhacir* no. 10, 22 January 1910.

23. Behlül Özkan, *From the Abode of Islam to the Turkish Vatan: The Making of a National Homeland in Turkey* (New Haven, CT: Yale University Press, 2012), 39–40.

24. Varnalı Ahmed Hilmi, 'Muhacir Hemşehirlerime', *Muhacir* no. 1, 22 December 1909.

25. Rashid Rida, 'Must Muslims Leave Austro-Hungarian Bosnia', trans. Alan Verskin, in Verskin, *Oppressed in the Land? Fatwas on Muslims Living under Non-Muslim Rule from the Middle Ages to the Present* (Princeton, NJ: Markus Wiener Publishers, 2013), 113–27.

26. Ahmed Şukri, 'Izah-i Meram', *Muhacir* no. 2, 25 December 1909.

27. Ibid.

28. Ahmed Şukri, 'Bosna ve Hersek İslam Kardeşlerimize', *Muhacir* no. 8, 15 January 1910.

29. Ibid.

30. 'Hicret Etmeli mi? Etmemeli mi? Hatime', *Muhacir* no. 24, 13 March, 1910.

31. Dobrucalı Şukri, 'Hicret Meselesi', *Muhacir* no. 25, 16 March 1910.

32. Lofçalı Mehmet Hulusi, 'İfade-i Hususiye', *Muhacir* no. 1, 22 December 1909.

33. Osmancık, 'Muhacir Hemşehirlerimize Hitab', *Muhacir* no. 20, 26 February 1910. Members of the RMIC held events intended to foster such unity. For example, a letter from the society's Gümülcine Branch described the success of a wrestling competition and national games event the branch sponsored in May 1910. Thousands of people from surrounding towns and villages had attended, allowing for 'migrants and original inhabitants' to meet one another, and, as the governor of Edirne described, to gather together, as 'children of the homeland' without distinction of type or sect. 'Gümülcine'deki Merkezimizden Mektub', *Muhacir* no. 54, 25 June 1910.

34. Ömer Fevzi, 'Muhaceret-i Hakikiye', *Muhacir* no. 17, 16 February 1910.

35. Quran 2:195. 'do not throw [yourselves] with your [own] hands into destruction [by refraining]'.

36. Ömer Fevzi, 'Muhaceret-i Hakikiye'.
37. MMZC 1.1.4.82, 16 Mayıs 1325/29 May 1909, 11.
38. Ibid., 12.
39. MMZC 1.2.2.34, 20 Kânunusani 1325/2 February 1910, 92.
40. MMZC 1.2.2.35, 23 Kânunusani 1325/5 February 1910, 125–7.
41. Ibid., 127.
42. MMZC 1.1.2.39, 25 Şubat 1324/10 March 1909, 224–5.
43. Mehmed Talat was still 'Mehmed Talat Bey' in 1909, but I have opted to refer to 'Talat Pasha' since this is how he is widely known and to disambiguate him from another MP of the same name.
44. MMZC 1.1.2.42, 4 Mart 1325/17 March 1909, 327.
45. MMZC 1.1.6.133, 1 August 1325/14 August 1909, 401.
46. MMZC 1.2.5.97, 12 Mayıs 1326/25 May 1910, 479–80.
47. Ibid., 480. Rıza Tevfik also expressed support for Zionism. See Fishman, *Jews and Palestinians*, 178.
48. Can, *Spiritual Subjects*.
49. See Yosmaoğlu, *Blood Ties*.
50. MMZC 1.2.5.97, 481–2.
51. MMZC 1.3.1.7 13 Teşrinisani 1326/26 November 1910, 160.
52. Barış Zeren notes that unlike many of his cohort of Macedo-Bulgarian MPs, Dorev remained in parliament until the eve of the Balkan Wars, reflecting his sincere attachment to the promise of the constitution. Zeren, 'Between Constitution, Empire, and Nation: An Intellectual Trajectory of Pancho Dorev and his Legalist Paradigm', in *The Turkish Connection: Global Intellectual Histories of the Late Ottoman Empire and Republican Turkey*, ed. Deniz Kuru and Hazal Papuccular (Boston: De Gruyter, 2022), 52.
53. MMZC 1.3.6.100, 17 May 1911, 602–3.
54. MMZC 1.3.6.99, 3 Mayıs 1327/16 May 1911, 557. Quoted in Fishman, *Jews and Palestinians*, 188–9.
55. Fishman, *Jews and Palestinians*, 188.
56. For a discussion of Vlahov's political perspectives and intellectual milieu, see Pelin Tiglay, 'The Ideological Melting Pot: Salonican Socialists and "Empire" during the Second Constitutional Period (1908–1912)', *Etudes Balkaniques* 2022, no. 4 (2022): 609–39.
57. MMZC 1.3.6.100, 4 Mayıs 1327/17 May 1911, 610.
58. Ibid., 611.
59. For a discussion of the articles Vlahov referenced, see Samuel Dolbee and Shay Hazkani, 'Unlikely Identities: Abu Ibrahim and the Politics of Possibility in Late Ottoman Palestine', *Jerusalem Quarterly* 63–4 (2015): 24–39.
60. MMZC 1.3.6.100, 610–11.
61. MMZC 1.2.5.97, 25 May 1910, 483.
62. Ibid., 484.
63. Ibid., 482.

Muhacir *as Possibility*

64. MMZC 1.3.1.7, 159–60.
65. MMZC 1.2.5.97, 484.
66. MMZC 1.3.1.7, 165–6.
67. Ibid., 161.
68. Ibid., 163.
69. Ibid., 165.
70. MMZC 1.2.2.35, 128.
71. MMZC 1.2.5.97, 480–1.
72. MMZC 1.3.6.100, 610.
73. Ibid.
74. MMZC 1.3.6.101, 675. The question of whether the CUP government actively incited Muslim migration was another topic of frequent debate.
75. Ibid., 675–7.
76. Rather than an exaggeration, Ibrahim Hakkı's reference to an 80 per cent death rate reflected estimates from the 1880s of the horrific outcomes of *muhacir* settlement in Çukurova in the years prior. See Gratien, *Unsettled Plain*, 69.
77. MMZC 1.2.5.97, 483.
78. MMZC 1.3.1.7, 161.
79. Ibid., 163.
80. Ibid., 162.
81. Ibid., 166–7.

Conclusion
Categories of Movement and Categories of Belonging

Who was a *muhacir*? What does that term reveal about Ottoman governance? This book has considered those questions across sixty years of Ottoman history. The six decades spanning the mid-nineteenth to the early-twentieth centuries were marked by tremendous changes in the empire's territorial breadth, in the capacity of the state to intervene in individuals' lives, and in how Ottoman subjects understood themselves within Ottoman society. During that time, millions of individuals immigrated to and settled in Ottoman territory, contributing to tremendous demographic, economic, cultural and political changes. Migrants transformed Ottoman society, and so too did the governance of migration. The shifting meaning of *muhacir* reflected and contributed to those changes. Across that period, the *muhacir* evoked multiple and overlapping connotations, ideas and social roles, yet certain aspects of the meaning of the *muhacir* persisted across time. Across sixty years, Ottoman reformers, statesmen and officials identified the migrant for what they promised. The category of *muhacir* stemmed from movement across borders; however, the promise of the *muhacir* was tied to stasis. By becoming unambiguously Ottoman subjects, settling in permanent locations and developing Ottoman land, the ideal *muhacir* – productive, tax-paying and loyal – was to breathe new life into the Ottoman economy and strengthen Ottoman sovereignty. A persistent aspect of the *muhacir* emerged as well from reformers' certainty that the state could and should manage mobility to realise migrants' potential. That guiding assumption determined how Ottoman officials envisioned the ideal *muhacir* over time and how they developed the tools, techniques and interventions of the modern state.

Governmentality and Migration Administration

Beginning in the eighteenth century, statesmen in the Ottoman Empire began to enact centralising measures and developed the apparatus, infrastructure,

Conclusion

tools and techniques of a modern state. Their reforms emerged from a new rationality of governance – governmentality, identified by Michel Foucault as intrinsic to the survival of the modern state – which positioned population as the 'ultimate end of government'.[1] The population became an entity with characteristics that could be identified, understood and manipulated through new techniques and tactics intended to intervene in the lives and consciousness of individuals. The art of government relied upon rendering the population 'legible', that is, organising people 'in a manner that permit[ed] them to be identified, observed, recorded, counted, aggregated, and monitored'.[2]

The management of human mobility arose from and contributed to the development of governmentality within the empire. In the mid-nineteenth century, Ottoman statesmen sought to encourage immigration to increase the empire's population density and agricultural productivity, and the Tanzimat Council, the empire's main legislative body from 1854–61, issued the 1857 Migrant Regulations (*Muhacirin Nizamnamesi*) in an attempt to attract European settlers to the empire during the nineteenth-century global migration boom. The 1857 regulations were a formal assertion of the Ottoman state's right and responsibility to control movement across the border. As an invitation to colonists to settle in the empire, the regulations emerged from a logic of facilitating and enabling migration. Nonetheless, by seeking to formalise, standardise and oversee the process of immigration, Ottoman statesmen simultaneously endorsed a logic of constraining it in accordance with specific parameters.

Beginning in the 1860s and persisting until the dissolution of the empire, episodes of mass immigration overwhelmed the administrative and logistical capacity of the Ottoman state. In the face of the expansion of the Russian Empire, multiple wars, territorial change and intercommunal violence, millions of individuals crossed into Ottoman territory. Though the 1857 Migrant Regulations were intended to attract self-sufficient colonists to the empire, many of those who arrived during moments of mass migration were in need of emergency shelter, food and medical treatment. In 1860, the Tanzimat Council established the Migrant Commission to centrally coordinate the vast and complex project of immigrant reception, aid and settlement. Alongside developing tools and policies to address the immediate needs of those who arrived in the empire, officials within the Migrant Commission sought to turn impoverished immigrants into the productive colonists envisioned in 1857. Their efforts to do so tied the distribution of resources, in the form of short-term aid and long-term assistance, to the category of *muhacir*.

Governing Migration in the Late Ottoman Empire

The *muhacirin* overseen by the Migrant Commission remained a means to change Ottoman society and to strengthen the Ottoman state, but migrants were also subject to techniques intended to mould them into ideal subjects. Officials developed strategies to render Ottoman territory, migrants and the broader population more legible and governable, such as cadastral surveys, property registers and detailed plans for villages and housing. Administrators' attempts to settle large numbers of newcomers encountered perennial problems, including migrant disease, departure and death; delayed settlement; insufficient and harmful land allotments; and land disputes, instability and conflict. Officials' response to moments of crisis and administrative failure contributed to the development of techniques to overcome these issues. For instance, to stem the spread of disease and to convert newcomers into healthy, productive settlers, officials developed institutions and techniques to contain, spatially arrange and tabulate populations of concern. These projects further extended the state's presence in the lives of its subjects.

Thus, migration administration was tied closely to governmentality, and officials managed migrants, migration and settlement to develop the Ottoman population for the benefit of the Ottoman state. Administrators intervened in the population at the empire's borders and in its interior, deployed migrants to create a more uniform, legible property regime, and developed techniques to manage and manipulate migrant and non-migrant behaviour.

Social Engineering and the Muhacir

At the border and in the distribution of land and aid, migration administration provided sites for statesmen and officials to identify and subject the population to social engineering. At its most fundamental level, social engineering requires identifying and acting upon groups within the population in order to eliminate certain behaviours and ways of being. Such efforts are directed at those considered beneficial to the state as well as those deemed detrimental. By the twentieth century, the categories that administrators used to mould the population 'into an ideal image' often included ethnic, religious and national classifications.[3] Nonetheless, the history of late Ottoman migration administration suggests other categories in play prior to and alongside those classifications. Highlighting how statesmen and officials defined and sought to manage the ideal *muhacir* at various moments reveals contingencies and possibilities in how Ottoman officials envisioned the model Ottoman subject and society. Ottoman migration management reflected internal politics and concerns, but it was

Conclusion

never an entirely domestic affair. Migration policy reflected statesmen's concerns about Ottoman sovereignty, territorial loss and the empire's status vis-à-vis the Great Powers. Those factors shaped the attributes of the ideal Ottoman and the ideal *muhacir* as, over time, statesmen, administrators, officials and other Ottoman subjects adopted new criteria in their vision for Ottoman society, identified groups as capable and incapable of reform, and relied on prescriptive and proscriptive techniques to manipulate those groups.

The 1857 Migrant Regulations established the most important attributes of the *muahcir* as productivity and subjecthood. The regulations identified the *muhacir* as, first and foremost, a colonist, essential to statesmen's efforts to develop the empire's economy. Settlers received free land, over which they established full ownership after a period of twenty years, and multi-year exemptions from taxation and military conscription. The law required Ottoman consular agents to complete a character check and to verify that applicants met a capital requirement. The Capitulations and the European protégé system placed the Ottoman Empire within an inter-imperial competition for subjects, which rendered migrants' establishment of unambiguous Ottoman subjecthood crucial in the 1857 regulations and in subsequent laws. Thus, in 1857, the Tanzimat Council established the ideal *muhacir* as a hardworking, law-abiding, self-sufficient and permanent settler. This ideal informed the work of officials in the Migrant Commission and its later institutional iterations.

As noted above, Ottoman administrators' responses to moments of mass migration attached the distribution of resources to migration policy and to the category of the *muhacir*. The attachment of aid to migrant management further indicated the means by which officials classified, understood and acted upon the population. As officials sought to defray the costs of aid and settlement, they generated and applied categories to the migrant population itself. These categories split the population along lines of self-sufficiency and predicted productivity, captured by attributes such as age, gender, disability, social ties and existing wealth. The expectation of productivity unfolded as well when officials demarcated space for migrant settlement. Placing migrants, especially those whom administrators perceived as particularly productive and 'civilised', was a means to inspire, correct and develop the empire's rural population.

Inter-imperial competition and threats to Ottoman sovereignty contributed to the political significance of the *muhacir* following the 1877–8 Russo-Ottoman War and the Treaty of Berlin. As a result of the war, the empire lost most of its territory in the Balkans. The success of former Ottoman subjects in asserting their independence in Bulgaria, Romania,

Serbia and Montenegro sharpened some statesmen's perception of non-Muslim subjects in Rumelia and Anatolia as security threats. The Treaty of Berlin's minority protection clauses and its proposed reform plan for Eastern Anatolia further elevated the strategic importance administrators attached to the demographic distribution of ethnic and religious groups within the empire. In the 1880s and 1890s, the emergence of Armenian, Macedonian and Bulgarian revolutionary organisations and European powers' renewed calls for reform in Eastern Anatolia influenced the Hamidian state's embrace of Islamic Ottomanism. The regime established a Commission for Muslim Migrants in order to facilitate Muslim immigration and issued a new set of Migrant Regulations to increase border control and to reflect the reality that the empire had shifted away from encouraging European immigration. During the Hamidian period, the ideal *muhacir* was Muslim, and as the Hamidian state sought to promote Muslim economic development at the expense of other groups, migrant settlement contributed to the dispossession of non-Muslim subjects in Rumelia and Anatolia.

By the beginning of the Second Constitutional Period, aid had been a component of *muhacir* management for five decades, such that Ottoman parliamentarians understood the distribution of aid as fundamental to '*muhacir*' as an administrative category. Following the 1908 Young Turk Revolution, the Ottoman government initially reopened its borders, lifted a ban on Armenian immigration, welcomed back those who had fled from the violent excesses of the Hamidian regime and dropped the modifier 'Muslim' from the Migrant Commission. These policies aligned with the expectation, shared by many within the Young Turk movement, that Ottoman unity fostered by the equality of groups within the empire could overcome the problems created by the previous regime. Despite its embrace of Ottomanism in principle, from 1909–11, the Ottoman Interior Ministry used the distinction between *muhacirin* – in theory, anyone who met the expectations of Ottoman immigration law, but in practice, mostly Balkan Muslims – and 'returners' – non-Muslim Ottoman emigres who were denied re-entry during the Hamidian era, to justify reserving government assistance for the former.

Critique, Generative Failure and the Consolidation of the Ottoman State

The gap between ideal and outcome is fundamental to governance and state development, as 'the "will to govern", [is] fueled by the constant registration of "failure", the discrepancy between ambition and outcome, and

Conclusion

the constant injunction to do better next time'.[4] This book has explored how the officials who oversaw immigration and settlement were multifaceted individuals. They articulated visions of good governance and identified their work as serving to promote the empire's sovereignty, economy and progress; nonetheless, their perspectives and actions were shaped by their personalities and their own interests. Perhaps unsurprisingly, when their large-scale plans for change encountered challenges and unwelcome outcomes, they critiqued their colleagues and other Ottoman subjects on similar grounds. A fundamental proposal of modern governance is that it can muster administrative, infrastructural and technological expertise to manage the population. Ottoman officials wielded that presupposition to cast human error, ignorance and corruption, rather than plans themselves, as the root cause of failures in migrant management.

The story of migration administration is not a story of a fully formed, unified, autonomous state acting upon society, not least because 'the state' never exists as such. The state 'does not have this unity, this individuality, this rigorous functionality'.[5] Nevertheless, an element of the power of 'the state' is its image as a coherent entity external to, elevated above and acting upon society. In this book, I have considered how the history of migration management, and in particular, the gaps between administrators' ideals and the realities they encountered contributed not only to the development of techniques of rule but also to the image of the unified, autonomous, rational Ottoman state. Ottoman migration administration reveals the processes that give rise to that conceptualisation and its broader acceptance within society. The process of registering failure and seeking 'to do better next time' elevated forms of calculation, registration and documentation intended to depersonalise and render rational the workings of the state. Ottoman administrators, migrants and other Ottoman subjects participated in the process of critiquing and developing projects to improve governance.

Migration administration was crucial in Ottoman officials' claims to legitimacy through efficacy and expertise within and beyond the empire. The stakes of failure in migrant settlement were high, encompassing horrific death rates, epidemic disease, land disputes, banditry, intercommunal conflict and alienation of subjects. During the Tanzimat era, careful and effective administration was a component of how Ottoman officials sought to appeal to the empire's heterogeneous population. In subsequent decades, the fate of the *muhacir* was an element in diplomatic discussions and Ottoman claims to sovereignty. For example, Great Power politics influenced aspects of how Ottoman officials approached the administrative and infrastructural difficulties of responding to mass migration.

Governing Migration in the Late Ottoman Empire

Officials undertook measures to address public health and migrant welfare not only to resolve issues of stability and epidemic disease but also to frame the Ottoman state as efficacious, capable and civilised. In the early Hamidian period, self-representation to the population and to the Great Powers contributed to the expansion of official and semi-official aid and relief efforts.

The accrual of expertise – gained through experience and re-entrenched following the diagnosis of failure – ultimately rendered certain aspects of migration management hegemonic and seemingly outside the realm of politics. This is clear in administrators' identification of the environment as crucial to successful settlement. While environmental factors are mentioned in settlement plans and instructions dating to the mid-1850s, migrant death and suffering caused by their placement in malarial environments, on rocky soil and in insufficient allotments rendered 'failure to acclimate' a frequent and effective means for them to petition for relocation. By the 1870s, officials foregrounded the principle that migrants had a greater chance of success if they were settled in areas environmentally similar to that of their place of origin, and by the 1880s, officials thus categorised migrants by their ecological origin and attempted to match them to territory based on that criteria. During the Second Constitutional Era, this science of settlement, established as a result of extensive suffering and horrific death rates, allowed the CUP government to deny the charge of discriminatory settlement policies in Rumelia.

Migration Administration and Population Politics at the End of Empire

Mass migration, and the Ottoman state's attempts to manage it, persisted beyond the timeframe of this book. Expulsions from the Ottoman Empire and its successor states continued into World War I. During the Armenian Genocide, Ottoman officials viewed the Armenian population as an existential threat to their empire. Deportations and massacre led to the death of an estimated one million people. The IAMM, renamed the General Directorate of Tribes and Migrants (Aşair ve Muhacirin Müdüriyeti Umumiyesi, AMMU) during World War I, was involved in deportation and settlement. The institution collected demographic information, and the director of the IAMM, Şükrü Kaya, 'personally organized and oversaw most of the deportations' of Armenians and Kurds beginning in 1915.[6] The CUP intended Kurdish resettlement in Western Anatolia to lead to their rapid adoption of Turkish. To that end, the organisation placed limits on the concentration of the Kurdish population in places they were

Conclusion

settled. The IAMM/AMMU simultaneously coordinated the placement of Muslims displaced from the Balkans. Like the Kurdish resettlement plan, the migrant settlement process was intended to change the newcomers by dispersing them.[7] Muslim refugees of World War I were once more subjects and objects of social engineering, as the IAMM/AMMU's settlement of migrants contributed to the mass transfer of Armenian property intended to establish a Turkish national economy.[8]

Governmentality and social engineering are integral to the violence enacted by the Ottoman state in the empire's final decade. Late Ottoman genocides and the politics of genocide denial have cast a long shadow over histories of the late Ottoman Empire, obscuring how displacement, expulsion and massacre in Southeastern Europe and Anatolia are intertwined.[9] Considering these events as overlapping processes need not place competing experiences of victimhood in opposition, as has been a tactic of genocide denial.[10] Instead, considering genocide in light of a longer history of population politics can shed light on the emergence of a 'genocidal moment'.[11] The 'genocidal moments' of the Young Turk era emerged from existing practices of social engineering, based on an established relationship between the Ottoman state, Ottoman territory and the Ottoman population. The rationale of governance and underlying logic of social engineering, that is, that the state can and should identify and manipulate the characteristics of its population, was durable across regimes. In this way, continuities from the Ottoman Empire to the Turkish Republic are analogous to those Peter Holquist has identified in the transition from the Russian Tsarist to the Bolshevik eras, a continuity of 'preconditions and tools for operating on the social body through techniques of violence'.[12]

Officials in the Ottoman Empire conceived of the population as a knowable entity and a target of state policies of improvement, or social engineering. The *muhacir* comprised a crucial component of Ottoman population politics across the second half of the nineteenth century. This book has shown that, over time, internal and external social and political contexts shifted the characteristics of the ideal *muhacir* for Ottoman officials, yet their underlying conceptualisation of the utility of the *muhacir* was durable. The creation of the Migrant Commission and its subsequent institutional iterations over the decades allowed officials to envision, if not to fully enact, systematic and centralised responses to mass immigration. Though individuals fleeing from conditions of war, conflict and massacre may seem more intuitively 'refugees' than 'colonisers', from the perspective of the central state and its officials, the potential for immigrants to remake Ottoman society remained significant regardless of the causes of their movement. As Ottoman statesmen felt the pressure of limited sovereignty

Governing Migration in the Late Ottoman Empire

and as they became increasingly drawn to language of religious, ethnic and national exclusion, the parameters of the ideal *muhacir* shifted.

Late Ottoman society did not trudge towards an ultimate, primordial showdown between Turks and Armenians. Far from inevitable, genocide was a contingent event even in the early stages of World War I.[13] Instead, the practice of social engineering inherent to Ottoman immigrant settlement functioned within Ottoman population politics to create possibilities of social expulsion. Kurdish tribes and Circassian immigrants in Eastern Anatolia highlight the range of these possibilities. Both groups were notorious as participants in inter-communal conflict, land grabs and genocide; they were also subject to social engineering in the nineteenth century and deportation in the twentieth.[14] When Ottoman officials became convinced that the displacement, massacre and assimilation of certain groups was the route to saving the empire, they mobilised existing pathways of social expulsion, statistical knowledge about Ottoman territory and the infrastructure of population removal. Engagement with the population as a site of governance in the nineteenth century made possible the mass expulsions of the twentieth century.

The Enduring Significance of Labels

World War I and its aftermath contributed to the international governance, terminology and categorisation of migrants. The immediate aftermath of the war was a moment when other terms like *exile* and *émigré* withered away, and 'the refugee' took on 'the central role in the field of human displacement'.[15] Twenty million people were displaced in Europe as a result of the war. In order to coordinate relief and repatriation, the League of Nations established its High Commission for Refugees, beginning the consolidation of an intergovernmental institutional response to forced displacement. In 1922, Fridtjof Nansen, the High Commissioner for Refugees, created an identity certificate to allow greater interstate movement for some 800,000 Russian refugees. In 1924, the commission extended the Nansen Passports to Armenian refugees. While the Nansen Passport allowed for freedom of movement, it also regularised the status of refugees as distinct from citizens and other migrants.[16]

In 1923, Greece and the newly established Republic of Turkey signed the Convention on the Exchange of Populations, which led to the permanent relocation of nearly two million individuals. The internationally sanctioned forced population movement designated the 'Turkish nationals of the Greek Orthodox religion' in Turkish territory and 'Greek nationals of the Moslem religion' in Greece as subject to forced relocation.

Conclusion

The convention banned Greek-Orthodox Ottoman subjects who had already fled the empire from returning, and one and a half million Greek Orthodox Christians ended up in Greece. Half a million Muslim 'Turks' settled in Turkey, where they were placed on the 'abandoned' property of former Ottoman subjects, though the process of *mübadil* (exchanged person) settlement was 'negotiated against a background of local resistance and competing objectives of other institutions of the Turkish state'.[17] The convention reflected an internationally shared belief that religious and ethnic minorities within nation states inherently created conditions of instability. The logic of the Population Exchange assumed religion was enough to guarantee a sense of belonging. Nevertheless, the social divisions between migrant and non-migrant and the labels of *mübadil*, *muhacir* and refugee persisted for decades in Republican Turkey and in Greek cities and towns.[18]

The question of who is a migrant and who is a refugee, and the meanings attached to those terms, continue to shape practices of inclusion and exclusion around the world, including within Ottoman successor states. For example, within the Turkish Republic, ethno-nationalism set the terms of migration and citizenship after independence. Ayşe Parla asserts that Turkey is unique in moving beyond a preference for immigrants to have certain ethnic status to legally defining 'immigrant' (*göçmen*) in terms of ethnicity.[19] Settlement Laws in 1926, 1934 and 2006 restricted migration to individuals who were ethnically or culturally Turkish. After World War I, the Turkish government settled Balkan Muslims on Armenians' 'abandoned' property and used the settlers in Western Anatolia to stave off irredentist claims from other Balkan states.[20] As 'ethnic kin', Muslim immigrants from the Balkans retained a privileged position in migration law until 1990. The Turkish government treated Balkan migrants as repatriates rather than refugees, including the 300,000 forced migrants who fled Bulgaria in 1989 in the midst of violent assimilation campaigns.[21]

Legal categories likewise play a role in contemporary population movements. Since 2011, Turkey has received millions of individuals fleeing the Syrian Civil War and for several years has been the world's top refugee-hosting country. Nevertheless, Turkey retains the geographical limitations written into the UN's 1951 Refugee Convention, which restricts official refugee and asylum status to individuals fleeing from Europe. Turkish authorities designate non-European asylum seekers 'conditional refugees'; the UNHCR determines legal refugee status in order to move migrants to third countries. Turkey's restricted use of the term 'refugee' affected its policies towards its largest refugee population. Syrians are not eligible for refugee status in Turkey. Instead, as a result of the 2013 Law on

Governing Migration in the Late Ottoman Empire

Foreigners and International Protection, Turkey offers Syrians 'temporary protection status'. While Syrians do not need to apply individually for asylum, the status has left them stranded somewhere between refugee and guest, confined them to their provinces of registration and denied even individuals born in Turkey a clear pathway to full citizenship.[22] In 2016, the Turkish government proposed offering naturalisation to Syrians who met educational, capital and skill criteria, but the process remains highly contentious. In the midst of a years-long economic crisis, resentment over the distribution of aid to non-citizens and rising xenophobia rendered Syrians a key issue in the lead-up to Turkey's 2023 presidential and parliamentary elections.

Whether in the Ottoman Empire or in contemporary states, the labels used to differentiate among mobile individuals do not describe innate characteristics of the individuals to whom they are applied. Terms used in national, regional and international contexts to categorise movement – for example im/migrant, refugee, nomad, pilgrim, tourist – emerge from specific social orders at specific moments.[23] Those terms offer insight into the societies and individuals who employ them. As a concept in use prior to the emergence of the migrant/refugee binary, the changing meaning of the *muhacir* captures global historical patterns, such as the consolidation of states' right to control movement into their territories and the ensuing elevation of causality to determine migrant labels. The concept also captures specificities of Ottoman sovereignty and Ottoman society. The history of migration administration reveals an Ottoman state developing the tools of population management and social engineering. The history of a regime in motion, Ottoman migration administration highlights the interplay of internal and external forces in ever-changing parameters of inclusion and exclusion.

Notes

1. Foucault, 'Governmentality', 100.
2. Scott, *Seeing Like a State*, 183.
3. Weiner, 'Nature, Nurture, and Memory', 1116.
4. Rose and Miller, 'Political Power beyond the State', 191.
5. Foucault, 'Governmentality', 103.
6. Üngör, 'Turkey for the Turks', 295.
7. Ibid., 299.
8. Uğur Ümit Üngür and Mehmet Polatel, *Confiscation and Destruction: The Young Turk Seizure of Armenian Property* (London: Continuum International Publishing Group, 2011).

Conclusion

9. Dominik J. Schaller and Jürgen Zimmerer, 'Late Ottoman Genocides: The Dissolution of the Ottoman Empire and Young Turkish Population and Extermination Policies – Introduction', *Journal of Genocide Research* 10, no. 1 (2008): 7–14.

10. Justin McCarthy's *Death and Exile: The Ethnic Cleansing of Ottoman Muslims, 1821–1922* (Princeton, NJ: Darwin University Press, 1995) is an example of one such work. David Gutman describes several facets of denialism within Ottoman historiography in 'Ottoman Historiography and the End of the Genocide Taboo: Writing the Armenian Genocide into Late Ottoman History', *JOTSA* 2, no. 1 (2015): 167–83.

11. A. Dirk Moses, 'An Antipodean Genocide? The Origins of the Genocidal Moment in the Colonization of Australia', *Journal of Genocide Research* 2, no. 1 (2000): 89–106.

12. Holquist, 'To Count, to Extract', 128.

13. Suny, *They Can Live in the Desert*.

14. Bloxham, 'Internal Colonization', 328–33; Üngör, *Making of Modern Turkey*, 107–66.

15. Soğuk, *States and Strangers*, 103.

16. Ibid., 131.

17. Ellinor Morack, 'Refugees, Locals and "The" State: Property Compensation in the Province of Izmir Following the Greco-Turkish Population Exchange of 1923', *JOTSA* 2, no. 1 (2015): 163.

18. See Renee Hirschon, ed., *Crossing the Aegean: An Appraisal of the 1923 Compulsory Population Exchange between Greece and Turkey* (New York: Berghahn Books, 2003).

19. Ayşe Parla, *Precarious Hope: Migration and the Limits of Belonging in Turkey* (Stanford, CA: Stanford University Press, 2019), 17.

20. See Öztan, 'Settlement Law of 1934'.

21. Parla, *Precarious Hope*.

22. Feyzi Baban, Suzan Ilcan and Kim Rygiel, 'Syrian Refugees in Turkey: Pathways to Precarity, Differential Inclusion, and Negotiated Citizenship Rights', *Journal of Ethnic and Migration Studies* 43, no. 1 (2017): 45–51.

23. Nail, *The Figure of the Migrant*, 16.

Bibliography

Primary Sources

ARCHIVAL SOURCES

BAŞBAKANLIK OSMANLI ARŞIVI, ISTANBUL, TURKEY

A.DVN.MKL	Sadaret Divan Mukavelenameler
A.MKT.MHM	Sadaret Mektubi Mühimme Kalemi Evrakı
A.MKT.NZD	Sadaret Mektubi Kalemi Nezaret ve Devair Evrakı
A.MKT.UM	Sadaret Mektubi Kalemi Umum Vilayat Evrakı
BEO	Babıali Evrak Odası Evrakı
C.DH	Cevdet, Dahiliye
DH.İ.UM	Dahiliye Nezareti, İdare-i Umumiye Evrakı
DH.MHC	Dahiliye Nezareti, Muhacirin Komisyonu
DH.MKT	Dahiliye Nezareti, Mektubi Kalemi
HR.ID	Hariciye Nezareti, İdare
HR.TO	Harciye Nezareti, Tercüme Odası Evrakı
I.DH	İrade – Dahiliye
I.HR	İrade – Hariciye
I.HUS	İrade – Hususi
I.MMS	İrade – Meclis-i Mahsus
I.MVL	İrade – Meclis-i Vala
MF.MKT	Maarif Nezareti Mektubi Kalemi
MVL	Meclis-i Vala Evrakı
ŞD	Şura-yı Devlet Evrakı
Y.A.HUS	Yıldız, Sadaret Hususi Maruzat Evrakı
Y.A.RES	Yıldız, Sadaret Resmi Maruzat Evrakı
Y.MTV	Yıldız, Mütenevvi Maruzat Evrakı
Y.PRK.KOM	Yıldız Perakende Evrakı Komisyonlar Maruzatı
Y.PRK.OMZ	Yıldız Perakende Evrakı Orman, Maadin ve Ziraat Nezareti Maruzatı

Bibliography

Y.PRK.ŞD Yıldız Perakende Evrakı Şura-yı Devlet Maruzatı
Y.PRK.UM Yıldız Perakende Evrakı Umumi

ATATÜRK KITAPLIĞI

THE NATIONAL ARCHIVES, RICHMOND, UK
FO   The Foreign Office
FO 78   General Correspondence, Turkey
FO 195   Embassy and Consulates, Turkey, General Correspondence

Officially Published Primary Sources

Düstur: İkinci Tertip (Code of Laws: Second Series), Istanbul: 1908–18
Meclis-i Ayan Zabıt Ceridesi
Meclis-i Mebusan Zabıt Ceridesi
Salname-yi Devlet-i Aliye-yi Osmaniye
 11. 1273/1856
 12. 1274/1857
 28. 1290/1873
 29. 1291/1874
 30. 1292/1875
 36. 1297/1880
 37. 1299/1881
 38. 1300/1882
 39. 1301/1883
 40. 1302/1884
 41. 1303/1885
 42. 1304/1886
 43. 1305/1887

Newspapers

Muhacir, Istanbul, Turkey
New York Times, New York, United States
The Times, London, United Kingdom

Other Published Primary Sources

Burdett-Coutts, 'Preface'. In *Woman's Mission: A Series of Congress Papers on the Philanthropic Work of Women by Eminent Writers*, edited by Angela Burdett-Coutts, ix–xxi. New York: Scribner's Sons, 1893.
Burdett-Coutts, 'Woman the Missionary of Industry'. In *Woman's Mission: A Series of Congress Papers on the Philanthropic Work of Women by Eminent Writers*, edited by Angela Burdett-Coutts, 284–289. New York: Scribner's Sons, 1893.

Dunstan, H. Mainwaring. *The Turkish Compassionate Fund: An Account of Its Origin, Working, and Results*. London: Remington and Co., 1883.

Gladstone, William E. *Bulgarian Horrors and the Question of the East*. London: John Murray, 1876.

Great Britain. *Papers Respecting the Settlement of Circassian Emigrants in Turkey*. London: Harrison and Son, 1864.

Great Britain. *Ninth Annual Report of The Local Government Board, 1879–1880 Supplement Containing Report and Papers Submitted by the Medical Officer on the Quarantine in the Red Sea*, vol. 9. London: George E. Eyre and William Spottiswoode, 1881.

Ongley F. and Horace Miller. *The Ottoman Land Code*. London: William Clowes and Sons, 1892.

Osmanlı Belgelerinde Kafkas Göçleri, vols 1 and 2. Istanbul: Osmanlı Arşivi Daire Başkanlığı, 2012.

Redhouse, James. *An English and Turkish Dictionary in Two Parts, English and Turkish and Turkish and English, in which the Turkish Words are Represented in the Oriental Character, as Well as Their Correct Pronunciation and Accentuation Shewn in English Letters, on the Plan Adopted by the Author in his 'Vade-Mecum of Ottoman Colloquial Language'*. London: Bernard Quaritch, 1856.

Redhouse, James. *A Lexicon, English and Turkish: Shewing, in Turkish, The Literal, Figurative, Colloquial and Technical Significations of the English Terms, Indicating Their Pronunciation in a New and Systematic Manner; and Preceded by A Sketch of English Etymology, to Facilitate to Turkish Students the Acquisition of the English Language*. London: Bernard Quaritch, 1861.

Redhouse, James. *A Lexicon, English and Turkish: Shewing, in Turkish, The Literal, Figurative, Colloquial and Technical Significations of the English Terms, Indicating Their Pronunciation in a New and Systematic Manner; and Preceded by A Sketch of English Etymology, to Facilitate to Turkish Students the Acquisition of the English Language*, 2nd ed. Constantinople: A. H. Boyajian, 1877.

Redhouse, James. *Redhouse's Turkish Dictionary in Two Parts, English and Turkish and Turkish and English, in which the Turkish Words are Represented in the Oriental Character, as Well as Their Correct Pronunciation and Accentuation Shewn in English Letters, on the Plan Adopted by the Author in his 'Vade-Mecum of Ottoman Colloquial Language'*, 2nd ed., edited by Charles Wells. London: Bernard Quaritch, 1880.

Roberts, Randal. *Asia Minor and the Caucasus*. Boston: James R. Osgood and Company, 1877.

Sami, Şemsettin. *Kamus-ı Fransavi: Türkçeden Fransızcaya Lügat, Dictionnaire Turc-Français*. Istanbul: Mahran Matbaası, 1883.

Sami, Şemsettin. *Kamus-ı Türki: Kaffe-yi Lügat-i Türkiye ile Lisan-i Türkide Müstamil Kelimat ve Istılahat-ı Arabiye ve Farisiye ve Ecnebiyeyi Cami Olarak Lisanımızın Mükemmel Lügat Kitabıdır*. Istanbul: İkdam Matbaası, 1318/1900–1.

Bibliography

Süreyya, Mehmed. *Sicill-i Osmani, yahut, Tezkire-yi Meşahir-i Osmaniye*, vol. 4. Istanbul: Matbaa-i Amire, 1308/1893.

Us, Hakkı Tarik, ed. *Meclis-i Meb'usan, 1293 = 1877; Zabıt Ceridesi*, vol. 2. Istanbul: Vakit Gazete Matbaa-Kütüphane, 1954.

Van Lennep, Henry John. *Travels in Little-Known Parts of Asia Minor*, vol. 1. London: John Murray, 1870.

Zacaroff, Cariclee. 'The "Turkish Compassionate Fund"'. In *The Congress of Women Held in the Woman's Building, World's Chicago Exposition, Chicago, U.S.A.*, edited by Mary Kavanaugh Oldham, 618–622. Chicago: Monarch Book Company, 1894.

Secondary Sources

Abrahamyan, Victoria. 'Citizen Strangers: Identity Labelling and Discourse in the French Mandatory Syria, 1920–193'. *Journal of Migration History* 6, no. 1 (2020): 40–61.

Akçam, Taner. *The Young Turks' Crime against Humanity: The Armenian Genocide and Ethnic Cleansing in the Ottoman Empire*. Princeton, NJ: Princeton University Press, 2012.

Akcasu, Ebru. 'Migrants to Citizens: An Evaluation of the Expansionist Features of Hamidian Ottomanism, 1876–1909'. *Die Welt des Islams* 56, no. 3/4 (2015): 388–414.

Al-Arnaut, Muhamed Mufaku. 'Islam and Muslims in Bosnia, 1878–1918: Two "Hijras" and Two "Fatwas"'. *Journal of Islamic Studies* 5, no. 2 (1994): 242–53.

Albrecht, Sarah. *Dar al-Islam Revisited: Territoriality in Contemporary Islamic Legal Discourse on Muslims in the West*. Leiden: Brill, 2018.

Anderson, Dorothy. *The Balkan Volunteers*. London: Hutchinson, 1968.

Astourian, Stephen. 'The Silence of the Land: Agrarian Relations, Ethnicity, and Power'. In *A Question of Genocide: Armenians and Turks at the End of the Ottoman Empire*, edited by Ronald Suny, Fatma Müge Göçek and Norman Naimark, 55–81. New York: Oxford University Press, 2011.

Aydın, Cemil. *The Idea of the Muslim World: A Global Intellectual History*. Cambridge, MA: Harvard University Press, 2017.

Baban, Feyzi, Suzan Ilcan and Kim Rygiel. 'Syrian Refugees in Turkey: Pathways to Precarity, Differential Inclusion, and Negotiated Citizenship Rights'. *Journal of Ethnic and Migration Studies* 43, no. 1 (2017): 45–57.

Badem, Candan. *The Ottoman Crimean War (1853–1856)*. Leiden: Brill, 2010.

Bakewell, Oliver. 'Conceptualising Displacement and Migration: Processes, Conditions, and Categories'. In *The Migration-Displacement Nexus: Patterns, Processes, and Policies*, edited by Khalid Koser and Susan Martin, 14–28. Oxford: Berghahn Books, 2011.

Balkelis, Tomas. 'In Search of a Native Realm: The Return of World War One Refugees to Lithuania, 1918–24'. In *Homelands: War, Population, and*

Statehood in Eastern Europe and Russia 1918–1924, edited by Nick Baron and Peter Gatrell, 74–97. London: Anthem Press, 2004.

Balsoy, Gülhan. 'The Solitary Female Refugees and the Widows' Asylum (Kırmızı Kışla) in Late-Nineteenth Century Istanbul'. *JOTSA* 6, no. 2 (2019): 73–90.

Banivanua-Mar, Tracey, and Penelope Edmonds, eds. *Making Settler Colonial Space: Perspectives on Race, Place, and Identity*. Basingstoke: Palgrave Macmillan, 2010.

Banko, Lauren. 'Refugees, Displaced Migrants, and Territorialization in Interwar Palestine'. *Mashriq & Mahjar* 5, no. 2 (2018): 19–49.

Banner, Stuart. *Possessing the Pacific Land, Settlers, and Indigenous People from Australia to Alaska*. Cambridge, MA: Harvard University Press, 2007.

Barakat, Nora. 'An Empty Land? Nomads and Property Administration in Hamidian Syria'. PhD diss., University of California, Berkeley, 2015.

Barnett, Michael. *Empire of Humanity: A History of Humanitarianism*. Ithaca, NY: Cornell University Press, 2011.

Barrett, Thomas. *At the Edge of Empire: The Terek Cossacks and the North Caucasus Frontier, 1700–1860*. Boulder, CO: Westview Press, 1999.

Bashford, Alison. 'Immigration Restriction: Rethinking Period and Place from Settler Colonies to Postcolonial Nations'. *Journal of Global History* 9, no. 1 (2014): 26–48.

Bashford, Alison, and Jane McAdam. 'The Right to Asylum: Britain's 1905 Aliens Act and the Evolution of Refugee Law'. *Law and History Review* 32, no. 2 (2014): 309–50.

Bauman, Zygmunt. 'In the Court Where Multi-Ethnic Polities Are on Trial the Jury Is Still Out'. Interview by Sergei Glebov. *Ab Imperio* 2008, no. 1 (2008): 19–34.

Bell, Blake. 'Homestead National Monument of America and the 150th Anniversary of the Homestead Act'. *Western Historical Quarterly* 43, no. 1 (2012): 72–8.

Bell, Blake. 'America's Invitation to the World'. Accessed 5 July 2020, https://www.nps.gov/home/upload/Immigration-White-Paper.pdf.

Birdal, Murat. *The Political Economy of Ottoman Public Debt: Insolvency and European Financial Control in the Late Nineteenth Century*. London: I. B. Tauris, 2010.

Bloxham, Donald. 'Internal Colonization, Inter-Imperial Conflict and the Armenian Genocide'. In *Empire, Colony, Genocide: Conquest, Occupation, and Subaltern Resistance in World History*, edited by A. Dirk Moses, 325–42. New York: Berghahn Books, 2008.

Blumi, Isa. *Ottoman Refugees, 1878–1939: Migration in a Post-Imperial World*. London: Bloomsbury Academic, 2013.

Bosma, Ulbe. 'Beyond the Atlantic: Connecting Migration and World History in the Age of Imperialism, 1840–1940'. *International Review of Social History* 52, no. 1 (2007): 116–23.

Bibliography

Boucher, Anna, and Justin Gest. *Crossroads: Comparative Immigration Regimes in a World of Demographic Change*. Cambridge: Cambridge University Press, 2018.

Braude, Benjamin. 'Foundation Myths of the *Millet* System'. In *Christians and Jews in the Ottoman Empire*, abridged ed., edited by Benjamin Braude, 65–86. Boulder, CO: Lynne Rienner, 2014.

Breyfogle, Nicholas. 'Enduring Imperium: Russia/Soviet Union/Eurasia as Multiethnic, Multiconfessional Space'. *Ab Imperio*, 2008, no. 1 (2008): 109–12.

Bullough, Oliver. *Let Our Fame Be Great: Journeys among the Defiant People of the Caucasus*. London: Penguin Books, 2012.

Bulmuş, Birsen. *Plague, Quarantines, and Geopolitics in the Ottoman Empire*. Edinburgh: Edinburgh University Press, 2012.

Çadırcı, Musa. 'Türkiye'de Muhtarlık Teşkilatının Kurulması Üzerine bir İnceleme'. *Belleten* 34 no. 135 (1970): 409–20.

Campos, Michelle. *Ottoman Brothers: Muslims, Christians, and Jews in Early Twentieth-Century Palestine*. Stanford, CA: Stanford University Press, 2011.

Can, Lale. *Spiritual Subjects: Central Asian Pilgrims and the Ottoman Hajj at the End of Empire*. Stanford, CA: Stanford University Press, 2020.

Can, Lale, Michael Christopher Low, Kent F. Schull and Robert Zens, eds. *The Subjects of Ottoman International Law*. Bloomington: Indiana University Press, 2020.

Castles, Stephen, Hein de Haas and Mark J. Miller. *The Age of Migration: International Movements in the Modern World*, 5th ed. New York: Guilford Press, 2014.

Chang, Kornel. 'Enforcing Transnational White Solidarity: Asian Migration and the Formation of the U.S.-Canadian Boundary'. *American Quarterly* 60, no. 3 (2008): 671–96.

Chatty, Dawn. *Displacement and Dispossession in the Modern Middle East*. Cambridge: Cambridge University Press, 2010.

Chochiev, Georgi. 'XIX. Yüzyılın İkinci Yarısında Osmanlı İmparatorluğu'nda Kuzey Kafkas Göçmenlerin Toplumsal Uyarlanmasına Dair Bazı Görüşler'. *Kebikeç* 23 (2007): 407–56.

Çelik, Zeynep. *The Remaking of Istanbul: Portrait of an Ottoman City in the Nineteenth Century*. Berkeley: University of California Press, 1986.

Çelik, Züriye. 'Osmanlının Zor Yıllarında Göçmenlerinin Türk Basınındaki Sesi: "Muhacir" Gazetesi (1909–1910)'. *Türkiyat Araştırmaları Dergisi 2010* no. 28 (2010): 405–12.

Çetinkaya, Gökhan. *Ottoman Administration of Iraq, 1890–1908*. London: Routledge, 2006.

Çetinkaya, Y. Doğan. *The Young Turks and the Boycott Movement: Nationalism, Protest, and the Working Class in the Formation of Modern Turkey*. London: I. B. Tauris, 2014.

Çetinkaya, Y. Doğan. 'Illustrated Atrocity: The Stigmatisation of Non-Muslims through Images in the Ottoman Empire during the Balkan Wars'. *Journal of Modern European History* 12, no. 4 (2014): 460–78.

Cohen, Julia. *Becoming Ottomans: Sephardi Jews and Imperial Citizenship in the Modern Era*. New York: Oxford University Press, 2014.

Craib, Raymond B. *Cartographic Mexico: A History of State Fixations and Fugitive Landscapes*. Durham, NC: Duke University Press, 2004.

Cuthell, David Cameron. 'The Muhacirin Komisyonu: An Agent in the Transformation of Ottoman Anatolia, 1860–1866'. PhD diss., Columbia University, 2005.

Delaney, David. *Territory: A Short Introduction*. Oxford: Blackwell Publishing, 2005.

Denzel, Markus. *Handbook of World Exchange Rates, 1590–1914*. Farnham: Ashgate, 2010.

Der Matossian, Bedross. *Shattered Dreams of Revolution: From Liberty to Violence in the Late Ottoman Empire*. Stanford, CA: Stanford University Press, 2014.

Der Matossian, Bedross. *The Horrors of Adana: Revolution and Violence in the Early Twentieth Century*. Stanford, CA: Stanford University Press, 2022.

Deringil, Selim. *The Well-Protected Domains: Ideology and the Legitimation of Power in the Ottoman Empire, 1876–1909*. London: I. B. Tauris, 1998.

Deringil, Selim. '"They Live in a State of Nomadism and Savagery": The Late Ottoman Empire and the Post-Colonial Debate'. *Comparative Studies in Society and History* 45.2 (2003): 311–42.

Dimitriadis, Sotirios. 'Transforming a Late-Ottoman Port-City: Salonica, 1876–1912'. In *Well-Connected Domains: Towards an Entangled Ottoman History*, edited by Pascal Firges, Tobias P. Graf, Christian Roth and Gülay Tulasoğlu, 207–21. Leiden: Brill, 2014.

Dinçyürek, Sena Hatip. *A 'Compassionate' Episode in Anglo-Ottoman History: British Relief to the '93 Refugees (1877–1878)*. Istanbul: Libra Kitapçılık ve Yayıncılık, 2013.

Dobreva, Margarita. 'Circassian Colonization in the Danube Vilayet and Social Integration (Preliminary Notes)'. *OTAM* 33 (2013): 1–30.

Dolbee, Samuel, and Shay Hazkani. 'Unlikely Identities: Abu Ibrahim and the Politics of Possibility in Late Ottoman Palestine'. *Jerusalem Quarterly* 63–4 (2015): 24–39.

Douglas, Mary. *Purity and Danger: An Analysis of Concepts of Pollution and Taboo*, Routledge Classics ed. London: Routledge, 2005.

Dündar, Fuat. 'Balkan Savaşı Sonrasında Kurulmaya Çalışılan Muhacir Köyleri'. *Toplumsal Tarih* 14, no. 82 (2000): 52–4.

Dündar, Fuat. *İttihat ve Terakki'nin Müslümanları İskan Politikası (1913–1918)*. Istanbul: İletişim Yayınları, 2001.

Dündar, Fuat. *Crime of Numbers: The Role of Statistics in the Armenian Question (1878–1918)*. New Brunswick, NJ: Transaction Publishers, 2010.

Eldem, Edhem. 'Ottoman Financial Integration with Europe: Foreign Loans, the Ottoman Bank, and the Ottoman Public Debt'. *European Review* 13, no. 3 (2005): 431–45.

Bibliography

Erdem, Ufuk. *Osmanlı'dan Cumhuriyet'e Muhacir Komisyonları ve Faaliyetleri (1860–1923)*. Ankara: Türk Tarih Kurumu Yayınları, 2018.

Eren, Ahmet Cevat. *Türkiye'de Göç ve Göçmen Meseleleri: Tanzimat Devri, İlk Kurulan Göçmen Komisyonu, Çıkarılan Tüzükler*. Istanbul: Nurgök Matbaası, 1966.

Ertem, Özge. 'Eating the Last Seed: Famine, Empire, Survival and Order in Ottoman Anatolia in the Late Nineteenth Century'. PhD diss., European University Institute, 2012.

Evered, Emine Ö. *Empire and Education under the Ottomans: Politics, Reform, and Resistance from the Tanzimat to the Young Turks*. London: I. B. Tauris, 2012.

Feldman, Ilana. 'Difficult Distinctions: Refugee Law, Humanitarian Practice, and Political Identification in Gaza'. *Cultural Anthropology* 22, no. 1 (2007): 129–69.

Fisher, Alan. 'Emigration of Muslims from the Russian Empire in the Years after the Crimean War'. *Jahrbürcher für Geschichte Osteuropas* 35, no. 3 (1987): 356–71.

Fishman, Louis A. *Jews and Palestinians in the Late Ottoman Era, 1908–1914: Claiming the Homeland*. Edinburgh: Edinburgh University Press, 2020.

Foucault, Michel. 'Governmentality'. In *The Foucault Effect: Studies in Governmentality*, edited by Graham Burchell, Colin Gordon and Peter Miller, 87–104. Chicago: The University of Chicago Press, 1991.

Foucault, Michel. *Discipline and Punish: The Birth of the Prison*, 2nd ed., translated by Alan Sheridan. New York: Vintage, 1995.

Gatrell, Peter. *The Making of the Modern Refugee*. Oxford: Oxford University Press, 2013.

Gingeras, Ryan. *Sorrowful Shores: Violence, Ethnicity, and the End of the Ottoman Empire 1912–1923*. New York: Oxford University Press, 2011.

Ginio, Eyal. *The Ottoman Culture of Defeat: The Balkan Wars and Their Aftermath*. New York: Oxford University Press, 2016.

Gövsa, İbrahim Alaettin. *Türk Meşhurları Ansiklopedisi: Edebiyatta, Sanatta, İlimde, Harpte, Politikada ve her Sahada Şöhret Kazanmış Olan Türklerin Hayat Eserleri*. Istanbul: Yedigün Neşriyatı, 1946.

Gratien, Chris. 'The Ottoman Quagmire: Malaria, Swamps, and Settlement in the Late Ottoman Mediterranean'. *IJMES* 49, no. 4 (2017): 583–604.

Gratien, Chris. *The Unsettled Plain: An Environmental History of the Late Ottoman Frontier*. Stanford, CA: Stanford University Press, 2022.

Gül, Murat, and Richard Lamb. 'Mapping, Regularizing and Modernizing Ottoman Istanbul: Aspects of the Genesis of the 1839 Development Policy'. *Urban History* 31, no. 3 (2004): 420–36.

Gürsel, Zeynep Devrim. 'Classifying the Cartozians: Rethinking the Politics of Visibility Alongside Ottoman Subjecthood and American Citizenship'. *photographies* 15, no. 3 (2022): 349–80.

Gutman, David. 'Ottoman Historiography and the End of the Genocide Taboo: Writing the Armenian Genocide into Late Ottoman History'. *Journal of the Ottoman and Turkish Studies Association* 2, no. 1 (2015): 167–83.

Governing Migration in the Late Ottoman Empire

Gutman, David. *The Politics of Armenian Migration to North America, 1885–1915: Sojourners, Smugglers, and Dubious Citizens.* Edinburgh: Edinburgh University Press, 2019.

Hacısalioğlu, Mehmet. 'Bulgaristan'da Bağımsızlıktan Günümüze Yer İsimlerinin Değiştirilmeleri'. In *Balkanlar'da Islam Medeniyeti II. Milletlerarası Sempozyumu Tebliğleri Tiran, Arnavutluk 4–7 Aralık 2003*, edited by Ali Çaksu, 177–89. Istanbul: İslam Tarih, Sanat ve Kültür Araştırma Merkezi, 2006.

Hamed-Troyansky, Vladimir. 'Imperial Refugee: Resettlement of Muslims from Russia in the Ottoman Empire, 1860–1914'. PhD diss., Stanford University, 2018.

Hamlin, Rebecca. *Crossing: How We Label and React to People on the Move.* Stanford, CA: Stanford University Press, 2021.

Hanioğlu, M. Şükrü. *A Brief History of the Late Ottoman Empire.* Princeton, NJ: Princeton University Press, 2008.

Hanley, Will. 'What Ottoman Nationality Was and Was Not'. *Journal of the Ottoman and Turkish Studies Association* 3, no. 2 (2016): 277–98.

Hanley, Will. *Identifying with Nationality: Europeans, Ottomans, and Egyptians in Alexandria.* New York: Columbia University Press, 2017.

Hannah, Matthew C. 'Space and Social Control in the Administration of the Oglala Lakota ("Sioux"), 1871–1879'. *Journal of Historical Geography* 19, no. 4 (1993): 412–32.

Hartnett, Lynne Ann. 'Alien or Refugee? The Politics of Russian Émigré Claims to British Asylum at the Turn of the Twentieth Century'. *Journal of Migration History* 3 (2017): 229–53.

Healey, Edna. *Lady Unknown: The Life of Angela Burdett-Coutts*, 1st American ed. New York: Coward, McCann & Geoghegan, 1978.

Hernandez, Jose Angel. *Mexican American Colonization during the Nineteenth Century: A History of the U.S.-Mexico Borderlands.* New York: Cambridge University Press, 2012.

Herzog, Christoph. 'Notes on the Development of Turkish and Oriental Studies in the German Speaking Lands'. *Türkiye Araştırmaları Literatür Dergisi* 8 no. 15 (2010): 7–76.

Herzog, Cristoph. 'Migration and the State: On Ottoman Regulations concerning Migration since the Age of Mahmud II'. In *The City in the Ottoman Empire: Migration and the Making of Urban Modernity*, edited by Ulrike Freitag, Malte Fuhrmann, Nora Lafi and Florian Riedler, 117–34. London: Routledge, 2011.

Hirschon, Renee. *Crossing the Aegean: An Appraisal of the 1923 Compulsory Population Exchange between Greece and Turkey.* New York: Berghahn Books, 2003.

Hoerder, Dirk. *Cultures in Contact: World Migrations in the Second Millennium.* Durham, NC: Duke University Press, 2002.

Holquist, Peter. 'To Count, to Extract, and to Exterminate: Population Statistics and Population Politics in Late Imperial and Soviet Russia'. In *A State of*

Bibliography

Nations: Empire and Nation-Making in the Age of Lenin and Stalin, edited by Ronald Suny and Terry Martin, 111–44. New York: Oxford University Press, 2001.

Huber, Valeska. 'The Unification of the Globe by Disease? The International Sanitary Conferences on Cholera, 1851–1894'. *The Historical Journal* 49, no. 2 (2006): 453–76.

Hunt, Catalina. 'Changing Identities at the Fringes of the Late Ottoman Empire: The Muslims of Dobruca, 1839–1914'. PhD diss., The Ohio State University, 2015.

Hütteroth, Wolf-Dieter. 'The Influence of Social Structure on Land Division and Settlement in Inner Anatolia'. In *Turkey: Geographic and Social Perspectives*, edited by Peter Bendict, Erol Tümerlekin and Fatma Mansur, 19–47. Leiden: Brill, 1974.

İpek, Nedim. *Rumeli'den Anadolu'ya Türk Göçleri, 1877–1890*. Ankara: Türk Tarih Kurumu, 1994.

İpek, Nedim. 'Trablusgarb ve Bingazi Mültecileri (1911–1912)'. *19 Mayıs Üniversitesi Eğitim Fakültesi Dergisi* 9 (1994): 90–109.

İpek, Nedim. 'Göçmen Köylerine Dair'. *Tarih ve Toplum* 25, no. 150 (1996): 15–21.

Kale, Başak. 'Transforming an Empire: The Ottoman Empire's Immigration and Settlement Policies in the Nineteenth and Early Twentieth Centuries'. *Middle Eastern Studies* 50, no. 2 (2014): 252–71.

Kane, Eileen. *Russian Hajj: Empire and the Pilgrimage to Mecca*. Ithaca, NY: Cornell University Press, 2015.

Karpat, Kemal. 'The Status of the Muslim under European Rule: The Eviction and Settlement of the Cerkes'. *Journal of Muslim Minority Affairs* 1, no. 2 (1979): 7–27.

Karpat, Kemal. *Ottoman Population, 1830–1914: Demographic and Social Characteristics*. Madison: University of Wisconsin Press, 1985.

Karpat, Kemal. 'The Crimean Emigration of 1856–1862 and the Settlement and Urban Development of Dobruca'. In *Passé Turco-Tatar, Présent Soviétique: Études Offertes à Alexandre Bennigsen*, edited by Ch. Lemercier-Quelquejay, G. Veinstein and S. E. Wimbush, 275–306. Paris: Éditions Peeters, 1986.

Karpat, Kemal. 'The *Hijra* from Russia and the Balkans: The Process of Self-definition in the Late Ottoman State'. In *Muslim Travellers: Pilgrimage, Migration, and the Religious Imagination*, edited by Dale F. Eickelman and James Piscatori, 131–52. Los Angeles: University of California Press, 1990.

Karpat, Kemal. *The Politicization of Islam: Reconstructing Identity, State, Faith and Community in the Late Ottoman Empire*. Oxford: Oxford University Press, 2001.

Karpat, Kemal. *Studies on Ottoman Social and Political History: Selected Articles and Essays*. Leiden: Brill, 2002.

Kasaba, Reşat. *A Moveable Empire: Ottoman Nomads, Migrants, and Refugees*. Seattle: University of Washington Press, 2009.

Khalid, Adeeb. 'Pan-Islamism in Practice: The Rhetoric of Muslim Unity and Its Uses'. In *Late Ottoman Society: The Intellectual Legacy*, edited by Elisabeth Özdalga, 201–224. London: Routledge, 2005.

Khosravi, Shahram. *'Illegal' Traveller: An Auto-Ethnography of Borders*. Basingstoke: Palgrave Macmillan, 2010.

King, Charles. *The Black Sea: A History*. Oxford: Oxford University Press, 2004.

King, Charles. *The Ghost of Freedom: A History of the Caucasus*. Oxford: Oxford University Press, 2008.

Kırımlı, Hakan. 'Emigrations from the Crimea to the Ottoman Empire during the Crimean War'. *Middle Eastern Studies* 44, no. 5 (2008): 751–73.

Klein, Janet. *The Margins of Empire: Kurdish Militias in the Ottoman Tribal Zone*. Stanford, CA: Stanford University Press, 2011.

Kocacık, Faruk. 'XIX. Yüzyılda Göçmen Köylerine İlişkin Bazı Yapı Planları'. *İstanbul Üniversitesi Edebiyat Fakültesi Tarih Dergisi* 32 (1979): 415–26.

Kocacık, Faruk. 'Balkanlar'dan Anadolu'ya Yönelik Göçler'. *The Journal of Ottoman Studies* 1 (1980): 137–90.

Koçunyan, Aylin. 'The *Millet* System and the Challenge of Other Confessional Models, 1856–1865'. *Ab Imperio 2017* 1 (2017): 59–85.

Kozelsky, Mara. 'Casualties of Conflict: Crimean Tatars during the Crimean War'. *Slavic Review* 67, no. 4 (2008): 866–91.

Kuehn, Thomas. *Empire, Islam, and the Politics of Difference: Ottoman Rule in Yemen, 1849–1919*. Leiden: Brill, 2011.

Küsükbatır, Hamit. 'Altunizade İsmail Zühdü Paşa'. *TDV İslam Ansiklopedesi*. Accessed 17 March 2023, https://islamansiklopedisi.org.tr/altunizade-ismail-zuhdu-pasa.

Lester, Alan, and Fae Dussart. *Colonization and the Origins of Humanitarian Governance: Protecting Aborigines across the Nineteenth-Century British Empire*. Cambridge: Cambridge University Press, 2014.

Li, Tania Murray. *The Will to Improve: Governmentality, Development, and the Practice of Politics*. Durham, NC: Duke University Press, 2007.

Lorenz, Fredrick Walter. 'The "Second Egypt": Cretan Refugees, Agricultural Development, and Frontier Expansion in Ottoman Cyrenaica, 1897–1904'. *International Journal of Middle East Studies* 53, no. 1 (2021): 89–105.

Low, Michael Christopher. *Imperial Mecca: Ottoman Arabia and the Indian Ocean Hajj*. New York: Columbia University Press, 2020.

Makdisi, Ussama. *The Culture of Sectarianism: Community, History, and Violence in Nineteenth Century Lebanon*. Berkeley: University of California Press, 2000.

Makdisi, Ussama. 'Ottoman Orientalism'. *American Historical Review* 107, no. 3 (2002): 768–96.

Maksudyan, Nazan. 'Orphans, Cities, and the State: Vocational Orphanages (*Islahhanes*) and Reform in the Late Ottoman Urban Space'. *International Journal of Middle East Studies* 43, no. 3 (2011): 493–511.

Maksudyan, Naza. *Orphans and Destitute Children in the Late Ottoman Empire*. Syracuse, NY: Syracuse University Press, 2014.

Bibliography

Malkki, Liisa. 'National Geographic: The Rooting of Peoples and the Territorialization of National Identity among Scholars and Refugees'. *Cultural Anthropology* 7, no. 1 (1992): 24–44.

Manasek, Jared. 'Empire Displaced: Ottoman-Hapsburg Forced Migration and the Near Eastern Crisis, 1875–1878'. PhD diss., Columbia University, 2013.

Manasek, Jared. 'Protection, Repatriation, and Categorization: Refugees and Empire at the End of the Nineteenth Century'. *Journal of Refugee Studies* 30, no. 2 (2017): 301–17.

Manesek, Jared. 'Refugee Return and State Legitimization: Habsburgs, Ottomans, and the Case of Bosnia and Herzegovina, 1875–1878'. *Journal of Modern European History* 19, no. 1 (2021): 63–79.

Marrus, Michael. *The Unwanted: European Refugees from the First World War through the Cold War*, 2nd ed. Philadelphia: Temple University Press: 2002.

Masud, Muhammad Khalid. 'The Obligation to Migrate: The Doctrine of *hijra* in Islamic Law'. In *Muslim Travellers: Pilgrimage, Migration, and the Religious Imagination*, edited by Dale F. Eickelman and James Piscatori, 29–49. Los Angeles: University of California Press, 1990.

Mazak, Mehmet, and Fatih Gürdal. *Osmanlı'dan Günümüze Temizlik Tarihi: Tanzifat-ı İstanbul*. Istanbul: Yeditepe Yayınevi, 2011.

Mazower, Mark. *Governing the World: The History of an Idea*. New York: The Penguin Press, 2012.

McCarthy, Justin. *Death and Exile: The Ethnic Cleansing of Ottoman Muslims, 1821–1922*. Princeton, NJ: Darwin University Press, 1995.

McKeown, Adam. 'Global Migration, 1846–1940'. *Journal of World History* 15, no. 2 (2004): 155–89.

McKeown, Adam. *Melancholy Order: Asian Migration and the Globalization of Borders*. New York: Columbia University Press, 2008.

Methodieva, Milena. *Between Empire and Nation: Muslim Reform in the Balkans*. Stanford, CA: Stanford University Press, 2021.

Meyer, James. 'Immigration, Return, and the Politics of Citizenship: Russian Muslims in the Ottoman Empire, 1860–1914'. *International Journal of Middle East Studies* 39, no.1 (2007): 15–32.

Meyer, James. *Turks across Empires: Marketing Muslim Identity in the Russian-Ottoman Borderlands, 1856–1914*. Oxford: Oxford University Press, 2014.

Miller, Peter, and Nikolas Rose. *Governing the Present: Administering Economic, Social, and Personal Life*. Oxford: Polity Press, 2008.

Minkov, Anton. 'Ottoman *Tapu* Title Deeds in the Eighteenth and Nineteenth Centuries: Origin, Typology and Diplomatics'. *Islamic Law and Society* 7, no.1 (2000): 65–101.

Mirkova, Anna. '"Population Politics" at the End of Empire: Migration and Sovereignty in Ottoman Eastern Rumelia, 1877–1886'. *Comparative Studies in Society and History* 55, no. 4 (2013): 955–85.

Mirkova, Anna. *Muslim Land: Christian Labor: Transforming Ottoman Imperial Subjects into Bulgarian National Citizens, c. 1878–1939.* New York: Central European University Press, 2017.

Mitchell, Dean. *Governmentality: Power and Rule in Modern Society.* London: Sage, 1999.

Mitchell, Timothy. *Rule of Experts: Egypt, Techno-Politics, Modernity.* Berkeley: University of California Press, 2002.

Mongia, Radhika. 'Historicizing State Sovereignty: Inequality and the Form of Equivalence'. *Comparative Studies in Society and History* 49, no. 2 (2007): 384–411.

Mongia, Radhika. *Indian Migration and Empire: A Colonial Genealogy of the Modern State.* Durham, NC: Duke University Press, 2018.

Moon, David. 'Peasant Migration and the Settlement of Russia's Frontiers, 1550–1897'. *The Historical Journal* 40, no. 4 (1997): 859–93.

Morack, Ellinor. 'Refugees, Locals and "The" State: Property Compensation in the Province of Izmir Following the Greco-Turkish Population Exchange of 1923'. *Journal of the Ottoman and Turkish Studies Association* 2, no. 1 (2015): 147–66.

Moses, A. Dirk. 'An Antipodean Genocide? The Origins of the Genocidal Moment in the Colonization of Australia'. *Journal of Genocide Research* 2, no. 1 (2000): 89–106.

Moulin, Anne Marie, and Yeşim Işıl Ulman, eds. *Perilous Modernity: History of Medicine in the Ottoman Empire and the Middle East from the 19th Century onwards.* Istanbul: Gorgias Press and The Isis Press, 2010.

Moya, Jose. *Cousins and Strangers: Spanish Immigrants in Buenos Aires, 1850–1930.* Berkeley: University of California Press, 1998.

Naganwa, Norihiro. 'Tatars and Imperialist Wars: From the Tsars' Servitors to the Red Warriors'. *Ab Imperio 2020*, no. 1 (2020): 164–96.

Nail, Thomas. *The Figure of the Migrant.* Stanford, CA: Stanford University Press, 2015.

Oğuz, Mustafa. 'Osmanlı Devleti'nde Devlet Adamı Kitliği (Kaht-ı Rical) Hakkında II. Abdülhamid'e Sunulan Bir Rapor'. *Türklük Bilimi Araştırmaları* 2008, no. 24 (2008): 99–134.

Öke, Mim Kemal. 'The Ottoman Empire, Zionism, and the Question of Palestine (1880–1908)'. *International Journal of Middle East Studies* 14, no. 3 (1982): 329–341.

Özbek, Nadir. *Osmanlı İmporatorluğu'nda Sosyal Devlet: Siyaset, İktidar, ve Meşrutiyet 1876–1914.* Istanbul: İletişim Yayıncılık, 2002.

Özbek, Nadir. 'Philanthropic Activity, Ottoman Patriotism, and the Hamidian Regime, 1876–1909'. *IJMES* 37, no. 1 (2005): 59–81.

Özcan, Azmi. *Pan-Islamism: Indian Muslims, the Ottomans and Britain (1877–1924).* Leiden: Brill, 1997.

Özel, Oktay. 'Population Changes in Ottoman Anatolia During the 16th and 17th Centuries: The "Demographic Crisis" Reconsidered'. *International Journal of Middle East Studies* 36, no. 2 (2004): 185–205.

Bibliography

Özel, Oktay. 'Migration and Power Politics: The Settlement of Georgian Immigrants in Turkey (1878–1908)'. *Middle Eastern Studies* 46, no. 4 (2010): 477–96.

Özkan, Behlül. *From the Abode of Islam to the Turkish Vatan: The Making of a National Homeland in Turkey*. New Haven, CT: Yale University Press, 2012.

Öztan, Ramazan Hakkı. 'Point of No Return? Prospects of Empire after the Ottoman Defeat in the Balkan Wars (1912–1913)'. *International Journal of Middle East Studies* 50, no. 1 (2018): 65–84.

Öztan, Ramazan Hakkı. 'Settlement Law of 1934; Turkish Nationalism in the Age of Revisionism'. *Journal of Migration History* 6, no. 1 (2020): 82–103.

Öztan, Ramazan Hakkı, and Alp Yenen, eds. *Age of Rogues: Rebels, Revolutionaries and Racketeers at the Frontiers of Empires*. Edinburgh: Edinburgh University Press, 2021.

Pamuk, Şevket. *A Monetary History of the Ottoman Empire*. New York: Cambridge University Press, 2000.

Panayi, Panikos. 'Imperial Collapse and the Creation of Refugees in Twentieth-Century Europe'. In *Refugees and the End of Empire: Imperial Collapse and Forced Migration in the Twentieth Century*, edited by Panikos Panayi and Pippa Virdee, 3–27. Basingstoke: Palgrave Macmillan, 2011.

Parla, Ayşe. *Precarious Hope: Migration and the Limits of Belonging in Turkey*. Stanford, CA: Stanford University Press, 2019.

Petrov, Milen V. '*Tanzimat* for the Countryside: Midhat Paşa and the *Vilayet* of Danube, 1864–1868'. PhD diss., Princeton University, 2006.

Pinson, Mark. 'Demographic Warfare – An Aspect of Ottoman and Russian Policy, 1854–1866'. PhD diss., Harvard University, 1970.

Pinson, Mark. 'Ottoman Colonization of the Circassions in Rumeli after the Crimean War', *Etudes Balkaniques* 3 (1972): 71–9.

Pinson, Mark. 'Ottoman Colonization of Crimean Tatars in Bulgaria, 1854–1862'. In *VII. Türk Tarih Kongresi (Ankara: 25–29 Eylül 1970). Kongreye Sunulan Bildiriler*, vol 2, 1040–58. Ankara: Türk Tarih Kurumu Basımevi, 1973.

Pinson, Mark. 'Ottoman Bulgaria in the First Tanzimat Period: The Revolts in Nish (1841) and Vidin (1850)'. *Middle Eastern Studies* 11, no. 2 (1975): 103–46.

Quataert, Donald. 'Limited Revolution: The Impact of the Anatolian Railway on Turkish Transportation and the Provisioning of Istanbul, 1890–1908'. *The Business History Review* 51, no. 2 (1977): 139–60.

Quataert, Donald. *Ottoman Manufacturing in the Age of the Industrial Revolution*. Cambridge: Cambridge University Press, 1993.

Quataert, Donald. 'The Age of Reforms: 1812–1914'. In *An Economic and Social History of the Ottoman Empire*, vol. 2, edited by Halil İnalcık and Donald Quataert, 759–943. Cambridge: Cambridge University Press, 1994.

Reinkowski, Maurus. 'The State's Security and the Subject's Prosperity: Notions of Order in Ottoman Bureaucratic Correspondence (19th Century)'. In *Legitimizing the Order: The Ottoman Rhetoric of State Power*, edited by Hakan T. Karateke and Maurus Reinkowski, 195–212. Leiden: Brill, 2005.

Robarts, Andrew. *Migration and Disease in the Black Sea Region: Ottoman-Russian Relations in the Late Eighteenth and Early Nineteenth Centuries.* London: Bloomsbury Academic, 2017.

Robson, Laura. *States of Separation: Transfer, Partition, and the Making of the Modern Middle East.* Oakland: University of California Press, 2017.

Rodogno, Davide. *Against Massacre: Humanitarian Interventions in the Ottoman Empire, 1815–1914.* Princeton, NJ: Princeton University Press, 2012.

Rogan, Eugene L. 'Aşiret Mektebi: Abdülhamid II's School for Tribes (1892–1907)'. *International Journal of Middle East Studies* 28, no. 1 (1996): 83–107.

Rogan, Eugene. *Frontiers of the State in the Late Ottoman Empire: Transjordan, 1850–1921.* Cambridge: Cambridge University Press, 1999.

Rose, Nikolas, and Peter Miller. 'Political Power beyond the State: Problematics of Government'. *The British Journal of Sociology* 43, no. 2 (1992): 173–205.

Rosser-Own, Sarah A. S. Isla. 'The First "Circassian Exodus" to the Ottoman Empire (1858–1867), and the Ottoman Response, Based on the Accounts of Contemporary British Observers'. Masters thesis, School of Oriental and African Studies, University of London, 2007.

Ruprecht, Adrian. 'The Great Eastern Crisis (1875–1878) as a Global Humanitarian Moment'. *Journal of Global History* 16, no. 2 (2021): 159–84.

Sabol, Steven. *'The Touch of Civilization': Comparing American and Russian Internal Colonization.* Boulder: University Press of Colorado, 2017.

Sack, Robert. *Human Territoriality: Its Theory and History.* Cambridge: Cambridge University Press, 1986.

Sahara, Tetsuya. 'Two Different Images: Bulgarian and English Sources on the Batak Massacre'. In *War and Diplomacy: The Russo-Turkish War of 1877–1878 and the Treaty of Berlin*, edited by M. Hakan Yavuz and Peter Sluglett, 479–510. Salt Lake City: University of Utah Press, 2011.

Saraçoğlu, M. Safa. *Nineteenth-Century Local Governance in Ottoman Bulgaria: Politics in Provincial Councils.* Edinburgh: Edinburgh University Press, 2018.

Saydam, Abdullah. *Kırım ve Kafkas Göçleri, 1856–1876.* Ankara: Türk Tarih Kurumu, 1997.

Saydam, Abdullah. 'Osmanlıların Siyasi İlticalara Bakışı ya da 1849 Macar-Leh Mültecileri Meselesi'. *Belleten* 61, no. 231 (August, 1997): 339–85.

Scalettaris, Giulia. 'Refugee Studies and the International Refugee Regime: A Reflection on a Desirable Separation'. *Refugee Survey Quarterly* 26, no. 3 (2007): 36–50.

Schaller, Dominik J., and Jürgen Zimmerer. 'Late Ottoman Genocides: The Dissolution of the Ottoman Empire and Young Turkish Population and Extermination Policies – Introduction'. *Journal of Genocide Research* 10, no. 1 (2008): 7–14.

Schweig, Alexander. 'Tracking Technology and Society along the Ottoman Anatolian Railroad, 1890–1914'. PhD diss., University of Arizona, 2019.

Scott, James. *Seeing Like a State: How Certain Schemes to Improve the Human Condition Have Failed.* New Haven, CT: Yale University Press, 1998.

Bibliography

Schull, Kent. *Prisons in the Late Ottoman Empire*. Edinburgh: Edinburgh University Press, 2014.

Şeker, Nesim. 'Demographic Engineering in the Late Ottoman Empire and the Armenians'. *Middle Eastern Studies* 43, no. 3 (2007): 461–74.

Shaw, Stanford. 'The Central Legislative Councils in the Nineteenth Century Ottoman Reform Movement before 1876'. *International Journal of Middle East Studies* 1, no. 1 (1970): 51–84.

Shaw, Stanford. 'A Promise of Reform: Two Complimentary Documents'. *International Journal of Middle East Studies* 4, no. 3 (1973): 359–65.

Shaw, Stanford. 'The Nineteenth Century Ottoman Tax Reforms and Revenue System'. *International Journal of Middle East Studies* 6, no. 4 (1975): 421–59.

Shaw, Stanford. 'Ottoman Expenditures and Budgets in the Late Nineteenth and Early Twentieth Centuries'. *International Journal of Middle East Studies* 9, no. 3 (1978): 373–8.

Shaw, Stanford, and Ezel Kural Shaw. *History of the Ottoman Empire and Modern Turkey*, vol. 2: *Reform Revolution, and Republic: The Rise of Modern Turkey, 1808–1875*. Cambridge: Cambridge University Press, 1977.

Siegelbaum, Lewis, and Leslie Page Moch. *Broad Is My Native Land: Repertoires and Regimes of Migration in Russia's Twentieth Century*. Cornell, NY: Cornell University Press, 2014.

Soğuk, Nevzat. *States and Strangers: Refugees and the Displacements of Statecraft*. Minneapolis: Minneapolis University Press, 1999.

Sunderland, Willard. *Taming the Wild Field: Colonization and Empire on the Russian Steppe*. Ithaca, NY: Cornell University Press, 2004.

Suny, Ronald. *They Can Live in the Desert but Nowhere Else*. Princeton, NJ: Princeton University Press, 2015.

Tan, Seda. 'Osmanlı Devleti'nde At Yetiştiriciliği (1842–1918)'. PhD diss., Akdeniz Üniversitesi, 2015.

Taparata, Evan. '"Refugees as You Call Them": The Politics of Refugee Recognition in the Nineteenth-Century United States'. *Journal of American Ethnic History* 38, no. 2 (2019): 9–35.

Terzibaşoğlu, Yucel. 'Landlords, Nomads, and Refugees: Struggles over Land and Population Movement in North-Western Anatolia, 1877–1914'. PhD diss., University of London, 2003.

Terzibaşoğlu, Yucel. 'Land-Disputes and Ethno-Politics: Northwestern Anatolia, 1877–1912'. In *Land Rights, Ethno-Nationality and Sovereignty in History*, edited by Stanley Engerman and Jacob Metzer, 153–80. London: Routledge, 2004.

Tiglay, Pelin. 'The Ideological Melting Pot: Salonican Socialists and "Empire" during the Second Constitutional Period (1908–1912)'. *Etudes Balkaniques* 2022, no. 4 (2022): 609–39.

Torpey, John. *The Invention of the Passport: Surveillance, Citizenship, and the State*. Cambridge: Cambridge University Press, 2000.

Tusan, Michelle. *Smyrna's Ashes: Humanitarianism, Genocide, and the Birth of the Middle East*. Berkeley: University of California Press, 2012.

Governing Migration in the Late Ottoman Empire

Üngör, Uğur Ümit. *The Making of Modern Turkey: Nation and State in Eastern Anatolia, 1913–1950.* Oxford: Oxford University Press, 2011.

Üngör, Uğur Ümit. '"Turkey for the Turks": Demographic Engineering in Eastern Anatolia, 1914–1945'. In *A Question of Genocide: Armenians and Turks at the End of the Ottoman Empire*, edited by Ronald Suny, Fatma Müge Göçek and Norman Naimark, 287–305. New York: Oxford University Press, 2011.

Üngür, Uğur Ümit, and Mehmet Polatel. *Confiscation and Destruction: The Young Turk Seizure of Armenian Property.* London: Continuum International Publishing Group, 2011.

Verskin, Alan. *Oppressed in the Land? Fatwas on Muslims Living under Non-Muslim Rule from the Middle Ages to the Present.* Princeton, NJ: Markus Wiener Publishers, 2013.

Watenpaugh, Keith. *Bread from Stones: The Middle East and the Making of Modern Humanitarianism.* Oakland, CA: University of California Press, 2015.

Weiner, Amir. 'Nature, Nurture, and Memory in a Socialist Utopia: Delineating the Soviet Socio-Ethnic Body in the Age of Socialism'. *The American Historical Review* 104, no. 4 (1999): 1114–55.

Weiner, Amir, ed. *Landscaping the Human Garden: Twentieth-Century Population Management in a Comparative Framework.* Stanford, CA: Stanford University Press, 2003.

Weitz, Eric D. 'From the Vienna to the Paris System: International Politics and the Entangled Histories of Human Rights, Forced Deportations, and Civilizing Missions'. *The American Historical Review* 113, no. 5 (2008): 1313–43.

White, Benjamin. *The Emergence of Minorities in the Middle East: The Politics of Community in French Mandate Syria.* Edinburgh: Edinburgh University Press, 2011.

White, Sam. *The Climate of Rebellion in the Early Modern Ottoman Empire.* New York: Cambridge University Press, 2011.

Williams, Brian Glyn. 'Hijra and Forced Migration from Nineteenth-Century Russia to the Ottoman Empire: A Critical Analysis of the Great Crimean Tatar Emigration of 1860–1861'. *Cahiers du Monde Russe* 41, no. 1 (2000): 79–108.

Williams, Brian Glyn. *The Crimean Tatars: From Soviet Union to Putin's Conquest.* Oxford: Oxford University Press, 2016.

Yılmaz, Özgür. 'An Italian Physician in the Caucasian Migration of 1864: The Mission of Dr. Barozzi in Trabzon and Samsun'. *Journal of Modern Turkish History Studies* 9, no. 28 (2014): 5–44.

Yörük, Ali Adem. 'Introduction'. In *Nusretü'l-Hamid Ala Siyaseti-l-Abid Mikyasü'l Ahlak: Sülükü'l-Malik Tercümleri*, edited by Ali Adem Yörük, 15–35. Istanbul Bilnet Matbaacılık ve Yayıncılık, 2020.

Yosmaoğlu, İpek K. 'Counting Bodies, Shaping Souls: The 1903 Census and National Identity in Ottoman Macedonia'. *International Journal of Middle East Studies* 38, no.1 (2006): 55–77.

Yosmaoğlu, İpek. *Blood Ties: Religion, Violence, and the Politics of Nationhood in Ottoman Macedonia, 1878–1908.* Ithaca, NY: Cornell University Press, 2014.

Bibliography

Zandi-Sayek, Sibel. *Ottoman Izmir: The Rise of a Cosmopolitan Port, 1840–1880*. Minneapolis: University of Minnesota Press, 2012.

Zeren, Barış. 'Between Constitution, Empire, and Nation: An Intellectual Trajectory of Pancho Dorev and His Legalist Paradigm'. In *The Turkish Connection: Global Intellectual Histories of the Late Ottoman Empire and Republican Turkey*, edited by Deniz Kuru and Hazal Papuccular, 49–78. Boston: De Gruyter, 2022.

Zetter, Roger. 'Refugees and Refugee Studies: A Label and an Agenda, Editorial Introduction' to the Journal of Refugees Studies. *Journal of Refugee Studies* 1, no. 1 (1988): 1–6.

Zetter, Roger. 'Labelling Refugees: Forming and Transforming a Bureaucratic Identity'. *Journal of Refugee Studies* 4, no. 1 (1991): 39–62.

Zolberg, Aristide. 'The Formation of New States as a Refugee-Generating Process'. *The Annals of the American Academy of Political and Social Science* 467, no. 1 (1983): 24–38.

Zolberg, Aristide. *A Nation by Design: Immigration Policy in the Fashioning of America*. Cambridge, MA: Harvard University Press, 2006.

Zurcher, Erik Jan. 'The Balkan Wars and the Refugee Leadership of the Early Turkish Republic'. In *War and Nationalism: The Balkan Wars, 1912–1913, and the Sociopolitical Implications*, edited by M. Hakan Yavuz and Isa Blumi, 665–78. Salt Lake City: University of Utah Press, 2013.

Index

Note: *f* indicates figure, *t* indicates table

Abdülaziz (sultan), 68, 115
Abdülhamid II (sultan), 70, 115, 116,
    117, 126
  CUP, 203
  Hamidiye Regiments, 184–5
  image management, 100, 116, 118,
    121
  Islamism, 177, 180, 195
  philanthropy, 119, 120, 121, 123
  reform, 141
  sovereignty, 195
  'Victims of Russian Atrocities'
    album, 98–9, 100, 120, 124
  Zionism, 53, 186
  see also Hamidian era
Abdülmecid I (sultan), 7, 74
Abkhazian migrants, 113
acclimation, 80, 81–2; *see also*
    environmental factors
'Address to Our Migrant Compatriots'
    (Osmancık), 216
administration, 7–8, 15,168, 215, 228,
    238–40, 243, 244–6
  critiques, 229
  identity documentation, 193, 194,
    195, 204, 246
  improving, 230

land registration, 152–4, 156, 160,
    162
  see also governance
age, 70, 93n, 124, 125
agriculture, 28, 147, 151, 155
  colonies, 38–9, 40
Ahmed Hilmi, Varnalı, 211, 212
Ahmet (settlement commissioner),
    147–9, 163, 164
  empty land, 150–2
  Islamism, 182, 184, 185, 187
Ahmet Rıza, 220
aid, 70–1, 86, 218–21, 239, 241, 242
  Bulwer, Henry, 49
  İane-i Muhacirin Encumeni
    (Migrant Aid Committee), 122,
    123, 126
  International Aid Committee for
    Refugees from the Provinces
    (Comité International de Secours
    aux Refugies des Provinces), 121
  Migrant Aid Commission
    (Muhacirin İane Komisyonu),
    183
  regimes, 66–76
  see also philanthropy
Aliens Act, 196

Index

Altunizade Ismail Zühdü, 122–3
American migrants, 51, 53; *see also*
US
AMMU (General Directorate of
Tribes and Migrants [Aşair
ve Muhacirin Müdüriyeti
Umumiyesi]), 1, 244–5
Anatolia, 34–5, 37, 158, 227, 242
development, 184–5, 191
land surveys, 139, 142
migrants, 158
settlement, 71–2, 73, 74, 77, 139,
142, 149–53, 159, 160, 227
settlement challenges, 78–82
see also Eastern Anatolia; West
Anatolia
Anatolian Railway Company
(Chemins de fer Ottoman
d'Anatolie [CFOA]), 142–3*f*
Ankara, 142–3*f*, 147–9, 155–6, 164,
165*f*, 166*f*
anti-*hijra* doctrine, 214
Armenians
Armenian Question, 139, 176,
177–8, 183–5, 186
deportation, 244
emigration restrictions, 186, 187
genocide, 209, 244
massacre, 185, 206
Nansen Passports, 246
return migrants, 176, 186, 219,
220–1, 222
assimilation, 73, 87, 206
asylum, 43, 196
asylum seekers, 3, 43
Austria-Hungary, 20n, 41, 190
Azapagic, Mehmed Teufik Azab, 190
Azmi, Abdullah (Torun), 227

Baggio, Alexander, 38, 53
Balchik, 48
Balkan migrants, 121, 182, 207
benefits of, 151, 164, 168, 182, 184,
230

Christians, 46, 124
disease/death, 103
ethnicity, 247
Muslims, 114, 118, 120–1, 124,
182, 191–2, 212, 214–15, 245,
247
settlement, 139, 147, 184, 247
Balkan Wars (1912–13), 15, 120–1,
207, 208
Balkans, the, 115, 178–9*f*, 212,
214–15
maps, 64*f*, 179*f*
Barozzi, Dr, 100–1, 104, 106–7, 108,
109, 110
Batumi migrants, 78
Bauman, Zygmunt, 10
Berlin Congress *see* Treaty of Berlin
Bitlis, 176, 183–4
Blumi, Isa, 5
Board of Health *see* Constantinople
Superior Health Council
border control, 12, 53–4, 176, 177–8,
195–7
hijra, 187–8, 196
migrant distinctions, 187
Bosnia and Herzegovina, 114, 116,
190, 206, 212, 213–14
Bosnian migrants, 47, 144, 155–6,
164, 165, 190
boycotts, 207
Bulgaria, 77, 86, 114, 178, 183,
190–1, 206
atrocities, 208
hijra, 212, 214
return migration from, 222, 223,
226
'Bulgarian Horrors and the Question
of the East, The' (Gladstone,
William), 118
Bulwer, Henry 49, 111
Burdett-Coutts, Angela, 120, 124
bureaucracy *see* administration
bureaucrats, 65–6; *see also* migration
institutions

269

burial practices, 101, 107, 109–10, 111
al-Bustani, Sulayman, 219–20

'Call to Migrants, A' (Fevzi, Haci
     Ömer), 203
Capitulations, the, 33–4, 105, 241
categories, 85–7, 88*f*, 144, 152, 241
     legal, 247–8
Caucasus, 14, 42
Cavit, Mehmet, 217, 218–19
CFOA (Chemins de fer Ottoman
     d'Anatolie [Anatolian Railway
     Company]), 142–3*f*
children, 98, 124–5; *see also* age;
     orphanages/orphans
Christianity, 118, 120
Circassian migrants, 14, 39, 41–2, 49,
     65, 90, 158–9
     crime, 77–8, 158, 159
     expulsion, 246
     Great Britain, 118
     housing, 102–3
     land appropriation, 161
     mortality, 100–1, 102, 112
     settlement, 71, 72, 73, 74–5, 76
     violence, 118
citizenship, 3; *see also* subjecthood
civilisation, 67, 87, 99–100, 114, 116,
     118–19
     Muzaffer Pasha, 171
     planning regularity, 168
     settlement, 73–4
     Swiss, 31
cleanliness *see* sanitation
climate, 80, 103, 148, 151
coerced migration *see* forced
     migration
colonisation, 25–56
     crisis, 47–50
     emigration prevention 189
     empty land, 149
     German, 155
     imperial humanitarianism, 119–21,
          122, 124

infectionism, 106
Islam, 188
labelling, 43–7
migration regimes, 50–4
obstacles, 36–42
population development, 27–36
commerce, 108–9
Commission for Muslim Migrants
     (Muhacirin-i İslamiye
     Komisyonu), 18, 168, 176, 186,
     196, 204
Committee of Union and Progress
     (CUP), 203–4, 206, 207–8, 244
conditions *see* victimhood
confinement, 110–13, 125; *see also*
     quarantine
conflict, 15; *see also* land; revolution;
     war
Constantinople Superior Health
     Council, 17, 99–100, 105–6, 113,
     114, 127
Convention on the Exchange of
     Populations, 246–7
corruption, 78, 107, 158–60; *see also*
     failure
cotton, 38–9, 51
counter-revolution (1909), 206
crime, 77–8, 157; *see also* dishonesty
Crimean Tatar migrants 13–14, 39,
     41–2, 46, 48–9
     Gasprinskii, Ismail, 190, 192
     hijra, 188–9, 190, 192–3, 194–5
     restrictions, 194–5
     Rumelia, 65
     settlement, 73
     Williams, Brian Glyn, 188–9, 192
Crimean War, 14, 27, 41, 48
crisis, 15, 47–50, 108–9
     strategies, 117
CUP (Committee of Union and
     Progress), 203–4, 206, 207–8,
     244
Çürüksulu Ali Pasha, 158–9
Cyprus, 38–9

Index

Daily Telegraph, 120
Dalchef, Hristo, 222–3, 225, 226
Danube Province, 65, 85–6, 92n
data collection *see* mapping
demographic engineering, 44
deportation, 244, 246
Dickson, Edward, 102, 105–6, 108,
109, 112
diplomacy, 178–9; *see also* Eastern
Question
Directorate for the Settlement of
Tribes and Migrants (İskan-ı
Aşair ve Muhacirin Müdüriyeti
[IAMM]), 207, 244
disease, 79, 80, 100–1, 102, 103
Barozzi, Dr, 108
cleanliness, 109
confinement, 110–13
ignorance, 118–19
infectionism, 105–6
medical assistance, 115
migrants to blame for, 109
quarantine, 105, 106, 108, 110,
111
Samsun, 111
social control, 100, 105–6
spread prevention, 111–12
Trabzon, 106, 108–10
Uşak, 108
see also public health
dishonesty, 109; *see also* corruption
dispersal, 73–4; *see also* space
Divriği, 78
Diyarbakir, 183–4
Dobruca, 48, 65, 75, 77
documentation *see* administration
Dorev, Pancho, 223, 227
Dunstan, H. Mainwaring, 124
Düzce, 77, 80, 161

Eastern Anatolia, 73, 139, 183–4, 242
Eastern Crisis, 114–17, 118, 119,
120–6
Eastern Question, 6, 115

Eastern Rumelia, 116, 178, 183,
190–1
economy, 141, 217–25, 229
cotton, 38–9, 51
OPDA, 141
productivity, 86–7, 124–5, 150–2,
182
Tanzimat era, 27–8, 32, 39
taxation, 32–3, 39, 71, 74, 78
trade 182
see also commerce; expenditure
Edhem, Bezci, 209–11, 212
'Father and Child's Conversation,
A', 209
Elif (Russo-Ottoman War refugee),
98, 99
emigration restrictions, 186, 187, 189,
192, 194–5, 197
employment, 49, 71, 124–5
empty land, 55, 149–52, 162–3
entrepreneurs, 38
environmental factors, 80, 103, 144,
147–8, 150, 151–2, 230–1, 244
equality, 25, 33, 51, 206, 221
Erzurum, 183–4
ethnic cleansing, 10–11
ethnicity, 178–9, 247
ethno-nationalism, 208
Europe, 5, 6, 107, 117–18, 195
Capitulations, the, 33–4, 105
exiles, 45
expenditure, 70–1, 77, 229, 230–1
aid, 70–1
settlement, 70–1, 72, 77, 85–7,
217–19, 222–3
expertise, 138–54, 225–32, 243, 244

failure, 11–13, 134–71, 205, 230,
242–4
administrative, 228
categories, 144, 147
empty land, 149–52, 162–3
environmental factors, 144, 147–8,
150

271

failure (*cont.*)
  expertise, 138–54
  land claims, 144, 147–50, 152, 154, 156, 160–3
  land discovery, 138, 142, 144
  land disputes, 134–8, 156–7, 160–2
  land management, 148–9
  land registration, 152–4, 156, 160, 162
  land surveys, 138–9, 141–2, 144
  plans, 156–60
  reform, 141–4, 149
  settlement challenges, 76–82, 138, 157–60
  settlement contesting, 155–63
  space organisation, 163–8
  spatial relationships, 138
  'will to improve', 12, 169, 228–30
  see also problems
families, 81
famine, 78, 101
'Father and Child's Conversation, A' (Edhem, Bezci), 209–10
Ferid Pasha, Mehmet, 176
Fevzi, Haci Ömer, 203–4, 207, 216–17, 231–2
  'Call to Migrants, A', 203
  'True Emigration', 216
firariler (deserters), 45, 59n
Fishman, Louis, 224
Florentine migrants, 36–7
Fonvielle, Arthur de, 102
food, 70, 77
forced migration, 3, 4, 5, 20n, 42, 43, 50, 223
  Convention on the Exchange of Populations, 246–7
  League of Nations High Commission for Refugees, 246
  see also *hijra*
forced relocation, 246–7
Foucault, Michel, 10, 239
'free' migration, 50–1
Fuat Pasha, 49, 51, 67

Garipler Mezarlığı/Cemetery, 134–8
Gasparini, Dormann, 30–2
Gasprinskii, Ismail, 190, 192, 195
Gemlik, 184
gender, 124, 125
General Directorate of Tribes and Migrants (Aşair ve Muhacirin Müdüriyeti Umumiyesi [AMMU]), 1, 244–5
General Migrant Administration (İdare-i Umumiye-i Muhacirin), 70
genocide, 10–11, 13, 245, 246
  Armenian, 185, 244
German migrants, 29–30, 41, 46, 48, 155
Gladstone, William, 121, 124
  'Bulgarian Horrors and the Question of the East, The', 118
göçmenler (immigrants), 20n, 247
governance, 12, 13, 66, 67, 82, 169, 170, 242–3
  gardener metaphor, 10–11, 12, 197
  governmentality, 10, 11, 12, 238–40, 245
  humanitarianism, 119
  see also failure; leadership
Great Britain
  Aliens Act, 196
  Circassian migrants, 118
  commerce, 108–9
  emigration restrictions, 186
  imperial humanitarianism, 119–21, 122, 124
  infectionism, 105–6
  philanthropy, 120, 121
Greece, 206, 207, 208
  Convention on the Exchange of Populations, 246–7
Gülhane Rescript, 7, 33

hajj, 9, 116, 180–1, 192
Hakkı, Ibrahim, 225–6, 227, 228–9, 230

Index

Hamidian era, 7, 8, 196, 198, 227, 242
  Islamic Ottomanism, 9, 180, 181
  migration regime, 181–3
  Islamism, 177, 180–1, 182–7
  Muslim migrants, 193–4
  failure, 11–12, 228
Hamidiye Regiments, 184–5
Hasan Saidi Pasha, 164
Hasbi, Muharrem, 217–18
health *see* public health
High Commission for Migrants
  (Muhacirin Komisyon-ı Alisi),
  185–6
hijra 44, 178, 181, 187–95, 197
  limits, 191–5, 196
  Muhacir newspaper, 212, 213–15,
  216
  Rida, Rashid, 213
histories of migration, 3–4, 5, 7–8, 11,
  13, 45, 50–4
homeland (*vatan*), 210, 211
housing, 76–7, 102–3
  design blueprints, 164, 165*f*, 166*f*–8
  disputes, 134–8
  Hasan Saidi Pasha, 164, 165*f*
  management, 149
Hulusi, Lofçalı Mehmet, 204, 215
humanitarianism, 67, 116, 119–23
al-Husayni, Said, 224, 225

IAMM (Directorate for the Settlement
  of Tribes and Migrants [İskan-ı
  Aşair ve Muhacirin Müdüriyeti]),
  207, 244
İane-i Muhacirin Encumeni (Migrant
  Aid Committee), 122, 123, 126
Ibrahim (Parliament), 227, 231
identity, 8, 197, 208
  border control, 195–6
  documentation, 193, 194, 195, 204,
  246
  state, 217–18
ignorance, 118–19, 151, 198
İlyas Sami, 228

image management, 110–11, 116, 118,
  121
images, use of 98–9, 100
imperial humanitarianism, 119–21,
  122, 124
Imperial Reform Edict (*Islahat
  Fermanı*), 25, 33, 40, 194
IMRO (Internal Macedonian
  (-Adrianople) Revolutionary
  Organization), 222
India, 121, 124
infectionism, 105–6
inheritance, 34
Internal Macedonian (-Adrianople)
  Revolutionary Organization
  (IMRO), 222
International Aid Committee for
  Refugees from the Provinces
  (Comité International de Secours
  aux Refugies des Provinces), 121,
  122
internationalism, 99, 105
Irish migrants 38, 39
irregular migrants, 3
irrigation, 139, 140*f*, 141–2
Islam, 8–9, 44, 52, 117–18, 176–98
  anti-Muslim feeling, 120, 121, 208
  Fevzi, Haci Ömer, 203
  hajj, 116, 180–1
  Hamidian era, 177, 180–1, 182–7
  India, 121
  Islamic Ottomanism, 9, 180, 181–2,
  242
  millet system, 33
  Ottoman Islamism, 177, 187, 209
  pan-Islamism, 180–1
  politics, 178–81
  in Russia, 192–3
  Şukri, Ahmed, 214
  see also *hijra*; Muslims
Islamic Ottomanism, 9, 180, 181–2,
  242
  Armenian migration, 176, 177–8,
  183–7

273

Governing Migration in the Late Ottoman Empire

Ispartalıyan, Stephan/Istepan, 219
Istanbul, 103, 112–13, 115
Istanbul Municipality (Şehremaneti), 68, 124, 134, 135
Italian migrants, 26, 36–7
Italy, 207
İzzeddin, 68

Jewish migrants, 53, 186, 187, 224–5

Kemal, Namık, 211
Keun (British Vice Consul), 155
Keygam (Der Garabedian), 218–19, 220–1, 225, 226
al-Khalidi, Ruhi, 224
Kırmızı Kışla, 125, 126
Konya, 155
Kostaki Musurus Pasha, 39
Köstence, 76–7, 87–90
  conditions, 191
Kurds, 73, 184–5, 244–5, 246

labelling, 2–5, 43–7, 197, 246–8; *see also* terminology
labour, 49, 71
land, 32–3
  administration, 184
  allotment, 147
  availability, 158, 225–6
  claims, 144, 147–50, 152, 154, 156, 160–3, 218–21
  compensation, 161–2
  cultivation, 149–50
  discovery, 138, 142, 144
  disputes, 77, 87–9, 134–8, 156–7, 160–2
  distribution, 29, 147, 157
  empty, 149–52, 162–3
  inheritance, 34
  management, 148–9
  mapping, 82–90
  naming, 153
  Nusret Bey/Pasha, 64–6
  quality, 79–80, 81

  registration, 152–4, 156, 160, 162
  speculation, 143–4
  surveys, 36, 37–8, 82–90, 138–9, 141–2, 144, 148
  transfer reform, 74
Land Code (1858), 32, 147, 149, 162
Lane, Thomas, 38–9, 45
Layard, Austen Henry, 62, 120–1
League of Nations High Commission for Refugees, 246
legal categories, 247–8; *see also* labelling; terminology
legal status, 153, 160, 247–8
legislation, 3, 4, 8; *see also* migration regulations
Lester, Alan and Dussart, Fae, 119
Liberal Entente, 207
liberality, 51, 52, 53
local communities, 170
  difficulties, 78, 87–9, 155, 158, 159
  displacing, 223
  Köstence, 87–90
  land disputes, 77, 87–9, 134–8, 156–7, 160–2
  petitions, 78
  productivity, 150–2
  reliance on, 72
  spatial relationships, 72–3
loyalty, 8, 73, 87, 195

Macedonian Question, 183, 222
Mahmud II (sultan), 7, 104
malaria, 79, 233, 244
Malatya, 139, 140*f*, 142
Mamuretülaziz, 183–4
mapping, 82–90, 125–6, 141, 144
maps, 64*f*, 153, 164, 179*f*
Mecidiye, 47–9, 75, 76
  conditions, 101–2
medicine, 115
Mehmet Vehbi (Çelik), 220
Midhat, Ahmed Şevfik, 62, 65, 90, 125
  Danube Vilayet, 85–6

Index

registers, 86–7, 88*f*
settlement costs, 86
Migrant Administration (Muhacirin
    İdaresi), 69–70
Migrant Aid Commission (Muhacirin
    İane Komisyonu), 183
Migrant Commission (Muhacirin
    Komisyonu), 9, 63, 68–9, 70, 78,
    239–40, 245
migrant/refugee binary, 4–5, 45
Migrant Regulations (*Muhacirin
    Nizammamesi*) (1857), 26, 50,
    52–3, 54, 55–6, 193, 194, 239,
    241
  agricultural colonies, 38–9
  Anatolia, 34–5, 37
  colonisation, 45, 47, 49
  Florentine migrants, 36–7
  influence, 42–3, 44
  Irish migrants 38, 39
  labels, 43–7
  Land Code (1858), 32
  land, 32–3
  liberality, 52
  mass migration, 42
  Mecidiye, 47–9
  migrant labels, 43–7
  1902 revisions, 193–4
  obstacles, 36–42
  population development, 27–36
  preparation, 36–7
  Prussian migrants, 25–6, 28, 29
  selection, 35
  subjecthood, 33–4, 40–1, 45
  taxation, 32–3, 39
  terminology, 46–7
migrants see *muhacirin*
migration institutions, 68–70; *see
    also* bureaucrats; Migrant
    Commission
migration regimes, 9–13, 181–3
  aid regimes, 66–76
  failure, 11–13
  governmentality, 10, 11, 12

liberality and restriction, 50–4
migrant distinctions, 187
social engineering, 10–11, 12–13
migration regulations, 26
Migrant Settlement Regulations
    (*İskan-ı Muhacirin Nizamnamesi*)
    (1913), 1
Mongia, Ridhika, 50, 52
of 1902, 193–4
see also Migrant Regulations
    (*Muhacirin Nizamnamesi*) (1857)
migrations 13–15, 25, 41–3, 66–7,
    239, 243–4
Abkhazians, 113
aid, 49, 68, 75, 86
Austro-Hungarians, 41
Bosnian, 47, 144, 155–6, 164, 165,
    190
Bulgarian, 191
conditions *see* victimhood
dangers, 229
East Rumelian, 191
Florentine, 36–7
Germans, 29–30, 41, 46, 48, 155
global, 26, 50
health, 101
Irish, 38, 39
Jewish, 53, 186, 187, 224–5
Kurdish, 73
numbers, 50
Prussians, 25–6, 28, 29
restriction, 53–4
rumours, 109
Russo-Ottoman War, 115
Swiss, 30–1
transatlantic, 25, 29–30, 31–2,
    50–1, 224, 229
Uşak, 108
see also Balkan migrants;
    Circassian migrants; Muslim
    migrants; Tatar migrants
millet system, 30, 33, 40
mobility, 3, 8–9
causes of, 5, 6

275

Mongia, Ridhika, 50, 52
Mordtmann, Andreas David, 29–30, 40
mortality, 79, 100–4, 112
motivation, 4, 45, 47; *see also* labelling; terminology
Muhacir newspaper, 203, 204–5, 209, 211, 232–5
  hijra, 212, 213–14, 216
  purpose, 215
  society, 215–17
muhacirin (migrants), 5, 6, 45, 238
  as colonist *see* colonisation
  definition/meaning/use of term 1–2, 6, 20, 34, 45–7, 50, 198, 205, 210–11, 216–17
  Fevzi, Haci Ömer, 203, 216–17
  as failure *see* failure
  grief/loss, 210, 211, 212
  identifying as, 109
  as Muslim *see* Islam
  population politics, 245–6
  as possibility *see* potential
  potential of, 205
  as problem *see* problems
  religious significance of term, 44
  as resources, 49, 65
  significance of, 209, 233
  social engineering, 240–2
  as threat, 105, 107–8, 109, 110, 111, 114
  as victim *see* victimhood
muhajirun (*muhacirin*) (early followers of Muhammad), 44, 46, 188, 203
Muhammad (prophet), 46, 188, 216
mülteciler (refugees), 45
  definition/meaning/use of term 1–2, 20n, 46–7
  see also refugees
Murad V (sultan), 115, 178
Muş, 184
Musa Pasha (Circassian), 157, 158, 159

Muslim migrants, 182, 183–96, 220, 225–7, 242
  AMMU/IAMM, 245
  assisting, 67, 116, 120, 121, 124
  Balkans, the, 114, 118, 120–1, 124, 182, 191–2, 212, 214–15, 245, 247
  Commission for Muslim Migrants (Muhacirin-i İslamiye Komisyonu), 18, 168, 176, 186, 196
  discrimination, 227
  ethnicity, 247
  expenditure, 222–3
  facilitating, 183–7
  Fevzi, Haci Ömer, 203
  forced relocation, 246–7
  Hakkı, Ibrahim, 225–6
  hijra 44, 178, 181, 187–95, 196, 197, 212
  numbers, 15, 50
  portrayal, 114, 117–18
  Russian Empire, 14, 42
  Talat, Mehmed (Parliament), 227–8
  Turkism, 208
  see also Muslims; RMIC
Muslims, 8, 13
  anti-Muslim feeling, 120, 121, 208
  Indian, 121
  millet system, 33
  portrayal, 114, 117–18
  under non-Muslim rule, 213, 214
  see also Islam; Muslim migrants
Mustafa Nuri Pasha, 134, 135
Muzaffer Pasha, 141–2, 149, 163
  empty land, 150
  environmental factors, 150, 151
  irrigation project, 139, 140*f*
  land speculation, 143–4
  land surveys, 138–9, 142, 144, 147

Nail, Thomas, 5–6
Nansen Passports, 246

Index

nationalism, 180, 208–9
nationality, 8–9, 180; *see also*
  subjecthood
Nationality Law, 34, 40, 59n, 180
Nogay Tatars, 13–14, 41–2, 65, 71,
  72
  settlement, 73, 74–5
nomadic pastoralists, 7, 14, 73
North America, 51; *see also* US
Nusret Bey/Pasha, 49, 62–6, 67–8
  legacy, 91
  mapping, 83–5
  memoranda of, 90
  Migrant Administration, 69–70
  Migrant Commission, 63–5, 69, 70,
    72, 76
  public health, 75, 102
  resignation, 86
  sanitation, 102, 104
  settlement, 70, 72, 73, 74–5, 76,
    90–1
  successes, 74–5, 83, 102

obligatory migration see *hijra*
officials, 157, 158, 243
OPDA (Ottoman Public Debt
  Administration), 141
orphanages/orphans, 86, 125
Osmancık
  'Address to Our Migrant
    Compatriots', 216
Ottoman Islamism, 177, 187, 209
Ottoman Public Debt Administration
  (OPDA), 141
Ottoman Quarantine Council (Meclis-i
  Tahaffuz), 105
Ottomanism, 8, 9, 205, 208, 209, 212,
  215–17, 225–8, 242
  Dalchef, Hristo, 223
  Dorev, Pancho, 223
  Zohrap, Krikor, 220
overcrowding, 101–2, 103, 110–11,
  112
Ozenbashli, Seyit Abdullah, 192

Palestine, 12, 53, 186, 224, 225
pan-Islamism, 180–1; *see also*
  Hamidian era; Islam; Ottoman
  Islamism
passports, 193, 194, 195, 204, 246
patriarchal philanthropy, 116, 119–23
petitions, 78–81
Petrov, Milen, 90
philanthropy, 116–17, 119–23, 124,
  126; *see also* aid
planning, 164, 165f, 166f–8; *see also*
  space
Police Ministry (Zaptiye Nezareti), 68
politics, 154, 158, 225–32
  CUP, 203–4, 206, 207–8, 244
  expenditure, 217–24, 229, 230–1
  foreign policy, 207
  Liberal Entente, 207
  Macedonian Question, 222
  major events, 178–9
  population, 245–6
  Young Turk movement, 7, 8, 203,
    204, 206–7, 209, 211, 242
  Zionism, 186, 224–5
  see also governance
population, the 10–11, 32, 148
  Anatolia, 34–5
  development, 27–36
  exchanges, 67
  global trends, 25
  governmentality, 239
  growth, 232
  information, 15, 125–6, 148, 153,
    199n
  mapping, 82–90, 125–6, 148
  politics, 245–6
  social engineering, 10–11, 12–13,
    32
  potential, 203–33
    economy, 217–25
    expertise, 225–32
    post-Hamidian future, 209–17
    Second Constitutional Era, 206–9
  poverty, 78–80, 224–5, 232

problems, 62–92, 240; *see also* failure
aid regimes, 66–76
mapping people and land, 82–90
obstacles, 36–42
settlement challenges, 76–82, 138, 157–60
productivity, 86–7, 124–5, 150–2, 182
propaganda, 208
Protégé Law, 34, 40
Prussian migrants, 25–6, 28, 29
public health, 99, 100, 104–14
Constantinople Superior Health Council, 17, 99–100, 105–6, 113, 114, 127
medicine, 115
Nusret Bey/Pasha, 75, 102
Sarıyer, 137

quarantine, 105, 106, 108, 110, 111, 113

race, 51, 52–3, 117–18
railways, 142–3
Redhouse, James, 46
reform, 90, 91, 141–4, 149, 169
reform era, 6–7, 9
refugees, 196, 246
as resources, 49, 65
definition/meaning/use of term, 5, 45–6, 50, 247
labelling, 2–5, 43–7
legal status, 247–8
Syrian, 247–8
see also *mülteciler*
registration, 153–4
Reinkowski, Maurus, 87
religion, 44, 46–7, 152, 177–8, 183, 196–7
Christianity, 118, 120
deprivation, 197–8
discrimination, 220, 227
Eastern Crisis, 117
forced relocation, 246–7
freedom of, 212–14

Greece, 246–7
land claims, 163
legal opinions, 189
millet system, 33, 40
Turkey, 246–7
see also Islam
regularity *see* space
relocation, 79–82, 89
Reşid, 134, 135, 138
return migration, 77, 177, 186, 215, 219–23, 226, 227, 242
Hakkı, Ibrahim, 227, 228
revolution, 183–4, 203–4
Anatolia, 184–5
Armenian, 176, 183–4
Constitutional Revolution (1908), 203
counter-revolution, 206
Macedonia, 222
taxation, 74
see also conflict; war
Rida, Rashid, 213
Rıza Nur, 229
Rıza Tevfik (Bölükbaşı), 221, 226, 232
RMIC (Rumeli Muhacirin-i Islamiye Cemiyeti [Society for Rumelian Muslim Migrants]) 203, 204–5, 208, 209, 211, 212, 233; see also *Muhacir* newspaper
roads, 103–4
Roberts, Randal, 103–4
Rumelia, 63, 65, 67–8, 222, 227, 242
environmental factors, 230, 231
land availability, 225–6
Muslims, 213–14
refugees, 155
settlement challenges, 78–82, 222, 223
see also Eastern Rumelia; RMIC
rumours, 37, 109, 112
Russian Empire, 13–15, 20n, 42, 184
Circassian migrants, 118
emigration restrictions, 186, 192, 194

Index

Gasprinskii, Ismail, 190
  Muslim military service, 192, 193
  population exchanges, 67
  'Victims of Russian Atrocities'
    album, 98–9, 100, 120, 124
  see also Crimean Tatar migrants
Russo-Ottoman War (1877–8), 14–15,
  98–9, 114–15, 178, 216, 241
  Great Britain, 120, 121
  philanthropy, 120, 121
Rüstem, 30, 31, 38

sacrifice, 209, 210, 211, 227
Samsun, 100–1
  conditions, 111, 112, 113
  mortality, 102
  quarantine and sanitation, 106, 107
sanitation, 104, 106, 109, 137
Sarıyer, 134–8
Saydam, Abdallah, 71
Sebah, Pascal, 98
  'Victims of Russian Atrocities'
    album, 98–9, 100, 120, 124
Second Constitutional Era, 206–33,
  242
  economy, 217–25
  expertise, 225–32
  post-Hamidian future, 209–17
sedentarisation, 67, 73, 87, 207
Selim III (sultan), 7
Şemsettin, Sami, 47
settlement, 7, 152
  aid and investment, 49, 70–6, 86
  Balkan migrants, 139
  challenges, 76–82, 138, 157–60
  contesting, 155–63
  dispersal, 73–4
  employment, 49, 71
  environmental factors, 80, 103, 144,
    147–8, 150, 151–2, 230–1, 244
  expenditure, 70–1, 72, 77, 85–7,
    217–19, 222–3
  housing, 76–7
  land allotment, 147

land discovery, 138, 142, 144
land disputes, 77, 87–9, 134–8,
  156–7, 160–2
land management 148–9
migrant demands, 71–2, 89–90, 156
migrant wealth, 85, 86
Muzaffer Pasha, 142, 144
officials, 157, 158
policies, 226, 229
regulations, 148
removals, 135
Sarıyer, 134–8
space organisation, 163–8
spatial relationships, 72–3, 138
transfers, 79–82, 89
Sivas Province, 78, 157–8, 159, 160,
  183–4
Sivrihisar, 147–9, 150–2, 164
Smith, J. Hosford, 51, 52
social engineering, 10–11, 12–13, 138,
  205, 233, 240–2
  expulsion, 246
  Migrant Regulations (*Muhacirin
    Nizamnamesi*) (1857), 32–3, 34,
    35
  populations of concern, 124
  violence, 245, 246
social stability, 226
society, 215–17
Society for Rumelian Muslim
  Migrants (Rumeli Muhacirin-i
  Islamiye Cemiyeti [RMIC]) *see*
  RMIC
sovereignty, 4, 8–9, 33–4, 123, 195
space
  designating, 138, 142, 144
  organisation, 163–8
  regularity, 166–8
  spatial relationships, 72–3
  see also land
state, the, 4, 115, 243–4
  failure, 169
  fictions, 162
  formation of, 4, 43–4, 55

state, the (*cont.*)
  gardener metaphor, 10–11, 12, 197
  humanity, 67
  identity, 217–18
  loyalty, 8, 73, 87, 195
  migrant/refugee binary, 4–5
  modern Ottoman state, making of,
    6–9
  order, 87
  sovereignty, 4, 8–9, 33–4, 123,
    195
  state control, 54
  stud farms, 138–9, 141–2, 143*f*,
    144, 145*f*, 146*t*
  subjecthood, 8–9, 33–4, 40–1, 45,
    195–6, 214
  subjects, relationship with, 226–7
  unity, 206, 215–16, 243
  see also Ottomanism
status, 2, 153, 160, 247–8
Stevens, Francis Illif, 102, 109, 110
stud farms, 138–9, 141–2, 143*f*, 144,
  145*f*, 146*t*
subjecthood, 8–9, 33–4, 40–1, 45,
  195–6, 214
subjects, state, relationship with,
  226–7
Şukri, Ahmed, 204, 213–14, 215
Suleyman (Miralay), 159–60, 181–2,
  185, 187
Supreme Council (Meclis-i Vala), 45,
  73–4
surveillance, 168
surveys, 36, 37–8, 82–90, 138–9,
  141–2, 144, 148
Swiss migrants, 30–1
Syrian refugees, 247–8

Tahsin (Captain), 38
Talat, Mehmed (Parliament), 227–8
Talat Pasha (Mehmed Talat), 220,
  227, 231
Tanzimat era, 7, 8, 25–43, 243
  agriculture, 28

Austro-Hungarian migrants, 41
Capitulations, the, 33–4, 105
civilising, 87
economy, 27–8, 32–3, 39
Florentine migrants, 36–7
German migrants, 29–30, 41
Gülhane Rescript, 7, 33
Imperial Reform Edict (*Islahat
  Fermanı*), 25, 33, 40, 194
Land Code (1858), 32
legislative bodies, 27
mass migration, 41–2
Migrant Commission (Muhacirin
  Komisyonu), 9, 63, 68–9, 70, 78,
  239–40, 245
migration institutions, 68–70
millet system, 33, 40
Muslim migrants, 182
Nationality Law, 34, 40, 59n, 180
Protégé Law, 34, 40
Prussian migrants, 25–6, 28, 29
reform, 90
refugees as resources, 49
Swiss migrants, 30–1
see also Migrant Regulations
  (*Muhacirin Nizamnamesi*)
  (1857); problems
Tarabar, Muhammad Zahir al-Din,
  213
Tatar migrants
  conditions, 101
  Crimean, 13–14, 39, 41–2, 46,
    48–9, 188–9, 190, 192–3, 194–5
  Nogay, 13–14, 41–2, 65, 71, 72, 73,
    74–5
  Rumelian, 63, 65
  settlement, 76
Tausch, Pierre, 36, 37
taxation, 32–3, 39, 71
  corruption, 78
  revolution, 74
TCF (Turkish Compassionate Fund),
  120–1, 122, 124
technology, 142

Index

terminology, 1–2, 20, 34, 45–7, 246–8; *see also* labelling
territorialisation, 156, 171n; *see also* space
territory, 178
  loss of, 206–7
  Muslim, 188–9
Terzibaşoğlu, Yücel, 162–3
Trabzon, 108, 109
  land disputes, 161
  mortality, 102
  quarantine and sanitation, 106, 107
Trade Ministry (Ticaret Nezareti), 68
transatlantic migration, 25, 29–30, 31–2, 50–1, 224, 229
transportation, 102–3, 112
  conditions, 101, 102, 103–4, 112–13
  expenditure, 70–1
  railways, 142–3*f*
  roads, 103–4
Treaty of Berlin, 115, 116, 123, 152, 178–9, 183, 241, 242
  Armenian Question, 139, 183
  Bosnia, 190
  OPDA, 141
Treaty of Küçük Kaynarca, 13
Treaty of San Stefano, 115
Tripoli, 167*f*, 207
'True Emigration' (Fevzi, Haci Ömer), 216
Tulça, 41
Turkey, 247–8
  Convention on the Exchange of Populations, 246–7
Turkification, 8, 207–8
Turkish Compassionate Fund (TCF), 120–1, 122, 124

UNHCR (United Nations High Commissioner for Refugees), 3, 43, 247
United Nations High Commissioner for Refugees (UNHCR), 3, 43, 247

United States (US) *see* US
urban planning, 166*f*, 167
US (United States), 30, 43–4, 54–5, 224
  American migrants, 51, 53
  frontier, the, 55
  Homestead Act, 56
  Homestead National Monument, 54–5
  race, 51, 52
Uşak, 108

Van, 183–4
van Lennep, Henry John, 112
vatan (homeland), 210, 211
victimhood, 98–128
  Adapazarı, 197–8
  civilisation, 87, 114, 116, 118–19
  Constantinople Superior Health Council, 17, 99–100, 105–6, 113, 114, 127
  Eastern Crisis, 114–17, 118, 119, 120–6
  health, 99–100, 104–14
  humanitarianism, 67, 116
  imperial humanitarianism, 119–21, 122, 124
  media attention, 110–11, 117–18, 120, 121
  mortality, 79, 100–4, 232
  patriarchal philanthropy, 116, 119–23
  philanthropy, 116–17, 119–23, 124, 126
  portrayal of, 123–4
  poverty, 78–80, 224–5, 232
  productivity, 124–5
  race, 117
  welfare, 116–17, 119
  see also violence
'Victims of Russian Atrocities' album (Sebah, Pascal), 98–9, 100, 120, 124
Vidin, 74, 83

village design, 164–8
violence, 98–9, 118, 161, 206, 245
   Anatolia, 185
   Armenia, 185, 244
   Christians, 117, 118
   genocide, 10–11, 13, 185, 244, 245, 246
visitor status, 79, 195
Vlahov, Dimitar, 224–5, 228
'voluntary' migration, 3, 4, 5

war, 99, 185
   Balkan Wars (1912–13), 15, 115, 120–1, 207, 208
   Crimean War, 14, 27, 48
   World War I, 246
   see also revolution; Russo-Ottoman War
welfare, 116–17, 119; *see also* aid; philanthropy

West Anatolia, 159–60, 181–2
widow asylums, 125
Williams, Brian Glyn, 188–9, 192
Wilson, Charles William, 158, 159
women, 124, 125, 126
Women's Work Establishment (WWE) 124, 126
World War I, 246
WWE (Women's Work Establishment) 124, 126

Yaver, 107
Young Turk movement, 7, 8, 203, 204, 206–7, 209, 211, 242
Yusuf İzzeddin, 68

Zionism, 186, 224–5, 228
Zohrap, Krikor, 220, 225, 226